Medical Understandings of Emotions in Antiquity

Trends in Classics –
Supplementary Volumes

Edited by
Franco Montanari and Antonios Rengakos

Associate Editors
Stavros Frangoulidis · Fausto Montana · Lara Pagani
Serena Perrone · Evina Sistakou · Christos Tsagalis

Scientific Committee
Alberto Bernabé · Margarethe Billerbeck
Claude Calame · Kathleen Coleman · Jonas Grethlein
Philip R. Hardie · Stephen J. Harrison · Stephen Hinds
Richard Hunter · Giuseppe Mastromarco
Gregory Nagy · Theodore D. Papanghelis
Giusto Picone · Alessandro Schiesaro
Tim Whitmarsh · Bernhard Zimmermann

Volume 131

Medical Understandings of Emotions in Antiquity

Theory, Practice, Suffering
Ancient Emotions III

Edited by
George Kazantzidis and Dimos Spatharas

DE GRUYTER

Ancient Emotions, edited by George Kazantzidis and Dimos Spatharas within the series *Trends in Classics Supplementary Volumes*, investigates the history of emotions in classical antiquity, providing a home for interdisciplinary approaches to ancient emotions and exploring the inter-faces between emotions and significant aspects of ancient literature and culture.

ISBN 978-3-11-153433-6
e-ISBN (PDF) 978-3-11-077193-0
e-ISBN (EPUB) 978-3-11-077201-2
ISSN 1868-4785

Library of Congress Control Number: 2022932967

Bibliographic information published by the Deutsche Nationalbibliothek
The Deutsche Nationalbibliothek lists this publication in the Deutsche Nationalbibliografie; detailed bibliographic data are available on the Internet at http://dnb.dnb.de.

© 2024 Walter de Gruyter GmbH, Berlin/Boston
This volume is text- and page-identical with the hardback published in 2022.
Editorial Office: Alessia Ferreccio and Katerina Zianna
Logo: Christopher Schneider, Laufen

www.degruyter.com

For M. and M.
G.K

For my father
D.S.

Preface

This volume arose from the 2017 Crete/Patras *Ancient Emotions* II Conference on *Medical Understandings of Emotions* which took place at the University of Patras. The event and the present volume, including thoroughly revised versions of the papers read at Patras, address an under-explored topic, i.e. medical conceptualizations of ancient emotions. In view of emotions' predominance in modern medical practice — health psychology is a sub-field of clinical psychology — and the epidemic of mental diseases, such as depression and anxiety disorders, in Western societies, the topic of this volume is pertinent to modern concerns about health in the societies we live in. Equally importantly, our desire to explore medical conceptualizations of emotions was prompted by our curiosity about the possible similarities or differences between ancient and modern medical discourses, the definition of pathological emotions, and the ways in which ancient patients experienced and expressed sentiments caused by suffering and pain. The editors of this volume hope that contributors' discussion of emotions in the doctors will enhance our understanding of the ways in which ancient cultures construed the category emotion and that it will shed fresh light on issues which are pivotal to the study of ancient emotions, such as the implications of the mind/body dichotomy, the possible interfaces between professional and folk understandings of sentiments or the relationship between ancient medicine and philosophy.

During the volume's production, which partly coincided with the COVID-19 pandemic, we have accrued several debts. We are grateful to the volume's contributors for their collegial spirit and their patience. We also want to extend our thanks to the Departments of Philology of the Universities of Crete and Patras for their support. Last but not least, we want to thank warmly the general editors of the Trends in Classics series, Professors Montanari and Rengakos, for making this volume and the sub-series *Ancient Emotions* possible.

G.K.
D.S.

Contents

Preface —— VII

George Kazantzidis and Dimos Spatharas
Introduction —— 1

Part I: Emotions Across Medicine and Philosophy

Peter N. Singer
What is a *Pathos?* Where Medicine Meets Philosophy —— 17

Dimos Spatharas
Drugs and Psychotropic Words in Gorgias' *Encomium of Helen* —— 43

Spyridon Rangos
Wonder and Perplexity across Medicine and Philosophy in Classical Greece —— 59

Part II: Emotions in the Medical Room

Elizabeth Craik
The Doctor's Dilemma: Addressing Irrational Fears —— 117

Jennifer Kosak
Shame and Concealment in the Hippocratic Corpus —— 123

Chiara Thumiger
The Body to be Hidden: Shame and Ancient Medicine —— 145

George Kazantzidis
Reading and Misreading Medical Emotions: Some Cases of Female Patients in the Hippocratic *Epidemics* —— 173

Part III: Medico-philosophical Treatments of Emotion

Teun Tieleman
Posidonius and the Pneumatists: The Aetiology of Emotions and Diseases —— 201

David Kaufman
Galen on Non-Rational Motivation and the Freedom from Emotions: A Reading of *Affections of the Soul* —— 229

Julien Devinant
Disorders of the Soul: Emotions and Clinical Conditions in Galen —— 247

Susan P. Mattern
The Atlas Patient: Galen on Melancholia and Psychosis —— 271

List of Contributors —— 287
Index Rerum et Nominum —— 289
Index Auctorum Antiquorum et Locorum —— 295

George Kazantzidis and Dimos Spatharas
Introduction

1 Preliminaries

Our project on medical understandings of emotions was conceived and partly executed before the COVID-19 pandemic. Hence, none of our contributors employs this distressing global experience as comparative ground for his or her arguments. The fact that the papers included in this volume were produced before the threatening emergence of the pandemic is felicitous. For one thing, all those who were involved in this project may now feel the urge to revisit their conclusions on the basis of their experience of medical history in the making. Readers may also be tempted to compare ancient scripts of patients' emotions with the emotions caused by the pandemic. With the outburst of COVID-19, globalization took on a new meaning, insofar as secluded citizens across the world became possible transmitters and patients of the new virus. Our 2017 COVID-19-free curiosity about the under-explored issue of how ancient medical authors treated or pathologized emotions and how they depicted their patients' emotionally charged sufferings or hopes morphed into a living experience with significant affective aspects.

Fear, anxiety, panic, hope, distress, sorrow, grief, anger, and gratitude (to mention some emotions) have been — and still are — pivotal to both professionals' and non-professionals' discourse about the pandemic since 2020. During the pandemic, health professionals, often underpaid, were elevated to the status of resilient heroes in a battle with an invisible enemy — battle metaphors are indeed very common in medical language (e.g. people 'beat cancer', a disease sometimes qualified as 'aggressive').[1] Self-centered Galen or other ancient doctors would no doubt have relished with pride the spectacle of thousands of citizens applauding doctors and nurses from their balconies. The rise of conspiracy theories or the emergence of irrational responses (it is reported that Boris Johnson wanted to be injected with the virus on live TV, but later contracted COVID-19 in the usual way and was, thus, urgently sent to the hospital) would perhaps make Thucydides, a pioneer in medical psychology, give us a knowing wink.

---

[1] See Sontag 1978.

2 Thinking about Medical Understandings of Emotions

In this section, we outline some of the questions that we want to ask ancient authors about the ways in which they conceptualize emotions and suggest reasons which make medical understandings of emotions a topic that deserves investigation.

As has been noted (Holmes 2010: 110), medical writers in antiquity sketch doctors as disembodied agents of knowledge, while patients are positioned between knowledgeably observing doctors and the object of observation, i.e. their bodies. The objectification of the suffering body in ancient medical writers may explain why doctors typically depict themselves as emotionally neutral agents of knowledge. As it happens, the image of the detached doctor in ancient medical treatises is in key with lay understandings of doctors' responses to pain and illness.

In Demosthenes' *Against Conon* (Dem. 54), young Ariston claims that he was beaten violently by his opponent, Conon, in the agora of Athens. According to the speaker's narrative, Conon and his friends staged a comic performance whose script relied on the humiliation of young Ariston (8–9). After the attack, Ariston was unable to stand on his feet and was carried by passers-by to his house. When his mother and the female slaves saw his maltreated body, they begun shrieking and wailing (9). Their response is reminiscent of female lamentations and thus invests the passage with tragic overtones which are intended to anticipate Conon's attempt to trivialize the incident in the agora and present it as an instance of playful aggression among young Athenians. But when Ariston describes the doctor's 'diagnosis' after the public examination of his wounds at the public baths (11–12), the language of the speech becomes saliently 'professional' and emotionally detached. Unlike the inarticulate wailing of the household's women and Ariston's violently forced silence, the doctor who examined him uttered the following words:

> μετὰ δὲ ταῦτα τῶν μὲν οἰδημάτων τῶν ἐν τῷ προσώπῳ καὶ τῶν ἑλκῶν οὐδὲν ἔφη φοβεῖσθαι λίαν ὁ ἰατρός, πυρετοὶ δὲ παρηκολούθουν μοι συνεχεῖς καὶ ἀλγήματα, ὅλου μὲν τοῦ σώματος πάνυ σφοδρὰ καὶ δεινά, μάλιστα δὲ τῶν πλευρῶν καὶ τοῦ ἤτρου, καὶ τῶν σιτίων ἀπεκεκλείμην. καὶ ὡς μὲν ὁ ἰατρὸς ἔφη, εἰ μὴ κάθαρσις αἵματος αὐτομάτη μοι πάνυ πολλὴ συνέβη περιωδύνῳ ὄντι καὶ ἀπορουμένῳ ἤδη, κἂν ἔμπυος γενόμενος διεφθάρην· νῦν δὲ τοῦτ' ἔσωσεν τὸ αἷμ' ἀποχωρῆσαν. ὡς οὖν καὶ ταῦτ' ἀληθῆ λέγω, καὶ παρηκολούθησέ μοι τοιαύτη νόσος ἐξ ἧς εἰς τοὔσχατον ἦλθον, ἐξ ὧν ὑπὸ τούτων ἔλαβον πληγῶν, λέγε τὴν τοῦ ἰατροῦ μαρτυρίαν καὶ τὴν τῶν ἐπισκοπούντων.
>
> Dem. 54.11–12

> Afterwards the doctor said he was not too worried by the swellings on my face and my cuts, but continuous fever followed and pains, terrible pains throughout my body, but especially in my sides and belly, and I lost my appetite. And as the doctor said, if I hadn't spontaneously lost a great deal of blood — I was already suffering intense pain and in despair — I would have died from an abscess. But this loss of blood saved me. [To the clerk] Read out the depositions of the doctor and my visitors to show that what I say is true, that my illness, a result of the blows I suffered at their hands, was so severe that I nearly died.
>
> Transl. Victor Bers

This passage speaks of Demosthenes' masterful deployment of persuasive strategies. The quasi-technical medical jargon is intended to impress his audience and enhance the rhetorical *deinôsis* which enables Ariston to present the attack that he suffered as an instance of insolent violence which could have caused his death. But equally important for the purposes of our discussion are the differences in internal audiences' responses to Ariston's wounded body.

Ariston, the victim of the attack, is distinctively focalized through his suffering body. Note that during the attack in the agora, he is unable to respond verbally to his opponent's obscenities or, for that matter, stand on his feet. The women of his household lament over his maltreated body, as if what they see is the wounded body of a dead man. A sense of urgency also emerges from bystanders' initiative to call a doctor and Ariston's friends' and relatives' alacrity when they see wounded Ariston on their way home after a sympotic gathering. Compare, now, the doctor's emotionally detached language, characterized by relatively complex syntax and the use of carefully chosen medical terminology, with Ariston's silence and women's loud and inarticulate expressions of grief and panic. Note also the difference in the doctor's approach to the bruises on the victim's face with the defendant's own emphasis on the black eye and the lesions on his lips caused by his opponent's blows. For the doctor, who is indifferent to the social implications of aggression, Ariston's bruised face *is not* a cause of concern. Indeed, the phrase οὐδέν ... φοβεῖσθαι λίαν (11) seems to be an appeasing response to bystanders' wrong understanding of Ariston's wounded face as a disquieting symptom. The doctor's words are meant to instruct non-professionals and notably emphasize what the doctors call *apostasis*, "the isolation and expulsion of corrupted humors" (Holmes 2010: 154) or possible harm in the victim's internal and thus invisible organs.[2] Indeed, hemorrhage, the cause of bystanders' distress and fear, was, according to the doctor, the reason of Ariston's recovery.

---

2 On the identification of *apostasis* with the doctor's explanation of Ariston's recovery, see Holmes 2010: 150.

The passage under review reveals several aspects of cultural understandings revolving around medical practice, understandings in which emotions seem to play a pivotal role. Internal audiences' responses of panic, fear, and distress to Ariston's body (which are of course intended to make the dikasts realize the gravity of the attack) offer the appropriate background on which Demosthenes projects the doctor's soberness. The passersby and the doctor see the same body, but their attention is directed to different parts or 'symptoms'. What Demosthenes wants to establish is that Conon's attack could have caused Ariston's death and he does so by making the doctor display his professionalism by highlighting the beneficial effects of 'symptoms' which arouse laymen's panic. Like the doctor who defends medicine in the distinctively epideictic treatise *De arte*, Demosthenes' doctor might pridefully have asserted: "what eludes the sight of the eyes is captured by the sight of the mind" (11.2, transl., Mann).[3] As Mann points out (2012: 196), "[T]here is neither implication of, nor need for, an insensible world known only to the mind ... Where medical matters are concerned, the mind knows only what is sensible, even if it is not at the moment directly sensed".

A topic that we also wanted to discuss in this volume, and, indeed, one that displays obvious interfaces with ancient philosophical treatments of emotions, is the ways in which ancient medicine pathologizes emotions and the implications of sentiments' medicalization for the formation of the conceptual category of insanity. In non-medical literature, medical metaphors commonly map intense emotional experiences and their repercussions upon the lexical fields of disease or illness. These literary uses reflect cultural understandings of emotions which are particularly important for the historian of ancient emotion concepts, especially because not all emotions are metaphorically conceptualized as diseases. E.g. anger, erotic love, and, perhaps less frequently, envy are usual suspects in the metaphorical conceptualization of emotions as diseases. In addition, the cultural understandings reflected in medical metaphors for emotions are commonly deployed by philosophers who understand emotions as an impediment to the attainment of a full and happy life. These metaphors reflect pivotal aspects of how agents perceived or canonized their affective experiences. The conceptualization of *erôs* as a disease, for example, is a recurring issue in Plato's *Phaedrus*, a dialogue which illustrates lucidly how philosophical discourse appropriates folk

---

[3] ὅσα γὰρ τὴν τῶν ὀμμάτων ὄψιν ἐκφεύγει, ταῦτα τῇ τῆς γνώμης ὄψει κεκράτηται, 11.2. Cp. also Holmes (2010: 129–30): "Despite inflecting it differently in different contexts, then, the medical writers consistently use the symptom to connect the visible and invisible dimensions of the physical body, implicating suffering in a world of somatic stuffs and forces that can be neither easily observed nor intuitively known, while, at the same time, bringing that world to light".

understandings of emotions reflected in the metaphors that poets commonly employ to refer to the phenomenology of the emotion and its overwhelming effects on its agents.[4]

Disease metaphors show that specific emotions are typically understood as external forces reducing the agent to a state of helpless passivity (as is the case with the English verb 'lovesick'). In other instances, disease metaphors reflect the uncontrollability of emotions, a quality which is directly relevant to their intensity. Although not always identified with madness, emotions such as anger and erotic love elicit forms of behaviour which are commensurate with the irrational behaviour that characterizes insanity. The fact that one of the most common source domains for disease metaphors of emotion is madness (and madness *is* commonly identified as a disease) is partly due to the fact that in ancient thought, especially in systematic approaches to emotions and their implications for the quest of virtue and happiness *pathê* are understood as a driving force which must be either moderated or extirpated. But one may note that as early as Gorgias of Leontini strong emotional experiences are *identified* as the causes of insanity. In his attempt to establish the overwhelming power of images to generate emotions in the *Encomium of Helen*, Gorgias claims that in some cases frightful sights cause people to lose their minds (16–17) and engage in irrational and counterintuitive actions which harm their own interests. This 'definition' of madness, relying as it does on the 'absurd' and self-harming behaviour that it causes, is quite common in ancient thought. Moreover, Gorgias' description of the psychological impact of frightful images through the example of combat terror is strikingly similar with Shay's classification of changes in behaviour and character prompted by Combat Trauma.[5] This is not, of course, to say that Gorgias was aware of the PTSD and, indeed, we know very little about how ancient societies responded to people who 'lost it' because of their exposure to shocking images in the battlefield. A possible exception is provided by epic and tragedy, where heroes like Achilles, Heracles or Hecuba endorse violent and self-harming types of behaviour which are directly related to combat violence.[6] Yet, we know disappointingly little about how people responded to the 'hysterical' blindness — caused by combat trauma — of a man who got well after his visit at the Asclepeion in Epidaurus.[7]

---

4 See Cairns 2013.
5 Shay 2002. On the similarities between Gorgias' approach and Shay's classification, see Tritle 2009: 198.
6 See the excellent discussion by Fisher (2018, esp. 62–63).
7 On this case, combat trauma in antiquity, and Gorgias' *Helen*, see Tritle 2009.

The understanding of strong emotional experiences as an elicitor of madness or as a condition which can metonymically be described as madness is longstanding in ancient Greek thought. Aristotle, for example, claims that strong emotional experiences, such as 'angers' (θυμοί) affect the body and cause mania (*EN* 1147a 12–18). Similarly, in a less quoted passage from the *De somniis* (460b 4–16) Aristotle points out that the intensity of emotions is directly relevant to the gravity of the cognitive impairment that they cause.[8] Interestingly, in that passage Aristotle compares emotions' impact on judgment with the visual illusions caused by strong fever which make patients perceive through their senses things that do not exist (or rather things which exist only as a result of patients' arbitrary and selective combination of the signs that they see). In the Stoic anti-emotionalist tradition, emotions are conceived as madness, but this does not mean that the Stoics identify the insanity of uncontrollable emotional experiences with the 'pathological' madness caused by bodily factors.[9]

Emotions' implications for medicine are not however restricted to 'psychopathology', i.e. what we would label mental/behavioural disorders, neurosis or psychosis. Although an orthodox Stoic would advocate the benefits of his philosophical therapy for a critically ill patient (and would also probably take his/her extreme fear for death as a form of insanity), some contributors in this volume emphasize aspects of patients' emotional experiences in their own right. As we saw, in the ancient societies that we want to explore doctors do not seem to be particularly sensitive to patients' sentiments. This may be due to the fact that the extant medical treatises 'objectify' patients by treating them primarily as somatic entities rather than as *persons*. Hence, medical writers do not share the emphasis that modern medicine places on the psychological consequences of bodily illness and their effects on patients' recovery. If we are to believe Gorgias' words in Plato's homonymous dialogue (Pl. *Grg.* 456a7–c7), it is thanks to the sophist's eloquence that patients overcome their fear for dreadful, albeit necessary surgical procedures (see Spatharas' essay in this volume).[10] Gorgias' boastful comparison

---

[8] For discussion, see Spatharas 2019: 40–41.
[9] See Ahonen 2018.
[10] On medical psychology, cp. the following definition: "Medical psychology has historically been defined as the branch of psychology concerned with the application of psychological principles to the practice of medicine. Medical psychology shares with the fields of health psychology and behavioral medicine an interest in the ways in which biological, psychological, and social factors interact to influence health. Medical psychologists use psychological theories and principles in order to improve the health and well-being of patients with physical illness". (King P.S. 2013. "Medical Psychology," In *Encyclopedia of Behavioral Medicine*, edd. M.D. Gellman and J.R. Turner. Springer, New York, NY: 1357.

of rhetoric with medicine must, no doubt, be explained in relation to Plato's own programme in the dialogue *Gorgias* emphasizing ethical concerns about civic discourse. But the passage also indicates how the public nature of medical procedures in antiquity is a welcoming environment for performers such as Gorgias, who takes advantage of the medical epideixis to advocate the effectiveness of his art. The stress that this passage lays on rhetoric's rather than medicine's 'power' (*dunamis*, a recurring word in medical texts) to exercise control on patients' sentiments reflects medical authors' reticence about patients' feelings. And as is commonly the case, patients' feelings in this passage are focalized through the eyes of external observers: doctors who are unable to proceed because of patients' panic and the eloquent rhetor who appeases them through persuasive manipulation of their emotions.

3 Outline of the Volume

This volume falls into three major sections. The first section — entitled "Emotions Across Medicine and Philosophy" — consists of chapters which discuss various ways in which emotions can provide us with a heuristic tool for the exploration of the dialogue — sometimes complementary, at other times antagonistic — between medicine and philosophy in antiquity. In the first chapter, "What is a *pathos*? Where Medicine meets Philosophy", Peter N. Singer investigates the core conception and fundamental nature of *pathos* (*psuchês*) in Greek thought — warning us that 'affection of the soul' is a far better translation in English, compared, that is, to 'emotion'. Singer starts his discussion with the crucial observation that while the "use of *pathê psuchês* as a standard term to refer to a category of items — including fear, anger, pity, hatred — readily translatable as 'emotions' is already present in Aristotle, it is not so in Plato"; while the soul in Plato is said to have 'health' and 'disease' (*nosos*), it is not straightforwardly designated as having *pathê* or *pathêmata*. Still, a careful investigation of the term *pathos* in the Platonic corpus reveals certain semantic attributes of the term, which later become fundamental in Galen's conception of the 'affections of the soul': among them, Singer draws particular attention to Plato's association of *pathos* with an unpleasant experience; its use as an indicator of passivity as opposed to activity; and its regular occurrence in contexts which denote physical affectedness. Galen's discussion of *pathê psuchês* is shown by Singer to engage in dialogue with the previous philosophical tradition in a variety of ways. Thus, while Galen's 'therapy of the soul' owes admittedly a lot to Chrysippus, his very claim that a *pathos* of the soul belongs to or arises in its non-rational part is strongly asserted against the Stoics, who denied the existence of such a part and proposed that all *pathê* are or involve errors of judgment. Galen is more Platonic on this point: his adoption of the model of a tripartite soul (as opposed to the 'monistic' view of the Stoics) allows him effectively to speak of *pathos* in direct association with the uncontrolled behaviour of the soul's (non-rational) 'spirited' and 'desiderative' part. At the same time, Galen's understanding of *pathos* as something unambiguously negative and undesirable is distinctly Stoic, and is pursued as thought against the Aristotelian position where there may be an *appropriate* level of *pathos*. Singer subsequently concludes his chapter by paying emphasis on the strongly physical sense in which *pathos* is understood by Galen: the term is suggestive of an ongoing inappropriate motion; this motion affects parts of the soul and, potentially, it can end up impinging on the whole body, either by subjecting it to whimsically affective turns and twists, or by causing an actual bodily illness. What Galen is essentially trying to do in this case — according to Singer — is map the concept of *pathos* in its physical or medical understanding onto the concept of *pathos* in its ethical understanding. In the second chapter, entitled "Drugs and Psychotropic Words in Gorgias' *Encomium of Helen*", Dimos Spatharas investigates Gorgias' — philosophically inflexed — claim that the therapeutic power of speech (evident, amongst others, in its effective treatment of wearing and exhausting emotions) "bears the same relation to the ordering of the soul as the ordering of drugs bears to the constitution of the bodies". Gorgias' axiomatic statement constitutes one of the first declarations of the so-called 'medical analogy' — a concept that provides the background for several other chapters in this volume. Although this analogy is normally treated by scholars as implying some kind of contrast between physiology and psychology (medicine deals in material drugs, philosophy deals in disembodied words; medicine cares for the 'body', philosophy cares for the 'soul'), Spatharas argues that Gorgias conceives of the emotive potentialities of *logos* in distinctively physiological terms. To the extent that *logos* grants with visibility invisible things, thus making them perceptible to the eye of belief, it assumes the status of a physical entity which is materially impressed upon people. In this sense, a subject's emotional manipulation through words resembles his treatment through drugs not in a vaguely metaphorical way: the analogy drawn by Gorgias is premised on a bodily continuum, different parts and aspects of which respond variously to different kinds of therapy. The evidence from Gorgias brings to the fore a major issue that the present volume wishes to address: namely, the fact that emotions, under certain circumstances, acquire the status of pathological entities which call for an expert's therapeutic intervention. The third and concluding chapter of this first part of the volume takes a slightly different direction: it focuses on a specific kind of *pathos* and explores how philosophers and physicians are affected by it (or remain unaffected, for that matter) in the course of their respective intellectual pursuits. In his contribution, entitled "Wonder and Perplexity across Medicine and Philosophy in Classical Greece", Spyridon Rangos examines the ways in which *thaumazein* turns out to be fundamental for the agenda of classical philosophy, while remaining by contrast of little relevance to Hippocratic medicine. Thus, both Plato and Aristotle locate wonder at the beginning of the philosopher's quest, and they conceive of it as "an indispensable affection for philosophical reflection to get started". However, while Aristotle — as Rangos argues — seems to think that wonder is entirely overcome with the advent of knowledge, Plato believes that wonder can only be elevated in rank or sublimated, never fully transcended; his philosopher lives in alternate states of admiration and awe, of perplexity and puzzlement. Another important difference is that Aristotle thinks that wonder, though pre-eminently a philosopher's mental and affective disposition, is an emotion common to *all* human beings: *thaumazein* comes close to being identified with universal *curiosity*, and the primary objects thought to induce and promote it the most are strange, unusual, and exceptional events which undermine our assumptions and force us to research. In Plato's dialogues, by contrast, wonder addresses and is caused by reflection on the usual and the ordinary when, all of a sudden, it loses its all-too-common and familiar appearance and turns into an unintelligible puzzle. Despite these differences, wonder remains for both philosophers a creative force of energy. On the contrary, as Rangos shows, *thauma* is cast in an entirely negative light in the Hippocratic Corpus. Physicians consider wonder an impediment to knowledge, and they profess time and again their ability to dispel it by disclosing fully the mysteries of the human body. While the first three chapters in this section discuss *pathos* as a topic that is closely investigated by both philosophers and physicians, Rangos' chapter illuminates the ways in which *pathos* — in the specific form of wonder shapes the circumstances under which the medical and the philosophical quest for truth is carried out. And in this respect, it is important to note that philosophy transpires to be more 'emotional' than medicine: a philosopher's attempt to get a grip on truth is permeated — cognitively as well as affectively — by instances of wonder; a Hippocratic physician, on the other hand, in his attempt to achieve an optimum state of clinical detachment leaves wonder — along with other emotions — out of his inquiries.

The second section of the volume, entitled "Emotions in the Medical Room", consists of four chapters which are predominantly focused on the Hippocratic Corpus. In the first of these chapters, entitled "The Doctor's Dilemma: Addressing Irrational Fears", Elizabeth Craik starts by noting the intense correlation between mental and physical conditions in the Hippocratic writings, as this becomes evident both in the pragmatic case histories reported throughout the *Epidemics* and in the theoretical observations made in the *Aphorisms*. Among the mental conditions, according to Craik, 'fear' features prominently, most often in the form of irrational phobias, dream terrors, and nightmares. Irrational fears in *On the Sacred Disease* and *On Diseases of Girls* are highlighted by Craik as a case in point, and they are explored with particular regard to the supposed aetiology of, and recommended therapy for, such problems and associated precipitating conditions. In this context, the author draws attention to the fact that mental and emotional, like physical, conditions are treated by *katharsis*, the clearance of excessive, undesirable matter in the body. This consequently leads her to the contention that, at some level at least, the medical notion of addressing emotional disturbance by means of 'clearing' the body from stuff that needs to be purged is intrinsically linked to Aristotle's ideas about the emotions, and more specifically to his model of the cathartic treatment of fear and pity proposed in the *Poetics*.

While Craik's chapter deals with a type of emotion — that of (irrational) fear — which emerges as a *symptom* in the course of illness, the next two chapters deal with an emotion that shapes the patient's perception of and *reaction* to his or her illness. In "Shame and Concealment in the Hippocratic Corpus", Jennifer Kosak discusses the surprising fact that while one encounters all sorts of debilitating and, in theory at least, embarrassing medical conditions in the Hippocratic Corpus, physicians very rarely read 'shame' in these situations; as she characteristically points out, if those patients — whose case histories are reported in classical medical sources — felt shame, "these writers aren't telling". "Just having a disease", Kosak observes, "or becoming sick does not appear to be a source of shame; even when the medical writers mention patient behaviour, such as disobedience or intemperance, that might cause or exacerbate the illness, they do not indicate that the patients feel shame, or should feel shame, because of their actions". There is one notable exception, and this is the unusual emphasis placed on shame in *On the Sacred Disease* where we read that those patients who are accustomed to having epileptic attacks, sense in advance when they are about to be seized, and flee from their fellow humans, seeking the privacy of hidden places; this they do because of shame. According to Kosak, the medical author's attention to the psychology of shame in this instance is noteworthy: it is definitely related to the dehumanizing lack of self-control suffered by patients during their seizures and it certainly has something to do with the overall extraordinary nature of this particular disease. The patient's hiding away from the public eye is then sensitively linked by Kosak with some telling case histories from the Hippocratic *Epidemics* where we read of (female) patients who, in the course of displaying signs of emotional distress, are described as 'veiling' themselves at some point. Rather than dismiss this as a cursory detail, Kosak suggests that we should treat it as a marked gesture: what we have here are not just patients trying to warm themselves up because of their fever or chill; the act of veiling may be taken to implicate a far more complex emotional script that points ultimately to the uncomfortable position in which the patient finds herself and her reaction with feelings of shame.

In the next chapter, entitled "The Body to be Hidden: Shame and Ancient Medicine", Chiara Thumiger starts from the general claim that "basic strong emotions that concern the survival of one's body and bodily integrity are irreducible part of the experience of being ill", adding that "shame, as the strongest, non-negotiable discomfort deriving from the perception of one's bodily flaws being exposed to the outside world belongs to the same discussion". In a way similar to Kosak, Thumiger then continues with the observation that, unlike Greek tragedy's representation of illness as a profoundly shame-inducing experience, classical medical sources only rarely comment on shame as an attendant feeling of the sick. According to her reading of the exceptional testimony found in *On the Sacred Disease*, the medical author in that case is not so much interested in the emotion of shame as part of the phenomenology of illness; rather, his unusual digression into the depths of patient psychology serves the purpose of establishing that the reason why epileptics run away every time they are about to be seized has nothing to do with their 'fear' of the divine (supposed by charlatans and religious healers to hide behind the attack): it is simply a natural reaction that results from their embarrassment. After looking at some instances of female patients who cover up themselves ("what emerges from these passages", she argues, "is a desire to shield and protect the body in reaction to a state of vulnerability and danger"), Thumiger moves on to later medical sources, and more specifically to the nosological treatises of Aretaeus of Cappadocia. What one finds in this case is a growing medical interest in social values of decorum, honour, and, overall, appropriate behaviour; consequently, the idea of illness as a shame-inducing event is time and again thrown into sharp relief — such development is aptly contrasted with the Hippocratics' silence on the subject. Relatedly, lack of shame — in imperial and late antique medical sources — is seen to turn into a symptom of specific pathological conditions, some of them believed to be affecting not only the body but also the mind of the patient.

In this section's final chapter, "Reading and Misreading Medical Emotions: Some Cases of Female Patients in the Hippocratic *Epidemics*", George Kazantzidis observes that while emotions feature quite often in the case histories of the Hippocratic *Epidemics*, the general tendency in scholarship has been to treat them, almost exclusively, as affective disorders that make their presence felt in the course of, and as an immediate result of *physical* illness. He then goes on to argue that, while the bodily origin and nature of emotions in classical medicine are indeed incontestable, in some cases a patient's emotional profile reveals more about his or her 'psychology' than is usually assumed to do. By focusing on some intriguing cases of female patients reported in the Hippocratic *Epidemics*, Kazantzidis shows that there are instances where the narrative suggests — or, at least, leaves us enough space to assume — that the emotions displayed by a patient are deeply anchored to their behavioral traits; they are manifestations, in other words, of the mood patterns and the emotional make-up that characterize them as individuals. This then leads him to the conclusion that on occasions we can use medical emotions as ways of recovering the ancient patient's identity and character — a character that is all too often believed to be suppressed and become obliterated under the sweeping presence of bodily symptoms which constitute the experience of what we call 'illness'.

The third and final section of the volume, entitled "Medico-philosophical Treatments of Emotion", explores ancient understandings of emotions *qua* pathological occurrences both in strictly philosophical contexts (Stoicism/Posidonius) but also in medical contexts which clearly interact with and are heavily influenced by the philosophical notion of a "therapy of the soul" (Galen). In the first of these chapters, entitled "Posidonius and the Pneumatists: The Aetiology of Emotions and Diseases", Teun Tieleman focuses on the important figure of Posidonius of Apamea. Based on a report by Galen, which establishes a link between Athenaeus of Attaleia — the founder of the Pneumatist school of medicine — and Posidonius, Tieleman argues that the distinction between three different types of causes of illness, which is ascribed to Athenaeus, ultimately derives from the renowned Stoic. Posidonius' distinction between a cohesive, an immediate and a predisposing cause is linked by Tieleman to the Stoics' more general inquiries into the interplay between body and soul, and into the causal explanation of mental phenomena such as the emotions. Particular attention is drawn in this context to Posidonius' Περὶ παθῶν (variously translated as *On Affections* or *On Emotions*) in which its author appears to have taken issue with Chrysippus' famous analogy between diseases of the body and diseases of the soul. On the basis of the evidence which once again survives in Galen, Posidonius turns out to have placed extra emphasis on the notion of a (weak) person's 'proneness' to emotional outbursts. In this sense, the analogy could be rephrased in the following terms: a diseased soul does not necessarily resemble a diseased body, but rather an over-sensitive body which, though healthy, is vulnerable to becoming affected with illness. Posidonius — according to

Tieleman — appears to have conceived of this state of vulnerability as a *predisposing* cause of illness.

In the next chapter, entitled "Galen on Non-Rational Motivation and the Freedom from Emotions: A Reading of *Affections of the Soul*", David Kaufman explores Galen's view on emotions in relation to the following famous positions that survived from antiquity: the Stoic view that ordinary emotions contribute nothing at all to a virtuous life; and the Peripatetic view that such emotions, at least if they are suitably moderate and concordant with the agent's practical reasoning, play a crucial role in virtuous action. Kaufman highlights the fact that Galen's position in this debate is rather puzzling: on the one hand, he argues that appropriate non-rational motivation plays an ineliminable and valuable role in a virtuous life; on the other hand, he also argues in favour of the ideal of *apatheia*, the complete freedom from emotions, and develops a detailed method of moral education intended to cultivate it. Although previous scholarship has found Galen's claim that we ought to free ourselves from the emotions to sit uneasily with his view that the non-rational parts of the soul have a fundamental role to play in virtuous motivation, Kaufman argues that his considered position, developed most fully in *Affections of the Soul*, makes a cogent and sophisticated contribution to the *apatheia/metriopatheia* debate, which differs from both Stoic *apatheia* and Peripatetic *metriopatheia*. In Kaufman's words: "When Galen urges us to extirpate the emotions, he is not recommending that we eliminate all non-rational motivation, but instead that we eliminate excessive and inappropriate instances of it. Indeed, far from urging us to eliminate non-rational motivation altogether, Galen takes spirit and appetite to play crucial roles in virtuous motivation". Galen's account is helpful in this sense as a model of how an author might develop an ideal of *apatheia* while maintaining their commitment to Platonic psychology.

In the next chapter, entitled "Disorders of the Soul: Emotions and Clinical Conditions in Galen", Julien Devinant starts with the observation that "by the time Galen was writing, a connection was already well established between clinical disorders of the soul and emotions — that is, illnesses such as *phrenitis*, *mania*, or melancholy, and *pathê* such as fear, anger, or sorrow". However, as he notes, the exact nature of this connection was not plainly explained, so much so that sometimes it becomes extremely difficult to tell "whether our sources take all these conditions as sorts, stages, or aspects of one and the same phenomenon, or even as distinct experiences bearing mere resemblance to each other". Even Galen's position on the subject — according to Devinant — is far from clear. This seems to be complicated by the fact that recent scholarship has highlighted a possibly unresolved tension between the ethical treatises, relying on a Platonic tripartite conception of the soul, and the medical writings, presenting a brain-centred treatment of mental conditions. To resolve this tension, Devinant insists that we should not confuse the two sets of 'psychic affections', and proceeds to show that, as far as Galen is concerned, emotions and medical affections of the soul, albeit strongly interrelated, are categorically distinct: they are neither 'psychic' nor 'affections' in the exact same sense. "Ethics and medicine", as Devinant illustrates in this chapter, "address different *types* of issues: the former is concerned with misuses of an otherwise functional soul, while the latter takes care of patients whose souls are themselves unable to function correctly".

In the last chapter of the volume, entitled "The Atlas Patient: Galen on Melancholia and Psychosis", Susan Mattern focuses on a type of patient who belongs to the latter of the two categories discussed by Devinant: that of a person whose soul and mind have been so damaged that they are virtually unable to function properly. The Atlas patient is obsessed with the idea that the mythical figure that holds the sky on his shoulders will become tired and the skies will collapse. This extremely interesting case of psychosis is shown by Mattern to belong to a wider category of hallucinations and delusions which are believed to affect those suffering from *melancholia*. Her case study thus brings to the fore how mental and emotional disturbance is deeply rooted in the body (in that specific case, the brain's function is damaged by black bile). At the same time, the Atlas patient — defined as he is by his constant 'fear' that the skies will fall — exemplifies the crucial (experiential as well as diagnostic) role played by emotions in certain mental disorders and illustrates how the conceptual category of mental illness can be structured and ordered across distinctive affective profiles.

Bibliography

Ahonen, M. 2018. "Making the Distinction: The Stoic View of Mental Illness", in: Thumiger and Singer (eds.), 343–364.
Cairns, D.L. 2013. "The Imagery of *Eros* in Plato's *Phaedrus*", in: E. Sanders *et al.* (ed.), *Eros in Ancient Greece*, 233–250. Oxford: Oxford University Press.
Holmes, B. 2010. *The Symptom and the Subject: The Emergence of the Physical Body in Ancient Greece*. Princeton: Princeton University Press.
Mann, J. 2012. *Hippocrates*, On the Art of Medicine. Leiden: Brill.
Shay, Jonathan. 2002. *Odysseus in America: Combat Trauma and the Trials of Homecoming*. New York.
Sontag, S. 1978. *Illness as Metaphor*. New York: Doubleday.
Spatharas, D. 2019. *Persuasion and Emotions in the Public Discourse of Classical Athens*. Berlin: De Gruyter.
Tritle, L.A. 2009. "Gorgias, the *Encomium of Helen*, and the Trauma of War", *Clio's Psyche* 16.2: 195–199.

Part I: Emotions Across Medicine and Philosophy

Peter N. Singer
What is a *Pathos*? Where Medicine Meets Philosophy

Abstract: What is happening to us when we experience a powerful emotion? Is *pathos* primarily an ethical or a medical concept — or does it admit of a coherent psycho-physical account? Galen provides a particularly fruitful site for the investigation of these questions, as both a prominent participant in the philosophical discourse on the emotions and a medical theorizer of the relationship between *pathê psuchês* and physical and physiological phenomena. This paper explores Galen's physiological and ethical approach to the emotions on the basis of a wide range of Galenic texts, while at the same time situating his conception of *pathos* within the philosophical tradition, in particular in relation to Plato, Platonism and the Stoics. It identifies in Galen's thought both a strong *parallelism* between the accounts of 'body' and 'soul' functions and pathologies and a strong understanding of the *pathê* as *themselves* physical events.

1 Introduction

What is it to have a passion? Even within the modern period, the word has a bewildering variety of contexts and connotations, shifting both meaning and moral implications in dramatic ways. In everyday contemporary English to have a passion, or to be passionate, is something which bears overwhelmingly positive connotations — those of a life-affirming enthusiasm or devotion, whether to a person, or to an activity or cause. But we may contrast this with another usage, probably only a few decades out of date, whereby the term 'passionate' is typically coupled with 'rage', and 'to be in a passion' denotes, precisely, that negative and uncontrollable emotion of anger. Or, still more strikingly, with another, even earlier, usage — still familiar to us in the phrase 'the passion of Christ' — where the term refers rather to a profound or extreme form of suffering.

Warmest thanks go to George Kazantzidis and Dimos Spatharas for the opportunity to participate in the conference at Patras in December 2017 from which this paper arose, and to the participants at that conference for helpful discussion. I also gratefully acknowledge the support of the Wellcome Trust for the research project during which the paper was written.

https://doi.org/10.1515/9783110771937-002

That polysemic nature of Latin *passio* (and its various European cognates) is partially traceable to the term's function as a translation of the Greek *pathos* (of which, of course, it is also a cognate). If we turn, then, to the Greek term itself, this too undergoes transformations, and displays a similarly complex and dramatic multiplicity. To the widely differing connotations borne by modern European 'passion' words, briefly indicated above (alongside which we should put those borne by the terms 'passive' and 'passivity') we should add those of the Greek derivatives 'pathetic' and 'pathology' — and of course of the English word given by the transliterated form 'pathos' itself. The Greek term is notoriously plural in translation, too. To 'passion' we may add as possibilities 'affection', 'affect', 'suffering', 'experience', 'ailment', 'disease'[1] — and, of course, 'emotion'.

There is a growing body of recent work on the emotions in the ancient world, which, however, has tended either to consider the methodology with which one should approach the study of the emotions or to explore individual particular emotions (or both), rather than to investigate the core conception of *pathos* itself.[2] Relatedly, there has been (with some exceptions) little discussion of the issue of translation just mentioned: much recent work does not question, or at least does not find seriously problematic, the equation — which, as I shall argue, is fundamentally distortive — of the Greek *pathos* with the modern English term 'emotion'.[3]

So, what is a *pathos*, and a *pathos* of the soul (*psuchê*) in particular? And what is it, especially, at the points where philosophical analysis interacts with medical understandings? Quite a lot has been written about the *pathê psuchês*, both in Galen and in the Hellenistic philosophical background that precedes and coexists with Galen, especially in relation to Stoic ethics and theory of action, as well as to the discourse of the 'therapy of the soul', or cure of the passions or affections.

---

1 The latter two will be more likely in medical contexts — but, as we shall see below, 'medical' and 'ethical' senses are potentially closely intertwined. (And it should not be forgotten that Cicero preferred the translation *morbus* also in the ethical contexts.) For broader historical discussion of the semantic range of 'passions' and 'emotions' in the modern period, see Dixon (2003).
2 Prominent examples of such work are: Braund and Gill (1997); Cairns and Fulkerson (2015); Caston and Kaster (2016); Chaniotis (2012); Chaniotis and Ducrey (2016); Harris (2001); Kaster (2005); Knuuttila (2004); Konstan (2006); Rosenwein (2006); Sorabji (2000).
3 A useful but brief account of the translation issue is given by Harris (2001: 4 n. 3; cf. 84 and 93). The equation of *pathos* with 'emotion', even for Plato, is regarded as unproblematic by Rosenwein (2006: 33), whose focus is admittedly mainly with later periods. See further below n. 25 on Stoicism and Sorabji. For important discussions of the problems of translatability between ancient and modern emotion categories see Lloyd (2007); Cairns (2008); Introduction to Cairns and Fulkerson (2015).

This chapter will also consider both Galen and that philosophical background, but will aim to do two things less often attempted, but of considerable interest for the history and development of this crucial term itself, for its use within both medical and philosophical discourses, and for its role in the history of the emotions.

Those two (related) things are:
a) to examine aspects of the fundamental nature of *pathos* in Greek thought — to look at it definitionally and in terms of its core conception, considering the early, in particular Platonic, usage, which, I shall argue, is crucial also to a full understanding of its use in Hellenistic and post-Hellenistic contexts;
b) to highlight the *physical* nature of *pathos*, the sense in which it is a bodily, as much as or more than a mental or ethical concept, and investigate how this too may assist with our understanding of it.

That, then, will be the thematic focus; textually, the central focus will be Galen, though we shall also pay considerable attention to Stoic thought and to other relevant texts and discussions amongst Galen's medical-philosophical predecessors.

In the process I believe that some important features will emerge of the function and usage of this ancient word for 'emotion' — a word which, indeed, is so translated only at the risk of considerable distortion or confusion — as well as some clarity as to how it is used in medical and philosophical contexts, and how and why those uses are inextricably intertwined.

2 The Background: Plato

We begin, then, with Plato. As I shall argue, Plato's usage is of central importance for the later conception of the *pathê psuchês*. And yet we do not find the *pathê psuchês* themselves in Plato. While the noun *pathos* and the verb *paschein* are sometimes used in the context of accounts of both emotion and perception, and are used in formulations which relate them in some (not always entirely clear) way to the soul, neither on its own nor in conjunction with *psuchê* has the term acquired a generalized sense corresponding to emotion (or passion, affection, etc.).[4] It seems, further, that the use of the term in the *plural* in such a sense is not

---

4 The point is succinctly summarized by Gosling (1975).

found before Aristotle.[5] To the extent that there *is* a general term or terms corresponding to our 'emotions' in Plato, this is represented rather by the pairing *hêdonai–lupai*, 'pleasures and pains'; some of what we understand by the term, moreover, will also be covered by *epithumiai*, 'desires'. There is, of course, much more that could be said on the conception of *pathos* in Plato, and nothing approaching a full account can be attempted here; but we shall say a little more shortly.

The main point for our present purposes, however, is that while this use of *pathê psuchês* as a standard term to refer to a category of items — including fear, anger, pity, hatred — readily translatable as 'emotions' is already present in Aristotle, it is not so in Plato. In a very well-known passage of *De anima*, Aristotle poses the question whether these *pathê* of the soul all also involve the body.

> T1
> ἔοικε δὲ καὶ τὰ τῆς ψυχῆς πάθη πάντα εἶναι μετὰ σώματος, θυμός, πραότης, φόβος, ἔλεος, θάρσος, ἔτι χαρὰ καὶ τὸ φιλεῖν τε καὶ μισεῖν· ἅμα γὰρ τούτοις πάσχει τι τὸ σῶμα ... διαφερόντως δ' ἂν ὁρίσαιντο ὁ φυσικὸς [τε] καὶ ὁ διαλεκτικὸς ἕκαστον αὐτῶν, οἷον ὀργὴ τί ἐστιν· ὁ μὲν γὰρ ὄρεξιν ἀντιλυπήσεως ἤ τι τοιοῦτον, ὁ δὲ ζέσιν τοῦ περὶ καρδίαν αἵματος.
>
> It seems that the *pathê psuchês* all involve the body: rage, meekness, fear, pity, confidence, also kindness and loving and hating; for the body undergoes something in these ... But the student of nature and the dialectician will define each of them differently, the nature of anger for instance; for the former will say it is an appetite for retribution or something of the sort, the latter that it is a boiling of the blood in the region of the heart.[6]
>
> *De anima* 1.1, 403a16–33

The precise nature of this proposition regarding the relationship of the mental and the physical is a major question for Aristotle's philosophy of mind, and in general beyond our scope in this paper.[7] Yet it is clear, at least, that Aristotle thinks it appropriate and uncontroversial to use the terminology of *ta tês psuchês pathê*, i.e. in some sense to attribute *pathê* to the soul; indeed he raises the

---

5 As remarked by Harris (2001).
6 Translations are my own unless otherwise stated.
7 The interpretation of Aristotle's philosophy of mind, in particular his understanding of the mind–body relationship, has been the subject of vigorous and extensive scholarly discussion in recent years. A small selection of the most important contributions is: Nussbaum and Rorty (1992) (especially the essays of Burnyeat; Frede; Nussbaum and Putnam; Sorabji); Menn (2002); Caston (2005) (with a comprehensive survey of recent views, in particular on the issue of perception); Shields (2009).

question whether all its *pathê*, or only some of them, also co-involve the body.[8] It also seems likely — from the completely unproblematized way in which this topic of discussion is introduced — that this terminology is by now well-known and widespread, at least in Aristotle's *milieu*.[9] (As I shall argue further below, the new usage also seems related to a fundamentally different attitude to *pathos* of the soul from that found either in Plato or in Hellenistic successors, in particular the Stoics and Galen — that is to say, to the conception of such *pathos* as in itself value-neutral rather than undesirable.)

In any case, Plato's usage predates, or at least is markedly distinct from, this 'technical' or standardized usage, familiar to us also from later philosophy. In Plato the term *pathos* is almost never coupled with *psuchê* in the genitive in such a phrase. It is interesting in this context to note some of the terms which *are* so coupled, by Plato — things which he thinks can fairly straightforwardly be attributed to the soul. These include strength, weakness, justice, wickedness, parts or forms and internal conflict (*stasis*).[10] Indeed, the soul may — using even more clearly physical or medical language — be said to have, health, condition (*hexis*), and indeed specific locations in the body; it can even have disease (*nosos*) and treatment (*therapeia*). Yet it is not — at least not generally or straightforwardly — said to have *pathê* or *pathêmata*.

How, then, *does* Plato use the term *pathos*? To summarize, one may make a classification into four main usages or senses of *pathos* and its cognates:

a) an 'everyday' usage, referring in very general terms to an event or experience;
b) a negative sense: a bad thing, unpleasant experience, punishment;
c) to indicate *passivity* as opposed to *activity*;
d) a bodily sense: to denote *physical* affectedness.

---

8 But I do not here enter into the question, what kind of *motion* of the soul, if any, is involved in this attribution. Aristotle's *De anima* may be interpreted — as powerfully argued by Menn (2002) — as centrally motivated to *deny* that the soul itself takes part in any motion, and indeed to part company from Plato on this very point — an interpretation which might seem tendentially to reverse the thrust of the argument below, contrasting Platonic or Neoplatonic unaffectedness with the Aristotelian view. For my present argument, however, it is sufficient that the Aristotelian usage, at least, straightforwardly attributes *pathos* to the soul, and that in this usage *pathos* is itself of neutral rather than of negative value.

9 An alternative interpretation (in my view less plausible, for the reason stated) is that it is Aristotle himself who has developed this new terminology.

10 The qualification should be made, at least for the last four of these items, that Plato will at times argue that they are features of the soul due to its embodiment, thus not belonging to it in its truest nature: cf. the references to *Timaeus* 44a–b and *Republic* 610b below.

The first of these senses is of less importance to us, except to the extent that it draws attention to the general, theoretically unloaded, use of the term, and to the extent that it blends into the second sense. Many examples of (a) could be given: it will suffice here to recall Socrates recounting his own youthful experience (τὰ ἐμὰ πάθη) of enthusiasm, followed by disillusionment, on encountering the philosophy of Anaxagoras (*Phaedo* 96a), or Aristodemus in the preamble to the *Symposium* "saying that something ridiculous happened to him" (τι ἔφη αὐτόθι γελοῖον παθεῖν, 174e).

The last three senses, meanwhile, are of particular importance to us, all corresponding to aspects of *pathos* which we shall see to be fundamental also in Galen. Two examples — again, out of many available — of (b) are the statement of the necessity of an individual undergoing whatever sanctions are imposed by the state at *Crito* 51b (πάσχειν, ἐάν τι προστάττῃ παθεῖν) and the reference to people "undergoing the greatest, most painful and most fearful sufferings because of their wrong-doings" (διὰ τὰς ἁμαρτίας τὰ μέγιστα καὶ ὀδυνηρότατα καὶ φοβερώτατα πάθη πάσχοντας) at *Gorgias* 525c. Use (c) may be seen in *Phaedrus* in the account of how an enquiry into any subject (here, the nature of certain desires or appetites) should proceed.

T2
σκοπεῖν τὴν δύναμιν αὐτοῦ, τίνα πρὸς τί πέφυκεν εἰς τὸ δρᾶν ἔχον ἢ τίνα εἰς τὸ παθεῖν ὑπὸ τοῦ.

consider what capacity it has, either of acting or of being acted upon, and in respect of what things.

Phaedrus 270d

Here the verbs *dran* and *paschein* correspond respectively to 'acting' and 'being acted upon'.[11]

We then come to sense (d); and here we observe the extent to which *pathê* are experiences or events that take place in the body — albeit ones which in some cases, and in some sense at least, may co-involve the soul.

T3
καὶ διὰ δὴ ταῦτα πάντα τὰ παθήματα νῦν κατ' ἀρχάς τε ἄνους ψυχὴ γίγνεται τὸ πρῶτον, ὅταν εἰς σῶμα ἐνδεθῇ θνητόν.

And it is because of all these *pathêmata* [sc. arising through mortal embodiment] that the soul becomes mindless when it is first bound into a mortal body.

Timaeus 44a–b

---

11 Cf. the pairing, 'actions or undergoings' (ποιημάτων εἴτε παθημάτων) at *Republic* 4, 437b.

We note here that the *pathêmata* are not themselves 'of the soul'; the term is applied either to bodily events or to the whole sequence of happenings in the course of which the soul is incarnated (we may compare with this the account of the 'diseases of the soul' which come about because of bodily condition at 86b-d). Relatedly — or conversely — the point is emphasized in book 10 of the *Republic* (610b) that the soul is in the most important sense *not* affected — does not itself become less just or pious — as a result of what are, in fact, *pathêmata of the body*.

This leads on to the question of the soul's *co*-involvement in *pathos*, which is indeed somewhat complicated.

T4
ψυχὴ παντὸς ἀνθρώπου ἀναγκάζεται ἅμα τε ἡσθῆναι ἢ λυπηθῆναι σφόδρα ἐπί τῳ καὶ ἡγεῖσθαι, περὶ ὅ ἂν μάλιστα τοῦτο πάσχῃ, τοῦτο ἐναργέστατόν τε εἶναι καὶ ἀληθέστατον ... οὐκοῦν ἐν τούτῳ τῷ πάθει μάλιστα καταδεῖται ψυχὴ ὑπὸ σώματος;

The soul of every human being is compelled, in the experience of great pleasure or pain in relation to something, at the same time to believe that the object in relation to which it suffers this most especially is the clearest and truest ... in the case of this *pathos*, then, is not soul powerfully fettered by the body?

Phaedo 83c–d

We see a strong sense in which *pathos* arises in or from the body, as well as some unclarity (to put it at its mildest) as to exactly how or to what extent the soul is involved in it. A further text of central importance for this discussion is *Philebus*. Detailed analysis of both these texts is beyond our scope; but a few points may be made in summary. One is that in key passages of both *Phaedo* and *Philebus* where the soul is described as affected by a motion of the body, the context is an account of perception, not of emotion (e.g. *Philebus* 33d2–34a5). Another is that, while in one passage Socrates in *Philebus* insists precisely that emotion of a certain kind belongs to the soul and not the body, the term in play there is *epithumia*, not *pathos* (esp. *Philebus* 35c6–d2) Thirdly, as already indicated, while there are some formulations which do seem to describe the soul as in some way undergoing or involved in *pathos* — or at least as co-involved with in it with the body — there seems to be a reluctance to state this straightforwardly.[12]

---

12 The argument of *Philebus* in relation to pleasures and pains, desires, the relationship of these to body and soul, and the role of *pathos* in the whole picture, is complex and impossible to summarize succinctly; the entire passage 31b–55b is in various ways relevant.

3 Neoplatonist Digression

The reluctance to attribute *pathê* to the soul is related to the Platonic view that soul is in its very nature active, a self-mover and a source of motion in bodies, which are, by contrast, in themselves passive. It may be instructive here to consider some Neoplatonic, in particular Plotinian, texts. While it may be taken to be anachronistic to use the views of later Platonist philosophers to shed light on Plato, Plotinus' very rich exploration of the problems of the soul–body relationship can — to put it at its weakest — prove fruitful in throwing into relief and elucidating certain perspectives which are tendentially present in the text of Plato himself. Indeed, there is strong support for the notion of the soul as principle or cause of motion in *Phaedrus* (245c5–9) and *Laws* (10, 896a–897d); relevant too is the view of the soul as bringer of life in the 'final argument' of the *Phaedo*, 102–107. But the thought is developed much more fully in Neoplatonism. As seen in the following texts,[13] Plotinus will argue that the soul, properly speaking, engages in *energeia*, rather than being subject to *pathos*, which is proper rather to the body.

> T5
> πῶς ἂν πάθος ἐγγένοιτο ἐν ἀριθμῷ ἢ λόγῳ; ἀλλὰ μᾶλλον λόγους ἀλόγους καὶ ἀπαθῆ πάθη δεῖ ἐπιγίνεσθαι αὐτῇ οἴεσθαι, καὶ ταῦτα τὰ ἀπὸ τῶν σωμάτων μετενηνεγμένα ἀντικειμένως ληπτέον ἕκαστα καὶ κατ' ἀναλογίαν μετενηνεγμένα, καὶ ἔχουσαν οὐκ ἔχειν καὶ πάσχουσαν οὐ πάσχειν.
>
> How could affections arise in a number or in a rational principle? We should rather think that non-rational reasonings, or unaffected affections, arise in it, and we should take it that these things, which are transferred from the body, are transferred in an opposed sense and by correspondence – that it has them while not having them, and suffers (undergoes affection) while not doing so.
>
> *Enneads* 3.6.1.33–7

> T6
> οἷον ἐν τῇ τομῇ τεμνομένου τοῦ σώματος ἡ μὲν διαίρεσις κατὰ τὸν ὄγκον, ἡ δὲ ἀγανάκτησις κατὰ τὸν ὄγκον τῷ μὴ μόνον ὄγκον, ἀλλὰ καὶ τοιόνδε ὄγκον εἶναι· ἐκεῖ δὲ καὶ ἡ φλεγμονή· ᾔσθετο δὲ ἡ ψυχὴ παραλαβοῦσα τῷ ἐφεξῆς οἷον κεῖσθαι. πᾶσα δὲ ᾔσθετο τὸ ἐκεῖ πάθος οὐκ αὐτὴ παθοῦσα.
>
> When a body is cut, the division is within the physical mass of the body, but the annoyance belongs to that mass by virtue of its not being just a physical mass, but also a physical mass

---

[13] Alongside these passages, particularly relevant are also e.g. *Enneads* 1.2.5.1–14, 3.6.2.54–9, 3.6.3.22–5, 4.4.28.

disposed in a certain way. This, too, is where inflammation is; but the soul takes it on through as it were lying next to it, and so perceives it. But the soul as a whole perceives the *pathos* there, while not itself suffering.

Enneads 4.4.19.8–13.

T7

καὶ λῦπαι καὶ ὀργαὶ καὶ ἡδοναὶ ἐπιυθμίαι τε καὶ φόβοι πῶς οὐ τροπαὶ καὶ πάθη ἐνόντα καὶ κινούμενα; ... ἀλλὰ χρὴ συγχωροῦντας ζητεῖν ὅ τι ἐστὶ τὸ τρεπόμενον. κινδυνεύομεν γὰρ περὶ ψυχὴν ταῦτα λέγοντες ὅμοιόν τι ὑπολαμβάνειν, ὡς εἰ τὴν ψυχὴν λέγομεν ἐρυθριᾶν ... διὰ ψυχὴν μὲν ταῦτα τὰ πάθη, περὶ δὲ τὴν ἄλλην σύστασίν ἐστι γιγνόμενα. ἀλλ' ἡ μὲν αἰσχύνη ἐν ψυχῇ δόξης αἰσχροῦ γενομένης· τὸ δὲ σῶμα ... ὑπὸ τῇ ψυχῇ ὂν καὶ οὐ ταὐτὸν ἀψύχῳ ἐτράπη κατὰ τὸ αἷμα εὐκίνητον ὄν.

Distress, anger, pleasure, desire, fear — how could these not be changes and affections present [in the soul] and moving there? ... But, while conceding this, we should enquire what it is that is changed. If we say this of the soul, we risk formulating a proposition similar to one where we would say that the soul blushes ... these affections are because of the soul, but are brought about in another composition. Shame comes about in the soul when there arises the opinion that there is something shameful; but the body ... is subject to the soul and, not being the same as a lifeless body, is changed in its blood, by virtue of the readiness of this to motion.

Enneads 3.6.3.1–15

So, we do speak — people certainly did speak, by Plotinus' time — in an everyday way of the *pathê* of the soul; but Plotinus' view is that to do so is to use a somewhat loose circumlocution to describe what is actually happening. Properly speaking, the *pathos* belongs to the body: only this is actually *affected*. There is thus an imprecision or contradiction inherent in the very term *pathê psuchês*. The precise nature of the experience, and of the relationship between soul and body involved in it, is not straightforward: we note the tortured language to which Plotinus resorts in an effort to do justice to it (ἀπαθῆ πάθη, 'unaffected affections'; πάσχουσαν οὐ πάσχειν, 'suffers ... while not doing so' in T5). What the soul is doing during (what we call) its *pathos* is in fact *moving* in some way (it can have *kinêsis*, but not *pathos*) — a motion which bears some relationship with that *pathos* of the body. Another way of looking at is that such *pathos* comes about through a failure of the non-rational soul to follow the *logoi* of the rational: what is essentially involved here is a judgement (*krisis*), not a 'being affected'. As Noble puts it,[14] Plotinus' strategy in relation to the "mistaken view that the soul is

---

14 Noble (2016), offering a very helpful and lucid analysis of the relative role of body and soul in Plotinus' '*pathos* of soul'. On Plotinus' emotions see also Emilsson (1998), and on his theory of the soul more broadly Remes (2007), Caluori (2015).

affected in the passions" is to claim "either the affections in us are misattributed to the soul, or the motions in soul are misidentified as affections". Yet, as Noble also insists, it is important not to make the mistake of thinking that *pathos psuchês* is, or is just, a bodily thing: although the use of the term *pathos* for this motion represents a transferred usage from its proper bodily context *pathos psuchês* (as it is called) is indeed a kind of motion of the soul. In fact, what are called 'passionate' states of the soul are actually cognitive states, specifically of the nutritive soul.

It is of course not legitimate to project this fully-formed view back on to Plato. But Plotinus' formulations may help us focus on features which do indeed seem central to Plato's approach too, namely the bodily nature of *pathos* as well as its connotations of passivity. A possible response to this might be that for Plato emotion is, indeed, fundamentally a bodily event. But such a response, while containing an element of truth, would be a distortive simplification: as we have seen, it is true both that Plato (and Plotinus) at points consider some emotional experiences as involving a judgement of the soul, and that some things which we would call emotions have no bodily component and are certainly not properly called *pathos*: most clearly, the desires, *epithumiai*, attributed to the rational part of the soul at *Republic* 9, 580d-e.

The main points that arise from this consideration of Plato in relation to Neoplatonist developments are that (i) *pathos* is considered as fundamentally bodily in nature; (ii) there is a crucial relationship with the notion of passivity; and (iii) any straightforward equation of *pathos* with our 'emotion' must fail. A fourth point (iv), which is very clear in Plato (though less so in Plotinus), is that *pathos* — when it *is* used to refer to some kind of emotional experience — refers to negative ones. There undoubtedly are (again, unless one is committed to an unusually restricted sense of the term 'emotion') positive emotions in Plato; but these will not be referred to by the term *pathos*.

4 *Pathos Psuchês* in Galen: Some Essential Features

Let us then jump forward from Plato, five centuries or so, to Galen. In doing so we must of course bear in mind that some important things have emerged in between — both the Epicurean and the Stoic schools, to begin with, and, more specifically, the writings of Chrysippus and Posidonius; and, relatedly, a whole tradition of discussion and treatment of the *pathê* of the soul. This 'therapeutic' discourse is richly exemplified, in Galen's time and in the generation immediately before him, by such figures as Plutarch, Epictetus, Marcus Aurelius. But it is also true that *Platonic* language and terminology and indeed specific Platonic texts are of fundamental importance to Galen in the development of his own theory and practice. And Galen participates in this discourse of 'cure of the affections', especially in a couple of short works, *The Diagnosis and Cure of the Affections Peculiar to Each Person's Soul* (hereafter '*Affections*') and *Freedom from Distress*.[15]

Let us consider some of the central characteristics of the *pathê psuchês* in Galen. First, crucially, a *pathos* of the soul belongs to or arises in its *non-rational* part. This is strongly asserted against the Stoics, who deny the existence of a non-rational part of the soul, and thus take it that all *pathê* are or involve errors of judgement, and against Epicureans, who he says have obscured the distinction.[16]

Important, secondly — and Platonically — is that there are in fact *two* non-rational parts of the soul. Galen, following Plato, divides the soul into rational, 'spirited' (*thumos* or *thumoeides*) and desiderative (*epithumêtikon*). The former is responsible for our tendency to anger, as well as to pride, and our noble, brave or warlike instincts; the latter for our desires for food, drink and sex. Both may function at an appropriate level, or alternatively at an inappropriate, uncontrolled level; in the latter case they are in a state of *pathos*.

T8
δύο γὰρ ἔχομεν ἐν ταῖς ψυχαῖς δυνάμεις ἀλόγους, μίαν μέν, ἧς θυμοῦσθαι παραχρῆμα καὶ ὀργίζεσθαι τοῖς δόξασί τι πλημμελεῖν εἰς ἡμᾶς ἔργον ἐστί ... ἄλλη δ' ἐστιν ἐν ἡμῖν δύναμις ἄλογος ἐπὶ τὸ φαινόμενον ἡδὺ προπετῶς φερομένη.

For we have two non-rational capacities in our soul. The action of the first is to become immediately enraged and angry at people who seem to us to be doing us some wrong. Our other non-rational capacity is dragged rashly towards anything which appears pleasant.
Affections 6 (20 de Boer = V.28–9 K.)

The way that we exert discipline, and thus avoid *pathos*, is different in the two cases. The spirited is potentially influenced by reason, and has essentially good instincts; the desiderative, like a wild animal, can only be subjugated, not educated. The rational soul must indeed enlist the help of the former — likened to a noble horse, or dog — to control the latter.

---

15 On this 'therapeutic' discourse see the fundamental work of Hadot (1995), as well as Nussbaum (1994); Graver (2009a), (2009b); and, specifically in relation to Galen, Gill (2010) and Singer (2018), (2019).
16 This is certainly his view of the Epicurean Antonius at *Affections* 1 (3–4 de Boer = V.3 K.).

T9
The rational soul cannot restrain the desiderative without calling upon the spirited for help ... The relationship ... is analogous to that of the dog to the hunter, or of the horse to the rider, for although they assist him to do their will, they sometimes move at the wrong time and to an undue degree. ... Education makes the spirited soul compliant and the desiderative weak.

Character Traits 1 (27–8 Kraus, Arabic text trans. Davies, in Singer 2013)[17]

Interesting for our purposes is a passage earlier on in the first text cited above:

T10
ἐπειδὴ τὰ μὲν ἁμαρτήματα διὰ ψευδῆ δόξαν γίγνοται, τὰ δὲ πάθη διὰ τὴν ἄλογον ὁρμήν, ἔδοξέ μοι πρότερον ἑαυτὸν ἐλευθερῶσαι τῶν παθῶν· εἰκὸς γάρ πως καὶ διὰ ταῦτα ψευδῶς ἡμᾶς δοξάζειν. ἔστι δὲ πάθη ψυχῆς ... θυμὸς καὶ ὀργὴ καὶ φόβος καὶ λύπη καὶ φθόνος καὶ ἐπιθυμία σφοδρά.

Since errors arise from false belief, while affections arise from non-rational impulse ... one should first free oneself from the affections: it is not unlikely that these may themselves in some way be a cause of our forming false beliefs. [A]ffections of the soul are: ... rage, anger, fear, distress, envy, vehement desire.

Affections 3 (6–7 de Boer = V. 7 K.)

Here Galen clarifies the identity of the most central *pathê*, i.e. the excessive non-rational impulses. But while defining this domain of the non-rational in the soul, he also points to a complexity of interaction within the apparently binary rational/non-rational model with which he started. *Pathê*, though in their nature events in the non-rational soul, may cause false beliefs, that is, errors in the rational soul.

Moving from the theoretical model to the practical or therapeutic account, we get quite a lot of detail, both in *Affections* and in *Freedom from Distress*, on the techniques or interventions that should be used to moderate or cure the *pathê* – the 'therapy of the emotions'.[18] These techniques prominently include: a daily self-assessment; the employment of an independent monitor to observe one's actions and give frank criticism; the *praemeditatio malorum*, or daily consideration of the worst that may befall; contemplation of models of exemplars; the recitation, whether internalized or out loud, of certain poetic texts to reinforce these processes.[19]

---

17 Cf. similarly *Affections* 6 (19 de Boer = V.28 K.).
18 This practical 'therapy' and its background in the Greek philosophic tradition has been well discussed by Gill 2010; see also Singer 2013, 2018, 2019.
19 For a fuller account see especially Singer 2018.

Pathos psuchês for Galen is an out-of-control emotional response: it drags you along, it takes over. It impairs, temporarily removes or 'crowds out' correct judgement; it may cause violent behaviour later regretted. Galen gives vivid examples of such events: his Cretan friend who almost kills two of his slaves in a fit of temper; the emperor Hadrian, who put out the eye of one of his slaves with a *stilus*.[20] The notion of the rational soul being potentially pulled out of its way by uncontrolled forces — as described in the first text cited in this section — is central to Galen's understanding of what *pathos* is.

We know, then, quite a lot about *pathos psuchês*, in terms of its causes, its experiential nature, its effects and the way in which we should handle it. But can we get closer to a definition, to an understanding of the underlying reality? What sort of event *is* this *pathos* which has these momentous effects and demands these important interventions? What is actually going on inside you?

5 Stoic Accounts of *Pathos Psuchês* in Relation to Galen

It may be helpful to take a step sideways, and look at some Stoic definitional accounts of *pathos* — both because these accounts are very clearly in the background to Galen's thought, and because they engage closely with the question, which is of particular interest to us here, of the relationship of 'body' and 'soul' elements in *pathos*.

Of course, as already observed, much of Galen's ethical writing consists of a defence of the Platonic tripartite soul against the misguided 'monistic' view of the Stoics, especially Chrysippus. Yet he is clearly indebted to the Stoic and Epicurean traditions on the *pathê*, from which the discourse of 'therapy of the soul' primarily arose; and indeed much of his central work on the *pathê*, in *The Doctrines of Hippocrates and Plato* (henceforth *PHP*), is a closely argued account of and engagement (admittedly hostile) with Chrysippus' texts on the subject.

What do the Stoic texts tell us about the nature of the *pathê*? One thing is that they are in their nature negative; they are undesirable. That is a Stoic understanding of *pathos* that Galen adopts, against the Aristotelian position where there may be an *appropriate* level of *pathos*. I leave aside here any detailed discussion of this Aristotelian ethical–psychological model and of how his approach

---

20 *Affections* 4 (13–15 de Boer = V.17–20 K.).

might be compared with Galen's. But there is, at least, a fundamental distinction in linguistic usage.

Galen must agree with Aristotle that there is an appropriate degree of emotive response, in the sense that the two non-rational parts of the soul have a role to play, rather than needing simply to be eliminated. But he will not, as Aristotle would, refer to such appropriate emotive response as a kind of *pathos*. It is for this reason, too, surely, that Galen — as noted by a number of scholars[21] — makes no mention of the notion of *metriopatheia* or 'moderation of the *pathê*', which had become a term of art in the Platonic–Aristotelian tradition of his time.

Galen's approximate contemporaries the 'Middle Platonists', by contrast, drawing on Platonic tripartition on the one hand and Aristotelian ethics on the other, allot an explicit positive role to certain natural *pathê*. For them, the correct calibration of the *pathê* naturally arising in both of the two non-rational parts — always under the overall control of the rational — constitutes an essential element in virtue or ethical health.[22]

For Galen, however, while some form of non-rational response *can* be appropriate, *pathos* of the soul never can: it is always a bad thing. It would not, therefore, make sense for Galen to speak of its appropriate moderation.[23]

While this may seem at one level a semantic point, it is also a matter of considerable importance for the ethical model elaborated. For while there are undoubtedly desirable non-rational soul responses, and in that sense 'emotions', for Galen, there is no detailed account of them, certainly no sophisticated elaboration of their range and precise extent, as in the *Nicomachean Ethics*.[24]

---

[21] See Singer (2013: 22 with n. 53) for discussion with further references.

[22] The view is well summarized by Plutarch, *Ethical Virtue* 443c–d, insisting that *pathos* should not be eliminated altogether, and identifying a role for it in ethical virtue; see also Alcinous, *Didaskalikos* 30.3, 30.5. See Boys-Stones (2017) for a wide range of relevant text and for discussion; see also Singer (forthcoming).

[23] There is perhaps a little more uncertainty or flexibility in Galen's position than this simplified account allows. Galen does indeed seem, as Kaufman (2014) has discussed, to talk of an appropriate level of *lupê* in *Freedom from Distress*. That thought, however, is not fully developed by Galen; and his views in that work seems consistent with the view that a certain degree of *lupê* is in certain circumstances humanly *inevitable* and *allowable*, rather than that it is actually *appropriate*. He thus presents himself as adopting broadly the same attitude to *lupê* (which is surely, in this context, a variety of or even equivalent to *pathos*: on this point see Singer (2019)) as the Stoics, but without their hardline extremism.

[24] Certainly in general Galen does not present correct emotional responses, in an Aristotelian way, as means or midpoints. There is, however, an exception: in *Mixtures* he suggests that virtuous characters can be understood as consisting in midpoints between excesses; strikingly, though, the context is bodily mixture, where the notion of good balance is central to his thinking;

In his attitude to *pathos*, then, Galen, I suggest, adopts the Stoic, negative sense of the term, in spite of his strong theoretical disagreement with the Stoic psychological model. But it is also the case — as we have seen earlier — that this sense of *pathos* as something always or predominantly negative is one which is strongly Platonic.

The above considerations, incidentally, point to one of the strongest senses in which the still widespread translation 'emotions' is misleading for *pathê*. It is often stated that the Stoics wished to eradicate all emotions; but this is true only of the particular kind of emotional response which they define as *pathos*.[25] It is clear that there is a range of, in our terms, emotional response which is acceptable and indeed desirable, from a Stoic point of view. Translating *pathos* as 'emotion' risks seriously distorting the nature of the Stoic approach. (And a similar argument applies, albeit within different psychological models, for both Plato and Galen.)

But is there a still closer similarity between Galen's and the Stoic account? Let us look more closely at some of the Stoic definitional accounts.

T11
πάθος δ' εἶναί φασιν ὁρμὴν πλεονάζουσαν καὶ ἀπειθῆ τῷ αἱροῦντι λόγῳ ἢ κίνησιν ψυχῆς <ἄλογον> παρὰ φύσιν ... πᾶσαν πτοίαν πάθος εἶναι, <καὶ> πάλιν <πᾶν> πάθος πτοίαν.

[The Stoics] say that *pathos* is impulse which is excessive and disobedient to the dictates of reason, or a movement of the soul which is <irrational and> contrary to nature ... therefore every fluttering is a *pathos*, and likewise every *pathos* is a fluttering.

Stobaeus II.88–90 (= LS 65A part, their trans., adapted)

T12
λύπη μὲν οὖν ἐστιν ἄλογος συστολή· ἢ δόξα πρόσφατος κακοῦ παρουσίας, ἐφ' ᾧ οἴονται δεῖν συστέλλεσθαι. φόβος δὲ ἄλογος ἔκκλισις· ἢ φυγὴ ἀπὸ προσδοκωμένου δεινοῦ. ἐπιθυμία δὲ ἄλογος ὄρεξις· ἢ δίωξις προδοκωμένου ἀγαθοῦ. ἡδονὴ δὲ ἄλογος ἔπαρσις· ἢ δόξα πρόσφατος ἀγαθοῦ παρουσίας, ἐφ' ᾧ οἴονται δεῖν ἐπαίρεσθαι.

---

and the discussion or psychological or ethical excellence has been added as an extension of that. See *Mixtures* 2.1 (42 Helmreich=I.576 K.), with Singer and van der Eijk (2018: 106 n. 20).

25 E.g. Sorabji (2000: 17) states that the Stoics wanted to 'eradicate emotion'; but his detailed account (29–54) makes clear that there is room in the Stoic system for a range of responses which (as indeed he explicitly admits, 49) *we* would call emotions. The fact that "Chrysippus is entitled to treat them separately" is, of course, an argument against their being counted as *pathê* by the Stoics, but not for us to continue translating that term as 'emotions'. A helpful corrective is supplied by Gill (2016), directly discussing the 'positive emotions' of Stoicism and by Graver (2007), (2009a) and (2017), the latter two pieces exploring still further the sometimes surprising range of emotional responses envisaged for the Stoic sage.

> Distress is an irrational contraction, or a fresh opinion that something bad is present, at which people think it right to be contracted. Fear is an irrational shrinking, or avoidance of an expected danger. Appetite is an irrational stretching, or pursuit of an expected good. Pleasure is an irrational swelling, or a fresh opinion that something good is present, at which people think it right to be swollen.
>
> [ps.-]Andronicus, *De passionibus* 1 (= LS 65B)

What is notable here is that we have both a physical or bodily account of the *pathos and* an account in terms of intentional content. That *pathos* is in some sense a psycho-physical event seems to be central to its understanding — even if the precise nature of the psycho-physical event or precise relationship between cognitive and bodily elements, may be difficult or controversial.[26] It is sufficient for our purposes to note that there is a complex definition of *pathos* in terms of its mental and physical aspects in early Stoicism. This same problem — that a *pathos psuchês* is a psycho-physical event in some sense, but that be difficult to establish in *precisely* what sense — will be a pertinent one for Galen too.

6 *Pathos* in Galen: Soul–Body Parallelism (1)

Turning back to Galen, then, let us proceed by considering, first, what he says definitionally about the concept of *pathos* in general terms, and then, some of his more detailed remarks about the *pathos* of the soul in its relationship to bodily events.

On the general conception of *pathos*, he is very explicit. As he explains in book 6 of *PHP*, there are in fact two fundamental senses of the distinction between the terms *energeia* and *pathos*, and two correlated senses in which a subject X is said to undergo a *pathos*, as follows.

(1) X undergoes a motion which is not caused by X:

> T13
> ἡ μὲν οὖν ἐνέργεια κίνησίς ἐστι δραστική, δραστικὴν δ' ὀνομάζω τὴν ἐξ ἑαυτοῦ, τὸ δὲ πάθος ἐν ἑτέρῳ κίνησίς ἐστιν ἐξ ἑτέρου.

---

[26] There is a considerable literature exploring these complexities, and in particular the questions (a) whether a Stoic passion is a physical experience following upon an opinion, or whether the judgement itself constitutes the emotion, this judgement however being inextricably connected to a physical event; (b) whether the answer to that is the same for all the early Stoics, or whether — as Galen claims — there is an important difference here between Zeno and Chrysippus. For Galen's claim of an inconsistency in Chrysippus see *PHP* 4.2 (238–40 De Lacy = V.366–8 K. = Long and Sedley 65D, part); for discussion see especially Sorabji (1998); Gill (2005), (2006); Price (2005).

The *energeia* is an active motion, and by active I mean 'from itself', while the *pathos* is a motion *in* one subject *from* another.

PHP 6.1 (360 De Lacy = V.506–7 K.)

(2) X undergoes a motion contrary to nature:

T14
τὴν μὲν ἐνέργειαν κατὰ φύσιν τινὰ κίνησιν ... τὸ δὲ πάθος παρὰ φύσιν.

Energeia is a normal motion ... *pathos* an abnormal one.

PHP 6.1 (362 De Lacy = V.507 K.)

If, for example, I pick up a pen, then this event is, in sense (1), a *pathos* of the pen, but an *energeia* of my hand or arm. The *energeia* is of that which initiated the motion, and the *pathos* of the object that was moved, or caught up in the motion.

Sense (2) is, of course, that which gives rise to our modern terms 'pathology' and 'pathological': a *pathos* is a motion of X *para phusin*, contrary to nature, whereas its *energeia* is its normal motion, its motion *kata phusin*. In sense (2), then, *pathos* occurs when something goes *wrong* with a motion of X, even if that motion *is* X's own, proper motion, its *energeia* in sense (1). An example is given by the pulse. Pulsation is the proper motion — a sense-(1) *energeia*, not a sense-(1) *pathos* — of the heart. If, however, there is something wrong with the pulse — if it has become too strong or too weak — then, while its pulsation will still be an *energeia* in sense (1), it will be a *pathos* in sense (2), simply because there is something pathological about it: it is a distorted version of that proper motion.

This, then, is a general account of the concepts of *energeia* and *pathos*, in terms of the kinds of motion that they are. Further important information is provided elsewhere.

T15
ἐν κινήσει πάντως εἶναι τὸ πάθημα ... τὸ σύμπτωμα δὲ οὐκ ἐν κινήσει μόνον, ἀλλὰ καὶ καθ' ἕξιν τινὰ ... ἔσται δὴ πάθος μὲν ἡ περὶ τὴν ὕλην ἀλλοίωσις ἢ κίνησις ἔτι γινομένη, ἡ δ' ὑπομένουσα, διάθεσις.

A *pathêma* ... is always in motion ... whereas a *sumptōma* may also consist in a condition (*hexis*) ... Let us say, indeed, that a *pathos* is *alteration in respect to the matter, or motion still coming about*, while a motion that endures is rather a disposition.

Distinct Types of Symptom 2 (VII.53–4 K.)

Here Galen is offering definitions of different conceptual categories related to disease. Essential to the notion of *pathos* — and distinguishing it from other pathological categories — is again that it consists in an ongoing motion.[27]

But — returning to our *PHP* text — it turns out that this fundamental understanding of *pathos* as either an abnormal physical motion, or a physical motion with its origin outside the body in question, is of direct relevance to the soul and its *pathê* too. Indeed, Galen moves immediately to discuss that further on in the same passage.[28]

Consider *thumos*, the second or middle part of the Platonic tripartite soul — that related to the virtues of bravery and nobility and in pathological cases to excessive anger and violence. In our sense (1), then, *thumos* is the *energeia* of that particular part of the soul. But, if its motions become out of control and unbalanced (ἔκφοροί τε καὶ ἄμετροι), and out of accord with nature (οὐ κατὰ φύσιν), then these motions are — according to our sense (2) of the term — not *energeiai*, but *pathê* (*PHP* 6.1, 362,31–364,2 De Lacy = V.509 K.). Adopting the language of the famous chariot analogy of the *Phaedrus*,[29] where the two horses correspond to *thumos* and *epithumia*, the two non-rational forces in the soul, we may say that, in a case of out-of-control anger, or indeed lust, the motion of the non-rational horse in question is a *pathos* in sense (2) but an *energeia* in sense (1). That is to say: the affective states of anger and sexual desire are the proper province of the two respective horses, but they are engaging in them in an inappropriate or abnormal (οὐ κατὰ φύσιν) way (*PHP* 6.1, 364,10–21 De Lacy = V.510 K.)

Let us note, however, what is happening to the poor old charioteer — the rational part of the soul — in such a case, if he reaches the stage of losing control and being overwhelmed by these motions from the non-rational. His movement "is not an *energeia* in either sense, but a *pathos* in both" (*PHP* 6.1, 364,19–20 De Lacy = V.510 K.): *pathos* in sense (1) because the *energeia* is from elsewhere, and *pathos* in sense (2) because the resulting motion is pathological or distorted.

The above discussion is of interest not just because it sheds light on the fundamental or more abstract notion of *pathos*, in terms of the kind of motion that it is, but also because it tells us more about how Galen understands a *pathos* in the

---

27 One may compare this account with that in *Affected Places* 1.2–3 (VIII.20–30 K.), asserting the diagnostic importance of establishing whether particular parts are affected primarily (*idiopatheia*), on the one hand, or secondarily or sympathetically (*sumpatheia*), on the other. Here too *pathos* is conceived as an unnatural or abnormal motion arising in a body, and potentially causing *pathos* in connected bodies.

28 The entire passage in question, too long to cite here *in extenso*, is *PHP* 6.1 (362–6 De Lacy = V.506–13 K.).

29 *Phaedrus* 253c7–254a7.

specific context of the soul. Runaway anger is a *pathos* of the *thumos*, because that is the part that has gone wrong, that has an inappropriate motion; but it is also a *pathos* of the whole soul (and indeed potentially the whole body), because these are dragged along by it, and this unnatural process of being dragged along constitutes *pathos*.

7 *Pathos* in Galen: Soul–Body Parallelism (2)

So, we have seen one way in which a physical understanding of *pathos*, in terms of the fundamental motions involved, underlies the understanding in the soul context too. Another very rich text, also from *PHP*, is of considerable interest here too. The context is — as so often in this text — that of an irritated polemic against the Stoics, in this case for errors made in their version of the analogy of health of soul and health of body. The text is intricate and complex in its detailed engagement with various targets. But one may present Galen's own conclusions, and his version of the analogy, in the following table, which summarizes the argument of *PHP* 5.2 (296 De Lacy = V.434 K.).

Health of soul	Health of body
Souls of the virtuous (σπουδαίων)	Bodies immune from *pathos* (ἀπαθέσι σώμασιν)
Souls of those making progress (προκοπτόντων)	Bodies in good condition (εὐεκτικοῖς)
Souls of intermediate people (μετρίων)	Bodies in health but not in good condition (ὑγιαίνουσι χωρὶς εὐεξίας)
Souls of the many/ordinary (πολλῶν τε καὶ φαύλων)	Bodies suffering disease on little provocation (ἐπὶ σμικρᾷ προφάσει νοσοῦσι)
Souls of people in grip of *pathos* (ἐν πάθει τινὶ καθεστώτων)	Actually diseased bodies (ἤδη νοσοῦσιν)

In this passage, Galen is trying to map the concept of *pathos* in its physical or medical understanding onto the concept of *pathos* in its ethical understanding: to provide a neat marriage or parallelism of the two. This neat parallelism encounters some difficulties, to an extent acknowledged by Galen himself.[30] But the

---

30 There is, first of all, no actual person who is *apathês* in the physical or medical sense, that is, not liable to disease. (And indeed, Galen casts considerable doubt on the notion that a person may be absolutely *apathês* in the ethical sense either: see e.g. *Freedom from Distress*, with the

ambition to advance a close analogy between health of soul and health of body remains — and with it, one particular sense of the close connection between physical and ethical *pathos*.

In this section and the previous one, then, we have seen one distinct sense of the importance of the physical conception of *pathos* for the ethical or mental: that of parallelism. That is to say: we are not in this context arguing — as may be argued for the Stoic accounts — that *pathos* of the soul actually is, or under some description is, a bodily event. Rather, what we have observed here is the way in which the bodily understanding of *pathos* — as a disease category and more specifically as a particular kind of physical motion — both *parallels* and *informs* the conceptualization of the soul *pathos*, in detail.

8 *Pathos psuchês* and its Physical Dimension; Concluding Remarks

But we also need to explore the sense in which there is *more* than just a parallelism. As we shall see in this final part of the chapter, the connection between physical and ethical domains is so close that an emotional or ethical *pathos* — a *pathos psuchês* — may actually *cause* a bodily illness, or indeed in the worst case, death. It may, even more strongly, be possible to argue that a *pathos psuchês* in its fundamental nature actually *is* a bodily event.

Before proceeding, let us note a further possible complexity, and path not taken, within the present discussion. In what follows we shall consider the items we have seen identified by Galen as *pathê psuchês* — such items as anger, fear, distress, shame. These are the *pathê psuchês* of the ethical tradition (going back in a similar form, as we have seen e.g. in T1, to Aristotle).

But there are also, for Galen, the ailments or impairments of the soul in the strictly *medical* sense — such items as *melancholia, phrenitis, mania, paraphrosunê*. These are, undoubtedly, *pathê* in the medical sense already observed, e.g. in T14 and T15 above. Nor should one forget, indeed, that *pathos* was a term in widespread use in the medical tradition, from Hippocratic texts onward, to refer simply to medical diseases or ailments. And those just mentioned certainly affect the *psuchê*: they are, specifically, malfunctions or abnormal states of the *psuchê*, or of certain of its capacities.

---

discussions of Kaufman (2014) and Singer (2019). Perhaps, however, he concedes to the Stoics at least that theoretical possibility.)

Now, Galen does not directly use the term of art *pathê psuchês* to refer to these specifically *medical* psychic ailments, confining it rather precisely to the terms of the ethical tradition, as just outlined; and our present discussion has confined itself to *pathê psuchês* in this narrower sense too. It seems that the closest that Galen gets to such a usage, in the medical context, is to refer to such illnesses as *pathê* that arise in the brain, and as *pathê* of the rational [*sc.* part of the soul], that is the *logistikon*.[31] Consideration of the relevance of *melancholia, mania*, etc. would take us far beyond what is possible within the present paper. One may however briefly summarize the situation in very broad terms by saying that there are fundamentally two models of analysis and related therapy for the *psuchê* in Galen: that where he works within the *pathê psuchês* tradition, analysing the soul and its shortcomings in ethical terms and recommending largely cognitive or habituative interventions for their remedy, and that where analysis and therapy are centred on bodily mixture and its optimal and suboptimal states, on the one hand, and on the brain and its functions or malfunctions, on the other (the latter having a close causal dependency on the former, and the main forms of intervention being diet, drugs, or bloodletting); but that there is, however, considerable complexity in the overlap between these two models.[32]

We return, then, to our narrower focus on the ethical *pathê psuchês*. As we saw above (T8–10), Galen approaches these from within a post-Platonic psychological model, and offers a range of therapeutic approaches to them, similar to others found in the ethical writings of his time. More distinctively Galenic, however, is the role that the *pathê* may have in the causation of physical disease. The point is a recurrent one in Galen's writings on health and its preservation; one example may suffice.

T16
θυμοὶ καὶ φροντίδες καὶ λῦπαι καὶ πάνθ' ὅσα τοιαῦτα μονονουχὶ καθ' ἑκάστην ῥοπὴν ὑπαλλάττοντα τὴν κρᾶσιν.

rages, worries, distress and all such things which pretty nearly transform the mixture through their every shift.

Matters of Health 1.5 (14 Koch=VI.28 K.)

In fact, the *pathê psuchês* can have severe medical consequences. Anger, as we see also in his ethical works, has unpleasant physical side-effects, such as

---

31 In *Affected Parts* 3.6; on this see Singer 2018.
32 A consideration of the relationship between all Galen's different accounts of the *psuchê*, in the context of its pathology and therapy, is made by Singer (2018); see also Devinant (2018).

frothing at the mouth and redness (as well as the disastrous ethical consequences we already noted above). But fear and distress or grief, and even occasionally joy, may have very serious, even fatal, results. And Galen has a precise physiological account of why this is so. A *pathos psuchês* typically involves certain motions of the heart and blood. We may see below how the different *pathê* each give rise to a specific progression of physical events, in terms of the motion of blood and the heart. The table that follows summarizes information from *Causes of Symptoms* 2.5 (VII.191–4 K.):

Pathos of soul	Concomitant physical manifestation
fear (φόβος)	blood and *pneuma* drawn inwards; cooling of body surface
rage (θυμός)	blood and *pneuma* pushed outwards to surface, with heating
anxiety (ἀγωνία)	uneven mixture of the two above
shame (αἰδώς)	first inward motion; then return to surface
distress (λύπη)	milder version of motions seen in fear

What can then happen, as Galen makes clear elsewhere too, is that the overall heating and drying which are associated with distress, in particular, may lead to fever, and even to death.[33] Related to this is the fact that such emotional disturbances — including erotic disturbances, as in the comparatively well-known example of the love-sick lady in *Prognosis* — have physical, and therefore diagnosable, manifestations in the pulse.

Can one go even further? Is there a sense in which a *pathos psuchês* actually *is* a physical event? Particularly relevant here are two further passages from the two texts last cited (the former, as we shall see, with a strong echo of T1 above).

T17
ὁ μέν γε θυμός ... οἶον ζέσις τίς ἐστι τοῦ κατὰ τὴν καρδίαν θερμοῦ –διὸ καὶ τὴν οὐσίαν αὐτοῦ τῶν φιλοσόφων οἱ δοκιμώτατοι τοιαύτην εἶναί φασι– συμβεβηκὸς γάρ τι καὶ οὐκ οὐσία τοῦ θυμοῦ ἐστιν ἡ τῆς ἀντιτιμωρήσεως ὄρεξις.

Rage is ... a kind of boiling of the hot in the heart; which is why the most reputable philosophers state that this is its essence; for the appetite for revenge is an incidental feature, and not the essence, of rage.

Matters of Health 2.9 (61 Koch = VI.138 K.)

---

[33] Relevant case-histories, involving death ultimately due to distress or grief, or in some cases even shame, appear in the *Commentary on Hippocrates' Epidemics VI* and in *Freedom from Distress*: see the discussion of Singer (2018).

T18
τῆς ψυχῆς τὴν οὐσίαν ... ἤτοι πρώτοις ὀργάνοις εἰς ἁπάσας τὰς ἐνεργείας χρῆσθαι πνεύματί τε καὶ αἵματι καὶ τῇ θερμασίᾳ τῇ κατὰ θάτερον καὶ συναμφότερον, ἢ ἐν αὐτοῖς τούτοις ὑπάρχειν.

the substance of the soul ... either uses *pneuma*, blood and the heat that is in both of them as the primary instruments for all its activities, or [actually] subsists in those things.
Causes of Symptoms 2.5 (VII.191 K.)

The question raised above is apparently answered in the affirmative by T17. It is obviously related to the broader one of Galen's physicalism — a question to which T18 gives an inconclusive answer, and which has been much discussed in recent literature.[34] Let us summarize the situation very briefly. There are texts, such as T17 and T18, which give a strong statement of the physical component in the pathology of the *psuchê*, as well as a strongly physicalist reading of Aristotle (T17 is essentially a 'strong misreading' of T1 above, distortively highlighting what is, for Aristotle, only one side of the coin — the account of the 'natural philosopher' as opposed to that of the 'dialectician'.)[35] There are also texts which suggest a soul–body identity thesis (especially that the soul is a particular mixture of the body, as especially in *The Soul's Dependence on the Body*; the identity of soul with *pneuma* is also entertained, as in T18); but such a position is not consistently maintained throughout the corpus, and it seems that an interactionist position, with a strong statement of the dependence of soul on body, corresponds most closely to Galen's overall view.

For present purposes, however, what is relevant is that we have identified two distinct senses of the importance of the physical in Galen's account of the *pathê psuchês*. First, in sections 6 and 7 above, we saw how the biological or physical model of *pathos* functions as a parallel, informing our understanding of the nature and operation of soul *pathos* in detailed ways: crucial in both cases is the notion of a *pathos* as a motion contrary to nature, and/or as a motion with an external source, with the capacity to disrupt or take over both a part and the whole organism or subject. In the present section, we have seen how *pathos psuchês* may be understood as at least partially a bodily event, with potentially severe bodily consequences.

---

[34] Amongst the considerable literature on the subject, see especially Hankinson (1993) and (2006); Gill (2010); Singer (2013); in relation to *pathos* the question is explored especially by Singer (2017).
[35] On this see by Singer (2014) and (2017); the physicalist interpretation of Aristotle is central to Galen's strongest physicalist argument in *The Soul's Dependence on the Body*, as discussed by Singer (2013: esp. 348–350).

More work may fruitfully be done on the early conception of *pathos*, and on the relationship of medical or physical to ethical usages in the classical period, especially in Plato. In the present chapter, I hope to have achieved three things: (1) drawn attention to the importance of that relationship, as well as the significance it has for the post-Platonic tradition, in both philosophy and medicine; (2) highlighted some of the specific connotations of the term *pathos*, in particular those of *negativity* of experience and those relating it to a *physical* or *bodily* motion, and relatedly the imperfect overlap between the Graeco-Roman *pathos psuchês* and our 'emotion'; (3) explored the detailed significance of this biologically or physically informed understanding of *pathos* for the Graeco-Roman philosophical discourse, in Galen in particular.

Bibliography

Ahonen, M. 2018. "Making the Distinction: The Stoic View of Mental Illness", in: Thumiger and Singer (eds.), 343–364.

Boys-Stones, G. 2017. *Platonist Philosophy 80 BC to AD 250: An Introduction and Selection of Sources in Translation*. Cambridge: Cambridge University Press.

Braund, S.M. and C. Gill (eds.) 1997. *The Passions in Roman Thought and Literature*. Cambridge: Cambridge University Press.

Brennan, T. "The Old Stoic Theory of the Emotions", in: Sihvola and Engberg-Pedersen (eds.), 21–70.

Cairns, D. 2008. "Look Both Ways: Studying Emotion in Ancient Greek", *Critical Quarterly* 50.4: 43–62.

Cairns, D. and L. Fulkerson (eds.) 2015. *Emotions Between Greece and Rome*. Bulletin of the Institute of Classical Studies Supplement. London: Institute of Classical Studies.

Caluori, D. 2015. *Plotinus on the Soul*. Cambridge: Cambridge University Press.

Caston, R.R. and R.A. Kaster (eds.) 2016. *Hope, Joy, and Affection in the Classical World*. Oxford: Oxford University Press.

Caston, V. 2005. "The Spirit and the Letter: Aristotle on Perception", in: Salles (ed.), 245–320.

Chaniotis, A. (ed.) 2012. *Unveiling Emotions: Sources and Methods for the Study of Emotions in the Greek World*. Heidelberger Althistorische Beiträge und Epigraphische Studien 52. Stuttgart: Franz Steiner Verlag.

Chaniotis, A. and P. Ducrey (eds.) 2014. *Unveiling Emotions II: Emotions in Greece and Rome: Texts, Images, Material Culture*. Heidelberger Althistorische Beiträge und Epigraphische Studien 55. Stuttgart: Franz Steiner Verlag.

Devinant, J. 2018. "Mental Disorders and Psychological Suffering in Galen's Cases", in: Thumiger and Singer (eds.), 198–221. Leiden: Brill.

Dixon, T. 2003. *From Passions to Emotions: The Creation of a Secular Psychological Category*. Cambridge: Cambridge University Press.

Emilsson, E.K. 1998. "Plotinus on the Emotions", in: Sihvola and Engberg-Pedersen (eds.), 339–363.

Frede, D. and B. Reis (eds.) 2009. *Body and Soul in Ancient Philosophy*. Berlin/New York: de Gruyter.
Gill, C. 2005. "Competing Readings of Stoic Emotions", in: Salles (ed.), 445–470.
Gill, C. 2006. "Psychophysical Holism in Stoicism and Epicureanism", in: King (ed.), 209–230.
Gill, C. 2009. "Galen and the Stoics: What Each Could Learn from the Other about Embodied Psychology", in: Frede and Reis (eds.), 409–423.
Gill, C. 2010. *Naturalistic Psychology in Galen and Stoicism*. Oxford: Oxford University Press.
Gill, C. 2016. "Positive Emotions in Stoicism: Are They Enough?", in: Caston and Kaster (eds.), 143–160.
Gosling, R. 1975. *Plato: Philebus, translated with notes and commentary*. Oxford: Clarendon Press.
Graver, M. 2007. *Stoicism and Emotion*. Chicago: University of Chicago Press.
Graver, M. 2009a. "The Weeping Wise: Stoic and Epicurean Consolations in Seneca's 99th Epistle", in: *Tears in the Roman World*, ed. T. Fögen, 235–252. Berlin/New York: de Gruyter.
Graver, M. 2009b. "Philosophy as Therapy", in: *Encyclopedia of Ancient Greece and Rome*, vol. 5, 273–274. Oxford: Oxford University Press.
Graver, M. 2017. "Pre-Emotions and Reader Emotions in Seneca", *Maia* 69.2: 281–296.
Hadot, P. 1995. *Philosophy as a Way of Life*, trans. M. Chase. Oxford: Blackwell.
Hankinson, R.J. 1993. "Actions and Passions: Affection, Emotion, and Moral Self-Management in Galen's Philosophical Psychology", in: J. Brunschwig and M. Nussbaum (eds.), *Passions and Perceptions: Studies in Hellenistic Philosophy of Mind*, 184–222. Cambridge: Cambridge University Press.
Hankinson, R.J. 2006. "Body and Soul in Galen", in: King (ed.), 232–258.
Harris, W. 2001. *Restraining Rage: The Ideology of Anger Control in Classical Antiquity*. Cambridge, MA: Harvard University Press.
Johnston, I. 2006. *Galen on Diseases and Symptoms*, translated with introduction and notes. Cambridge: Cambridge University Press.
Kaster, R.A. 2005. *Emotion, Restraint, and Community in Ancient Rome*. Oxford: Oxford University Press.
Kaufman, D.H. 2014. "Galen on the Therapy of Distress and the Limits of Emotional Therapy", *Oxford Studies in Ancient Philosophy* 47: 275–296.
King, R.A.H. (ed.) 2006. *Common to Body and Soul: Philosophical Approaches to Explaining Living Behaviour in Greco-Roman Antiquity*. Berlin: de Gruyter.
Knuuttila, S. 2004. *Emotions in Ancient and Medieval Philosophy*. Oxford: Oxford University Press.
Konstan, D. 2006. *The Emotions of the Ancient Greeks: Studies in Aristotle and Classical Literature*. Toronto: University of Toronto Press.
Lloyd, G.E.R. 2007. *Cognitive Variations: Reflections on the Unity and Diversity of the Human Mind*. Oxford: Oxford University Press.
Mattern, S.P. 2016. "Galen's Anxious Patients: *Lypê* as Anxiety Disorder", in: G. Petridou and C. Thumiger (eds.), *Homo Patiens: Approaches to the Patient in the Ancient World*, 203–223. Leiden: Brill.
Menn, S. 2002. "Aristotle's Definition of Soul and the Programme of the *De anima*", *Oxford Studies in Ancient Philosophy* 22: 83–139.
Noble, C.I. 2016. "Plotinus' Unaffectable Soul", *Oxford Studies in Ancient Philosophy* 51: 231–281.

Nussbaum, M.C. 1994. *The Therapy of Desire: Theory and Practice in Hellenistic Ethics*. Princeton, NJ: Princeton University Press.

Nussbaum, M.C. and A.O. Rorty (eds.) 1992. *Essays on Aristotle' s De anima*. Oxford: Oxford University Press.

Price, A.W. 2005. "Were Zeno and Chrysippus at Odds in Analysing Emotion?", in: Salles (ed.), 471–488.

Remes, P. 2007. *Plotinus on Self: The Philosophy of the 'We'*. Cambridge: Cambridge University Press.

Rosenwein, B.H. 2006. *Emotional Communities in the Early Middle Ages*. Ithaca, NY: Cornell University Press.

Salles, R. (ed.) 2005. *Metaphysics, Soul and Ethics in Ancient Thought*. Oxford: Clarendon Press.

Shields, C. 2009. "The Priority of the Soul in Aristotle's *De anima*: Mistaking Categories?", in: Frede and Reis (eds.), 267–290.

Sihvola, J. and T. Engberg-Pedersen (eds.) 1998. *The Emotions in Hellenistic Philosophy*. Dordrecht/Boston/London: Kluwer.

Singer, P.N. (ed.) 2013. *Galen: Psychological Writings*, translated with introduction and notes by V. Nutton, P.N. Singer and D. Davies, with the assistance of P. Tassinari. Cambridge: Cambridge University Press.

Singer, P.N. 2014. "Galen and the Philosophers: Philosophical Engagement, Shadowy Contemporaries, Aristotelian Transformations", in: *Philosophical Themes in Galen*, ed. P. Adamson, R. Hansberger and J. Wilberding, 7–38.

Singer, P.N. 2017. "The Essence of Rage: Galen on Emotional Disturbances and their Physical Correlates", in: R. Seaford, J. Wilkins and M. Wright (eds.), *Selfhood and the Soul: Essays on Ancient Thought and Literature in Honour of Christopher Gill*, 161–196. Oxford: Oxford University Press.

Singer, P.N. 2018. "Galen's Pathological Soul: Diagnosis and Therapy in Ethical and Medical Texts and Contexts", in: Thumiger and Singer (eds.), 381–420.

Singer, P.N. 2019. "A New Distress: Galen's Ethics in *Peri Alupias* and Beyond", in: C. Petit (ed.), *A Tale of Resilience: Galen's Περὶ ἀλυπίας (De indolentia) in Context*, 180–198. Leiden: Brill.

Singer, P.N. and van der Eijk, P.J. 2018. *Galen: Works on Human Nature, vol. I: Mixtures (De temperamentis)*, translated with introduction and notes. Cambridge: Cambridge University Press.

Singer, P.N. forthcoming. "Graeco-Roman Emotion Therapy: Medical Techniques, Biological Understandings", in: D. Cairns and C. Virág (eds.), *Emotions in Ancient Greece and Early China*.

Sorabji, R. 1998. "Chrysippus – Posidonius – Seneca: A High-Level Debate on Emotion", in: Sihvola and Engberg-Pedersen (eds.), 149–170.

Sorabji, R. 2000. *Emotion and Peace of Mind: From Stoic Agitation to Christian Temptation*. Oxford: Oxford University Press.

Thumiger, C. and P.N. Singer (eds.) 2018. *Mental Illness in Ancient Medicine: from Celsus to Paul of Aegina*. Leiden: Brill.

Tieleman, T. (1996) *Galen and Chrysippus on the Soul: Argument and Refutation in the De Placitis Books II-III*. Leiden: Brill.

Tieleman, T. (2003) *Chrysippus' On Affections: Reconstruction and Interpretation*. Leiden: Brill.

Dimos Spatharas
Drugs and Psychotropic Words in Gorgias' *Encomium of Helen*

Abstract: In this paper I discuss Gorgias' use of medical metaphors for emotion in the *Encomium of Helen*. I argue that the comparison of drugs' effects on the body with emotions' effects on the soul reflects metaphors' typical mapping of abstract notions onto our immediate, bodily experience. As I show through comparison of Gorgias' arguments about sights' psychological impact and speech's (*logos*) psychotropic qualities, Gorgias postulates a materialist soul whose emotional disposition is determined by the psychological charges of *logoi*. This model of explanation is compatible with cultural understandings of words' affective potentialities, but Gorgias seems to remodel it, thereby granting his speech with novelty, on the basis of intromissive theories about vision. His use of medical analogy to explain the affective power of words does not therefore reflect the identification of *logoi* with *pharmaka*, but the deployment of an embodied metaphor in an attempt to interpret a complicated physical process by appealing to the immediate, bodily effects caused by humoural changes.

> *Psychotropic Medication is drugs that have effects on psychological function.*
> NHS Data Model and Dictionary[1]

Εἰ πάντα γε εἰδείης, ὦ Σώκρατες, ὅτι ὡς ἔπος εἰπεῖν ἁπάσας τὰς δυνάμεις συλλαβοῦσα ὑφ' αὑτῇ ἔχει [sc. ἡ ῥητορική]. μέγα δέ σοι τεκμήριον ἐρῶ· πολλάκις γὰρ ἤδη ἔγωγε μετὰ τοῦ ἀδελφοῦ καὶ μετὰ τῶν ἄλλων ἰατρῶν εἰσελθὼν παρά τινα τῶν καμνόντων οὐχὶ ἐθέλοντα ἢ φάρμακον πιεῖν ἢ τεμεῖν ἢ καῦσαι παρασχεῖν τῷ ἰατρῷ, οὐ δυναμένου τοῦ ἰατροῦ πεῖσαι, ἐγὼ ἔπεισα, οὐκ ἄλλῃ τέχνῃ ἢ τῇ ῥητορικῇ. φημὶ δὲ καὶ εἰς πόλιν ὅπῃ βούλει ἐλθόντα ῥητορικὸν ἄνδρα καὶ ἰατρόν, εἰ δέοι λόγῳ διαγωνίζεσθαι ἐν ἐκκλησίᾳ ἢ ἐν ἄλλῳ τινὶ συλλόγῳ ὁπότερον δεῖ αἱρεθῆναι ἰατρόν, οὐδαμοῦ ἂν φανῆναι τὸν ἰατρόν, ἀλλ' αἱρεθῆναι ἂν τὸν εἰπεῖν δυνατόν, εἰ βούλοιτο. καὶ εἰ πρὸς ἄλλον γε δημιουργὸν ὁντινοῦν ἀγωνίζοιτο, πείσειεν ἂν αὑτὸν ἑλέσθαι ὁ ῥητορικὸς μᾶλλον ἢ ἄλλος ὁστισοῦν· οὐ γάρ ἐστιν περὶ ὅτου οὐκ ἂν πιθανώτερον εἴποι ὁ ῥητορικὸς ἢ ἄλλος ὁστισοῦν τῶν δημιουργῶν ἐν πλήθει. ἡ μὲν οὖν δύναμις τοσαύτη ἐστὶν καὶ τοιαύτη τῆς τέχνης

Pl. *Grg.* 456a7–c7.

A marvel, indeed, Socrates, if you only knew how rhetoric comprehends and holds under her sway all the inferior arts. Let me offer you a striking example of this. On several occa-

---

[1] https://datadictionary.nhs.uk/nhs_business_definitions/psychotropic_medication.html (consulted on June 8, 2021).

https://doi.org/10.1515/9783110771930-003

sions I have been with my brother Herodicus or some other physician to see one of his patients, who would not allow the physician to give him medicine, or apply a knife or hot iron to him; and I have persuaded him to do for me what he would not do for the physician just by the use of rhetoric. And I say that if a rhetorician and a physician were to go to any city, and had there to argue in the Ecclesia or any other assembly as to which of them should be elected state-physician, the physician would have no chance; but he who could speak would be chosen if he wished; and in a contest with a man of any other profession the rhetorician more than any one would have the power of getting himself chosen, for he can speak more persuasively to the multitude than any of them, and on any subject. Such is the nature and power of the art of rhetoric.

Transl. Benjamin Jowett

With these words Gorgias defends the superiority of rhetoric in the homonymous dialogue by Plato.² When he composed his speech under the title the *Encomium of Helen*, usually dated in the last thirty years of the 5th century BCE, Gorgias was perhaps unaware of the fact that he was practicing an art whose name was 'rhetoric' (ῥητορική).³ And he was surely unaware of the fact that Plato, born a year or so before Gorgias' arrival at Athens in 427, would time and again in his dialogues enlist medicine in support of his arguments against rhetoric.⁴ Yet, depending on the accuracy of our information concerning his extraordinary lifespan, Gorgias may have had the opportunity to read the dialogue under his name and admire the style of 'his' defence of rhetoric echoing the medical analogy through which he (i.e. Gorgias) emphasized the emotional power of words.⁵ For Gorgias' defence of rhetoric's overwhelming power saliently emphasizes the *emotional* impact of words. Eloquence removes patients' fear for extremely painful terrifying, but necessary medical practices and thus saves their lives.

Gorgias' comparison of rhetoric with medicine in Plato's dialogue is introduced (and concludes) with the word *dynameis* which belongs to the technical

---

2 On the interfaces between Gorgias' speeches and medical writers, see Jouanna 2012: ch.3; Spatharas 2007.
3 See Schiappa 1990; 1991: 39–63; 1992; 1993, for a criticism of Schiappa's approach, see Pendrick 1998. Schiappa's views are similar to Cole's (1991) view that rhetoric is systematized in the 4th century BCE.
4 Athenaeus (11.505d=Dk 82 15a) preserves an anecdote (no doubt unhistorical) that Gorgias responded to the contents of Plato's *Gorigas* with these words: "how well Plato knows how to mock!". The bibliography on Plato and medicine is vast, but see Frede 1987: 225–242; Lidz 1995; Holmes 2010a; Peponi 2020.
5 On Gorgias' life and dates, see Introduction to Spatharas 2001.

jargon of medicine.[6] It is commonly employed by ancient doctors to indicate drugs' or foods' 'capacity' (anachronistically, the effects of a drug's active substance). It is quite possible, but improvable on the basis of internal evidence, that the use of the word in Plato's dialogue is a deliberate allusion to Gorgias' own work. In his *Helen*, Gorgias employs *dunamis* twice to describe the effectiveness of magic spells and medicaments: in the first instance (8), magic *logos* is presented as possessing an inherent capacity to affect one's emotions while in the second (10) drugs are offered as an analogy on the basis of which Gorgias shows the psychotropic properties of persuasion. Furthermore, the use of *dunamis* perhaps echoes Gorgias' definition of speech (*logos*) as a dynast with a tiny body who is capable (*dunatai*) of divine deeds, most prominently the generation of listeners' emotions. Notably, the author of the Hippocratic treatise *Breaths* (3) qualifies air as a μέγιστος δυνάστης, who is "invisible to sight but visible to reasoning" (τῇ μὲν ὄψει ἀφανής, τῷ δὲ λογισμῷ φανερός; cp. *logos*' ἀφανεστάτῳ σώματι '[invisible body]' at *Helen* 8).[7]

This chapter finds its focus in Gorgias' own treatment of emotions in the *Encomium of Helen* and its possible interfaces with medical or other 'scientific' explanatory models developed during his lifespan. Yet, a note of caution is necessary: Gorgias is very unsystematic in the way that he treats the topics that attract his attention and it is practically impossible to trace in his writings the consistency that we commonly demand from later philosophers. This inconsistency is in my view only natural. Gorgias was not a philosopher who attempted to offer systematic definitions. He was primarily a spectacular performer of epideictic speeches which, as Gagarin (2001) has shown, were not primarily intended to persuade their audiences. Especially in the case of the *Encomium of Helen*, Gorgias' programmatically stated aim is to impress his audiences and offer them pleasure by treating a traditional topic (5) — typically the object of poetic compositions —, through logical reasoning (*logismos*), which, as the text

---

6 See Miller 1952; Plambock, G. 1964; von Staden 1998 (offering uses of *dunamis* in different medical contexts); Holmes 2010, 133–135 with n. 56. Holmes (2010: 135) points out that "Yet our limited evidence suggests that it is not the physicists but the physicians who are primarily responsible for transferring the term *dunamis* to physical stuff ... Nevertheless, it is telling that, in the *Phaedrus*, Plato defines the "Hippocratic" approach to nature in part as an inquiry into *dunameis* (270c10–d7) ... If we turn to the medical writers themselves, we see that many of them attribute a *dunamis* to virtually everything—foods, drinks, drugs, and therapies, as well as the constituent stuff s of the body, body parts such as the brain or the nostrils, and the whole body. In so doing, they extend and reframe the power of things around them, stuff s like honey, oil, and bran, as well as the seasons and the winds".
7 See Ford 2002: 179–182; Holmes 2010: 212, n. 68.

makes plain, consists in the examination of probabilities (*eikos*), rather than through storytelling. Hence, his opening statement, expressed in a *priamel*, that his speech is characterized by *kosmos* (1) and is, thereby, truthful, is a recognizable poetic pattern that enables him to highlight the authority of his speech and underscore poets' ignorance (*amathia*, 2) by flying into the face of poets by using their own weapons.[8]

In *Helen*, Gorgias identifies at least two emotions with morbid conditions: fear and erotic love. Gorgias does not employ in his writings a semantically coextensive word with the English term 'emotions', as is the case with Aristotle or other later authors.[9] Fearful sights, he suggests, impair logical reasoning and prompt insane behaviour (16–17), while erotic love is a disease (19). The conceptualization of erotic love as an illness is common in Greek cultural models of emotion and reflects both the intensity of the sentiment and its understanding as an uncontrollable and overpowering external force.[10] In addition, the metaphorical description of *erôs* as a disease reveals a typical feature of emotion metaphors or metonymies, namely their tendency to map emotions onto aspects of our embodied, immediate experience. The feeling components of an affect, the changes in the physiology of our bodies, and, generally, the 'output' elements of a sentiment's phenomenology typically inform the metaphors through which we convey our emotions.[11] But in view of the wider context of Gorgias' argumentation in *Helen* the limits between metaphoricity and physicality require investigation. Note for example that the qualification of *erôs* as a malady (*nosêma*) of the soul is followed by the emotion's qualification as an 'incapacity of the soul' (19). This formulation raises the question of whether the soul's cognitive impairment is caused by a physiological process.

In a paper on *Helen*, Porter (1993: 287–288) pointed out that "Gorgias simply fails to spell out the physiology by and through which language is presumed to operate psychologically". A crude comparison of Gorgias' discussion of *logos* with the paragraphs that he dedicates to the psychological impact of vision asserts Porter's complaint. Yet, as I have argued elsewhere (Spatharas 2019), for Gorgias *logos* is distinctively visual in so far as it elicits mental images whose affective qualities are not different from the images that we perceive through

---

8 On Gorgias' dependence on poetic claims to authority and truth, see Spatharas 2008.
9 Instead, he uses the phrase *pathêma* ('suffering') suffered by the soul; on the semantic range of the words *pathos* and *pathêma*, see Singer in this volume.
10 On madness and emotion metaphors in general, see Kövecses 2000: 37, 73–75. On Greek metaphors for *erôs*, see Cairns 2013.
11 See Cairns 2016; Kövecses 2000.

sensory perception. Gorgias' conceptualization of *logos* as distinctively visual emerges clearly in its personification at 8, where Gorgias grants him with a body, and at 13 where *logos* is presented as imprinting images on listeners' mind/soul (*psychê*). Furthermore, the emotive potentialities of *logos* are discussed in distinctively physiological terms in a passage where Gorgias compares speech with drugs (14). This comparison is similar to Gorgias' treatment of images' emotional impact relying on a combination of 'materialistic' folk and scientific models. As he says at 14, "the power of speech bears the same relation to the ordering of the soul as the ordering of drugs bear to constitution of bodies" (τὸν αὐτὸν δὲ λόγον ἔχει ἥ τε τοῦ λόγου δύναμις πρὸς τὴν τῆς ψυχῆς τάξιν ἥ τε τῶν φαρμάκων τάξις πρὸς τὴν τῶν σωμάτων φύσιν). As Segal has pointed out (1962: 141), the meaning of *taxis* in the second part of the analogy designates drugs' 'effectiveness' or 'capacity' and is therefore semantically coextensive with *dunamis*. Alternatively, *taxis* would mean 'prescription', as is the case in Plato's *Politicus* 294e, a meaning, however, which I was unable to find in the texts of the Hippocratic corpus. If *taxis* is a synonym of *dynamis*, then Gorgias establishes an analogy between different types of medicaments' power to cure or cause death and the power of different kinds of *logoi* to elicit negative or positive emotions respectively.[12]

In what sense, however, is speech *like* a drug? And, if Gorgias relies on medical explanatory models emphasizing the implications of bodily changes for the onset of emotional experience, why doesn't he employ humoural approach in such a way as to encompass bodily *and* mental/psychic changes alike? Correlatively, does the analogy imply a physicalist conceptualization of *logos* which would invite us to interpret — by inference — *logos* as a physical substance which rearranges a material soul? In addition, are negative emotions caused by *logos* conceived as a treatable malady of the soul? And if yes, does this *also*

---

[12] Ford argues that *taxis* "suggests Anaxagoras, for whom change was rearrangement, a matter of *taxis*, and the emotions were disturbances in the ordering of the soul" (2002: 180). Perhaps, but note that in Aristotle's explanation of Democritus' theory about the differences of objects consisting of the same atoms we also find the word *taxis* ('arrangement', 'ordering', DK 67A6). Different arrangements of different shapes produce different objects (as is the case with letters A and B (*schemata*) which may be ordered in such a way as to yield the combinations AB and BA. In view of Gorgias' dependence on Democritus' materialist understanding of the soul (see below), it is possible that the notion of the 'ordering' of drugs is based on his materialistic conceptualization of the soul. If this is so, the use of the term *tarasso*, typical in doctors' descriptions of humoural disturbance, to explain the impact of external stimuli (drugs, *logoi*, and images) upon the soul perhaps reflects a medicalized modification of Democritus' atomism (compatible with Gorgias' claims to epideictic novelty).

mean that the soul is understood in physical terms? These questions do not afford sweeping answers and it would be impossible to address them in full, especially because, as I pointed out, Gorgias does not offer a systematic analysis which would enable us to get a better grasp of his thought. The best I can do here is use Porter's complaint about the obscurity of Gorgias' treatment of *logos* as a guide and examine his discussion of the psychotropic qualities of speech on the basis of its similarities with his discussion about the emotional impact of images.

Gorgias' bipolar division of *pharmaka* into medicaments and poisons according to their effects on the body is mirrored in the bipolar division of images into those that elicit unpleasant emotions, such as fear, and into those, paintings and statues, which please the eye (18). It is also mirrored in his division of *logoi* into those which arouse vexatious emotions, sorrow and fear, and those which give courage and offer pleasure (14). Just like evil drugs, whose *taxis* is lethal, evil persuasion poisons and bewitches the soul. Gorgias' dependence on medical thinking in his treatment of *logoi* as *pharmaka* can be shown through comparison with a passage from Polybus' (Hippocrates' student) treatise *The nature of man*, the earliest Hippocratic work arguing for the notion that the nature of men consists of four humours. In that passage, Polybus emphasizes the power (*dunamis*) of different medicaments to affect differently the balance of humours in the body (οὐχ ἓν ταῦτα πάντα ἐστίν).[13] Polybus' locution is strikingly similar to Gorgias' notion that different *pharmaka* remove different humours from the body (ὥσπερ γὰρ τῶν φαρμάκων ἄλλους ἄλλα χυμοὺς ἐκ τοῦ σώματος ἐξάγει, 14). Equally important is that Polybus' locution 'each [pharmakon] has a power and a nature of its own' (**ἀλλ' ἕκαστον αὐτέων ἔχει δύναμίν τε καὶ φύσιν τὴν ἑωυτέου**) is similar with Gorgias' foundational notion that *because* of individual images' different nature sights cause different emotions (ἃ γὰρ ὁρῶμεν, **ἔχει φύσιν οὐχ ἣν ἡμεῖς θέλομεν, ἀλλ' ἣν ἕκαστον ἔτυχε**· διὰ δὲ τῆς ὄψεως ἡ ψυχὴ κἀν τοῖς τρόποις τυποῦται, 15). Gorgias' medical analogy thus seems to encompass the deployment of intromissive theories of vision on the basis of which he attempts to show that agents are unable to control the emotional states caused by what they see. As I argue in the next paragraphs, the

---

13 Γνοίης δ' ἂν τοῖσδε, ὅτι οὐχ ἓν ταῦτα πάντα ἐστίν, ἀλλ' **ἕκαστον αὐτέων ἔχει δύναμίν τε καὶ φύσιν τὴν ἑωυτέου**· ἢν γάρ τινι διδῷς ἀνθρώπῳ φάρμακον ὅ τι φλέγμα ἄγει, ἐμέεταί σοι φλέγμα, καὶ ἢν διδῷς φάρμακον ὅ τι χολὴν ἄγει, ἐμέεταί σοι χολή (5.16). The treatise is dated to the 5th century BCE and hence the ideas that it expresses could have been known to Gorgias. Note that the prescription of different medicaments is used as an empirical method through which the author shows that each humour has its own *phusis*.

analogies between Gorgias' treatment of the impact of *logos* and the impact of images upon the soul have significant implications for our understanding of the comparison of *logoi* with *pharmaka*.

As I have argued elsewhere (2019, ch.1), Gorgias' discussion of the emotional potentialities of images relies on a materialistic construal of the soul and reflects intromissive models of vision. In the discussion of the fourth cause that may explain Helen's travel to Troy (15-19), Gorgias argues that images enter into us through the eyes and 'stamp' or 'engrave' the soul thereby prompting it to experience pleasant or unpleasant emotions, according to their (i.e. images') nature. I shall have to revisit this argument, but for now it is important to stress that when Gorgias refers to images' effects upon the soul, he employs the verb 'disturbed' or 'upset' (ἐτάραξε), a word commonly employed by the doctors to describe humoural disturbance.[14] One may compare here a passage from *On breaths*, whose author uses a similar construction to describe air's disturbance of the blood (οὕτως ὁ ἀὴρ ταραχθεὶς ἀνετάραξε τὸ αἷμα , 14). Equally important implications for the physicalist understanding of *phsychê* emerge from the fact that in Gorgias' treatment of Helen sensory perception substitutes for its agent. In the concluding paragraphs of the speech (19), Gorgias claims that the sight of Paris' beauty pleased Helen's eye (rather than Helen),[15] thereby transmitting into her soul erotic desire. The physicality of vision is thus extended to the soul which is also conceived in material terms, insofar as the soul, just as humours or other bodily organs, can be the object of some sort of *tarachê*.[16] Another important instance where the soul is conceived in physical terms appears in a passage where Gorgias shows the power of incantations (10). In this passage he employs the word *dunamis* to describe incantations' effects on the soul. The soul is again construed as a physical entity, insofar as magic spells' *dunamis* is presented as 'joining together' (*syggignomenê*) with the soul's opinion and

---

14 See Holmes 2010: 213; Schiefsky 2005: 231, 252.
15 εἰ οὖν τῷ τοῦ Ἀλεξάνδρου σώματι **τὸ τῆς Ἑλένης ὄμμα ἡσθὲν** προθυμίαν καὶ ἅμιλλαν ἔρωτος τῇ ψυχῇ παρέδωκε, τί θαυμαστόν. On the use of θαυμαστόν, emphasizing the gravitas of a conclusion based on reasoning, see Rangos in this volume.
16 On intromissive models of vision, see Long 1966 and O'Brien 1970. On Theophrastus' account of Empedocles' explanation of colour perception in *De sensibus* 7, presenting colours as being transmitted to the eye 'by effluence' (φέρεσθαι), see Ierodiakonou 2005. For a recent overview of Empedocles' colour perception theory, see Rudolph 2106: 44–46. Cairns (2011) discusses the interfaces between scientific and cultural models of vision and their implications for the phenomenology of emotions (especially envy and *erôs*). On Gorgias and Empedocles' theory of vision, see Buccheim 1989, n. on 18.

changing the soul (μεθίστησι). The verb *methistêmi* is quite commonly used in the Hippocratic corpus to designate physical changes in the body.

If the soul is conceived as a physical entity affected psychologically by words and images in the way that the body is affected by drugs, the next point that requires clarification concerns the process through which the soul experiences emotions. This question invites us to revisit Gorgias' views about the emotive effects of vision. As we saw, Gorgias introduces his discussion of the fourth cause by emphasizing that individual images have the nature that they happen to have rather than the one that we would like them to have (ἃ γὰρ ὀρῶμεν, ἔχει φύσιν οὐχ ἣν ἡμεῖς θέλομεν, ἀλλ' ἣν ἕκαστον ἔτυχε, 15). As is commonly the case in ancient philosophy and literature, 'chance' (τύχη) is construed here as commensurate with 'necessity' (*ananke*).[17] As Guthrie (1965: 163) points out in his discussion of 'chance' and 'necessity' in Empedocles, "[I]t must be remembered that for a Greek chance and necessity could be much the same thing" and that for the Presocratics, "*Physis* ... is a natural necessity inherent in each separate thing or substance, not a law of interaction between them". The psychological potentialities of vision are introduced with the verb *tupoutai* ('imprint', 15) a word that Gorgias has already used to indicate *logos*' impact upon the soul, by emphasizing its emotional effects (13). Like speech, images 'mould' our souls according to their 'nature' and yield emotional experiences which are beyond our control, in so far as individual images' *phusis* (and their emotional charge) determines the emotion experienced by the soul.

Gorgias' discussion of the psychological impact of images relies on a mixture of intromissive folk cultural models of vision which conceptualize the eyes as a gate that lays us open to external dangers and emotional experiences and 'scientific' optical models developed by philosophers such as Empedocles and Democritus during Gorgias' lifespan. In what follows, I propose to argue that Gorgias' discussion of vision's emotional effects appeals to his listeners' common cultural knowledge about vision's importance for the onset of specific emotions, especially erotic love, and appropriates aspects of Democritean *eidôla* theory. On the basis of this theory we may tentatively draw some conclusions concerning Gorgias' arguments about the psychological effects of *logos* and the medical analogy that he employs to support his thesis.

Atomists' optics display several difficulties of interpretation, but according to some ancient sources discussing the psychological impact of vision indicate

---

17 Cp. ἦ γὰρ Τύχης βουλήμασι καὶ θεῶν βουλεύμασι καὶ Ἀνάγκης ψηφίσμασιν ἔπραξεν ἃ ἔπραξεν at 6, which is similar with Empedocles' lines: ἔστιν Ἀνάγκης χρῆμα, θεῶν ψήφισμα παλαιόν, / ἀίδιον (B 115DK). See Buccheim 1989 n. *ad loc.*

that, according to Democritus, the *eidôla* of the objects of perception bear emotional charge. The most illustrative among these pieces of evidence is a passage from Plutarch (682F-683A), where one of the interlocutors explains the transmission of envy and *baskania* ('the evil eye'). On his account, the *eidôla* emitted from enviers are 'full' of (ἀνάπλεα) senders' negative psychological disposition (μοχθηρίας καὶ βασκανίας). Furthermore, the speaker notably uses the word συνοικοῦντα, which implies that *eidôla* enter into the beholder's body and 'lodge in' it or even become parts of it, as ἐμπλασσόμενα (corresponding to Gorgias' notion of *tupos*) seems to suggest. It is also noteworthy that in the speaker's explanation of the evil eye the intrusion of *eidôla* into targets' bodies is used to explain, in a materialist fashion, the disturbance (ἐπιταράττειν, see discussion above) and harm (κακοῦν) that they inflict on targets' souls and bodies.

In a recent discussion of the passage under review, Warren (2007: 99) argued that "according to Democritus, *eidôla* given off by people, especially people in extreme emotional states, carry and preserve the imprint of that psychic state. When they lodge in the soul of someone else, therefore, this psychic imprint can affect the perceiver's soul too … In this way, therefore, Democritus is able to offer a physical, atomist account of the mechanism of interpersonal psychic harm". On Warren's understanding, thus, Democritus' physicalist explanation of the psychological impact of *eidôla* has important implications for atomist ethics and serves to explain instances, such as 'mass hysteria' or panic, where groups of people are overpowered simultaneously by the same emotion.[18]

Gorgias' (possible) appropriation of Democritus' physicalist approach may offer an example of how, as Morel argues, "la théorie des simulacres constitue une explication générale susceptible d'applications multiples" (1996: 319). My hypothesis that Gorgias uses for his own purposes Democritus' theory gains some support from the fact that, in his formulation at 17, indicating the psychological harm done by frightful images, he says that vision imprints on *phronêma* 'images of sights', i.e. copies of sights, rather than 'sights' themselves (εἰκόνας τῶν ὀρωμένων).[19] In other words, Gorgias not only seems to employ Democritus' notion of images' 'imprinting' of the soul, a notion that as far as I can see is unattested elsewhere in the Presocratics, but also seems to be in line with Democritus' view that the objects of sight emit 'images'. Furthermore, as we saw, both at the beginning and at the end of his argumentation about vision, Gorgias emphasizes the randomness of images' sights, which he associates with

---

18 On 'mass psychology' in Gorgias and Thucydides, see Hunter 1986.
19 Cp. Pl. *Tht.* 191c–d; *Phil.* 39a–b; Arist. *de An.* 2.424a19; Arist. *de An.* 3.425b23, 3.434a29; Stoics: *SVF* 2.53, 55, 56.

the emotions that they produce (cp. οὕτω τὰ μὲν λυπεῖν τὰ δὲ ποθεῖν *πέφυκε* τὴν ὄψιν, 18). Hence, Gorgias not only postulates viewers' passivity, but also seems to attribute to the images emitted by sights emotional charge which is transmitted to and imprinted on the soul. Furthermore, as is the case with Gaius' Democritean explanation of the affective power of enviers' gazes (ἐπιταράττειν) in Plutarch, Gorgias says that the frightful sight of the enemy's armour alarms vision (ἐταράχθη) and, in its own turn, vision disturbs the soul (ἐτάραξε, 16). Finally, the notion that the malicious *eidôla* of *baskania* lodge in beholders' souls (συνοικοῦντα) parallels Gorgias' use of the verb εἰσῳκίσθη to convey images' inhabitation in beholders' souls.

The traces of Democritus' theory about *eidôla* in Gorgias' theorization may also be discerned in his division of sights into two distinct categories according to their hedonic valence, a distinction which we also traced in the comparison of *logoi* with drugs: sights are either pleasurable or distressful. This bipolar division is encapsulated in Gorgias' concluding remark that, by their own nature (πέφυκε, 18), some images make vision experience sorrow (λυπεῖν), while others make it experience longing (ποθεῖν). The polarity distressful/pleasurable (sights) is also reflected in the examples adduced by Gorgias: panic caused by frightful sights (16–17), yearning and erotic desire as a response to the products of visual arts (17–18).

According to later doxographical evidence, Democritus recognized two distinct types of *eidôla*: those which are harmful and those which are beneficial.[20] Democritus' bipolar division of *eidôla*, emphasizing their impact on the viewer, perhaps served as the basis for Gorgias' antithetical classification of images – a classification dictated by natural necessity (πέφυκε) – according to the psychological effects that each member of this antithesis prompts. This hypothesis is supported by the fact that, as we saw, Gorgias' treatment underscores the role of 'chance' (τύχη) in the visual transmission of emotions. The randomness with which perceived 'images' operate to transmit emotions is also a characteristic of Democritus' theory positing the existence of two distinct types of *eidôla*. In Plutarch's and Sextus's accounts of *eidôla* theory,[21] Democritus is presented as

---

20 On whether *eidôla* are intentionally harmful, see Warren 2007: 98, n. 21 with further bibliography.

21 Plutarch: Δημόκριτος μὲν γὰρ (B166 DK) εὔχεσθαί φησι δεῖν, ὅπως εὐλόγχων εἰδώλων τυγχάνωμεν, *Aemilius Paulus* 1.4; τι δὲ Δημόκριτος (B166 DK) **εὐχόμενος 'εὐλόγχων εἰδώλων' τυγχάνειν**, *De defectu oraculorum* 419A. Δημόκριτος δὲ εἴδωλά τινά φησιν ἐμπελάζειν τοῖς ἀνθρώποις, καὶ τούτων τὰ μὲν εἶναι ἀγαθοποιά, τὰ δὲ κακοποιά (ἔνθεν καὶ **εὔχετο εὐλόγχων τυχεῖν εἰδώλων**). Sextus: Δημόκριτος δὲ εἴδωλά τινά φησιν ἐμπελάζειν τοῖς ἀνθρώποις, καὶ

praying to meet propitious *eidôla* (εὔχεσθαι). Both sources, thus, underscore beholders' inability to control the *eidôla* that they happen to meet. Indeed, in Sextus' account, the role of 'chance' is made explicit in his depiction of the contents of Democritus' prayers (εὔχετο εὐλόγχων τυχεῖν εἰδώλων). The qualification of 'positive' *eidôla* with a word indicating that the beholder's perception of either type of *eidôla* is random seems to correspond to Gorgias' emphasis on 'chance' (ἔτυχεν) that I discussed earlier.

We may now reconsider Gorgias' medical analogy concerning speeches' impact on the soul. In his discussion of the emotional effects of poetry — defined as *logos* with *metron* —, and magic spells (9–10), Gorgias says that sentiments are caused by *logoi* in general rather than by specific, inherent properties of *logoi*. That listeners' souls suffer sufferings of their own for the sufferings of others (9)[22] indicates that poetry's emotional impact is due to the materiality of corporeal *logos* which, like images, enter into the soul and cause her to experience specific sentiments (fearful *phrikê*, pity, and longing) encapsulated in the word *pathêma*.[23] The verb μετέστησεν (also used to signpost the transition to the example of magic spells, 10), which, as I pointed out earlier, has medical overtones, may suggest another instance of Democritean influence and imply a physical change in the soul. According to Democritus, teaching (διδαχή) rearranges a man and through rearrangement it creates his nature.[24] This is perhaps a physical process involving changes in the composition of the student's soul —

τούτων τὰ μὲν εἶναι ἀγαθοποιά, τὰ δὲ κακοποιά (ἔνθεν καὶ **εὔχετο εὐλόγχων τυχεῖν εἰδώλων**), *Adversus mathematicos* 9.19.

22 ἐπ' ἀλλοτρίων τε πραγμάτων καὶ σωμάτων εὐτυχίαις καὶ δυσπραγίαις ἴδιόν τι πάθημα διὰ τῶν λόγων ἔπαθεν ἡ ψυχή (9). On the similarities of this locution with a passage from the treatise *De flatibus* (1,6.90 L), where doctors are presented as experiencing sorrows arising from patients' suffering, see Kazantzidis 2017; Spatharas 2021: 50–51. The passage runs as follows: ὁ μὲν γὰρ ἰητρὸς ὁρῇ τε δεινά, θιγγάνει τε ἀηδέων, ἐπ' ἀλλοτρίῃσί τε ξυμφορῇσιν ἰδίας καρποῦται λύπας.

23 The word *pathêma* expressing the 'suffering' of the soul caused by poetry is commonly employed by medical writers to designate diseases' 'symptoms' (typically in the plural). See Holmes 2010: 11 n. 39. It is impossible to say with certainty if *pathêma* retains in Gorgias its medical overtones, but the frequency of the word's uses in the writings of doctors perhaps suggests that the author invited his audiences to construe the suffering soul in physical terms. Note that at 19 love inflicted by sights is described as a 'human disease' (ἀνθρώπινον νόσημα) and an 'ignorance of the soul' (ψυχῆς ἀγνόημα).

24 Cp. 68 B 33DK.

in the atomist sense of the word — through the impact of words and images.²⁵ As Warren points out (2007: 100), "it is not an implausible thought that Democritus considered teaching to involve the impact of the teacher's words and image on the pupil's soul, whether or not the vocabulary in this fragment conclusively demonstrates that this was indeed his view". Gorgias' notion that the soul is stamped by words and sights further underscores his materialist understanding of speech and soul alike. Furthermore, if his use of μετέστησεν is related to Democritus' rearrangement of the soul, or, for that matter, conveys physical change, as is commonly the case in the doctors, then it may be taken to indicate that emotional experience is a process requiring bodily alteration caused externally by embodied *logos*, which, on account of its corporeality, has a δύναμις (comparable to the *dunamis* of drugs).

As a performer of *epideictic* speeches, intended to impress listeners through novelty, Gorgias introduces himself as a public speaker or teacher who is able to enlist natural philosophy and medicine in support of his explanation of human behaviour. The response of his audiences to his treatment of a traditional topic would have been characterized by *ekplêxis*. But, as I suggested, his new, iconoclastic approach to Helen's responsibility, resting on reasoning (*logismos*) rather than on a new narrative account about the events that prompted her travel to Troy does not depart from folk cultural models of emotions. In their ordinary communication, Gorgias and his audiences spoke about erotic love and longing in terms of illness or madness²⁶ and participated in symposia where gazes were manipulated, possibly through the help of poems' recurrent references to the affective impact of the eye (cp., e.g., Ibycus 287 *PMG*), to express erotic interest or arouse desire;²⁷ and from their literary and theatrical *paideia* they knew that poetry arouses emotions and makes people feel compassion and shed tears for the sufferings of others. The novelty of Gorgias' approach thus lies in the deployment of physicalist approaches in support of arguments that draw on common cultural understandings of emotions.

In his work on the notion of *phuchê*, Claus (1981: 182) suggests that the eventual identification of *phsuchê* with 'person' can be explained by the fact that "[N]aturalistic views of the ψυχή ... seem to have been more directly connected to the development of the ψυχή as self. As opposed to direct or explicit

---

[25] It has been suggested that the verb μεταρυσμοῖ reflects the atomist notion of ῥυσμός, namely the shape of atoms within a compound (cp. Ar. *Met.* 985b 13–19). See Taylor 1999: 233, Warren 2007: 101–112.
[26] Cairns 2013.
[27] Cairns 2011. On symposia, vase-paintings, and gazes, see Grethlein 2016.

interest in the cognitive functions of ψυχή, the most important thread here may well have been the development of an oblique analogy between body and soul by which rationalistic ideas of the body and its φύσις are transferred to the soul". And a few lines later, Claus (1981: 182) points out that "consistent interest in the moral value of ψυχή and the earliest treatment of ψυχή as the correlative of σῶμα appear in Democritus, Gorgias, and the early medical texts ... The ψυχή acquires moral and personal connotations because it is regarded as the psychosomatic φύσις of a man, amenable to therapy and doctrines like those furnished by scientific medicine for the body". This semantic shift in the meaning of *psuchê*, a meaning, which, as I tried to show, emerges from Gorgias' discussion of emotions in *Helen*, raises an important question about the metaphoricity of the analogy between drugs and *logoi* at 14. If *logoi*, perceived, according to Gorgias by the mind's eye (13), share the materiality of images and, perhaps more importantly, if 'material' *logoi are* medicaments (or for that matter poisons) affecting listeners' 'physical' souls can we still treat the analogy at 14 as a metaphor? And, if, as is also the case with images, material *logoi qua pharmaka* bear emotional charge which they engrave or impress on material souls thereby affecting their constitution, why does Gorgias apply the *as if* line of thinking to words' implications for emotions rather than to sights' emotional impact?

Let me start from the second question, which, perhaps, affords a simpler answer. Ancient literature makes it plain that folk understandings of the psychological effects of sights, compatible with intromissive theories of vision, grant the objects of sensory perception with material qualities. This is especially the case with erotic love, whose onset is typically associated with gazes and their power to incite overwhelming desire. Succinctly, love in Greek antiquity is primarily a visual experience and, in view of the distinctively materialist understandings of vision, an haptic engagement.[28] This aspect of *erôs'* phenomenology, salient in poetry and other genres, enables Gorgias to fly in the face of the poets who, on account of their ignorance (ἀμαθία, 2), held Helen responsible for her elopement. But what about the limits of metaphoricity in Gorgias' construal of *logoi* as *pharmaka*? As we saw, metaphors are an integral element of concept formation in general.[29] The metaphors that we use for cancer, e.g. 'aggressive cancer' or for medicaments removing pain, e.g. 'painkillers', refer to complicated physiological processes, but are also indicative of the ways that we understand the categories pain or disease or of the ways in which we classify diseas-

---

28 See Cairns 2011: 37; Squire 2016: 16–17, with n. 70 including further literature.
29 See Lakoff and Johnson 1980; Lakoff 1987; Johnson 1987; Gibbs 2008.

es.[30] 'Aggressive cancer' is a phrase conceptualizing disease as an enemy in battle, while 'painkillers' invite a personified understanding of medicaments which treat our pain. In both cases, metaphoricity invests with lucid, experiential immediacy physiological or pharmaceutical processes which we are unable to perceive through our senses or describe in words other than those deriving from source domains which belong to experiences irrelevant to the targets, i.e. disease or pain.

In Gorgias' case, the deployment of the medical analogy that he uses at paragraph 14 is compatible with his understanding of *logos* as a physical entity which grants with visibility invisible things thereby making them perceptible to the eye of belief (13).[31] In other words, for Gorgias *logos* shares with images the ability to impress the soul, because material *logos* produces visual effects which disturb the soul. The metaphor of drugs for *logos* does not thus show that *logos* is immaterial. *Logos* disturbs the soul in the way that drugs rearrange our humoural constitution in purely physical terms. What the deployment of the metaphor shows, in my view, is that, the materiality of invisible *logos* (ἀφανεστάτῳ σώματι, 8) and the physiological processes through which it causes emotions are not accessible through sensory experience and that the verbal description of these processes requires their mapping onto notions more immediate and more experientially specific. Metaphorically understood then, speech (*logos*) *is* a toxic or a therapeutic drug and, thereby, it *can be* a healer of negative emotions. As Democritus probably said, "medicine heals the diseases of the body, while wisdom frees the soul from passions" (68 A23 DK, transl. Taylor).

Bibliography

Buchheim, T. 1989. *Gorgias von Leontinoi. Reden Fragmente und Testimonien*. Hamburg: Felix Meiner.
Cairns, D.L. 2008. "Look Both Ways: Studying Emotion in Ancient Greek", *Critical Quarterly* 50: 43–62.
Cairns, D.L. 2011. "Looks of Love and Loathing: Cultural Models of Vision and Emotion in Ancient Greek Culture", *Metis* 9: 37–50.

---

[30] On this issue, see the breathtaking work of Susan Sontag (1978).
[31] Gorgias' remarks are comparable to a passage from *De arte*, an epideictic defence of the art of medicine from the Hippocratic corpus. The author of this treatise claims that when doctors deal with 'hidden diseases', they use thinking (cp. Gorgias' λογισμός at 2) to make what is invisible visible to the mind of belief. On this passage see Spatharas 2007 and especially Mann 2012: 27–30.

Cairns, D.L. 2013. "The Imagery of *Eros* in Plato's *Phaedrus*", in: E. Sanders *et al.* (ed.), *Eros in ancient Greece*, 233–250. Oxford: Oxford University Press.

Claus, D.B. 1981. *Toward the Soul: An Inquiry into the Meaning of Psyche before Plato*. New Haven and London: Yale University Press.

Cole, T. 1991. *The Origins of Rhetoric in Ancient Greece*. Princeton: Princeton University Press.

Ford, A. 2002. *The Origins of Criticism: Literary Culture and Poetic Theory in Classical Greece*. Princeton: Princeton University Press.

Frede, M. 1987. *Essays in Ancient Philosophy*. Minneapolis: University of Minnesota Press.

Gagarin, M. 2001. "Did the Sophists Aim to Persuade?", *Rhetorica* 19: 275–291.

Grethlein, J. 2016. "Sight and Reflexivity: Theorizing Vision in Greek Vase-painting", in: M. Squire (ed.), *Sight and the Ancient Senses: The Senses in Antiquity*, 85–106. London/New York: Routledge.

Gibbs, R.W. (ed.) 2008. *The Cambridge Handbook of Metaphor and Thought*. Cambridge: Cambridge University Press.

Holmes, B. 2010. *The Symptom and the Subject: The Emergence of the Physical Body in Ancient Greece*. Princeton: Princeton University Press.

Holmes, B. 2010a. Holmes, Brooke. "Body, Soul, and the Medical Analogy in Plato", in: J. Peter Euben and Karen Bassi (eds.), *When Worlds Elide: Classics, Politics, Culture*. Lanham, Md: Lexington Books.

Hunter, V. 1973. *Thucydides: The Artful Reporter*. Toronto: Hakkert.

Ierodiakonou, K. 2005. "Empedocles on Colour and Colour Vision", *Oxford Studies in Ancient Philosophy* 29: 1–37.

Johnson, M. 1987. *The Body in the Mind*. Chicago: The University of Chicago Press.

Jouanna, J. 2012. *Greek Medicine from Hippocrates to Galen: Collected essays* [edited by P. van der Eijk]. Leiden: Brill.

Kazantzidis, G. (2016), "Empathy and the Limits of Disgust in the Hippocratic Corpus", in: D. Lateiner and D. Spatharas (eds.), *The Ancient Emotion of Disgust*. Oxford: Oxford University Press: 45–68.

Kövecses, Z. 2000. *Metaphor and Emotion: Language, Culture, and Body in Human Feeling*. Cambridge: Cambridge University Press.

Lakoff, G. 1987. *Women, Fire, and Dangerous Things: What Categories Reveal about the Mind*. Chicago: University of Chicago Press.

Lakoff, G. and M. Johnson. 1980. *Metaphors We Live By*. Chicago: University of Chicago Press.

Lidz, J.W. 1995. "Medicine as Metaphor in Plato", *The Journal of Medicine and Philosophy* 20.5: 527–541.

Long, A.A. 1966. "Thinking and Sense-Perception in Empedocles: Mysticism or Materialism", *CQ* 16: 256–276.

Miller, H.W. 1952. "*Dynamis* and *Physis* in *On Ancient Medicine*", *TAPA* 83: 184–197.

Morel, P.-M. 1996. *Democrite et la recherche des causes*. Paris: Klincksieck.

O'Brien, D. 1970. "The Effects of a Simile: Empedocles' Theories of Seeing and Breathing", *JHS* 90: 140–179.

Pendrick, J.G. 1998. "Plato and PHTOPIKH", *RhM* 141.1: 10–23.

Peponi, A.E. 2002. "Mixed Pleasures, Blended Discourses: Poetry, Medicine, and the Body in Plato's *Philebus* 46–47c", *ClAnt* 21: 135–160.

Plamböck, G. 1964. "Dynamis in Corpus Hippocraticum", Akademie der Wissenschaften und der Literatur, Mainz: Abhandlungen der Geistes- und Sozialwissenschaftlichen Klasse 2: 59–110.

Rudolph, K. 2016. "Sight and the Presocratics: Approaches to Visual Perception in Early Greek Philosophy", in: M. Squire (ed.), *Sight and the Ancient Senses: The Senses in Antiquity*, 36–53. London/New York: Routledge.
Schiappa, E. 1990. "Did Plato Coin Rhêtorikê", *AJP* 111: 457–470.
Schiappa, E. 1991. *Protagoras and Logos: A Study in Greek Philosophy and Rhetoric*. Columbia, South Carolina: University of South Carolina Press.
Schiappa, E. 1992. "Rhêtorikê: What's in a Name? Toward A Revised History of early Greek rhetorical theory", *Quarterly Journal of Speech* 78: 1–15.
Schiappa, E. 1993. "The Beginnings of Greek Rhetorical Theory", in: D. Zarefsky (ed.), *Rhetorical Movement: Essays in Honor of Leland M. Griffin*. Evanston: Northwestern University Press.
Schiappa, E. 1994. "Plato and ἡ καλουμέμνη ῥητορική: A response to O'Sullivan", *Mnemosyne* 47: 512–514.
Schiefsky, M. 2005. *Hippocrates On Ancient Medicine: Translated with Introduction and Commentary*. Leiden: Brill.
Sontag, S. 1978. *Illness as Metaphor*. New York: Doubleday.
Spatharas, D. 2001. Gorgiias: An edition of the extant texts and fragments with commentary and introduction (PhD diss.). Glasgow.
Spatharas, D. 2007. "Gorgias and the Hippocratic Treatise *De arte*", *C&M* 58: 159–163.
Spatharas, D. 2008. "Δόξα, γνώση και απάτη στον Γοργία", in: Ch. Balla (ed.), *Φιλοσοφία και ρητορική στην κλασική Αθήνα*. Herakleion: Crete University Press.
Spatharas, D. 2021. "The Social Construction of Disgust in Ancient Greece", in: A. Chaniotis (ed.), *Unveiling Emotions III*. Stuttgart: Steiner Verlag.
Squire, M. (ed.) 2016. *Sight and the Ancient Senses: The Senses in Antiquity*. London/New York: Routledge.
Taylor, C.C.W. 1999. *The Atomists: Leucippus and Democritus*. Toronto: Toronto University Press.
Von Staden, H. 1998. "Dynamis: The Hippocratics and Plato", in: K.J. Boudouris (ed.), *Philosophy and Medicine*, 262–279. Alimos, Greece.
Warren, J. 2007. "Democritus on Social and Psychological Harm", in: A. Brancacci and P.-M. Morel (eds.), *Democritus: Science, the Arts, and the Care of the Soul, Proceedings of the International Colloquium on Democritus (Paris, 18–20 September 2003)*: 87–104. Leiden/Boston: Brill.

Spyridon Rangos
Wonder and Perplexity across Medicine and Philosophy in Classical Greece

Abstract: In both Plato and Aristotle wonder (θαυμάζειν) is the characteristic mark of the true philosopher. It is described as a distressing mental affection (πάθος) generating perplexity (ἀπορεῖν), that has a positive result, nonetheless: it instigates thoughtful reflection on a theoretical issue and leads, ideally, to real knowledge. In the Hippocratic corpus, by contrast, wonder and perplexity are cast in a purely negative light: it is not the expert physician but the ignoramus and the charlatan who are said to be affected thereby. The chapter examines the most prominent references to the subjects, objects and conditions of wonder and perplexity in Plato's dialogues, Aristotle's treatises and the Hippocratic writings with a view to establishing a radical, though often ignored, difference between philosophy and medicine in approaching their respective goals and traditions.

1 Enter Eryximachus

Aristophanes has hiccups. Eryximachus prescribes three distinct remedies to him: to hold his breath for long, to do a thorough gargle with water, and to cause a sneeze or two by tickling his noise through a feather or something. Eryximachus is confident in his craft — and he is right. For after completing his

---

The first part of this chapter (on wonder and perplexity in Plato and Aristotle, 2.1–2.4 below) has had a long gestation period. Audiences in Crete, Athens, and Princeton have provided invaluable insights for its improvement. Special thanks should go to Benjamin Morison and Christian Wildberg, who have read and commented on an earlier draft, and to Stephanos Dimitriou, Dimitri Gonticas, Eleni Filippachi, Andrew Ford, Melissa Lane and Spyros Tegos for their oral suggestions. George Kazantzidis and Dimos Spatharas have given me the opportunity to extend my research to the Hippocratic authors and to attempt a comparison. The conference that they organized in Patras on "Medical Emotions in Antiquity" provided the forum to test the comparison. I would like to thank the participants of the conference, especially Elizabeth Craik, for their suggestions and encouragement. Last but not least, I am very grateful to the editors of the present volume and to Stasinos Stavrianeas for their written comments on the submitted draft.

speech in praise of Eros, Aristophanes, already restored to a healthy state, is ready to begin his. He says:

> καὶ μάλ' ἐπαύσατο [sc. ἡ λύγξ], οὐ μέντοι πρίν γε τὸν πταρμὸν προσενεχθῆναι αὐτῇ, ὥστε με **θαυμάζειν** εἰ τὸ κόσμιον τοῦ σώματος ἐπιθυμεῖ τοιούτων ψόφων καὶ γαργαλισμῶν, οἷον καὶ ὁ πταρμός ἐστιν.
>
> The hiccups have stopped all right — but not before I applied the sneeze treatment to them; which makes me *wonder* whether the orderly state of the body calls for such sounds and tickles as sneezes.[1]

Aristophanes is pulling Eryximachus' leg. We may well imagine the comic poet trying the three remedies and making the corresponding funny sounds during the deliverance of the sober doctor's earnest speech. The situation is deeply amusing. However, behind Aristophanes' tease we may also discern a sense of real perplexity: how come health, described as an orderly balance of opposite forces in the doctor's speech, be in need of such disorderly eruptions of imbalance as sneezes and the like? The empirical evidence of a successful treatment and the theoretical account of health seem to stand at odds with one another.

The reader may have recognized the scene. It comes from Plato's *Symposium* (185c–e, and 189a whence the quotation). The physician Eryximachus is portrayed as extremely confident, almost pompous, in his knowledge of medical things.[2] He doesn't ever seem to entertain doubts about his expertise or be seriously puzzled.[3] Aristophanes, by contrast, playfully wonders. His speech is a

---

[1] All translations of Platonic passages come from Cooper 1997 — in this case the translation, slightly modified, is by Nehamas and Woodruff (= Nehamas and Woodruff 1989: 23, emphasis added). Translations of Aristotelian texts come from Barnes 1984 and of Hippocratic writings, other than the *On Ancient Medicine* (for which I have used Schiefsky 2005a), from Jones 1923a–b. When no translator is mentioned, the translation is mine.

[2] Eryximachus distinguishes two kinds of Love, a benevolent and a harmful one, from reflection on the physician's craft (186a–b) which he defines as "simply the science of the effects of Love on repletion and depletion of the body" (186c). He then applies his insight about the dual nature of Love to a variety of technical domains (187a–188d): gymnastics, agriculture, music (extensively), astronomy, religion (especially sacrifice and divination), even ethics. He never questions his knowledge of medicine nor the legitimacy of his extrapolation from medicine to other crafts and from the human body to the world at large (188a–b). His speech is the only one in the *Symposium* in which *Erôs* assumes a really cosmic dimension and almost becomes a dual cosmological principle like Empedocles' Love and Strife. In comparison, even Diotima's perspective, based as it is on reflection on animate and mortal things (207a–208b), is much more limited.

[3] Eryximachus' speech has been the topic of some very careful treatments: Edelstein 1967: 153–171; Konstan and Young-Bruehl 1982; Rowe 1999, Green 2014, Candiotto 2015. Commenta-

parody of Hippocratic medicine quite generally and of Eryximachus' convictions in particular.[4] But it is also the humorous product of a serious wondering at erotic attraction, infatuation, sexuality, loyalty, and love. In the context of the *Symposium*, the intoxicated poet's comic myth is juxtaposed, and evidently contrasted, with the sober physician's solemn account. But who of the two has delved more deeply into the subject of Eros? Plato seems to suggest an answer through the way he portrays the two speakers. Moreover, though he has Diotima allude to all previous speeches later in the dialogue,[5] it is only to Aristophanes' mythical account that he does so in a way meant to catch the reader's attention. Aristophanes gets the point and protests.[6] He should be pleased. *His* speech is the only one considered worthy of an explicit correction. The reason probably is that it was a profound contribution to the subject of love, more profound in its playfulness than Eryximachus' self-indulgent account. Profundity, Plato implies, stems from an antecedent experience of heartfelt wonder — which our physician seems to lack.

As a matter of fact, Greek 'wonder' (the noun θαῦμα, the verb θαυμάζειν) is a very ambivalent experience that points in opposite directions, much like the faces of the strange primordial anthropoids in Aristophanes' comic myth.[7] Θαυμάζειν signifies surprise, admiration, astonishment, marvel, even amazement and awe; but it also denotes bewilderment, perplexity, puzzlement, bafflement, even stupefaction or stupor. The extent to which all these mental events may or may not be properly called 'emotions' highlights the distance between ancient and modern understandings of the mind. Perhaps more significantly, the fact that the Greeks used a single word for a whole range of psychological phenomena, which to us are rather discrete and even opposite, shows that our distinction of mental life into cognitive, affective and conative/desiderative sides, does not

---

tors (Bury ²1932: xxviii; Dover 1980: 105; Nehamas in Nehamas and Woodruff 1989: xvi; Robin ²1989: LI–LIII, LVI; Gill 1999: 23; Rowe 1998: 147; Hunter 2004: 54) generally agree about the masterful way Plato displays, and implicitly criticizes, Eryximachus' pomposity and his tendency "to formulate excessively general laws governing the phenomena of the universe" (Dover 1980: 105); but there are also scholars who take exception and see Eryximachus' speech as replete with intellectual rigour, at least for his time (see Edelstein 1967: 158; Konstan and Young-Bruehl 1982: 44). The two approaches are not necessarily incompatible: Plato may well have designed the speech as a serious exposition of scientific ideas worthy of thoughtful examination, and still take an ironical stance towards the uncritical outlook of their expositor.
4 Craik 2001b.
5 Rangos 2005.
6 *Symp.* 212c referring back to 205d–e.
7 Llewelyn 2001: 48.

necessarily correspond, Plato's tripartite soul notwithstanding, to the way of the Greeks. Θαυμάζειν is an unexpected mental occurrence, similar in a sense to our 'surprise', one of the seven universal emotions in Ekman's list, but likely to last longer than it and to have deeper (positive or negative) consequences. Unlike Ekman's surprise, θαυμάζειν is not primarily prompted by sudden sounds or movements but by things that 'catch the eye'. Its experience contains a cognitive, an emotive and perhaps also a desiderative component.

In epic poetry, the objects of θαυμάζειν and the things to which the formulaic expression θαῦμα ἰδέσθαι is applied are, for the most part, excellent products of human or divine craftsmanship but they may also be other unlikely events (such as the exceptional response of Odysseus' body to Circe's poison).[8] The surprise expressed by Greek θαῦμα/θαυμάζειν usually involves a sense of admiration for ingenuity or expertise. When in his famous *Funeral Speech* Thucydides has Pericles twice use the verb (II.39.5: ἀξίαν θαυμάζεσθαι, II.41.4: θαυμασθησόμεθα), he clearly means that Athens is worthy of *admiration* and that the Athenians will be duly *admired* for their collective achievements. By contrast, in the work of Herodotus, arguably the classical author with the keenest eye for objects of θαυμάζειν (θωμαστά, θώματα, θωμάσια), the admiration/astonishment aspect of the experience is counterbalanced by the perplexity/puzzlement aspect. Egypt is the land with the most numerous θωμάσια (Hdt. II.35.1), because it is there rather than anywhere else that the visitor will be overwhelmed by both admiration for technical accomplishments and perplexity about natural phenomena and human institutions.

At the outset of the pseudo-Aristotelian *Mechanics* we read (I. 847a11–13):

> Θαυμάζεται τῶν μὲν κατὰ φύσιν συμβαινόντων, ὅσων ἀγνοεῖται τὸ αἴτιον, τῶν δὲ παρὰ φύσιν, ὅσα γίνεται διὰ τέχνην πρὸς τὸ συμφέρον τοῖς ἀνθρώποις.
>
> Our wonder is excited, firstly, by phenomena which occur in accordance with nature but of which we do not know the cause, and secondly by those which are produced by art despite nature for the benefit of mankind.
>
> trans. E.S. Forster

Here the single verb θαυμάζεται is used for two kinds of things: for natural phenomena whose cause remains unknown and for objects of human craftsmanship whose cause is by definition known. In the former case, when the cause is

---

[8] Hom. *Il.* V.725, X.439, XVIII.83, 377, 467, 549 (cf. XIII.99, XV.286, XX.344), *Od.* VI.306, VII.45, VIII.366, X.326, XI.287, XIII.108, XVII.306 (cf. XIX.36), Hes. *Theog.* 575, 581, Emp. B 35.34 Diels-Kranz (cf. Prier 1989).

discovered, wonder is bound to be extinguished; for 'wonder' at natural phenomena means primarily ignorance and/or cognitive perplexity. In the latter case, by contrast, 'wonder' has the sense of admiration for the products of human ingenuity that have improved the material or cultural conditions of social life; 'wonder' in that sense is admiration for expert knowledge.

Quite generally, in the Greek experience of θαῦμα the evaluative judgement implicit in spontaneous admiration, indubitably an emotion, is often overwhelmed by a corresponding perplexity about how the admirable thing is fashioned or works and by an equally implicit desire to understand and emulate. We might have reasonably assumed, even without explicit evidence to support the assumption, which indeed there is (e.g. Aesch. *Eum.* 407), that a genuine mental event of θαυμάζειν left its visible traces on facial expression, especially on and around the eyes, and that consequently a viewer could read off the corresponding emotion from its visible signs. In any case, both the much broader question about how the Greeks generally distinguished emotions from desires and thoughts and the more circumscribed issue about how, if at all, the emotive aspect of the experience of θαυμάζειν was distinguished from its cognitive and conative aspects fall outside the scope of the present chapter. I shall, instead, focus on θαυμάζειν in Plato, Aristotle and the Hippocratic treatises in an attempt to see what kind of mental events it signifies, how it is supposed to come about, in what way it is related to ἀπορεῖν (for the connection between the two is indisputable in the Platonic, Aristotelian and Hippocratic corpora), and whether or not it is a commendable or a blameworthy state of mind.

2 Plato and Aristotle

2.1 Wonder in Plato

In contrast to Aristophanes' playful and artistically concealed wonder, Theaetetus is deeply and seriously perplexed:

{ΘΕΑΙ.} Καὶ νὴ τοὺς θεούς γε, ὦ Σώκρατες, **ὑπερφυῶς ὡς θαυμάζω** τί ποτ' ἐστὶ ταῦτα, καὶ ἐνίοτε ὡς ἀληθῶς βλέπων εἰς αὐτὰ **σκοτοδινιῶ**. {ΣΩ.} Θεόδωρος γάρ, ὦ φίλε, φαίνεται οὐ κακῶς τοπάζειν περὶ τῆς φύσεώς σου. **μάλα γὰρ φιλοσόφου τοῦτο τὸ πάθος, τὸ θαυμάζειν· οὐ γὰρ ἄλλη ἀρχὴ φιλοσοφίας ἢ αὕτη**, καὶ ἔοικεν ὁ τὴν Ἶριν Θαύμαντος ἔκγονον φήσας οὐ κακῶς γενεαλογεῖν.

Pl. *Theaet.* 155c–d

THEAET.: Oh yes, indeed, Socrates, I often *wonder like mad* what these things can mean; sometimes when I'm looking at them I begin to *feel quite giddy*. SOC.: I dare say you do, my dear boy. It seems that Theodorus was not far from the truth when he guessed what kind of person you are. *For this is an experience which is characteristic of a philosopher, this wondering: this is where philosophy begins and nowhere else.* And the man who made Iris the child of Thaumas was perhaps no bad genealogist.

trans. M. Levett – M.J. Burnyeat, emphasis added

Socrates[9] says that the particular emotion or mental state (πάθος) by which Theaetetus is currently affected, namely wondering (τὸ θαυμάζειν), is peculiar to the philosopher; "for there is no other starting-point for philosophy than that." In other words, Plato has Socrates extrapolate from the particular mental state currently affecting Theaetetus to a universal claim about the psychological origin of philosophy as such: wonder is the emotional mark of the true philosopher.[10] He also brings a mythical genealogy to bear on the relation of wonder to philosophy. By making Iris the daughter of Thaumas, Hesiod is supposed to have alluded to the intimate connection between wonder and philosophical reflection.[11]

---

9 Throughout this paper when I mention 'Socrates' I always refer to the Platonic character. Questions about the relation of this character to the historical figure fall outside the scope of my present concerns.

10 For an approach, in some respects quite similar to mine, to the question of what is involved in the *Theaetetus* claim about wonder, see now Candiotto and Politis 2020 (cf., more generally, Chrysakopoulou 2012). It is perhaps significant that the most widely read commentators of the dialogue have not paid due attention to the passage: Cornford (1935: 43, n. 1) has a small note that McDowell (1973: 137) basically repeats while Burnyeat (1990) keeps silent. For a really astonishing account of wonder in the *Theaetetus*, see the self-contained essay "Monstrous Wonder: The Advance of Nature" in Sallis 2016: 58–157.

11 Socrates' anonymous genealogist should be Hesiod (*Theog.* 265–266). It is not very clear, however, how Plato meant Hesiod's evidence to bear on the relation between wonder and philosophy. Cornford (1935: 43, n. 1) adduces the relations of Ἶρις to εἴρειν ('string together', hence, when what is strung together is words, 'speak meaningfully') and of λέγειν (as a synonym of εἴρειν) to dialectic from the *Cratylus* (408b and 398d, respectively) in order to conclude that Iris stands for philosophy. But to expect the reader to supply evidence from two distinct passages of the *Cratylus* in order correctly to understand an allegorical interpretation of a Hesiodic genealogy seems to be too far-fetched even for Plato. In Homer, besides being the famous winged messenger of the gods (e.g. *Il.* II.786, VIII.398), Iris also represents the rainbow (*Il.* XI.27–8, XVII.547–9), a 'sign', (τέρας) to mortals sent by Zeus. Her Hesiodic parents, Thaumas ('wondering' or 'wonderful') and Electra ('the shining one'), point to the same celestial phenomenon (West 1966: 242). It seems that Plato here disregards, though he mentions, the causal course of the genealogy (i.e. the fact that Thaumas is the father, not the son, of Iris in Hesiod's narrative) and implies that wonder (Thaumas) is caused, i.e. generated, by the rainbow (Iris) regarded both as an unexpected marvel and as a divine sign requiring interpretation.

The idea that philosophy begins in wonder has had a celebrated history in Western tradition. Thinkers as varied and diverse as Thomas Aquinas, Montaigne, Francis Bacon, Hobbes, Descartes, Wittgenstein and Heidegger have repeated the claim — not to mention some others, such as Gabriel Marcel, who have made wonder a central theme of their philosophies.[12] Not all of them approach wonder in exactly the same way. But they all think that Plato's observation carries more than a merely historical significance: it tells something about philosophizing *per se*; it rings a bell about the experience of doing philosophy. A rather widespread and popular approach to the saying that philosophy begins in wonder looks on admiration as the distinctive experience that generates philosophical reflection. To determine this view's proximity to, or distance from, Plato's original statement we need to take into account the context in which this pregnant saying is embedded, and its immediate legacy in Aristotle's *Metaphysics*; for this is the other source, second only to Plato, for the dissemination of the idea in the modern world. To bring the distinctive character (and even originality) of the saying into higher relief one may compare it with other ancient views about the motivation for doing philosophy, as Frede (2008) has done. Alternatively, one may contrast Plato's saying to Greek views about the beginning of research in a field such as medicine. In the present chapter we have opted for the second alternative. A comparison of philosophy with medicine on the subject of wonder is attempted in the last part of the chapter.

For the time being, let's step back and ask: what is Theaetetus' present affection? In his own words, the sense of wonder which is currently affecting him is a kind of dizziness, giddiness, light-headedness, i.e. mental confusion (σκοτοδινιῶ). Theaetetus is unable to make up his mind and find an acceptable solution to a particular problem. He is utterly perplexed and confused. He cannot proceed further. He is mentally paralysed. He has accepted the following three admissions (*Theaet.* 155a–c, immediately preceding the passage cited above): first, that nothing can ever become bigger or smaller than itself in magnitude or in number as long as it remains equal to itself; second, that if nothing is added to, or reduced from, a particular thing this thing can grow neither bigger nor smaller; and third, that it is impossible for something which was not F in the

---

[12] Cf. Llewelyn 2001, Deckard and Losonczi 2011, Vasalou 2012, Sherey 2013. A quick google search provides several (historical or thematic) Introductions to Philosophy with 'wonder' featuring in their titles. This shows the currency and prevalence of the idea. For the place of wonder in spirituality as the kind of life that stands in-between a purely secular stance and a narrowly religious outlook, see Fuller 2006 (summarized in Fuller 2012). Earlier attempts at a philosophical elucidation of wonder include Parsons 1969 and Hepburn 1980.

past but now is F to have become F without changing. Notwithstanding those three admissions, Theaetetus, who is an adolescent in his late teens at the dramatic date of the dialogue's main discussion (399 B.C.), is well aware that next year, when he grows taller, the relative height of Socrates to his will be different. Socrates' height next year will not change; for Socrates is neither too young nor too old (ἐμὲ τηλικόνδε ὄντα). Theaetetus' height, by contrast, will change because he is young and he is still growing up. But the relative height of Socrates will also change because of the actual change of Theaetetus' height. How is that possible if the three admissions previously accepted are all true?

It is empirically evident that the predicate "taller than Theaetetus" now truly applies to Socrates. It is equally evident that the predicate "shorter than Theaetetus" will truly apply to Socrates next year when Theaetetus will have grown taller. And it is also plain that Socrates himself will not have changed in the meantime. But "taller than Theaetetus" and "shorter than Theaetetus" are contrary predicates; and contrary predicates cannot, both, be true of the same subject without its having changed. This is Theaetetus' puzzlement. Theaetetus has empirical reasons to think that "shorter than Theaetetus" will be a true property of Socrates next year. He has also empirical reasons to think that Socrates will not have changed. And he has also reasons, though of a different kind, namely logical reasons, to think that nothing changes from being X to being Y (where X and Y are contrary predicates) without actually changing: for a change without a change sounds like a plain contradiction.

Earlier on in the same dialogue (154c), Socrates said that six dice, when placed next and compared to four dice, are "more" (in a ratio of 3:2, ἡμιολίους), but when placed next and compared to twelve dice, they are "less" (in a ratio of 1:2, ἡμίσεις).[13] But "more" and "less" are contrary predicates. How can the same thing be, without changing, both "more" and "less"? This is also an example of the perplexity that is currently affecting Theaetetus (ὅταν τὰ περὶ τῶν ἀστραγάλων λέγωμεν, 155b).

Quite generally, Theaetetus' mental confusion stems from a careful examination of the paradoxical nature of those predicates that Aristotle would place in the distinct category of πρός τι,[14] i.e. of relative terms such as "bigger", "dou-

---

13 Stern (2008: 99) finds it significant that Socrates uses the "harmonic" numbers 4, 6 and 12 (6 being the harmonic mean between 4 and 12) in his example and that he mentions numbers *of dice* rather than simply numbers.
14 *Cat.* 7, 6a36–8b24, *Metaph.* Δ.15, 1020b26–1021b11.

ble", "half", "father", "sister",[15] etc. which are incomplete in themselves and logically require a complement.

It is not only Socrates' interlocutor that is affected by θαυμάζειν. Socrates himself is also under its impact. In the *Symposium* (174d–175d), he is seized by a thoughtful mood, lags behind Aristodemus, stands for quite a while in front of the door of Agathon's neighbour, disregards the slave's requests to join the group, and enters the banquet belatedly. Aristodemus who knows him quite well says that this is a rather common habit (ἔθος) of his (175b). Apparently, the same kind of thoughtful immobility affected Socrates for more than twenty four hours during a military campaign, according to Alcibiades (*Symp.* 220c–d), thus stirring the petty curiosity of all those present. We do not learn the kind of problem that was puzzling Socrates' mind for such a long time but we do learn that he stood still, "glued to the same point" (as Nehamas and Woodruff nicely translate), looking for a solution (εἱστήκει σκοπῶν, εἱστήκει ζητῶν). In both cases, it seems no more likely that Socrates found the desired solution, as Agathon assumes (175d), than that he didn't. It is equally possible that the affection which prompted his deep meditation abandoned him as unexpectedly as it had seized him in the first place.

We can perhaps get a glimpse of the sort of problems tormenting Socrates from the *Phaedo* (96e–97b). He is unable to accept the idea that such empirical processes as the addition of one thing to another or the division of one thing into parts would possibly account for the fact that one thing becomes two. How is it possible, he asks (97a–b), for one thing to become two if another thing, which is itself one, is placed next to it? And what is it that becomes two: the first thing or the added one or both?

{ΣΩ.} θαυμάζω γὰρ εἰ ὅτε μὲν ἑκάτερον αὐτῶν χωρὶς ἀλλήλων ἦν, ἓν ἄρα ἑκάτερον ἦν καὶ οὐκ ἤστην τότε δύο, ἐπεὶ δ' ἐπλησίασαν ἀλλήλοις, αὕτη ἄρα αἰτία αὐτοῖς ἐγένετο τοῦ δύο γενέσθαι, ἡ σύνοδος τοῦ πλησίον ἀλλήλων τεθῆναι. οὐδέ γε ὡς ἐάν τις ἓν διασχίσῃ, δύναμαι ἔτι πείθεσθαι ὡς αὕτη αὖ αἰτία γέγονεν, ἡ σχίσις, τοῦ δύο γεγονέναι· ἐναντία γὰρ γίγνεται ἢ τότε αἰτία τοῦ δύο γίγνεσθαι. τότε μὲν γὰρ ὅτι συνήγετο πλησίον ἀλλήλων καὶ προσετίθετο ἕτερον ἑτέρῳ, νῦν δ' ὅτι ἀπάγεται καὶ χωρίζεται ἕτερον ἀφ' ἑτέρου.

---

15 The relative character of terms such as "father", "mother", "brother" and "sister" is exploited by Socrates in the *Symposium* (199d–e) as a crucial step for the refutation of Agathon's idea that the Eros is the most beautiful (κάλλιστος) and most virtuous (ἄριστος) of gods (195a). In Socrates'/Diotima's view (201e–204c), erotic love *qua* desire for the beautiful and the good is neither beautiful and good nor ugly and wicked, hence neither a god nor a mortal thing but an in-between daemon.

{SOC.} For I wonder that, when each of them is separate from the other, each of them is one, nor are they then two, but that, when they come near to one another, this is the cause of their becoming two, the coming together and being placed closer to one another. Nor can I any longer be persuaded that when one thing is divided, this division is the cause of its becoming two, for just now the cause of becoming two was the opposite. At that time it was their coming close together and one was added to the other, but now it is because one is taken and separated from the other.

trans. G.M.A. Grube, slightly modified

Note that the perplexities of Socrates and Theaetetus concern *theoretical issues*: the problem of how duality is generated from unity and the problem of so-called Cambridge changes,[16] respectively. Socrates and Theaetetus have not discovered some *new facts* which they cannot accommodate within their already established cognitive schemata. The cases that puzzle them are everyday occurrences known to all human beings such as the relative size of two persons, the relative magnitude of six dice, and the making of two things out of one thing when the latter is either added to another thing or divided into two pieces. It seems unlikely that the man of the street would be affected, let alone seriously puzzled, by similar questions. That is precisely why Socrates thinks that wondering is the true mark of a philosopher. Wonder renders problematic and unaccountable what is usual and even trivial, what belongs to everyday experience, what is routinely encountered in daily life but rarely, if at all, questioned. In Plato's understanding, to wonder is *not* to be perplexed about the extraordinary, the miraculous and the strange: wonder is bewilderment *in the face of the ordinary and the familiar*. Platonic wondering transforms what is usually and normally taken for granted into an unresolved problem and a serious issue for thought. Platonic wondering wonders at what obtains always or for the most part, not at exceptional, rare or otherwise remarkable events.

In the *Republic* (VII, 524d–525a), Socrates speaks again of number and the one. He says to Glaucon that if one thing is perceived in itself (καθ' αὑτὸ) by sight or any other sense, it does not pull the perceiver to the domain of true being (οὐκ ἂν ὁλκὸν εἴη ἐπὶ τὴν οὐσίαν). But if the same thing appears to be no more one than its opposite – i.e. either many (by its having parts) or less than

---

16 In early twentieth century some philosophers based on Cambridge (Bertrand Russell, John McTaggart) defined change as what happens to a given subject S_1 if and only if a particular predicate P is true of S_1 at temporal point t_1 but not true of S_1 at t_2. A logical consequence of this definition is that S_1 must be considered as having changed even if P is a relational predicate such as "taller than S_2" and it is S_2 that has actually become taller. The name "Cambridge changes" for changes of this kind is proposed by Gearch 1969, 71–72, and it has been gradually accepted as a technical term.

one (by its being a part of a larger whole) —, the mind is forced to be perplexed on this, to inquire and to ask, by mobilizing the relevant notion, what the one itself is, after all (ἀναγκάζοιτ' ἂν ἐν αὑτῷ ψυχὴ ἀπορεῖν καὶ ζητεῖν, κινοῦσα ἐν ἑαυτῇ τὴν ἔννοιαν, καὶ ἀνερωτᾶν τί ποτέ ἐστιν αὐτὸ τὸ ἕν). In this way, learning about the one (ἡ περὶ τὸ ἕν μάθησις) is part and parcel of those training processes that turn the mind to the contemplation of true being (ἐπὶ τὴν τοῦ ὄντος θέαν). As in the previous examples from the *Theaetetus* and the *Pheado*, Socrates wants to effect a widening of the mental vision of his interlocutors that may ideally elevate them from sensible to intelligible reality. The bafflement of the mind is an indispensable step to this end. To be perplexed is to find oneself in a mental situation where contrary views mutually cancel one another and no way out of the contradiction seems to be available. The mind is stuck and incapable of proceeding further. But are Socrates' interlocutors able to be really and deeply puzzled and thus ascend to the intelligible realm as Socrates suggests?

In the famous comparison of himself with a midwife (*Theaet.* 149a–151d), Socrates emphatically says that he converses only with people who are *already* pregnant with perplexities (151a–b).[17] Socrates does not regard himself as a ferti-

---

[17] The Anonymous Commentator of the *Theaetetus* (probably Eudorus of Alexandria) understands the young man's pregnancy to consist of 'natural concepts' (φυσικαὶ ἔννοιαι) (47.35–48.7, 52.44–53.36 Diels-Schubart). The Commentator aligns his interpretation with the doctrine of recollection in the *Meno*. Other ancient authors follow a similar approach (Plut. *Quest.Plat.* 1000 D-E, Proclus *In Alc.* 28.16–29.3). But the aporetic end of the dialogue (210a–d), in which the midwife figure recurs, shows that what Socrates has finally delivered from Theaetetus' pregnant mind are false views ("wind-eggs") about the essence of knowledge, the examination of which has indicated that they are not worth nurturing further (ἀνεμιαῖα ... καὶ οὐκ ἄξια τροφῆς). In an earlier recurrence of the midwifery theme (160e–161a), the newly-born child is said to be the equation of knowledge with perception, a view about knowledge that has to be subsequently examined, Socrates says, as to its truth (σκοπουμένους μὴ λάθῃ ἡμᾶς οὐκ ἄξιον ὄν τροφῆς τὸ γιγνόμενον ἀλλὰ ἀνεμιαῖόν τε καὶ ψεῦδος). Of the two distinct parts of Socrates' midwifery process, delivery and examination, the second is said *not* to correspond to a stage in the practice of actual midwives since it is not difficult to tell whether a human infant is genuine or a mere phantom (150a–b). In the case of Socratic midwifery, "by contrast, the greatest and most honourable work" (μέγιστόν τε καὶ κάλλιστον ἔργον) is precisely this examination. Since examination crucially involves questioning and the interlocutor's consent, it follows that "the argument which emerges from such an interchange of questions and answers is not formally the questioner's argument, an argument he formally endorses" (Frede 1992: 206) but an argument that belongs to the respondent and shows his mental state (cf. 157c–d). If so, then the reduction of the respondent to a state of perplexity by means of an argument that he endorses is the outcome of the respondent's own beliefs and as such a kind of birth that he gives, with Socrates' help, to his own perplexity. What Socratic midwifery brings to light is the inadequacy

lizing father who causes the "conception" of mental impasses in others but, rather, as a midwife who helps with their "delivery" and "birth". What he means is that through cross-examination he makes others aware of perplexities that were *already* affecting them without perhaps being fully realized and adequately formulated.[18] These perplexities have been aptly described as labour-pain *aporiai*, and they are significantly different from the impasses *inflicted* by Socrates on his interlocutors in earlier dialogues to the extent that labour-pain perplexities prominently feature in a young man's mental state *prior to* his cross-examination.[19] In the so-called Socratic dialogues, by contrast, a person, usually of mature age, who is proud and confident in his expertise about a particular topic (e.g. piety, courage, virtue etc.) and has never questioned his competence in that domain, is unable to give satisfactory answers to Socrates' questions and usually contradicts himself conspicuously. But, in most cases, he does not learn a lesson of humility or moderation for his claim to know.[20] Euthyphro, unmoved in his conviction that he knows what piety is, finds a pretext hurriedly to leave the discussion (*Euth.* 15e). Laches, annoyed by his inability to articulate his thoughts properly, insists that he intuitively knows what courage is but is unable to state it, he claims, due to a lack of training in arguments (*Lach.* 194A-b). Meno puts the blame for his inadequacy to define what virtue is onto Socrates' argumentative tricks (*Meno* 79e–80b). Thrasymachus[21] arrogantly scoffs at Socrates' attempt to disprove his thesis about justice, is irritated, wants to leave

---

of the interlocutor's views and, ultimately, his own latent confusion. The contrast between the *Theaetetus* and the *Meno* is elegantly brought out in Burnyeat 2012: 27–29 [= 1977: 9–11].

18 Sedley (2004: 8) is potentially misleading when he writes that "the painful puzzlement which he [sc. Socrates] *inflicts* on his interlocutors is in reality nothing less than their birth pangs" (emphasis added). Socrates, in fact, denies the common accusation against his practice as "*causing* people to be puzzled" (ποιῶ τοὺς ἀνθρώπους ἀπορεῖν) and introduces the midwife image as a better, though secret, description of what he actually does (149a). In line with what Socrates says, we must assume that prior to Socratic questioning the perplexities have already been in the interlocutor's mind in a latent, not fully conscious or articulated state. Perhaps this is what Sedley, too, means by the unfortunate formulation quoted above. Burnyeat (2012: 22, 30, 31 = 1977: 7, 11) more cautiously writes that Socrates "has an extraordinary way of *reducing* people to perplexity", "of *awakening* or *allaying* perplexity", "*arousing* and *allaying* the pains of perplexity" or that he "*induces* perplexity" (emphasis added).

19 Brown 2018: 92–95.

20 Szaif 2018: 31–33, 36–37.

21 By drawing an example from the *Republic* I do not have to assume that Book I was initially composed as an independent dialogue, possibly called *Thrasymachus*, which was later expanded into the *Republic* we know. For present purposes it suffices that *Rep.* I displays a character that shares the confidence of Socrates' interlocutors in the so-called Socratic dialogues.

Polemarchus' house, and finally concedes reluctantly to Socrates' suggestions (εἶεν, 'so be it') as if he were addressing an old woman narrating mythical tales: in short, Thrasymachus remains unconvinced throughout the dialogue.[22] In all these cases, Socrates' interlocutors are not deeply shaken by their proven inability to provide a consistent definition. Their impasse is an objective fact for the reader of the dialogues to ponder upon, not a subjective experience of the interlocutors themselves. I assume that in view of the *Theaetetus*' midwifery image Plato's point is that all these characters had *not* been pregnant with perplexities prior to encountering Socrates. They had not treated as problematic and perplexing the usual and the ordinary. They had not wondered. In short, no matter what they could do or teach, they were not lovers of wisdom or philosophical natures as Theaetetus.

Upon manifestation and birth, the true views contained in the perplexities of those already pregnant with them are kept alive and nurtured whereas the false ones (*Theaet.* 151c: εἴδωλον καὶ μὴ ἀληθές; cf. 150c: εἴδωλον καὶ ψεῦδος) are exposed and cast away like handicapped infants. At the end of the process, as with Theaetetus, the interlocutor is purged of the false views contained in his earlier puzzlement and relieved of the pains of labour that had been torturing him all along (210b–c). By achieving a state of improved self-knowledge about what little he knows and, more significantly, what he ignores he is now in a position to "conceive" *better* perplexities thanks to the present examination (βελτιόνων ἔσῃ πλήρης διὰ τὴν νῦν ἐξέτασιν), if he happens to become pregnant in the future, i.e. if he finds himself in a state of wonder again.

It might be tempting to explain away Theaetetus' sense of puzzlement by assuming that relational terms ("taller", "shorter", "more", "less", etc.) are not real predicates but incomplete linguistic items whose inadequate grasp generates mental confusion. On that account, there is nothing really wondrous if Socrates' size remains the same for an entire year and we may *still* meaningfully and truly say that a year ago Socrates was taller than Theaetetus but now he is shorter than Theaetetus, since Theaetetus has in the meantime grown taller. But I think that by treating those perplexities as paradoxes created by language *alone* and the inadequate grasp of relational terms we are entirely missing the philosopher's original sense of puzzlement to which Plato wants to draw our attention. A fictional example might be of some help for what I mean.

---

[22] Scoff and irritation: 340d–341c, 343a, 343d; desire to leave: 344d; concession: 350c–e, 351c6 (σοὶ χαρίζομαι), 351d7 (ἵνα σοι μὴ διαφέρωμαι), 352b3–4 (οὐ γὰρ ἔγωγέ σοι ἐναντιώσομαι), 354a; Socrates as an old myth-telling woman: 350e.

John was not a father. But three months ago his wife gave birth to a beautiful daughter. He became a father. He changed without changing. This is not a merely linguistic puzzle. His fatherhood has affected him deeply. It has changed the ways he looks at things, the ways he perceives the world, the way he lives. It has changed his perspective and his stance. It cannot be a merely linguistic error that has caused his new concerns. Fatherhood has changed his life though his wife lives away and he has never actually seen his daughter. Something happened out there and he is no longer the same person as before. There might be a deeply personal interest involved in his raising the question "how may I change without actually changing?" The question speaks to him personally and affects his life. But for this question to be raised John must have already experienced wonder at the state of affairs that is called "fatherhood". On Socrates' view, John is a philosopher because he views as problematic and worthy of thoughtful consideration what is an ordinary and matter-of-fact situation of everyday life. Though deeply affected by his own bewilderment, John addresses the question of fatherhood as a theoretical issue: his situation will not be altered in the least, it will neither improve nor worsen, if he happens to find an acceptable way out of the puzzle or remains caught in the paradox of fatherhood.

A more radical course than both the unreflective attitude of Socrates' interlocutors in the early dialogues and the labour pains of those pregnant with perplexities in the *Theaetetus* is steered by the Eleatic Stranger in the *Sophist* (244a) when he admits, and has Theaetetus agree, that in the past they thought they knew what Being is but now they are perplexed: ἡμεῖς δὲ πρὸ τοῦ μὲν ᾠόμεθα [sc. γιγνώσκεσθαι], νῦν δ' ἠπορήκαμεν. The Eleatic Stranger, who is neither a midwife like Socrates nor a self-delusive ignoramus, ironically places himself among the many (243a) and castigates all previous philosophers as mythmakers addressing children (242c–243a). In the wake of Parmenides' teaching he has realized the difficulties in postulating primary entities, whether one or more than one, in order to account for the phenomenal existence of a variety of things, i.e. for the one vs. many problem, and ultimately for the unity of Being. The Eleatic Stranger has conceived and given birth to the fundamental *aporia* of Being all by himself. He has not remained content with the prima facie plausible accounts of others, including "father" Parmenides' assumptions (241d–242a), but has delved deep into their inconsistencies. The inscrutability of Being has stared him in the face. And he is afraid lest he appear insane (μανικός) to Theaetetus (242a). Beginning his inquiry into the unthinkable nature of Non-being (238c), which he thought he understood well in the past (243b), he ends up, by means of an audacious argument (παρακινδυνευτικὸς λόγος, 242b), questioning Being itself (243d–246a). All previous assurances and certainties have been cast away. He stands in wonder. Perhaps he is not inappropriately called a 'stranger' and an 'alien' (ξένος). For his ways of thinking are strange and alienating, indeed. They destabilize our normal views and upset our familiarities. The Eleatic Stranger is Plato's philosopher *par excellence*. For he is singularly able, now and again, to wonder and to stand in wonder.

2.2 Wonder and Perplexity in Aristotle

In *Metaphysics* Alpha Aristotle repeats Plato's idea: the psychological origin of philosophy, both in the past and in the present, is wonder (A.2, 982b11–19):

> Ὅτι δ' οὐ ποιητική [sc. ἡ ζητουμένη ἐπιστήμη], δῆλον καὶ ἐκ τῶν πρώτων φιλοσοφησάντων· **διὰ γὰρ τὸ θαυμάζειν οἱ ἄνθρωποι καὶ νῦν καὶ τὸ πρῶτον ἤρξαντο φιλοσοφεῖν**, ἐξ ἀρχῆς μὲν τὰ πρόχειρα τῶν ἀτόπων **θαυμάσαντες**, εἶτα κατὰ μικρὸν οὕτω προϊόντες καὶ περὶ τῶν μειζόνων **διαπορήσαντες**, οἷον περί τε τῶν τῆς σελήνης παθημάτων καὶ τῶν περὶ τὸν ἥλιον καὶ ἄστρα καὶ περὶ τῆς τοῦ παντὸς γενέσεως. **ὁ δ' ἀπορῶν καὶ θαυμάζων οἴεται ἀγνοεῖν** (διὸ καὶ ὁ φιλόμυθος φιλόσοφός πώς ἐστιν· ὁ γὰρ μῦθος σύγκειται ἐκ θαυμασίων).

> That it [sc. the science we are seeking] is not a science of production is clear even from the history of the earliest philosophers. *For it is owing to their wonder that men both now begin and at first began to philosophize;* they *wondered* originally at the obvious difficulties, then advanced little by little and *stated difficulties* about the greater matters, e.g. about the phenomena of the moon and those of the sun and the stars, and about the genesis of the universe. And *a man who is puzzled and wonders* thinks himself ignorant (whence even the lover of myth is in a sense a lover of wisdom, for myth is composed of wonders).
>
> trans. W.D. Ross, emphasis added

Aristotle believes that the particular experience that once affected the first philosophers in Greece (τὸ πρῶτον)[23] — and even perhaps, prior to them, the inventors of the mathematical sciences in Egypt (A.1, 981b17–25) — is to be also found in each and every case of a philosopher in the present (τὸ νῦν): ontogenesis resumes phylogenesis.[24] As in Plato, the mental state of wonder is for Aristotle an indispensable psychological prerequisite for philosophical inquiry to get

---

23 The expression οἱ πρῶτοι φιλοσοφήσαντες of A.2, 982b11–12 is clarified in A.3, 983b6–25, where the same expression is used (b6–7): the first philosophers are the natural philosophers of Ionia, whose "founding father" (ὁ τῆς τοιαύτης ἀρχηγὸς φιλοσοφίας) is Thales of Miletus.
24 The point was brought home to me by Melissa Lane when an earlier draft of the first part of this chapter was presented at Princeton in autumn 2016.

started in the soul of any human being, past, present or (we may safely add) future.[25]

The kind of philosophy that Aristotle has in mind here is neither practical nor productive knowledge: it is theoretical knowledge, i.e. knowledge for the sake of knowing rather than knowledge for the sake of some practical advantage or benefit.[26] This is shown by what immediately follows Aristotle's quoted passage (A.2, 982b19–27):

> ὥστ' εἴπερ διὰ τὸ φεύγειν τὴν ἄγνοιαν ἐφιλοσόφησαν, φανερὸν ὅτι διὰ τὸ εἰδέναι τὸ ἐπίστασθαι ἐδίωκον καὶ οὐ χρήσεώς τινος ἕνεκεν. μαρτυρεῖ δὲ αὐτὸ τὸ συμβεβηκός· σχεδὸν γὰρ πάντων ὑπαρχόντων τῶν ἀναγκαίων καὶ πρὸς ῥᾳστώνην καὶ διαγωγὴν ἡ τοιαύτη φρόνησις ἤρξατο ζητεῖσθαι. δῆλον οὖν ὡς δι' οὐδεμίαν αὐτὴν ζητοῦμεν χρείαν ἑτέραν, ἀλλ' ὥσπερ ἄνθρωπος, φαμέν, ἐλεύθερος ὁ αὑτοῦ ἕνεκα καὶ μὴ ἄλλου ὤν, οὕτω καὶ αὐτὴν ὡς μόνην οὖσαν ἐλευθέραν τῶν ἐπιστημῶν· μόνη γὰρ αὕτη αὑτῆς ἕνεκέν ἐστιν.

> Therefore since they philosophized in order to escape from ignorance, evidently they were pursuing science in order to know, and not for any utilitarian end. And this is confirmed by the facts; for it was when almost all the necessities of life and the things that make for comfort and recreation were present, that such knowledge began to be sought. Evidently then we do not seek it for the sake of any other advantage; but as the man is free, we say, who exists for himself and not for another, so we pursue this as the only free science, for it alone exists for itself.
>
> trans. W.D. Ross

According to Aristotle, philosophy is not just any old search for ways to overcome the adversities of climate and the scarcity of food; nor is it, more generally, research conducted for the improvement of one's material or cultural conditions. It is clearly a non-instrumental and even *useless* kind of investigation for the mere pleasure of knowing, and, as such, it gets started only after the basic necessities of life have been adequately dealt with and the further desire for comfort and recreation has already been satisfied. For philosophy to get started leisure is presupposed.

The view developed here is not contradicted by Aristotle's belief, in the *Nicomachean Ethics* (X.7–8), that theoretical contemplation provides in fact 'well-

---

[25] The passage is examined in Bernadete 1978 and Schaeffer 1999. Aristotle's legacy about wonder in the development of the pseudo-Aristotelian *Problemata* is elegantly studied in Oikonomopoulou 2019.

[26] The priority of the theoretical over the practical branches of knowledge that we find in both Plato (*Rep.* VII, 527d–541b) and Aristotle (*Metaph.* A.1–2, 980a21–983a23; *EN* X.7–8, 1177a12–1179a32) was, it seems, an innovation of the fourth century B.C. defended by means of new arguments as well as a rhetorical appropriation of religious *theoria* (Nightingale 2004: 72–93).

being' (εὐδαιμονία) and that this kind of well-being is in many ways superior to the well-being provided by the exercise of ethical virtues. For one of the reasons in which the superiority of theoretical life is grounded is the fact that it alone is loved for its own sake (αὐτὴ μόνη δι' αὐτὴν ἀγαπᾶσθαι); practical activities, by contrast, even when virtuously performed, are loved both for themselves and for their outcomes (*N.E.* X.7, 1177b1–4). It follows that the person who engages in theoretical investigation not out of love for what it is but in anticipation of a subsequent well-being (identified perhaps with fame, social success, riches, and the like) will be frustrated: rather than a means to the further end of well-being, theoretical contemplation is one and the same with the well-being of theoretical life. The ultimate ground of Aristotle's high valuation of the theoretical life is the idea that this is the only truly free enterprise[27] — which is also the reason why theoretical contemplation is the sole activity said to befit gods' eminent life.[28]

The idea about the liberal character of theoretical contemplation is causally related to Aristotle's view that all human beings have a natural desire for knowledge quite irrespective of the benefits they may gain from it (*Metaph.* A.1, 980a21–24). But some people, we learn from the *Poetics* (4, 1448b11–17; cf. 9, 1451b5–7), feel more urgently than others the desire to understand and are better equipped to successfully conduct researches. These are the true philosophers, and to them alone the well-being of the theoretical life is addressed. However, rather than claiming that the psychological origin of philosophy is the natural desire for knowledge Aristotle says that the psychological origin of philosophy is wonder. Why? One reason might be that Aristotle is here closely dependent on Plato who has Socrates claim that the characteristic 'affection' (πάθος) of the philosopher is wonder. Another might be that Aristotle considers the desire to understand to be the necessary, and the experience of wonder the sufficient, condition for philosophical reflection to get started, or that it is the *experience* of wonder that triggers the natural desire to understand to a specifically philosophical activity. The two reasons are not incompatible. In fact, it seems that, while following Plato in claiming that wonder is the affection characteristic of both past and present philosophers, Aristotle thinks of wonder as a mental event predicated upon the desire to escape ignorance (διὰ τὸ φεύγειν τὴν ἄγνοιαν), as the quoted passage shows. If so, then the natural desire to know (which is the positive way of describing the desire to escape ignorance), although always a prerequisite, is not said to be the psychological origin of

---

27 As has been noted by commentators (e.g. Ross 1924: I.123, Broadie 2012: 63), Aristotle's notion of a free science has a distinctly Platonic pedigree (*Rep.* VI.499a, VII.536d–e).
28 *Metaph.* A.2, 982b24–983a11; *N.E.* X.8, 1178b7–32, 1179a23–32.

philosophy for the following three reasons. First, because Aristotle wants to speak of a *particular emotion* that triggers to activity the natural desire to understand. Second, because the easiness with which the desire to know is occasionally satisfied (as, for instance, when to know something is just to perceive this thing happening) precludes that this alone may be the psychological origin of philosophy whereas the tortuousness, implicit in the impasse of θαυμάζειν, may indeed count as the beginning of philosophical inquiry proper. Third, because Aristotle wants to emphasize the theoretical direction that the desire to understand must take if it is to count as a specifically philosophical desire, and this can only be guaranteed by the involvement of wonder.[29] In favour of such an interpretation we have Aristotle's own admission that philosophy is primarily a theoretical endeavour as well as his claim, at the beginning of *Metaphysics* A.1, that the natural love we have for the senses (and for sight in particular), quite apart from their practical usefulness, is a sure sign that the desire to know is natural indeed since we delight in seeing things not only in order to be properly oriented in our movements but also for the sake of knowledge alone. We shall soon see that while adopting Plato's viewpoint Aristotle is slightly, and almost imperceptibly, twisting it to a radically new direction.[30]

The claim that philosophy, in the sense of a search for theoretical understanding, begins in wonder may be taken in two distinct ways since the verb used here (θαυμάζειν) has two distinct, though interrelated, meanings: it may be taken to mean that philosophy begins with a sense of astonishment, admiration and even awe before the wonderful processes of nature, their beauty and orderliness; or, it may be taken to mean that philosophy begins with a sense of puzzlement and perplexity. The first is a feeling of psychological elation, delight, and even rapture. The second is a feeling of psychological unrest, confusion, and even turmoil. The first involves a kind of joy or pleasure, the second a kind of pain or distress. Aristotle has already used the verb in the first sense a bit earlier (*Metaph.* A.1, 981b14–15) when he said of the first inventors of crafts that it was reasonable to be admired (θαυμάζεσθαι) by people not only for the usefulness of their inventions but also as wise and excellent persons. However,

---

29 "The desire to understand" features in the title of what is probably the best concise introduction to Aristotle's philosophy to date. Lear (1988: 3) thinks, as I do, that for Aristotle "philosophy grows out of man's natural capacity to feel puzzlement and awe". To stand in wonder is, then, a more intense expression of the natural desire to understand.

30 In my opinion, Bernadete (1978: 213–214) is wrong to write about Aristotle's conception of wonder that "[t]he desire to know ... is an indispensable greediness to transform the opaque into the plain (information); but wonder is the recognition of the opaque in the plain." To my mind, this is true of Plato's, not Aristotle's, wonder.

although it is not uncommon for the phrase of the passage that concerns us here to be routinely cited in the same sense, Aristotle, like Plato's Socrates in the *Theaetetus*, clearly intends the second meaning. For, as he goes on to claim, humans were puzzled and perplexed, to begin with, by strange things close to hand (τὰ πρόχειρα τῶν ἀτόπων), but as time was passing they gradually became perplexed by major events such as the phases or eclipses of the moon, the movement of the stars, and even the question about the origin of the universe as a whole. Quite obviously, the participles θαυμάσαντες and διαπορήσαντες at 982b14–15 (cf. ὁ ἀπορῶν καὶ θαυμάζων at 982b17–18) are meant to be near-synonyms in the present context.[31] To wonder is to be perplexed; and to be perplexed is to be aware of some ignorance. Notice that Aristotle refers to ἄτοπα, literally 'things out of place' and, hence, 'strange' or 'paradoxical'. What Aristotle seems to have primarily in mind here are not instances of ordinary, usual, and normal things, but rather the opposite cases of unexpected and extraordinary events. Such must have seemed to the primitive mind not only the infrequent and irregular (partial or total) eclipses of the sun and the moon, but also the regular, on a monthly basis, phases of the moon and the no-less-regular annual revolutions of the sun along the ecliptic which are the causes of seasonal variation; for it is all these celestial phenomena that we should consider to be intended by παθήματα at 982b16. The impression that Aristotle primarily intends irregular and seemingly exceptional events is reinforced by the parallelism he draws between the lover-of-wisdom (φιλόσοφος) and the lover-of-tales (φιλόμυθος). The bewildering things (θαυμάσια) contained in mythical tales are narrative events (like the transformation of men into pigs or the appeasement of wild beasts through music) that unsettle our assumptions and surprise us as extraordinary and/or abnormal.[32] In the *Poetics* (9, 1452a3–11), Aristotle argues that a well-devised plot consists of a sequence of events that follow causally from one another but are still capable of subverting our expectations (παρὰ τὴν

---

31 Quite often in Aristotle's *Metaphysics* the verb διαπορεῖν has a more technical sense, indicative of a thoughtful exploration of the perplexity one finds oneself in (perhaps by raising pertinent questions about both *p* and *not-p* in an exhaustive way, so Rapp 2018: 117), and is thus different from simple ἀπορεῖν (e.g. B.1, 995a28, 35, b5, 996a17, K.1, 1059a19, b15, M.9, 1086a19; cf. *Top*. I.2, 101a35 and διηπορημένον in Pl. *Soph*. 250e), but this technical sense is not supported by the present passage (Ross 1924: I.198).

32 A very different interpretation is provided by Bos 1983, according to which the φιλόμυθος of our passage refers not to the listeners but to the fabricators of fantastic tales, i.e. to the poets, who attempt to provide explanations of natural events through the medium of anthropomorphic myths. On that reading, the θαυμάσια contained in (basically etiological) myths are objective facts of nature which arouse wonder in the soul of the myth-making poet.

δόξαν δι' ἄλληλα). For even in the case of causally unrelated, i.e. chance events, the 'most marvellous' (θαυμασιώτατα), Aristotle explains, are those that seem to have happened on purpose (ἐπίτηδες). If the lover-of-tales is, in a sense (πως), a lover-of-wisdom, this is because he loves to be surprised by the unusual and the exceptional. Already, this view of Aristotle's is quite removed from Plato's original conception of wonder.

The claim that philosophy begins in wonder is repeated later in the same chapter (A.2, 983a12–21) with some more illuminating examples:

ἄρχονται μὲν γάρ, ὥσπερ εἴπομεν, ἀπὸ τοῦ θαυμάζειν πάντες εἰ οὕτως ἔχει, καθάπερ <περὶ> [add. Jaeger] τῶν θαυμάτων ταὐτόματα τοῖς μήπω τεθεωρηκόσι τὴν αἰτίαν[33] ἢ περὶ τὰς τοῦ ἡλίου τροπὰς ἢ τὴν τῆς διαμέτρου ἀσυμμετρίαν (**θαυμαστὸν γὰρ εἶναι δοκεῖ πᾶσι εἴ τι τῷ ἐλαχίστῳ μὴ μετρεῖται**)· δεῖ δὲ εἰς τοὐναντίον καὶ τὸ ἄμεινον κατὰ τὴν παροιμίαν ἀποτελευτῆσαι, καθάπερ καὶ ἐν τούτοις ὅταν μάθωσιν· **οὐθὲν γὰρ ἂν οὕτως θαυμάσειεν ἀνὴρ γεωμετρικὸς ὡς εἰ γένοιτο ἡ διάμετρος μετρητή**.

For all men begin, as we said, by wondering that the matter is so, as in the case of marionettes seeming automatic to those who have not yet perceived the explanation, or the solstices or the incommensurability of the diagonal of a square with the side (for it seems wonderful to all men that there is a thing which cannot be measured even by the smallest unit). But we must end in the contrary and, according to the proverb, the better state, as is the case in these instances when men learn the cause; for there is nothing which would surprise a geometer so much as if the diagonal turned out to be commensurable.

trans. W.D. Ross modified, emphasis added

It is to be questioned whether we should supply ἄνθρωποι to qualify πάντες in the above passage, as Ross does. One might think that φιλόσοφοι is a better supplement if wondering is the distinctive mark of the philosopher in the sense that in his/her case the emotive-cum-desiderative experience of wonder actually issues into a conscious striving after cognitive understanding. Moreover, the examples mentioned in the passage (solstices, incommensurability) do not seem to qualify as states of affairs that all human beings approach as problematic and worthy of investigation. In any case, our undecidedness to determine this question indicates that Aristotle believes that the difference between the

---

[33] Following a suggestion made by Bonitz, Jaeger transposed the phrase τοῖς μήπω τεθεωρηκόσι τὴν αἰτίαν from the place it is found in all MSS (i.e. 983a14–15) to 983a16–17. Ross (1924: I.124) explains the supposed difficulty and sides with Jaeger. But if we retain the manuscripts' reading, as Primavesi does (2012: 474–475): "dativum iudicantis revera ad αὐτόματα spectantem"), τῶν θαυμάτων ταὐτόματα (a standard expression in Aristotle, cf. *G.A.* II.1, 734b10, II.5, 741b9) appear self-moving (and, hence, generate wonder) only to those who have not yet seen the real cause of their movement.

philosopher and the layman is *a matter of degree* (calculated on the basis of the intensity of the desire to understand and the frequency of the experience of wonder) rather than a matter of a mental quality or propensity that the one has and the other lacks. And in this, too, he seems to differ from Plato who thought that the philosophers are crucially characterized by the presence, rather than prominence, of wonder and perplexity in their mental lives. On the other hand, it is worth noticing that Aristotle does not mention, as Plato does, highly abstract notions like Cambridge changes and the generation of duality out of oneness. He mentions, rather, things such as self-moving puppets, i.e. bewildering shows that are meant to astonish any spectator and not just the philosopher.

All philosophers begin by wondering, we learn, whether something or other is the case (ἄρχονται γάρ, ὥσπερ εἴπομεν, ἀπὸ τοῦ θαυμάζειν πάντες εἰ οὕτως ἔχει). Examples include automata, solstices, and the incommensurability of a square's diagonal with respect to its side. The philosopher is puzzled about these phenomena, presumably because they conflict with some prior assumptions s/he has taken for granted. How can an inanimate puppet move itself? How and why does the sun annually change its course? Why is the square's diagonal incommensurable with its side? The first example seems to refute the empirical observation that only natural, and more particularly animate, things are self-moving. The second case stands at odds with the assumption that the sun's movement is uniform. The third observation conflicts with the presupposition that there is always a measure, however small, common to any two finite lengths. The solutions to those riddles must accordingly differ. In the first case, by raising the question about how puppets do actually move themselves the philosopher will probably observe more cautiously the case and will eventually come to realize that there are strings (or any other similarly devised equipment) that actually do the moving. In the second case, s/he will realize that the sun's annual course is indeed uniform, notwithstanding its apparent rest for a day or so at the solstices, and that the obliquity of the ecliptic is actually devised for the best result in nature (cf. A.2, 982b7: τὸ ἄριστον ἐν τῇ φύσει πάσῃ) since it allows coming-into-being and passing-away to occur in the sublunary region (*GC* II.10). The solution to the third perplexity is postponed till we have seen Aristotle's official view of what an *aporia*, if adequately formulated and thought through, consists in.

At the beginning of *Metaphysics* Beta Aristotle expounds his view about philosophical perplexity and the proper attitude to it. To be sure, he does not use the verb θαυμάζειν or any of its derivatives here. He speaks of ἀπορῆσαι, διαπορῆσαι, and ἀπορία. But given the intimate connection between θαυμάζειν and ἀπορεῖν in A.2 we may take his view about ἀπορεῖν in B.1 to be continuous with his view about θαυμάζειν as the psychological origin of philosophy in A.2. The passage runs as follows (B.1, 995a24–b4):[34]

> Ἀνάγκη πρὸς τὴν ἐπιζητουμένην ἐπιστήμην ἐπελθεῖν ἡμᾶς πρῶτον περὶ ὧν ἀπορῆσαι δεῖ πρῶτον· ταῦτα δ' ἐστὶν ὅσα τε περὶ αὐτῶν ἄλλως ὑπειλήφασί τινες, κἂν εἴ τι χωρὶς τούτων τυγχάνει παρεωραμένον. **ἔστι δὲ τοῖς εὐπορῆσαι βουλομένοις προὔργου τὸ διαπορῆσαι καλῶς· ἡ γὰρ ὕστερον εὐπορία λύσις τῶν πρότερον ἀπορουμένων ἐστί, λύειν δ' οὐκ ἔστιν ἀγνοοῦντας τὸν δεσμόν, ἀλλ' ἡ τῆς διανοίας ἀπορία δηλοῖ τοῦτο περὶ τοῦ πράγματος· ᾗ γὰρ ἀπορεῖ, ταύτῃ παραπλήσιον πέπονθε τοῖς δεδεμένοις· ἀδύνατον γὰρ ἀμφοτέρως προελθεῖν εἰς τὸ πρόσθεν.** διὸ δεῖ τὰς δυσχερείας τεθεωρηκέναι πάσας πρότερον, τούτων τε χάριν καὶ διὰ τὸ τοὺς ζητοῦντας ἄνευ τοῦ διαπορῆσαι πρῶτον ὁμοίους εἶναι τοῖς ποῖ δεῖ βαδίζειν ἀγνοοῦσι, καὶ πρὸς τούτοις οὐδ' εἴ ποτε τὸ ζητούμενον εὕρηκεν ἢ μὴ γιγνώσκειν· τὸ γὰρ τέλος τούτῳ μὲν οὐ δῆλον τῷ δὲ προηπορηκότι δῆλον. ἔτι δὲ βέλτιον ἀνάγκη ἔχειν πρὸς τὸ κρῖναι τὸν ὥσπερ ἀντιδίκων καὶ τῶν ἀμφισβητούντων λόγων ἀκηκοότα πάντων.

> We must, with a view to the science which we are seeking, first recount the subjects that should be first discussed. These include both the other opinions that some have held on certain points, and any points besides these that happen to have been overlooked. *For those who wish to get clear of difficulties it is advantageous to state the difficulties well; for the subsequent free play of thought implies the solution of the previous difficulties, and it is not possible to untie a knot which one does not know. But the difficulty of our thinking points to a knot in the object; for in so far as our thought is in difficulties, it is in like case with those who are tied up; for in either case it is impossible to go forward.* Therefore one should have surveyed all the difficulties beforehand, both for the reasons we have stated and because people who inquire without first stating the difficulties are like those who do not know where they have to go; besides, a man does not otherwise know even whether he has found what he is looking for or not; for the end is not clear to such a man, while to him who has first discussed the difficulties it is clear. Further, he who has heard all the contending arguments, as if they were the parties to a case, must be in a better position for judging.
>
> trans. W.D. Ross, emphasis added

According to Aristotle, the mental state of the person caught in *aporia* is like the physical state of a chained prisoner: s/he cannot proceed further; s/he is in a standstill; his/her thought is unable to resolve the issue at hand. This is the proper state of the wonderer. And it is an indispensable preliminary state. For, as Aristotle explains with an eye to *Meno*'s famous paradox about knowledge, the person who has not stayed with, and delved into, the *aporia* for long will be unable to recognise the solution once it presents itself. Like a wanderer who

---

[34] For a meticulous analysis of B.1, see Laks 2009 and Buddensiek 2018.

walks without walking to a particular destination, the person who has not devoted enough time and energy to the *aporia* will not realise that s/he has reached the desired solution once s/he happens to bump into it. The serious wonderer is, then, the very opposite of the wanderer. S/he looks methodically to the end by meticulously looking at the beginning of his/her helplessness in an effort to orient him/herself thereby. For in a certain sense, Aristotle seems to believe, the solution is already contained in the problem: it is a step forward beyond the puzzle because it is a step backward into the puzzle.

The preliminary questions that are pertinent to first philosophy, which Aristotle summarily mentions in the sequence of the chapter and analytically raises in the rest of the book, are all articulated in an, either/or, (πότερον/ἤ) form. This is very significant. To be properly in wonder is not to be simply unable to answer a particular question. To be properly in wonder is to have reasons for adopting answers which are contrary to each other, as with Plato's Theaetetus. The general form of the perplexities which Aristotle uses in book Beta is the following: is it the case that P or that S (where P and S are contrary statements)? For instance, "is it the case that it belongs to a single science to consider all the kinds of cause or is it rather the case that it belongs to several?" (#1); "is it the case that there exist only sensible substances or is it rather the case that there are also other substances besides these?" (#5); "is it the case that the kinds are the principles of things or is it rather the case that the primary constituents are the principles of things?" (#6).[35]

As Aristotle is well aware, the disjunctive form in which philosophical perplexities are cast stems from court practice where there are two litigants, the prosecutor and the defendant, and they oppose each other's claims. In the context of rhetorical arguments this is the so-called τόπος ἐκ τῶν ἐναντίων. In any case, the judicial model, which is undoubtedly in the foreground of Aristotle's conception of *aporia*, was arguably one of the main reasons for the development of rhetoric in ancient Greece, and in particular for the development of the so-called *dissoi logoi* or "double arguments" whereby the same orator would develop arguments *pro* and *contra* a certain thesis. It is the court practice that Aristotle has in mind in the *De Caelo* (I.10, 279b7–12) when he writes:

Ἅμα δὲ καὶ μᾶλλον ἂν εἴη πιστὰ τὰ μέλλοντα λεχθήσεσθαι προακηκοόσι τὰ τῶν ἀμφισβητούντων λόγων δικαιώματα. Τὸ γὰρ ἐρήμην καταδικάζεσθαι δοκεῖν ἧττον ἂν ἡμῖν ὑπάρχοι· καὶ γὰρ δεῖ διαιτητὰς ἀλλ' οὐκ ἀντιδίκους εἶναι τοὺς μέλλοντας τἀληθὲς κρίνειν ἱκανῶς.

---

[35] #1: B.1, 995b5–6 = B.2, 996a18–b26, #5: B.1, 995b14–15 = B.2, 997a34–998a19, #6: B.1, 995b27–29 = B.3, 998a20–b14.

> What is going to be said will be more credible to people who have already listened to the justifications of the competing arguments; for in this case we shall not seem to convict somebody *in absentia* [= without listening to their defence speech first]; for those who are going to adequately judge the truth should be arbiters rather than litigants.

The philosopher, as Aristotle conceives of his function and duty, is an arbiter of truth in the midst of competing arguments. He will not take sides in the dispute but will try, to the best of his ability, to resolve it.

The beginning of the *Topics* (I.1) announces that this is a project about how to formulate dialectical syllogisms, i.e. valid conclusions drawn from reputable opinions (*endoxa*). The following chapter (I.2) makes it clear that this method is useful in three domains: (i) as a way of training oneself in argumentation (πρὸς γυμνασίαν); (ii) in public controversies (πρὸς τὰς ἐντεύξεις); and (iii) in philosophical sciences (πρὸς τὰς κατὰ φιλοσοφίαν ἐπιστήμας). In all three cases, the dialectician will try to devise arguments in favour of his/her preferred thesis. But while discussing the usefulness of the dialectical method for the philosophical sciences (101a35–36), Aristotle says that we will be better equipped readily to discern what is true and what false in reputable opinions on a given subject if we have the capacity of going through the difficulties on either side of the dispute (δυνάμενοι πρὸς ἀμφότερα διαπορῆσαι ῥᾷον ἐν ἑκάστοις κατοψόμεθα τἀληθές τε καὶ τὸ ψεῦδος). The dialectical method of giving arguments *pro* and *contra* a certain thesis crucially depends on the agonistic character of debates.³⁶ Ideally, the arguments *pro* and *contra* should counterbalance each other before the intellectual process of the resolution of the issue at hand begins.

Later in the *Topics* (VI.6, 145b1–2), Aristotle castigates those who define *aporia* as "equality of contrary arguments" (ἡ ἀπορία ἰσότης ἐναντίων λογισμῶν). He does not disagree that in the aporetic state one experiences an equality of contrary arguments. Aristotle wants to make it clear that perplexity primarily is, and must therefore be defined as, an *affection* (πάθος) of the soul or mental *state*, and only secondarily as the particular mental state caused by an equality of contrary arguments.³⁷ In other words, whereas "equality of contrary arguments" is the proper *differentia* pertaining to *aporia*, "affection of the soul" is its proper *genus*. The aporetic state is the feeling of being unable to proceed further in the solution of a particular binary opposition. Aristotle's insistence

---

36 Rapp 2018: 114: "It therefore seems that the method by which we can construct dialectical *sullogismoi* or avoid being refuted by dialectical *sullogismoi* is primarily designed with a view to a sort of dialogical disputation or examination that involves an attacking or examining party on the one hand and a defending party on the other."
37 Cf. Rapp 2018: 120–121.

that *aporia* is an affection indicates that for a person to count as a philosopher the mental impasse created by contrary arguments must be not simply learned from a teacher or a book but *experienced* as one's own concern.

Now, in the whole of Book Beta Aristotle is very cautious to introduce his audience to such an equality of contrary arguments by just carefully presenting the arguments *pro* and *contra* a certain thesis but without giving any indication or hint as to where the desired solution should be sought. Irrespective of whether Aristotle had already solved the difficulties or was himself in a state of *aporia* concerning some or all of them as he was writing Book Beta,[38] it is important to notice that he thought it advisable not to tip the balance in favour of one or the other horn of each dilemma. He seems to think that the readers should themselves be exposed to the difficulties involved in each case and experience the epistemic state of being perplexed.

In principle, Aristotle believes that it is always possible to find the desired solution to a well-formulated disjunctive perplexity. Most of the 14 or 15[39] *aporiai* of book Beta are resolved, one way or another, in the rest of the *Metaphysics*. But in the context of book Beta itself no solution or hint at a solution is provided. For Aristotle thinks, as he writes in the introductory chapter, that the desired 'way through' (εὐπορία) can be found only if one has studied and carefully analysed the two horns of the initial dilemma by paying due attention to the arguments in favour and against each one of them.

To give just one example (from *Metaph*. A.2 above): the inexperienced person will be perplexed at the mathematician's incapacity to measure the diagonal of a square by means of a measure common both to it and to the side of the square. S/he will think that if a particular measure A will not do, then a shorter measure B will, and if not that, then certainly a still shorter, namely C. For the diagonal and the side are, both, limited in size. How can it be that two definitive magnitudes cannot be measured by any common measure whatsoever? This sounds absurd. Besides, for all practical purposes the diagonal and the side appear commeasurable. What the inexperienced person misses is the mathematical

---

38 The former option is perhaps more probable, and it has been upheld in the bibliography (e.g. by Mansion 1955: 162). But given the palimpsest nature of the *Metaphysics* the question cannot be decided.

39 Since there is a mismatch between the initial list of the *aporiai* in B.1 and their subsequent treatment in the rest of the book (B.2–6), there is a controversy about their actual number as well. In the latest detailed treatment of the book (i.e. the collection of essays in Crubellier and Laks 2009), the explicitly numbered *aporiai* are 14 but one *aporia*, not announced in B.1, gets the designation "12 bis" (= B.6, 1002b12–32) since it is thought to be an appendix to *aporia* #12 (Ross 1924: I.xvii, n. 1, I.223) and also "akin to problems 5 and 9" (Ross 1924: I.249).

proof which states that, no matter what the actual size of the square is, the diagonal will always turn out to be √2 times the side; and √2 is, in modern terminology, an irrational number and, in ancient Greek mathematics, no number at all.[40] The accomplished mathematician, by contrast, would be perplexed if the diagonal were indeed measurable (as Aristotle emphasizes in *Metaph.* A.2). For s/he knows the reason, i.e. the mathematical proof, and the reason explains why the diagonal is incommensurable with the side. The argument *contra* the thesis of incommensurability relies on the limitedness of the magnitudes and assumes that limited magnitudes are not only measurable but commensurable as well, as experience shows. The argument *pro* the same thesis relies on the mathematician's empirical inability to find a geometrically precise measure, no matter how small, to do the job and regards this fact as a clear indication that a common measure is impossible. If there is to be any solution at all, one or the other horn of the initial dilemma should be wholly or partly faulted, wholly or partly proven to have been falsely stated. To resolve the difficulty, that is, one should be able to see what is right and what wrong in the arguments *contra* and *contra*. In our example, from the argument *pro* one should retain "limitedness implies measurableness" and deny "measurableness implies common measure"; from the argument *pro* one should accept the conclusion but find a logical-demonstrative, rather than simply empirical, reason to support it, i.e. devise a mathematical proof. By examining the puzzle itself we may come up with the solution. The answer lies in the question.

Wonder does not feature in Aristotle's analysis of the emotions that the orator needs to know in order to be effective in *Rhetoric* II;[41] nor does it become the subject of any focused treatment anywhere else in the Aristotelian corpus. But the verb θαυμάζω and the verbal adjective θαυμαστόν are to be found all over the place. In the *De Caelo* (II.13, 294a12–16), for instance, speaking about the movement or rest of the Earth as a whole Aristotle writes:

> Τὸ μὲν οὖν ἀπορῆσαι πᾶσιν ἀναγκαῖον ἐπελθεῖν· τάχα γὰρ ἀλυποτέρας διανοίας τὸ μὴ θαυμάζειν πῶς ποτε μικρὸν μὲν μόριον τῆς γῆς, ἂν μετεωρισθὲν ἀφεθῇ, φέρεται καὶ μένειν οὐκ ἐθέλει, καὶ τὸ πλεῖον ἀεὶ θᾶττον, πᾶσαν δὲ τὴν γῆν εἴ τις ἀφείη μετεωρίσας, οὐκ ἂν φέροιτο.

> The difficulty must have occurred to everyone. It would indeed be a complacent mind that felt no surprise that, while a little bit of earth let loose in mid-air, moves and will not stay

---

[40] The explanation given here does not rely on the ancient proof of the incommensurability of the diagonal, for which see Knorr 1975: 21–61.
[41] Aristotle admits, however, that ἔκπληξις ('astonishment'), a prominent emotion in ancient rhetorical theory, is excessive θαυμασιότης (*Top.* IV.5, 126b13–19).

still, and the more there is of it, the faster it moves, the whole earth, free in mid-air, should show no movement at all.

trans. J.L. Stocks

The word translated as 'difficulty' is ἀπορῆσαι in the original; 'surprise' is θαυμάζειν; and the 'complacent mind' is ἀλυποτέρα διάνοια, a mind not willing to be in pain, a lazy, idle or sluggish mind. The opposite of such a mind is the philosopher's mind. For as Aristotle indicates a few lines later (294a19–20), "to be perplexed, then, has naturally become the way of doing philosophy for all philosophers" (ὥστε τὸ μὲν ἀπορεῖν εἰκότως ἐγένετο φιλοσόφημα πᾶσιν).[42]

More famously, in the *De partibus animalium* (I.5, 645a4–24) Aristotle claims that "there is something wondrous in all natural things" (ἐν πᾶσι γὰρ τοῖς φυσικοῖς ἔνεστί τι θαυμαστόν) or, as Ogle translates, "every realm of nature is marvellous". The context indicates that Aristotle wants to defend the study of zoology which, as he admits, is inferior to theology, by claiming that even in the lower domain of generation and corruption the nature responsible for fashioning the various species of animals provides amazing pleasures to those who can trace lines of causation and are philosophers by nature (ἡ δημιουργήσασα φύσις ἀμηχάνους ἡδονὰς παρέχει τοῖς δυναμένοις τὰς αἰτίας γνωρίζειν καὶ φύσει φιλοσόφοις). The wondrous or marvellous element that is inherent in all realms of nature is the cause of the philosopher's initial wonder which, when surpassed with the advent of causal knowledge, gives rise to the intellectual pleasure of understanding. In the *Rhetoric* (I.11, 1371a31–34) Aristotle writes:

> Καὶ τὸ μανθάνειν καὶ τὸ θαυμάζειν ἡδὺ ὡς ἐπὶ τὸ πολύ· ἐν μὲν γὰρ τῷ θαυμάζειν τὸ ἐπιθυμεῖν μαθεῖν ἐστιν, ὥστε τὸ θαυμαστὸν ἐπιθυμητόν, ἐν δὲ τῷ μανθάνειν <τὸ> εἰς τὸ κατὰ φύσιν καθίστασθαι.
>
> Learning things and wondering at things are also pleasant for the most part; wondering implies the desire of learning, so that the object of wonder is an object of desire; while in learning one is brought into one's natural condition.
>
> trans. Rhys Roberts

For Aristotle wonder is a precious and also partly pleasant affection because it instigates learning which leads to knowing and understanding. The state one finds oneself in when understanding is achieved is regarded as the natural con-

---

42 Stokes' translation of the sentence ("the difficulty then, has naturally passed into a commonplace of philosophy") misses the positive tone of Aristotle's original phrase, tends to downplay the importance ascribed to the mental state of being perplexed, and disregards the emphasis put on *all* (πᾶσι) philosophers.

dition for a human being to be because the desire to understand is natural and, famously, "nature does nothing in vain". That the desire is natural implies that the resources for its satisfaction are, in principle, at one's disposal.

In the same vein, Theophrastus, Aristotle's disciple and successor in the Lyceum, claims,[43] perhaps more optimistically, that sense-perception provides the intellect with data generating perplexities by means of which, even if the intellect cannot proceed further, "a light appears in the non-light" (ὅμως ἐμφαίνεταί τι φῶς ἐν τῷ μὴ φωτί) as people are seeking a solution. To be perplexed is to be already in a luminous mental state that properly guides research.

2.3 A Comparison and Some Further Context

According to Plato, the philosopher finds himself, now and again, in a state of genuine perplexity about issues that the man of the street finds utterly unproblematic. He detects sources of confusion all over the place. He takes nothing for granted. And occasionally he enters mental states indicating perplexity about his own very nature. In the *Phaedrus* (229e–230a), Socrates says that he has not time to spend speculating about the allegorical or literal meaning of traditional myths because he has more urgent things to do: to find out whether he is an animal more beastly and complex than the mythical Typhon or, rather, a creature somehow resembling the gods. Presumably, he has reasons to think that both horns of the dilemma can be supported by argument, and the way out of the *aporia* is not an easy matter.

All in all, both Plato and Aristotle think that wonder stands at the beginning of the philosopher's quest and is an indispensable affection for philosophical reflection to get started. Whether or not wonder is to be found, perhaps in a transformed and deepened guise, also at the end of the process of understanding is a very vexed question. There are some indications that Plato and Aristotle parted ways in this respect. Aristotle seems to think that wonder is entirely overcome with the advent of knowledge,[44] while Plato, by describing in the

---

43 Theophr. *Metaph.* 19, 8b12–16.
44 Broadie 2012: 67 thinks that Aristotle does not disambiguate between wonder in the sense of puzzlement (*aporia*) and wonder in the sense of awe (*thambos*) and that, as a result, when puzzlement is left behind, "there is still room for *thambos*." What she has primarily in mind is Aristotle's description of God's contemplative life in Λ.7, 1072b24–26, as something θαυμαστόν if it (though everlasting) resembles human contemplation, and as something θαυμασιώτερον if it is superior to human contemplation not only in being uninterrupted but in quality as well. Aristotle favours the second option. It seems that divine contemplation is described as some-

Symposium (210e) the Form of Beauty as "something wondrous in its very nature," seems to think that wonder can only be elevated in rank or sublimated, never fully transcended. Of all Forms the Form of Beauty is the most luminous in its earthly instantiations, we learn in the *Phaedrus* (250d), so that in its case, and in its case alone, the leap from the sensible to the intelligible realm is much easier than in the case of the so-called ethical Forms. But even this leap is described as an experience that happens *all of a sudden* and is by its own nature wondrous even for the accomplished philosopher (*Symp.* 210e) — allusions not only to the quality of the experience but also to the unexpected and highly uncertain character of its occurrence. We have, then, reasons to conclude that Plato's philosopher lives in alternate states of wonder, in the sense of admiration and awe, and wonder, in the sense of perplexity and puzzlement. To put it differently and more poetically for once, philosophical revelation stems from a profound experience of philosophical mystification. The mystery of Being discloses its truth only to those who are courageous enough to stay with the question and exclamation marks for long. Neither security nor restlessness are the true marks of the philosopher as Plato conceived him.

But there is another (though related) important difference between Plato and Aristotle. By linking wonder with the desire to know Aristotle thinks that wonder, though pre-eminently a feature of the philosopher, is an emotion common to *all* human beings. In Aristotle's writings, wonder comes close to being identified with universal *curiosity*, and the primary objects thought to induce and promote it the most are strange, unusual, and exceptional events which undermine our assumptions and force us to research. In Plato's dialogues, by contrast, and in the *Theaetetus* in particular, wonder addresses and is caused by reflection on the usual and the ordinary when, all of a sudden, it loses its all-too-common and familiar appearance and turns into an unintelligible puzzle. The critical distance that wonder effects from everyday reality and the corresponding "disruption of previous cognitive schemata"[45] create the space for the philosopher to question the most self-evident of things — and ultimately Being itself. As a contemporary philosopher has elegantly put it, in wonder "the subject is maximally aware of the value of the object, and only minimally aware, if at all, of its relationship to her own plans. That is why it [sc.

---

thing "wondrous" or "more wondrous" precisely because it is unavailable to human experience and as such understood only by analogy.
45 Fuller 2006: 13.

wonder] is likely to issue in contemplation, rather than any other sort of action toward the object."⁴⁶

3 Wonder and Perplexity in the Hippocratic Corpus

If we compare the positive evaluation of wonder as the mark of the true philosopher that we find in Plato and Aristotle with the negative evaluation of it in the Hippocratic corpus we may reach some interesting results about the relation of philosophy to medicine — and, more generally, science — in classical Greece.⁴⁷

The verb θαυμάζειν and the noun θαῦμα are to be found in many places of the Hippocratic corpus, especially in regular negative expressions such as μὴ θαυμάζειν,⁴⁸ οὐκ ἂν θαυμάσαιμι,⁴⁹ and οὐ θαῦμα.⁵⁰ They all mean the same thing, "no wonder that ...", and they are followed or preceded by a conditional sentence, an infinitive or a similar syntactical structure that specifies what should not surprise or overwhelm the expert practitioner. These numerous occurrences show the confidence of the medical authors in their expertise, and remind us of Eryximachus' similar frame of mind. The physician will not be surprised if a particular further symptom (e.g. delirium, sleeplessness, insanity, or even death) strikes the patient who is already under the influence of a certain disease. We may reasonably assume that these uses of θαυμάζειν are partly related to the epideictic nature of some treatises. In chronological proximity to the earlier parts of the Hippocratic corpus, Gorgias also uses the rhetorical question τί θαυμαστόν; when it comes to the power of Eros as the cause of Helen's elopement to Troy, in his self-advertising *Praise of Helen* (19). But rhetoric cannot be the only reason for the presence of the afore-mentioned locutions in the Hippocratic Corpus. A deep sense of expertise, as with Eryximachus, must be at least equally important.

---

46 Nussbaum 2001: 54.
47 A similarly focused study with respect to the evaluation of 'conjecture' (στοχάζεσθαι) across Hippocratic medicine and classical philosophy (Plato and Aristotle) is Boudon-Millot 2005. It is interesting to note that some of the results of her study and mine are strikingly parallel. Kazantzidis 2018 covers partly the same material as I do, and to the same general conclusions, but his avowed purpose (viz. to show that the female body in the Hippocratic corpus is "an open window to paradox") is very different. For a balanced view about the interrelationships of philosophy and medicine in antiquity, see Frede 1986.
48 *Morb.* 4.7.14, 4.19.19, 4.26.34, *Haem.* 5.6, *Mul.* 1.25.44, 3.213.83, *Prorrh.* 2.12.21.
49 *Prorrh.* 1.116.4, *Acut.* [Sp.] 8.19.
50 *Morb.* 4.11.6, 4.44.19, 4.47.23, *Cord.* 6.3, *Coac.* 80.2.

Quite generally, in the Hippocratic corpus θαυμάζω occurs both in the sense of being perplexed (e.g. *Art.* 7.3, *Vict.* 1.24.6) and in the sense of admiring (e.g. *Vict.* 1.24.8). The author of the *On Ancient Medicine* (*VM* 12.2) writes that people should not despise and reject the ancient art of healing on the grounds that it has not achieved every precision in all issues but they should, rather, 'admire' (θαυμάζειν) its discoveries because they have been made not by chance but by human ingenuity from a state of earlier ignorance. In a special case, the two meanings are combined: the author of the *On the Art of Medicine* says that people should rather admire the power of medicine when it manages to cure a patient affected by an unknown disease than be dumbfounded when it fails to heal incurable afflictions. What I have translated as "admire" and "be dumbfounded" in the previous sentence is, in the original text, the single occurrence of the verb θαυμάζω.[51]

On the other hand, though, the noun ἀπορίη and the verb ἀπορέω are frequently used in the Hippocratic corpus in the rather technical sense of having a discomfort or physical distress,[52] there are also instances in which these words have their more common sense of being at a loss or being puzzled/perplexed,[53] or even the more literal sense of having no (financial) means at one's disposal.[54]

The single most important text about wonder and perplexity as mental states or affections comes from the beginning of the treatise *On the Sacred Disease* (1.1–3):[55]

Περὶ μὲν τῆς ἱερῆς νούσου καλεομένης ὧδ' ἔχει· οὐδέν τί μοι δοκεῖ τῶν ἄλλων θειοτέρη εἶναι νούσων οὐδὲ ἱερωτέρη, ἀλλὰ φύσιν μὲν ἔχει καὶ τὰ λοιπὰ νουσήματα ὅθεν γίνεται, φύσιν δὲ αὕτη καὶ πρόφασιν. Οἱ δ' ἄνθρωποι ἐνόμισαν θεῖόν τι πρῆγμα εἶναι **ὑπὸ ἀπειρίης καὶ θαυμασιότητος**, ὅτι οὐδὲν ἔοικεν ἑτέροισι. Καὶ **κατὰ μὲν τὴν ἀπορίην αὐτοῖσι τοῦ μὴ γινώσκειν** τὸ θεῖον διασώζεται, **κατὰ δὲ τὴν εὐπορίην τοῦ τρόπου τῆς ἰήσιος ᾧ ἰῶνται**, ἀπόλλυται, ὅτι καθαρμοῖσί τε ἰῶνται καὶ ἐπαοιδῇσιν. **Εἰ δὲ διὰ τὸ θαυμάσιον θεῖον νομιεῖται**, πολλὰ τὰ ἱερὰ νουσήματα ἔσται τούτου εἵνεκεν καὶ οὐχὶ ἕν, ὡς ἐγὼ δείξω **ἕτερα οὐδὲν ἧσσον ἐόντα θαυμάσια οὐδὲ τερατώδεα**, ἃ οὐδεὶς νομίζει ἱρὰ εἶναι.

---

51 *Art.* 11.30–32: Ἐπεὶ τῆς γε τέχνης τὴν δύναμιν, ὁκόταν τινὰ τῶν τὰ ἄδηλα νοσεύντων ἀναστήσῃ, **θαυμάζειν ἀξιώτερον**, ἢ ὁκόταν ἐγχειρήσῃ τοῖς ἀδυνάτοις.
52 ἀπορίη: *VM* 19.29, *Epid.* 3.2.8.8, 5.1.42.3, 5.1.43.4, *Morb.* 3.15.3, *Int.* 49.8, *Dieb.Iudic.* 10.2; ἀπορέω: *Morb.* 3.7.10, 3.7.12.
53 ἀπορίη: *VM* 13.21, *Morb.Sacr.* 1.6, *Praec.* 8.7, 8.14 (πάσῃ γὰρ εὐπορίῃ ἀπορίη ἔνεστι – "for in all abundance there is lack". Jones (1923a: 325, n. 2) explains: "No matter how much help you have you can never have enough" – in all likelihood, a recognition of the limited power of medicine); ἀπορέω: *VM* 15.1, *Aer.* 2.5, *Fract.* 16.14, *Art.* 10.2, *Aff.* 39.5.
54 ἀπορίη: *Decent.* 7.9, 8.7; ἀπορέω: *Praec.* 6.5, 7.16.
55 I quote the latest edition of text in the Budé series: Jouanna 2003: 2.

About the disease called "sacred" this is how things stand. It is not, in my opinion, any more divine or more sacred than other diseases, but as the other illnesses, too, have a natural origin from which they are generated, so this disease has a natural origin and a moving cause. But humans thought that it is something divine *due to their inexperience and to their wonder at its peculiarity* that does not resemble other diseases at all. Now, while humans continue to believe in its divine origin *because they are at a loss to understand it*, they really disprove its divinity *by the facile method of healing which they adopt*, consisting as it does of purifications and incantations. *But if it is to be considered divine just because it is wonderful,* there will be, on account of that, not one sacred disease but many, as I will show other diseases, which nobody considers sacred, *being no less wonderful and portentous.*

trans. W.H.S. Jones modified to fit Jouanna's different text, emphasis added

As Jouanna argues at length,[56] the name "sacred disease" is not (or not only) a popular appellation of epilepsy but (also) the technical term by which the disease is invariably known to early Hippocratic doctors and other authors in the 5th and 4th centuries B.C.[57] To be sure, all these writers distance themselves from the claim, implicit in the very name of the disease, that it is caused by some divine agency: by using, as they mostly do, the qualification 'so-called' (καλεομένη *vel sim.*) they clearly reject its supposedly divine causation. But the term 'epilepsy' (ἐπίληψις/ἐπιληψίη) does not occur prior to Aristotle and the late texts of the Hippocratic corpus.[58] The author of the Aristotelian *Problem* 30 (953a15–16) goes as far as to ascribe the origin of the traditional name of the disease, which must have become obsolete by his time, to 'people of old' (οἱ ἀρχαῖοι) who, seeing that Heracles was affected thereby, called this malady 'sacred' (presumably because of Heracles' quasi-divine status).[59] The argumentative originality and rigour displayed by the author of the *On Sacred Disease* can be better appreciated if seen against the background of a technical term of medical practice rather than a popular appellation already discounted by specialists in the field.

The author claims that the so-called sacred disease is not fundamentally different in character from other diseases that are not called sacred. It, too, pos-

---

[56] Jouanna 2003: XXII–XXV, cf. p. 2, n. 1; Jouanna 1999: 182; Jouanna 2012: 98–100.
[57] *Aer.* 3.17, 4.20–21; *Flat.* 14.1; *Virg.* 1.4; *Prorrh.* 2.5.2; Hdt. III.33; Pl. *Tim.* 85b; *Laws* XI.916a; Theophr. *Plant.* IX.11.3.
[58] Arist. *Somn.* 457a8–9; *Aph.* 3.22.4; *Alim.* 25.3.
[59] The author speaks not of 'epilepsy' but of the "illnesses [in the plural] of the epileptic people" (τὰ ἀρρωστήματα τῶν ἐπιληπτικῶν): what he probably means is the various symptoms and manifestations not only of epilepsy proper but of all kinds of sudden seizures. Craik (2001: 191) thinks that the extent of illnesses covered by "sacred disease" in the Hippocratic treatise of the same name is much wider than *grand mal* epilepsy.

sesses a nature of its own like other diseases. The reason behind its being called sacred is to be found in the lack of experience (ἀπειρίη) and the state of wonder or even bafflement (θαυμασιότης) that affected people when they confronted its symptoms which are so unlike the symptoms of all other diseases. With a playful stroke of antithetical sarcasm the author states that, on the one hand, the mental perplexity (ἀπορίη) that this disease generates tends to preserve its apparently sacred character while, on the other hand, the facile treatment (εὐπορίη τοῦ τρόπου τῆς ἰήσιος) through purifications and incantations, by means of which the disease is supposedly cured, removes this same sacred character out of sight. Here the 'difficulty of passing through' (ἀπορίη) to medical knowledge proper is contrasted with the 'easy way-out' (εὐπορίη) of sham treatment, and the religious practitioners are accused of inconsistency and implicit contradiction. If diseases are called divine as a result of the mental bafflement they give rise to, then the sacred diseases will turn out to be many, and not just one. The author's contention is presumably based on the fact that most, if not all, diseases cause bafflement to the inexperienced multitude of common people.[60]

The rhetorical flourish of this introductory paragraph cannot be missed. The author attacks his rivals who profess to treat the disease through magical incantations and religious purifications head-on. With an intended wordplay between ἀπειρίη and ἀπορίη, their 'inexperience' (ἀπειρίη) is not meant as lack of acquaintance with many cases of afflicted patients but as 'lack of means' (ἀπορίη) for understanding causes and treating the disease effectively. Their θαυμασιότης, accordingly, is the mental confusion created by the singular peculiarity of the disease. But this perplexity or bafflement is hidden behind an apparent 'resourcefulness' (εὐπορίη) of religious-cum-magical methods. Unlike the Platonic Eros of the *Symposium,* which is said to be the offspring of 'Lack' (Πενία) and 'Resourcefulness' (Πόρος), the two contrasting terms of the medical author's opposition are not liable to a synthesis, nor do they generate a philosophical love of wisdom. His rivals' ἀπορίη is not pregnant perplexity seeking to overcome its own painful state, and their εὐπορίη not the outcome of an inquisitive intelligence that tries to capture an object of cognitive desire.

In the section that immediately follows the opening paragraph quoted above, the author gives examples of diseases, such as different kinds of fever, "about which people are not affected by wonder" (ὧν οὐ θαυμασίως γ' ἔχουσι). He later explains (1.4) that in his opinion "the people who first sacralized this

---

[60] Cf. the diseases called δυσκριτώτατα τοῖς ἀπείροισιν (*Morb.Sacr.* 17.4) which, as Jouanna (2003: 130) rightly claims, should be understood as "difficult to discern/know" (in view of the complement "to the inexperienced") rather than "of the most difficult crises".

disease" (οἱ πρῶτοι τοῦτο τὸ νόσημα ἀφιερώσαντες) were similar to "present-day magicians/sorcerers, purifiers, vagabonds and wandering charlatans who pretend to be extremely pious and to possess a superior kind of knowledge" (οἷοι καὶ νῦν εἰσι μάγοι τε καὶ καθάρται καὶ ἀγύρται καὶ ἀλαζόνες, ὁκόσοι προσποιέονται σφόδρα θεοσεβεῖς εἶναι καὶ πλέον τι εἰδέναι). The accumulation of no less than four marked nouns (μάγοι, καθάρται, ἀγύρται, ἀλαζόνες) is clearly meant to cast a derogatory shadow on these people and their activities. In fact, as Jouanna notes,[61] none of those nouns is used elsewhere in the Hippocratic corpus: with the exception of καθαρτής,[62] in contemporary and later texts they are all evaluative rather than merely descriptive, and the value they carry is always negative.[63] Their combined effect in our passage is strongly increased by the direct accusations of sham piety and fake knowledge.[64] In the following sentence the author claims that these people used the divine as a screen in order to hide their own 'helplessness' (ἀμηχανίη) and 'utter lack of knowledge' (οὐδὲν ἐπιστάμενοι).

Two points need to be made at this juncture. First, in the context of the *On Sacred Disease* as a whole, and especially in the first and last chapters of the treatise where an intended ring-composition is evident, the adjectives θαυμάσιον, ἄπορον, and ἀμήχανον are used as semi-synonymous terms. They describe, at one and the same time, both a mental affection, i.e. bafflement or deep perplexity, and the external cause of this affection, i.e. the actual state of

---

61 Jouanna 2003: 38–40.
62 In Soph. *El.* 70 Orestes claims to be the "purifier" of his paternal home sent in justice (δίκῃ) by the gods, and in Aristoph. *Wasps* 1043 the chorus describes the poet as ἀλεξίκακον τῆς χώρας τῆσδε καθαρτήν. It follows that καθαρτής, unlike the other three terms, could be used as a praiseworthy predicate.
63 It is perhaps significant that two of these four marked nouns (μάγος, ἀγύρτης) are cast against Teiresias by the furious Oedipus of Sophocles' play (*OT* 387–388) who accuses the seer for both ignorance and greed as the Hippocratic author accuses his opponents (Jouanna 2003: XXVIII; 2012: 184–185). In the conflict between the practically wise "tyrant" and the blind seer one may discern the same fierce opposition of mundane to religious authority that underlies the Hippocratic author's belief in the superiority of the scientific outlook (based on empirical observation and reason) over mantic mystification generated by obscure language and equivocal expressions (cf. *Sacr.Morb.* 1.4: λόγους ἐπιλέξαντες ἐπιτηδείους, *OT* 439: ὡς πάντ' ἄγαν αἰνικτὰ κἀσαφῆ λέγεις).
64 Wilamowitz's suppression of ὁκόσοι ... εἰδέναι as a later gloss on these four nouns (discussed in Jouanna 2003: 4, n. 2) is rightly rejected by all modern editors of the text. The accusation of fake knowledge and pretentiousness recurs in 1.5 (ὥς τι πλέον εἰδότες) and 1.8 (προσποιέονται πλέον τι εἰδέναι). The accusation of sham piety recurs (and is supported by arguments) in 1.8–9 and 1.12–13.

affairs that generates bafflement. In 18.1 the author repeats his earlier claim that "each disease has a natural origin" (φύσιν δὲ ἕκαστον ἔχει), adds that "it also has a power of its own" (καὶ δύναμιν ἀφ' ἑαυτοῦ) — δύναμις probably being a significant variation on the πρόφασις of 1.1[65] — in order to triumphantly declare in the end that "no disease is inscrutable nor unmanageable" (καὶ οὐδὲν ἄπορόν ἐστιν οὐδ' ἀμήχανον). Here the adjectives ἄπορον and ἀμήχανον are predicated of (only to be emphatically denied) not mental states but the diseases that cause such mental states: the incongruity between an actual state of affairs (such as a well-ordered disease that is in itself explicable) and a corresponding mental state (that should ideally be an understanding of what is the case) is the principal reason why our author refuses to allow religious healers any claim to knowledge (and even to human decency, for that matter). The "divinity" (or "sacredness") of the so-called "sacred disease" is another name for the inscrutability and unintelligibility erroneously ascribed to it. To the author's mind, the divine follows a patterned and intelligible course of action[66] that is no less evident in the symptomatology, development, and possible cure of the "sacred disease" than in the manifestation of all other illnesses that are assumed to be more easily explicable on purely human terms. Rather than being a springboard to knowledge, as in Plato and Aristotle, the baffled perplexity of the religious healers is the sole single cause of their persistent ignorance and the primary impediment to their advance to a state of knowledge.

The second point that needs to be stressed concerns the author's view about the 'first finders' (πρῶτοι εὑρεταί) of the sacred character of the disease or, as he describes them, "those who were the first to make this illness sacred" (οἱ πρῶτοι τοῦτο τὸ νόσημα ἀφιερώσαντες). Unlike Aristotle's πρῶτοι φιλοσοφήσαντες (cf. 2.2 above), the first inventors of the sacred character of the disease were not motivated by a desire to overcome their wonder at its apparently unintelligible character. Nor did they seek to explore the malady out of a disinterested curiosity about its symptomatology and structure, as Thucydides (2.47–54) famously did with the Athenian plague.[67] On the contrary, they were led to the

---

65 Jouanna 2003: 131 says that this is the only instance in the Hippocratic corpus where the pair of φύσις and δύναμις is applied to a disease. On the difference between φύσις and πρόφασις, see Jouanna 2003: 35; cf. van der Ejik 2005: 73. If he is right that πρόφασις means "cause déclenchente due aux facteurs extérieurs" or "cause extérieure occasionelle" (Festugière), then δύναμις is something different (e.g. the internal power of the disease as distinct from its origin, φύσις). But I am not convinced that πρόφασις in 1.1 should be taken in such a limited sense.
66 For the theology underlying the *Morb.Sacr.* see van der Eijk 2005: 45–73.
67 Cf. Craik 2001a with useful bibliography on the subject of the relation of Thucydides' description to the Hippocratic corpus.

fabrication of its sacred character out of a desire for profit: βίου δεόμενοι (1.8). Unlike the relative wealth of the first philosophers who had already met the bare necessities of life (according to Aristotle's account in *Metaphysics* A2), their financial state must have been one of relative poverty. And it was because they wanted to overcome material scarcity, not mental perplexity, that they took an interest in the disease in the first place. They would sell their pretended knowledge for a price since that knowledge was of a practical or (according to Aristotle's finer classification of three, rather than two, types of knowledge),[68] of a 'productive' (ποιητική) kind. It was never meant to be knowledge for knowledge's sake, i.e. theoretical knowledge. The first fabricators of the sacredness of the disease, however, created, according to the Hippocratic author, a legacy not unlike the legacy created by Aristotle's first philosophers. The common element in both legacies is (real or apparent) progress. The Hippocratic author admits that there has been ingenuity and variation in the treatment of the disease over time as in all other subjects (1.10). It stands to reason that the fine distinctions about the identity of the god affecting the patient that the religious healers of his day are reported to draw (1.11) did not appear all at once with the "first sacralizers" but developed over time. However, the ingenuity of the traditional healers seems to have been predicated on an antecedent fact: forgetfulness of the initial perplexity that seized the "first finders" and pushed them to "discover" the sacredness of the disease. What is handed over in the tradition of religious treatment is a certain practice or cluster of practices that may well be elaborated and refined over time. What is not handed over is an inquisitive stance based on real wonder. Plato and Aristotle, by contrast, notwithstanding their differences about the proper objects of perplexity, were in agreement that wonder and perplexity are indispensable mental affections if one is to count as a true philosopher.

We know how fundamental and foundational this text has been for the self-awareness of a medical theory and practice based exclusively on rational grounds and empirical evidence. The author distances himself from all magical cures that seek to manipulate divine powers. He thinks that the so-called sacred disease affects people with a particular idiosyncrasy (i.e. the phlegmatic), displays characteristic patterns of explainable symptoms, and is ultimately caused by purely physical factors (i.e. the blockage of the vessels that provide the brain with air by an excess of phlegm). "All diseases are human and all are divine", he writes in *Morb.Sacr.* 18.1, and most diseases are curable, he claims later (18.2–3), if the practitioner knows how to bring about a situation directly oppo-

---

[68] Arist. *NE* VI.2, 1139a27–b5, VI.4, 1140a1–23.

site to the one that has caused the disease. In his view, the expert physician knows how to change the prevalence of the hot in the patient's body into a prevalence of the cold or the prevalence of the dry into a prevalence of the wet (and vice versa, as the case may be) by the prescription, 'at the appropriate time' (καιρός), of a proper diet that will bring about the desired effect. No disease is 'inapproachable' (ἄπορον) or 'impossible to be properly treated' (ἀμήχανον). The natural and the divine orders are not separated by any fundamental breach of continuity; nor does divine intervention produce gaps in natural causality.[69] The author of the treatise thinks, like Aristotle,[70] that there is something holy and admirable in the processes of nature, and that the hand of "divinity" is to be found not in exceptional aberrations but in the orderly rules themselves according to which illnesses develop their potential. But contrary to Plato and Aristotle, he does not think that the affection of mental perplexity or wonder is a preliminary requirement in the direction of understanding the ways of nature and solving particular problems. His vocabulary indicates that wonder and perplexity are not the springboards of knowledge but rather its very denial and blockage. In much the same spirit, the author of the *On Regimen*, in his long digression on the dependence of the arts and crafts upon human nature,[71] states that "many people stand awe-struck (θαυμάζουσιν), whereas few know (γιγνώσκουσιν)".[72] Wondering is here the polar opposite of knowing, not the indispensable prerequisite to the latter's attainment.

Although there is a great variety of viewpoints and approaches to health and disease in the Hippocratic Collection, there seems to be a fundamental agreement among different authors about the mental state of the wondering person: perplexity indicates ignorance. There is not the slightest hint, as in the Platonic and Aristotelian writings, that one needs to experience wonder and perplexity before proceeding to knowledge. In this sense, the medical principle, present both in Eryximachus' speech and parts of the Hippocratic corpus,[73]

---

[69] cf. Edelstein 1967: 208–226; Jouanna 1999: 190–195; Jouanna 2012: 106–109. Lloyd (1979: 26–27) speaks of a "paradigm switch" according to which "the divine is in no sense *super*natural" (author's emphasis).
[70] *Divin.* 463b14: ἡ γὰρ φύσις δαιμονία, ἀλλ' οὐ θεία, cf. *PA* I.5, 645a4–23.
[71] Craik 2015: 271: "it is particularly hard to perceive the relevance of the long digression (1.11–24) on crafts (*techai*)".
[72] *Vict.* 1.24.1–6: Ἀγωνίη, παιδοτριβίη τοιόνδε· διδάσκουσι παρανομέειν κατὰ νόμον, ἀδικέειν δικαίως, ἐξαπατέειν, κλέπτειν, ἁρπάζειν, βιάζεσθαι τὰ κάλλιστα καὶ αἴσχιστα· ὁ μὴ ταῦτα ποιέων κακός, ὁ δὲ ταῦτα ποιέων ἀγαθός· ἐπίδειξις τῶν πολλῶν ἀφροσύνης, θεῶνται ταῦτα καὶ κρίνουσιν ἕνα ἐξ ἁπάντων ἀγαθόν, τοὺς δὲ ἄλλους κακούς· **πουλλοὶ θαυμάζουσιν, ὀλίγοι γινώσκουσιν**.
[73] Bury 1932: 47, Dover 1980: 106, Hunter 2004: 55–56; *Flat.* 1, *Nat.Hom.* 9, *Morb.Sacr.* 18.3.

according to which opposites are the cures of opposites, applies not only to diseases at large but also to the physician's perplexity as understood by the writers of the Hippocratic corpus: wonder and perplexity are *deficient* mental states that affect the ignorant practitioners, and as such they can only be "cured" by the *plentitude* of proper medical knowledge, i.e. knowledge of real causes. Wonder and perplexity testify to ignorance, lack of observational skills, and insufficient empirical research. They are not diseases, to be sure, but they are *like* diseases in that they hinder the proper functioning of the investigator's mind and tend to mystify it. Once proper causal knowledge about a particular illness is achieved, wonder and perplexity disappear altogether from the physician's mind. Wonder and perplexity are not the psychological starting-points of research but, rather, the mental states testifying to its absence.

4 A Comparison of Philosophical with Medical Wonder: A Case of Conflict?

We may now raise the question about the reasons behind such a glaring disparity between the medical authors and the philosophers on the issue of wonder. What prompted Plato and Aristotle to turn the affection *par excellence* of the ignorant layman, according to the account of the Hippocratic authors, into the most prominent feature of the true philosopher? Does this semantic difference indicate anything about the self-understanding of philosophy in the fourth century? In an attempt to provide an answer we may take our cue from another famous treatise, the work *On Ancient Medicine* or *Tradition in Medicine* (as it has more accurately been translated).[74]

According to the view expressed in this rather polemical essay,[75] the efficient doctor does not need to make assumptions about the existence of any primary element or pair of contraries, such as the hot, the cold, the wet, and the dry, in order to do his job well (*VM* 1.1–3):[76]

---

[74] J. Chadwick and W.N. Mann in Lloyd 1978.
[75] The question about who is attacked in *VM* is a hotly debated issue: cf. Lloyd 1991; Jouanna 1990: 22–33; Schiefsky 2005a: 55–62: "A strong case can be made that the difficulty of pinpointing the target of the author's attack is due to the fact that he is not criticizing a specific text or thinker at all, but rather a general trend or tendency in the medicine of his time" (56).
[76] I quote the latest edition of the text with Introduction and Commentary: Schiefsky 2005a (cf. Jouanna 1990).

Ὁκόσοι ἐπεχείρησαν περὶ ἰητρικῆς λέγειν ἢ γράφειν, ὑπόθεσιν σφίσιν αὐτέοισιν ὑποθέμενοι τῷ λόγῳ, θερμὸν, ἢ ψυχρὸν, ἢ ὑγρὸν, ἢ ξηρὸν, ἢ ἄλλ' ὅ τι ἂν ἐθέλωσιν, ἐς βραχὺ ἄγοντες, τὴν ἀρχὴν τῆς αἰτίης τοῖσιν ἀνθρώποισι τῶν νούσων τε καὶ τοῦ θανάτου, καὶ πᾶσι τὴν αὐτέην, ἓν ἢ δύο προθέμενοι, ἐν πολλοῖσι μὲν καὶ οἶσι λέγουσι καταφανέες εἰσὶν ἁμαρτάνοντες· μάλιστα δὲ ἄξιον μέμψασθαι, ὅτι ἀμφὶ τέχνης ἐούσης, ᾗ χρέονταί τε πάντες ἐπὶ τοῖσι μεγίστοισι καὶ τιμῶσι μάλιστα τοὺς ἀγαθοὺς χειροτέχνας καὶ δημιουργούς. Εἰσὶ δὲ δημιουργοί, οἱ μὲν φλαῦροι, οἱ δὲ πολλὸν διαφέροντες· ὅπερ, εἰ μὴ ἦν ἰητρικὴ ὅλως, μηδ' ἐν αὐτῇ ἔσκεπτο, μηδ' εὕροιτο μηδέν, οὐκ ἂν ἦν, ἀλλὰ πάντες ἂν ὁμοίως αὐτέης ἄπειροί τε καὶ ἀνεπιστήμονες ἦσαν, καὶ τύχῃ ἂν πάντα τὰ τῶν καμνόντων διῴκετο. Νῦν δ' οὐχ οὕτως ἔχει, ἀλλ' ὥσπερ καὶ τῶν ἄλλων τεχνέων πασέων οἱ δημιουργοὶ πολλὸν ἀλλήλων διαφέρουσι κατὰ χεῖρα καὶ κατὰ γνώμην, οὕτω δὴ καὶ ἐπὶ ἰητρικῆς. **Διὸ οὐκ ἠξίουν ἔγωγε καινῆς αὐτέην ὑποθέσιος δέεσθαι, ὥσπερ τὰ ἀφανέα τε καὶ ἀπορεόμενα· περὶ ὧν ἀνάγκη, ἤν τις ἐπιχειροίη λέγειν, ὑποθέσει χρέεσθαι· οἷον περὶ τῶν μετεώρων ἢ τῶν ὑπὸ γῆν** εἰ λέγοι τις καὶ γινώσκοι ὡς ἔχει, οὔτ' ἂν αὐτέῳ τῷ λέγοντι οὔτε τοῖσιν ἀκούουσι δῆλα ἂν εἴη, εἴ τε ἀληθέα ἐστὶν εἴτε μή· **οὐ γὰρ ἔστι πρὸς ὅ τι χρὴ ἐπανενέγκαντα εἰδέναι τὸ σαφές.**

All those who have undertaken to speak or write about medicine, having laid down as a hypothesis for their account hot or cold or wet or dry or anything else they want, narrowing down the primary cause of diseases and death for human beings and laying down the same one or two things as the cause in all cases, clearly go wrong in much that they say. But they are especially worthy of blame because their errors concern an art that really exists, one which all people make use of in the most important circumstances and whose good craftsmen and practitioners all hold in special honor. Some practitioners are bad, while others are much better. This would not be the case if medicine did not exist at all and if nothing had been examined or discovered in it; rather, all would be equally lacking in both experience and knowledge of it, and all the affairs of the sick would be governed by chance. But in fact this is not the case: just as practitioners of all the other arts differ greatly from one another in manual skill and in judgment, so too in the case of medicine. *For this reason I have deemed that medicine has no need of a newfangled hypothesis, as do obscure and dubious matters. Concerning these things it is necessary to make use of a hypothesis if one undertakes to say anything at all about them — for example, about things in the sky or under the earth.* If anyone should recognize and state how these things are, it would be clear neither to the speaker himself nor to his listeners whether what he says is true or not, *for there is nothing by referring to which one would necessarily attain clear knowledge.*

trans. M. Schiefsky, emphasis added

The author's argument is based on experience. There is a craft or science (τέχνη) called "medicine", he claims, according to which practitioners are evaluated as better or worse. The evaluation would not be possible if there were no *techne* providing the standard for such an evaluation. But this *techne* needs no hypothesis to be effective. The doctor's approach must be exclusively empirical. The 'right measure' (μέτρον) for healing is not a number or weight or any other standard fixed in advance, the author claims later in the treatise (*VM* 9.3), but the very sensation of the body of the patient. To say to patients who are badly affected by a diet based on uncooked wheat, raw meat, and plain water that they should replace the cold of their diet with the hot of a diet based on baked bread, cooked meat, and wine is as pointless as the opposite claim (*VM* 13.1–3). For who and on what grounds can determine whether the baker has taken away the hot or the cold, the wet or the dry, out of the wheat in order to prepare bread? Since bread is produced by a mixture of wheat with water (which is wet and cold) and fire (which is dry and hot), we may always raise the question whether the final product is hotter or colder, drier or wetter than the initial ingredients. All options are equally plausible. According to the author, no food or drink is exclusively hot or cold, wet or dry (*VM* 15.1). To ask a patient to eat or drink something hot or cold, wet or dry will raise, on the patient's part, the further question about the precise kind of food or drink that is such (*VM* 15.2).

To introduce postulates about the existence of primary elements or pairs of opposites is, in the author's view, totally immaterial for medical healing. By contrast, the author claims that such postulations pertain to the study of astronomical and geological phenomena (*VM* 1.3). Ὑπόθεσις should be understood in the primary sense of 'something put under' as a foundation for drawing consequences, i.e. as a supposition on which other things are based, hence as a principle of research.[77] The context indicates that the kind of "supposition" intended here concerns the existence of primary constituents (in the human body or the world at large), as in the kind of natural philosophy we call pre-Socratic.[78] The locution περὶ τῶν μετεώρων ἢ τῶν ὑπὸ γῆν denotes, in the fifth and the early fourth centuries, cosmological research and speculative natural philosophy quite generally.[79] The author believes that the postulation of hypotheses in cosmological research is related to the fact that the domains dealt with here are

---

[77] Jouanna 1990: 155; cf. Cooper 2004: 19–23 and Schiefsky 2005a: 120–126 for a more extended discussion.

[78] The only other appearance of the noun ὑπόθεσις in the Hippocratic corpus comes from the last chapter of the *On Winds* (ch. 15), a treatise in which the author sets himself the task of proving that all diseases can be explained with recourse to the single principle of 'breath' (φῦσα). Here ὑπόθεσις means 'basic claim'. The author refers back to the fundamental idea he has defended throughout the treatise, namely (ch. 2) that "the form as well as the cause of all diseases is one and the same" (ἔστι δὲ μία ἁπασέων νούσων καὶ ἰδέη καὶ αἰτίη ἡ αὐτή). The closest parallel to the *VM* use of ὑπόθεσις comes from the occurrence of the verb ὑποτίθεσθαι in the opening chapter of the *On Flesh*, a treatise with which the author of *VM* seems to be in dialogue and the general thesis of which (that there is a basic constituent of everything; in this case, heat) he tries to refute as indemonstrable.

[79] Jouanna 1990: 158 citing such texts as Pl. *Apol.* 18b, 19b, Aristoph. *Nub.* 188, 228 about the presumed practice of Socrates.

'out of sight and problematic' (ἀφανέα καὶ ἀπορεόμενα).⁸⁰ What he probably means is not that all related phenomena are beyond the reach of the senses — earthquakes and eclipses, for instance, are not — but that the causes of them all are beyond empirical validation, and so is the origin of the cosmos as a whole. Given the very nature of these domains, the investigators are forced to lay down 'novel postulates' (καιναὶ ὑποθέσεις). But, according to the author, there is no evident standard or criterion by virtue of which their postulates can be deemed true or false. What is more, the researchers themselves cannot be sure about the truth of their own "suppositions". Cosmology is not a well-established 'craft' or 'science' (τέχνη) like traditional medicine because its objects are not liable to empirical investigation.⁸¹ These objects are 'obscure' (ἀφανέα) and 'perplexing' (ἀπορεόμενα), and as such they drive those trying to deal with them into perplexity. Irrespective of claims made to the contrary, philosophers engaging in cosmology and speculative natural philosophy are, then, always perplexed. Their perplexity is another name for their fundamental ignorance. Their error is that they presume to be able to know what is humanly unknowable. In the other occurrences of the noun ἀπορίη and the verb ἀπορέω in this treatise (VM 13.3

---

80 In a similar spirit Gorgias (*Helen* 13) claims that natural philosophers (μετεωρολόγοι) substitute one opinion for another and thus manage to make 'untrustworthy and invisible things' (τὰ ἄπιστα καὶ ἄδηλα) evident to the eyes of belief (φαίνεσθαι τοῖς τῆς δόξης ὄμμασιν ἐποίησαν). On the similarities between the Hippocratic *De Arte* and Gorgias' *Helen*, see Spatharas 2007.

81 I tend to disagree with Cooper 2004: 35 who sees "no irony or disrespect when our author [= the author of *VM*] says that with any direct inquiry into the nature of the cosmos one has no choice but to proceed on the basis of an ὑπόθεσις" and "no dismissal of research into such questions". Cooper is forced to approach the author of *VM* as a person who would welcome inquiries into natural philosophy by the introduction of ὑποθέσεις, because he has previously argued that, if the two wings into which medical theory and practice was bifurcated from the third century B.C. onwards are to be anachronistically applied to a writer of the late fifth century B.C., the author of *VM* would be a Rationalist rather than an Empiricist (justifiably termed "Empiric" by Cooper 2004: 26, n. 33, so as to prevent confusion with the doctrines of modern empiricism and what we understand by "empiricist" or "empirical"). Schiefsky 2005a: 118 is of the same opinion as Cooper but his arguments are even less convincing. To claim that the author "acknowledges that one might 'recognize and state' (γινώσκοι καὶ λέγοι) the truth about such matters [i.e. 'things in the sky and under the earth']" is to miss the rhetorical force of the author's style and his subtle irony. The whole point of *VM* 1–2 is the determination of what can and what cannot be known with certainty. The author insists that medicine *is* 'a craft' (ἀμφὶ τέχνης ἐούσης) with a 'well-established method' (ὁδὸς εὑρημένη) and denies that there can be another kind of medicine (ἀδύνατον γάρ); by so doing, he implies a distinction between genuine crafts and other kinds of activities that cannot be called τέχναι.

and 15.1, respectively)[82] the meaning is equally negative: the mental state of perplexity indicates, and is a symptom of, ignorance.

The author argues against a new trend (καινὸς τρόπος) in medicine (*VM* 13.1; cf. *VM* 1.3: καινῆς ὑποθέσιος). This new trend consists in the postulation of hypotheses, which is in the author's opinion not only an unnecessary but also a possibly harmful move for proper treatment (*VM* 14.2). The author believes that this new trend has been crucially influenced by natural philosophy — although he never makes this claim explicit in so many words. The accusations he launches against the adoption of the methods of natural philosophy by medicine are twofold: on the one hand, as we saw, he castigates the use of hypotheses in medicine (*VM* 1) and, on the other, he criticizes those "doctors and sophists" who deny that one can know medicine and be able to provide treatment without a prior knowledge of man's nature (*VM* 20.1–2):

Λέγουσι δέ τινες καὶ ἰητροὶ καὶ σοφισταὶ ὡς οὐκ ἔνι δυνατὸν ἰητρικὴν εἰδέναι ὅστις μὴ οἶδεν ὅ τί ἐστιν ἄνθρωπος· ἀλλὰ τοῦτο δεῖ καταμαθεῖν τὸν μέλλοντα ὀρθῶς θεραπεύσειν τοὺς ἀνθρώπους. **Τείνει δὲ αὐτέοισιν ὁ λόγος ἐς φιλοσοφίην**, καθάπερ Ἐμπεδοκλῆς ἢ ἄλλοι οἳ περὶ φύσιος γεγράφασιν ἐξ ἀρχῆς ὅ τί ἐστιν ἄνθρωπος, καὶ ὅπως ἐγένετο πρῶτον καὶ ὅπως ξυνεπάγη. Ἐγὼ δὲ τουτέων μὲν ὅσα τινὶ εἴρηται σοφιστῇ ἢ ἰητρῷ ἢ γέγραπται περὶ φύσιος, ἧσσον νομίζω τῇ ἰητρικῇ τέχνῃ προσήκειν ἢ τῇ γραφικῇ. Νομίζω δὲ περὶ φύσιος γνῶναί τι σαφὲς οὐδαμόθεν ἄλλοθεν εἶναι ἢ ἐξ ἰητρικῆς. Τοῦτο δὲ οἷόν τε καταμαθεῖν, ὅταν αὐτέην τις τὴν ἰητρικὴν ὀρθῶς πᾶσαν περιλάβῃ, – μέχρι δὲ τουτέου πολλοῦ μοι δοκέει δεῖν– λέγω δὲ ταύτην τὴν ἱστορίην, εἰδέναι ἄνθρωπος τί ἐστι, καὶ δι' οἴας αἰτίας γίνεται, καὶ τἄλλα ἀκριβέως.

But some doctors and sophists say that it is impossible for anyone to know medicine who does not know what the human being is; anyone who is going to treat patients correctly must, they say, learn this. *Their account tends towards philosophy,* just like Empedocles or others who have written about nature from the beginning, what the human being is and how it originally came to be and from what things it was compounded. But I hold that whatever has been said or written about nature by a sophist or doctor pertains less to the art of medicine than to the art of writing, and also that it is impossible to have any clear knowledge about nature from any other source than medicine. This knowledge can be acquired when one has correctly grasped medicine itself in its entirety, but until then it is impossible – I mean this science that consists in knowing what the human being is and by what causes it comes to be and all the rest, with precision.

trans. M. Schiefsky, emphasis added

---

[82] There is yet another instance of ἀπορίη in the treatise (*VM* 19.5) but there the noun has the technical meaning of 'physical discomfort'. The adjective ἀπόρων (pl. gen. neut.) in *VM* 8.2, a second-hand correction of the reading ἀφόρων given in the two main manuscripts of *VM* and unduly retained by Jouanna (1990: 127 and n. 1), qualifies incurable or intolerable diseases. In *VM* 15.2 ἄπορον means 'impracticable'.

Here the abstract noun φιλοσοφία, probably the earliest occurrence of the term in extant Greek literature,[83] acquires a semi-technical sense: it denotes speculative investigations about things beyond the evidence of the senses. Empedocles, the only person mentioned by name in the whole treatise, occurs at this juncture as an example, and perhaps the prime representative, of the kind of natural inquiries whose influence on medicine the author castigates. So much is pretty evident.

However, it is not entirely clear how the two accusations that the author launches against his opponents (in chapters 1–2 and 20, respectively) are related to one another. The author uses different descriptions for the exponents of the kind of investigations that postulate hypotheses in medicine and the exponents of the kind of inquiries into nature that pretend to know better than traditional medicine what man is.[84] In the former case, he speaks of "those who have undertaken to speak or write about medicine, having laid down as a hypothesis for their account hot or cold, etc.", and thinks that such a "hypothetical" procedure pertains not to medicine but to cosmology quite generally. In the latter case, he refers twice to "both/either doctor(s) and/or sophist(s)" (*VM* 20.1: καὶ ἰητροὶ καὶ σοφισταί, 20.2: ἢ σοφιστῇ ἢ ἰητρῷ), speaks of φιλοσοφία in a rather dismissive way, mentions Empedocles by name, refers to written works 'on nature' (περὶ φύσιος) in which the constitution of humans (or, alternatively, the constitution of the universe) is explained 'from the beginning' (ἐξ ἀρχῆς), opposes 'the art of writing' (γραφική) to medicine, claims that the proper understanding of nature can only begin with traditional medicine, but does not mention hypotheses at all.[85] Moreover, the beginning of chapter 20 announces the termination of an earlier discussion (in a sentence immediately preceding the above quotation) so that it would seem reasonable to suppose that the people and the ideas referred to in this chapter are different from those mentioned in the opening chapters of the treatise.[86] The first question we need to raise is

---

[83] This claim, obviously, depends on the date in which *VM* is supposed to have been composed. I agree with those who maintain that the last quarter of the fifth century is the most likely period: Jouanna 1990: 81–85, Schiefsky 2005a: 63–64.
[84] Cf. Cooper 2004: 10–18.
[85] For the (implicit or explicit) claims made here, namely that (i) σοφιστής means not 'clever/wise man' but 'sophist', (ii) φιλοσοφία has a derogatory sense, (iii) the works intended are *On Nature*, rather than *On Human Nature*, (iv) ἐξ ἀρχῆς qualifies the subordinate clauses that follow its occurrence, rather than what comes before it, (v) γραφική means the 'art of writing' rather than 'painting', see the explanations provided below in the main text.
[86] This is, for instance, Jouanna's (1990: 22) view but it can be shown to be based on a false dichotomy.

whether or not the accusations made in chapters 1–2 and 20 are related to one another. The second question is whether or not the author refers to the same group of people in chapters 1–2 and 20, respectively.

To tackle, in a preliminary fashion, the second question first, the beginning of chapter 20 goes as follows: περὶ μὲν οὖν τούτων ἱκανῶς μοι ἡγεῦμαι ἐπιδεδεῖχθαι, "I think that I have sufficiently displayed how things stand with respect to these matters". What are the "matters" referred to here? They are all the claims made from the beginning of the treatise up to this point: namely, that there is an age-old science of medicine with its own proper method and distinct discoveries; that this science is of a purely empirical character; that the supposition of a primary element or pair of contraries is of no avail for medical cure and has not been part of the traditional science of medicine; that healthy and diseased people require different diets; that different constitutions of bodies ask for differential treatment; that bodily troubles are caused no less by inopportune low than by inopportune high diet; in sum, that traditional medicine is a science endowed with many useful discoveries during its long process of development, a science well-tested over the ages and sophisticated enough to provide patients and healthy people alike with all they need in order to have their health restored or preserved. Once this thesis about the efficiency and sophistication of traditional medicine has been sufficiently demonstrated, the author proceeds to speak *again* of inappropriate innovations, as he did in chapters 1–2. The innovations he has now in mind do not concern the postulation of unnecessary hypotheses. They concern the claim that one cannot properly cure a patient unless one knows in advance what human nature is. But the fact that the innovations dealt with here are different from the innovations of chapters 1–2 does not mean that the author attacks now an entirely different group of people. The two groups may be overlapping or identical. And there are reasons to think that at least some of the people who form the group the author attacks in chapter 20 are the same as those attacked in chapters 1–2. We have thus already moved into tackling the first of the two questions raised earlier, the one about the different descriptions of the author's opponents.

In the opening chapter of *VM* the author refers to "those who have undertaken to speak or write about medicine", their account being crucially based on their favourite "suppositions" (*VM* 1.1). Some of these lecturers or writers need not be doctors themselves. But it is clear that the author includes at least *some* medical practitioners in their group. For when he explicitly returns to this same group later in the treatise (*VM* 15.1; cf. 13.1), the author expresses his perplexity about the way these people manage to cure real patients in accordance with their 'suppositions' (ἀπορέω ... τίνα ποτὲ τρόπον θεραπεύουσι τοὺς ἀνθρώπους ὥσπερ ὑποτίθενται). His belief is either that they are unable to cure or, if they manage to do so, that they succeed in providing treatment only by actually dropping their theoretical suppositions about the hot and the cold, the dry and the wet (*VM* 15.2). In any case, the author regards (some of) these people as doctors. In *VM* 20.1 the author mentions a group of "both doctors and sophists"; a bit later (*VM* 20.2) he indicates that "sophists" need not be doctors nor doctors "sophists". But it is evident that, whether doctors or sophists or both, these people aim at providing not a theoretical foundation for the extant science of medicine but a new starting-point for proper treatment (τοῦτο δεῖ καταμαθεῖν τὸν μέλλοντα ὀρθῶς θεραπεύσειν τοὺς ἀνθρώπους), i.e. a new science of medicine crucially based on theoretical suppositions about the nature of human beings (and perhaps the origin and constitution of Nature at large). Like the traditional science of medicine this new science aims at curing patients – only more effectively than the traditional science does. It follows that the "doctors and sophists" mentioned in chapter 20 are identical or, at least, overlapping with "those who have undertaken to speak or write about medicine" referred to in chapters 1, 13 and 15. The two groups are not so clearly distinct as Jouanna (1990: 22) believes.

Furthermore, if we go beyond what the author explicitly states to what he presumably means, we can see not only that the two groups are overlapping, if not identical, but that their innovative claims are interrelated and mutually reinforcing one another, and also that the author's refutation of these claims rests on the same basic idea.

In chapter 1, the author accuses his opponents for doing what, in his view, pertains to cosmology and speculative natural philosophy quite generally, rather than medicine. In chapter 20, he says that his opponents' ideas tend towards "philosophy", by which term he means not "love of wisdom" quite generally but something much more specific: the speculative philosophical systems of people such as Empedocles whom he mentions by name. By claiming that his opponents' ideas tend towards "philosophy" the author means that they do not pertain to medicine proper. When he later says that such ideas pertain to γραφική, the context makes it clear that he cannot mean 'painting' here,[87] but

---

[87] To think, as Jouanna (1990: 208–209) and others suggest, that here we have a reference to Empedocles' use of the technique of pointillism in painting as an example of the way the four elements come together, without actually merging with one another, so as to form the great variety of sensible things (DK 31 B 23) is to make too much of a passing reference to γραφική in an author who does not so much insinuate as states. The verbs γεγράφασι and γέγραπται mentioned earlier indicate that γραφική here means the 'art of writing' (so correctly *LSJ*), even if there is no other such attested sense of the noun in the fifth and fourth centuries B.C.

rather the 'art of writing' quite generally. It follows that the investigation περὶ τῶν μετεώρων ἢ τῶν ὑπὸ γῆν of ch. 1 is identical with, or at least a substantial part of, the φιλοσοφία mentioned in ch. 20, and that the ideas put forward by such speculative investigators of nature are, to the author's mind, good enough for epideictic speeches (orally delivered but previously composed in writing) and other such written rhetoric but wholly inappropriate for the science of medicine.[88] But if this is so, then the term σοφιστής of ch. 20 is either used ironically or meant in a sense that anticipates its later, derogatory, use in authors such as Plato.[89] Φιλοσοφία and σοφιστής, both being *hapax legomena* in the Hippocratic corpus, are used by our author as designations of an unwise kind of 'wisdom' that substitutes what comes first in the order of cognition (i.e. the empirically evident variety of human constitutions or 'natures' — διαφέρουσιν οὖν τούτων αἱ φύσιες, *VM* 20.6 — in their diversified reactions to diet) with what may come to be known only later (i.e. a more universal but precise knowledge of what a human being is and how s/he comes to be what s/he is — εἰδέναι ἄνθρωπος τί ἐστι καὶ δι' οἵας αἰτίας γίνεται καὶ τἆλλα ἀκριβέως, *VM* 20.2).

So much for the fundamental idea on the basis of which the author of *VM* refutes his opponents in both chapter 1 and chapter 20. When we come to the ideas that he ascribes to his opponents and think about them in view of what is known as pre-Socratic natural philosophy, we will realize (i) that their postulation of primary elements or pairs of contraries in the constitution of the human body (mentioned in chapters 1–2, 13 and 15, and implied throughout the stretch of chapters 1–19) can only have arisen out of a speculative investigation of Nature at large of the kind envisaged in chapter 20 and, conversely, (ii) that their claim (introduced in chapter 20) to know human nature better than traditional medicine does can only have arisen out of a postulation of primary elements or pairs of opposites in the constitution of the human body of the kind envisaged in chapters 1–2, 13 and 15. The "philosophers" or "sophists" and the "doctors" mentioned in chapter 20 are, then, seen by the author of *VM* as reaching their innovative but erroneous views about human nature (mentioned in chapters 1 and 20) after they have themselves devised, or adopted from others, a specula-

---

[88] It should be noted that the careful composition in written form of a speech meant to be delivered orally often suggested to the Greeks an unreliable or even positively deceptive product. The prime representative of this view is of course Alcidamas, himself (ironically) the author of a surviving speech *On the Writers of Written Speeches or On Sophists*, but there must have been many others who shared the same suspicion.

[89] The ironical use or pejorative connotation of the word σοφιστής is present already in *Prometheus Bound* 944 (cf. 62). Jouanna 1990: 206 is, then, probably wrong to deny all pejorative undertones of the word prior to its application to the Sophists.

tive theory of the universe as a whole, a domain which is, to our author's mind, essentially 'obscure and perplexing' (ἀφανέα τε καὶ ἀπορεόμενα). Since the testimony of the senses is incapable of reaching out to things such as τὰ μετέωρα ἢ τὰ ὑπὸ γῆν, the postulation of hypotheses becomes perhaps a necessary procedure for cosmology. But the truth of the conclusions thus reached cannot be tested against some firm and unobjectionable criterion. The correct method of investigation would be to start from the empirical evidence of the impact different kinds of food have on different kinds of (healthy or diseased) people, and to reach conclusions about human nature on this very basis, as traditional medicine does.

The physician's empirical cognition of things within the reach of the senses is thus juxtaposed to the speculative philosopher's contemplation of non-perceptible things. The physician's inductive method is opposed to the philosopher's deduction from hypothetical first principles. The piecemeal but sober and secure knowledge of the physician is contrasted to the insecure, unstable, fluctuating, inherent perplexing and deeply destabilising hypothetical knowledge of the philosopher (or theoretical scientist).

The author of *VM* clearly believes that traditional medicine has made much progress since its first inception in the distant past (*VM* 2.1; cf. 3.3, 3.6, 4.2, 7.3, 8.3). It has already secured for itself a proper 'method' (ὁδός) and many important discoveries over the years, and will come to many more discoveries provided that its practitioners are willing to rely on accumulated knowledge and to make this the sure springboard for their further research. If, by contrast, doctors overlook the accumulated knowledge of the past and try to make a new beginning, failure is imminent (*VM* 2.2). The fact that traditional medicine has not yet achieved utter precision in all matters is not a reason for disrespecting its scientific status; rather than blaming the art of medicine for its failures people should admire the amazing progress it has made over the earlier stages of deep human ignorance (*VM* 12.2)

The author of *VM* clearly believes that the origin of traditional medicine lies in 'human necessity' (ἀνάγκη) and 'need' (χρείη).[90] If diseased people could benefit from the same kind of diet as healthy people, he writes in *VM* 3.1, medicine would not have been discovered. But as things stand, this is not the case. The origin of medicine lies in the hard fact that humans need different kinds of diet when ill and when in a healthy state: Νῦν δὲ αὐτὴ ἡ ἀνάγκη ἰατρικὴν ἐποίησεν ζητηθῆναί τε καὶ εὑρεθῆναι ἀνθρώποισιν, "But in fact necessity itself

---

90 *VM* 3.1–2, 3.4, 4.1, 7.1–3.

caused medicine to be sought for and discovered by human beings".[91] The author of *VM* sees a straight line of development from the remote discovery that cooked food is better than raw food for humans, i.e. from the distant breakthrough of a specifically human diet based on cooking, to present-day differential dietary prescriptions in accordance with the various constitutions, health states and habits of people fed (*VM* 3.3–12.2).

That the origin of traditional medicine lies in necessity and human needs means that traditional medicine is a practical, not a theoretical, kind of science. That traditional medicine is a science crucially characterized by progress means that accumulation of knowledge is an essential feature of this science. These two traits of traditional medicine, i.e. the fact that it sprang from human need and the fact that its knowledge is of a kind that can be accumulated and passed over from one generation to the next, may go a long way into explaining why the author of *VM* does not pay any attention to wonder and perplexity as positive mental states leading to knowledge but regards them only, if at all, as negative emotions indicative of ignorance.

The kind of medicine that the author of *VM* attacks is present in the Hippocratic Collection: the author of the treatise *On Regimen* (1.3), for instance, claims that all animals, including humans, are constituted by the same primary elements, namely fire and water, which are the primary elements of the world at large. This kind of "a philosophically minded medicine"[92] is held in high esteem by Aristotle. In *De sensu* 1, 436a19–b1, and again in *De respiratione* 27, 480b26–30, Aristotle says that the most accomplished philosophers of nature end up dealing with the principles of medicine and praises those intelligent physicians who take their principles from the study of nature.[93] This shows the discrepancy between those, like the author of *VM*, who thought of medicine as an independent science with its own proper method based on experience and those, like the author of the *On Regimen* and Aristotle, who subordinated it to the philosophical study of nature. But this discrepancy is but an aspect of a more significant difference: the difference between theoretical contemplation pursued for the

---

[91] For the possibly Democritean origins of this view see Jouanna 1995: 46–48, Schiefsky 2005a: 50, Menn 2015: 17–18; cf. Dunn 2005: 54–59.

[92] Jouanna 1999: 269.

[93] One might claim, and scholars have actually maintained, that the new trend of medicine attacked in *VM* is the kind of medicine praised as truly scientific and ascribed to Hippocrates in Plato's *Phaedrus* (270c), our earliest testimony to the physician of Cos. But since what is meant there by τῆς τοῦ ὅλου φύσεως is a much-disputed issue (cf. Jouanna 1995: 77–81), it might be advisable to suspend judgment on whether or not Plato is of the same opinion as Aristotle concerning the right kind of medicine.

sake of knowledge alone and practical research conducted for the sake of some tangible improvement of human life.

5 Exit

The evidence of the Hippocratic corpus indicates that wonder and perplexity are affections of ignorant people which are going to be fully overcome with the arrival of empirical knowledge. The testimony of the Platonic-Aristotelian tradition, by contrast, indicates that wonder and perplexity are mental states that specifically characterize exceptionally inquisitive minds, i.e. minds that take nothing for granted but, rather, tend to critically inquire everything, even the simplest everyday things. Remember that Theaetetus' dizziness stems from a perplexity about Socrates' relative height, a change that occurs without a changing (the so-called Cambridge changes of relative terms, see p. 70 above). Remember also that Aristotle is emphatic about the kind of philosophy that stems from wonder: it is the theoretical kind, and this theoretical kind of inquiry gets started only *after* the everyday necessities of human life (including comfort, recreation, and, presumably, relatively stable health conditions and a specifically human diet) have already been procured (see pp. 76–77 above). Theoretical knowledge does not fulfil any practical human need. It just stems from the natural desire to understand. This desire, though naturally present in all humans, characterizes some people more than others. Those crucially distinguished by it are the philosophers; and the philosopher is liable to wonder more intensely or more often (or both) than an ordinary person. According to Plato, the mental state of inner perplexity and disquieting wonder before the miracle of Being is never going to be fully transcended: it tends, rather, to always regenerate itself in ever higher configurations. According to the more optimistic and empirically minded Aristotle, who was – be it noted – a physician's son, wonder and perplexity mark the beginning, but not also the end, of theoretical research into physics (including biology), mathematics and first philosophy.

When Plato and Aristotle identify θαυμάζειν as the beginning of philosophy they do not have in mind a historical beginning, a beginning that goes back to early sixth century B.C. Ionia. They clearly refer to a basic 'disposition' or 'affection' (πάθος) that sets one onto the path of philosophical reflection and determines that one is a philosopher. But if the statement is unconditionally true, it will be true of all philosophers, including those, such as Thales and Anaximander, who were the first to do philosophy. And if the saying applies to them in exactly the same way that it applies to Theaetetus, it would follow that this disposition or affection, which distinguishes the philosopher from the common run of men, is not essentially influenced, let alone determined, by the progress or lack of progress that philosophy has made nor by the fact that one might be a heir of a philosophical tradition or no heir of a tradition at all.

If θαυμάζειν is the true mark of the philosopher and the very beginning of one's philosophical activity, this beginning should be an ever *new* beginning and as such not a beginning that points to a termination, through a process of gradual accumulation of knowledge, which will be the beginning's own annihilation. This beginning, then, is an *endless* beginning. Moreover, this very beginning as πάθος is not a beginning of one's own making, the product of one's own decision to do philosophy rather than engage in politics or do business. If nothing but θαυμάζειν is truly the ἀρχή φιλοσοφίας, then θαυμάζειν not only determines that one will do philosophy but also must 'govern' (ἄρχειν) the way in which one will proceed in doing philosophy.

For Plato what is true of Eros, namely that τὸ ποριζόμενον ἀεὶ ὑπερκρεῖ (*Symp*. 203e), "anything he [sc. Eros] finds his way to always slips away" (trans. Nehamas-Woodruff), seems to be also true of θαυμάζειν — if the latter is to be understood not only as the starting-point but also as the governing principle of philosophy. As the conquest of the beloved, if ever fully accomplished, will result in the death of Eros itself, so the acquisition of wisdom, if ever attained to the full, will indicate the death of φιλοσοφεῖν, hence also the termination of the beginning and governing principle of doing philosophy, i.e. of θαυμάζειν. But as things stand, neither the absolute quenching of Eros nor the extinction of θαυμάζειν is possible. What is, rather, possible, and even desirable, is the deepening and widening of the vision that has τὸ καλόν as its object. Diotima says that the Beautiful is essentially θαυμαστόν. It may also be that the wondrous is essentially καλόν. Be that as it may, the mental troubles that the wondrous provides are the birth pangs of the philosophically pregnant natures. And those natures tend to move from wonder to wonder.

Aristotle would, in all likelihood,[94] disagree. By changing the proper objects of wondering from ordinary occurrences of everyday life, as they were in Plato,

---

[94] There are some indications, especially in the *Metaphysics*, that his implicit disagreement with Plato on the experience of wondering might not have been as radical as it appears from a close-reading comparison of *Metaph*. A.2 with the *Theaetetus* passage. One such indication is his famous dictum about the ever-perplexing nature of being in Z.1, 1028b2–4: καὶ δὴ **καὶ τὸ πάλαι τε καὶ νῦν καὶ ἀεὶ ζητούμενον καὶ ἀεὶ ἀπορούμενον**, τί τὸ ὄν, τοῦτό ἐστι "τίς ἡ οὐσία;", "And indeed the question *which was raised of old and is raised now and always, and is always the subject of doubt*, viz. what being is, is just the question, what is substance?" (tr. Ross, emphasis added); another is the description of divine thought in Λ.7, 1072b24–28 in

to extraordinary or rare or spectacular events that generate perplexity Aristotle tended to approach philosophical investigation on the model of progressive scientific research. But even if this crucial difference between Plato and Aristotle on the subject of wonder is taken on board, it remains true to say that their conception of theoretical philosophy, or at least of its highest branch (i.e. metaphysics), is radically different from the conception of a practical science such as medicine that we find in the Hippocratic authors.

As Heidegger once put it, "to say philosophy originates in wonder means philosophy is wondrous in its essence and it becomes more wondrous the more it becomes what it really is".[95] But then, obviously, philosophy in *this* sense is the polar opposite of technology and the applied sciences that bring about technical progress. The difference between philosophers and medical authors on the subject of wonder and perplexity highlights, and perhaps springs from, the gap between philosophical *contemplation* and scientific *discovering*, between, on the one hand, the love of inquiring for the sake of knowing and, on the other, the wish to understand, and subdue, things for some practical advantage. The corresponding attitudes to nature and to the world as a whole differ substantially. To the serene contemplation of the philosopher's *gaze* is juxtaposed the expedient interference of the scientist's *hand*. The former is an attitude of respect and reverence; the latter an attitude of manipulation and control. In both cases nature is asked to speak her secrets. But in philosophical investigation she is cajoled to do so for the sake of her glorification; in scientific scrutiny she is forced to do so for the sake of her subordination. Aristophanes' comic wonder bespeaks a philosopher's inquisitiveness; Eryximachus' knowingness a technician's expertise.

Bibliography

Barnes, J. (ed.) 1984. *The Complete Works of Aristotle: The Revised Oxford Translation*. 2 vols. Princeton: Princeton University Press.
Bernadete, S. 1978. "On Wisdom and Philosophy: The First Two Chapters of Aristotle's *Metaphyiscs* A", *Review of Metaphysics* 32: 205–215.
Bos, A.P. 1983. "Aristotle on Myth and Philosophy", *Philosophia Reformata* 48: 1–18.

---

terms of wonder. One might even go as far as to interpret Aristotle's reported tendency to be more fond of tales as he grows older (fr. 668 Rose³) in view of his opinion (in *Metaph*. A.2, 982b19 quoted above) that tales are composed of wonders.
95 Heidegger 1995: 141.

Boudon-Millot, V. 2005. "Art, Science and Conjecture, from Hippocrates to Plato and Aristotle", in: Philip J. Van Den Eijk (ed.), *Hippocrates in Context*: 87–99. Leiden/Boston: Brill.
Broadie, S. 2012. "A Science of First Principles: *Metaphysics* A2", in: Carlos Steel (ed.), *Aristotle's* Metaphysics *Alpha (Symposium Aristotelicum)*, (with a New Critical Edition of the Greek Text by Oliver Primavesi): 43–67. Oxford: Oxford University Press.
Brown, L. 2018. "*Aporia* in Plato's *Theaetetus* and *Sophist*", in: George Karamanolis and Vasilis Politis (eds.), *The Aporetic Tradition in Ancient Philosophy*: 91–111. Cambridge/New York/Melbourne/New Delhi: Cambridge University Press.
Buddensiek, F. 2018. "*Aporia* in Aristotle's *Metaphysics Beta*", in: George Karamanolis and Vasilis Politis (eds.), *The Aporetic Tradition in Ancient Philosophy*: 137–154. Cambridge/New York/Melbourne/New Delhi: Cambridge University Press.
Burnyeat, M.F. 1990. *The Theaetetus of Plato (with a translation of Plato's* Theaetetus *by M. J. Levett, revised by Myles Burnyeat)*. Indianapolis/Cambridge: Hackett Publishing Company.
Burnyeat, M.F. 2012. "Socratic Midwifery, Platonic Inspiration", in: M.F. Burnyeat, *Explorations in Ancient and Modern Philosophy*, II. 21–35. Cambridge/New York/Melbourne/Madrid/Cape Town/Singapore/São Paolo/Delhi/Mexico City: Cambridge University Press [= *Bulletin of the Institute of Classical Studies* 24 (1977) 7–16].
Bury, R.G. ²1932. *The Symposium of Plato (Edited with Introduction, Critical Notes and Commentary)*. Cambridge: W. Heffer and Sons Ltd.
Cambiano, G. 2012. "The Desire to Know: *Metaphysics* A1", in: Carlos Steel (ed.), *Aristotle's* Metaphysics *Alpha (Symposium Aristotelicum)*, (with a New Critical Edition of the Greek Text by Oliver Primavesi): 1–42. Oxford: Oxford University Press.
Candiotto, L. 2015. "Plato's Cosmological Medicine in the Discourse of Eryximachus in the *Symposium*: The Responsibility of a Harmonic *Technē*", *Plato Journal* 15: 81–93.
Candiotto, L. and Politis, V. 2020. "Epistemic Wonder and the Beginning of the Enquiry: Plato's *Theaetetus* (155d2–4) and Its Wider Significance", in: Laura Candiotto and Olivier Renaut (eds.), *Emotions in Plato*: 19–38. Leiden/Boston: Brill.
Chrysakopoulou, S. 2012. "Wonder and the Beginning of Philosophy in Plato", in: S. Vasalou (ed.), *Practices of Wonder: Cross-Disciplinary Perspectives*: 88–120. Cambridge: James Clarke and Co.
Cooper, J.M. 1997. *Plato: Complete Works (Edited with Introduction and Notes by John M. Cooper; Associate Editor: D. S. Hutchinson)*. Indianapolis/Cambridge: Hackett.
Cooper, J.M. 2004. "Method and Science in *On Ancient Medicine*", in: J.M. Cooper, *Knowledge, Nature and the Good: Essays on Ancient Philosophy*: 3–42. Princeton/Oxford: Princeton University Press [= *Interpretation und Argument*, Helmut Linneweber-Lammerskitten and Georg Mohr (eds.): 25–57. Würzburg: Königshausen & Neumann, 2002].
Cornford, F.M. 1935. *Plato's Theory of Knowledge: The* Theaetetus *and the* Sophist *of Plato Translated with a Running Commentary*. London: Routledge and Kegan Paul Ltd.
Craik, E.M. 2001a. "Thucydides on the Plague: Physiology of Flux and Fixation", *Classical Quarterly* 51: 102–108.
Craik, E.M. 2001b. "Plato and Medical Texts: *Symposium* 185c–193d", *Classical Quarterly* 51: 109–114.
Craik, E.M. 2015. *The 'Hippocratic' Corpus: Content and Context*. London/New York: Routledge.
Crubellier, M. and A. Laks 2009. "Introduction", in: Michel Crubellier and André Laks (eds.), *Aristotle's* Metaphysics *Beta (Symposium Aristotelicum)*: 1–23. Oxford: Oxford University Press.

Deckard, M.F. and P. Losonczi (eds.) 2011. *Philosophy Begins in Wonder: An Introduction to Early Modern Philosophy, Theology and Science*. Cambridge: James Clarke and Co.

Dover, K. 1980. *Plato: Symposium*. Cambridge/New York/Melbourne: Cambridge University Press.

Dunn F. 2005. "*On Ancient Medicine* and its Intellectual Context", in: Philip J. Van Den Eijk (ed.), *Hippocrates in Context*: 49–67. Leiden/Boston: Brill.

Edelstein, L. 1967. *Ancient Medicine: Selected Papers of Ludwig Edelstein*, eds. Owsei Temkin and C. Lilian Tempkin. Baltimore: The Johns Hopkins Press.

Frede, M. 1987. "Philosophy and Medicine in Antiquity", in: M. Frede, *Essays in Ancient Philosophy*: 225–242. Minneapolis: University of Minnesota Press.

Frede, M. 1992. "Plato's Arguments and the Dialogue Form", in: James C. Klagge and Nicholas D. Smith (eds.), *Methods of Interpreting Plato and his Dialogues*, (= *Oxford Studies in Ancient Philosophy*, Supplementary Volume 1992): 201–219. Oxford/New York: Oxford University Press.

Frede, M. 2008. "Ο Σέξτος Εμπειρικός για τις απαρχές της φιλοσοφίας" (Greek translation of an unpublished English lecture), in: M. Frede, *Η αρχαία ελληνική φιλοσοφία: όψεις της ιστορίας και της ιστοριογραφίας της*, ed. Chloe Balla: 131–158. Athens: Ekkremes.

Fuller, R.C. 2006. *Wonder: From Emotion to Spirituality*. Chapel Hill: The University of North Carolina Press.

Fuller, R.C. 2012. "From Biology to Spirituality: The Emotional Dynamics of Wonder", in: S. Vasalou (ed.), *Practices of Wonder: Cross-Disciplinary Perspectives*: 64–87. Cambridge: James Clarke and Co.

Gearch, P. 1969. *God and the Soul*. London: Routledge.

Gill, C. 1999. *Plato: The Symposium (Translated with an Introduction and Notes)*. London/New York/Camberwell/Toronto/New Delhi/Auckland/Johannesburg: Penguin Books.

Green, J.D., Jr. 2014. *Health and Harmony: Eryximachus on the Science of Eros*. Unpublished M.A. Dissertation. The University of Texas at Austin.

Heidegger, M. 1995. *Basic Questions of Philosophy: Selected "Problems" of "Logic."* Translated by Richard Rojcewicz and André Schuwer. Bloomington and Indianapolis: Indiana University Press.

Hepburn, R.W. 1980. "The Inaugural Address: Wonder", *Aristotelian Society Supplementary Volume* 54: 1–23.

Hunter, R. 2004. *Plato's Symposium*. Oxford/New York: Oxford University Press.

Jones, W.H.S. 1923a. *Hippocrates: Ancient Medicine; Airs, Waters, Places; Epidemics 1 and 3; The Oath; Precepts; Nutriment* (*The Loeb Classical Library* No. 147). London/Cambridge (MA): Heinemann/Harvard University Press.

Jones, W.H.S. 1923b. *Hippocrates: Prognostic; Regimen in Acute Diseases; The Sacred Disease; The Art; Breaths; Law; Decorum, Physician (ch. 1); Dentition* (*The Loeb Classical Library* No. 148). London/Cambridge (MA): Heinemann/Harvard University Press.

Jouanna, J. 1990. *Hippocrate*, tome II, 1er partie: *L'ancienne médicine*, Paris: Les Belles Lettres.

Jouanna, J. 1999. *Hippocrates*, translated by M.B. DeBevoise. Baltimore: The Johns Hopkins University Press.

Jouanna, J. 2003. *Hippocrate*, tome II, 3e partie: *La maladie sacrée*. Paris: Les Belles Lettres.

Jouanna, J. 2012. *Greek Medicine from Hippocrates to Galen: Selected Papers,* translated by Neil Allies, edited with a Preface by Philip J. Van Den Eijk. Leiden/Boston: Brill.

Kazantzidis, G. 2018. "Medicine and the Paradox in the Hippocratic Corpus and Beyond", in: Maria Gerolemou (ed.), *Recognizing Miracles in Antiquity and Beyond* (Trends in Classics – Supplementary Volume 53), 31–61. Berlin: De Gruyter.

Knorr, W. 1975. *The Evolution of the Euclidean Elements: A Study of the Theory of Incommensurable Magnitudes and its Significance for Early Greek Geometry*. Dordrecht: Reidel.

Konstan, D. and E. Young-Bruehl 1982. "Eryximachus' Speech in the *Symposium*", *Apeiron* 16: 40–6.

Laks, A. 2009. "*Aporia Zero (Metaphysics B* 1, 995a–995b4)", in: Michel Crubellier and André Laks (eds.), *Aristotle's* Metaphysics *Beta (Symposium Aristotelicum)*: 25–46. Oxford: Oxford University Press.

Lear, J. 1988. *Aristotle: The Desire to Understand*. Cambridge: Cambridge University Press.

Llewelyn, J. 2001. "On the Saying that Philosophy Begins in *Thaumazein*", *Afterall: A Journal of Art, Context and Enquiry* 4: 48–57.

Lloyd, G.E.R. 1978. *Hippocratic Writings*. Edited with an Introduction by G.E.R. Lloyd; translated by J. Chadwick and W.N. Mann. London/New York/Camberwell/Toronto/New Delhi/Auckland/Johannesburg: Penguin Books.

Lloyd, G.E.R. 1979. *Magic, Reason and Experience: Studies in the Origins and Development of Greek Science*. Cambridge/New York/Melbourne: Cambridge University Press.

Lloyd, G.E.R. 1991. "Who Is Attacked in *On Ancient Medicine*?", in: G.E.R. Lloyd, *Methods and Problems in Greek Science: Selected Papers*: 49–69. Cambridge: Cambridge University Press [= *Phronesis* 8 (1963): 108–126].

McDowell, J. 1973. *Plato's Theaetetus (Translated with Notes)*. Oxford: Oxford University Press.

Mansion, S. 1955. "Les apories de la Métaphysique aristotélicienne", in: *Autour d'Aristote. Receuil d'études de philosophie ancienne et médiévale offert à Monseigneur A. Mansion*: 141–179. Louvain: Publications Universitaires de Louvain.

Menn, S. 2015. "Democritus, Aristotle, and the *Problemata*", in: Robert Mayhew (ed.), *The Aristotelian* Problemata Physica: 10–35. Leiden/Boston: Brill.

Metcalf, R. 2013. "The Elemental Sallis: On Wonder and Philosophy's 'Beginning'", *Journal of Speculative Philosophy* 27.2: 208–215.

Munson, R.V. 2001. *Telling Wonders: Ethnographic and Political Discourse in the Work of Herodotus*. Ann Arbor: The University of Michigan Press.

Nehamas, A. and P. Woodruff 1989. *Plato: Symposium (Translated with Introduction and Notes)*. Indianapolis/Cambridge: Hackett.

Nightingale, A.W. 2004. *Spectacles of Truth in Classical Greek Philosophy: Theoria in its Cultural Context*. Cambridge/New York/Melbourne/Madrid/Cape Town/Singapore/São Paulo: Cambridge University Press.

Nussbaum, M. 2001. *Upheavals of Thought: The Intelligence of Emotions*. Cambridge/New York/Oakleigh/Madrid/Cape Town: Cambridge University Press.

Oikonomopoulou, K. (2019). "Paradoxography and the pseudo-Aristotelian *Problemata*", in: George Kazantzidis (ed.), *Medicine and Paradoxography in Classical Antiquity*: 53–71. Berlin: De Gruyter.

Palmer, J. 2018. "Contradiction and *Aporia* in Early Greek Philosophy", in: George Karamanolis and Vasilis Politis (eds.), *The Aporetic Tradition in Ancient Philosophy*: 9–28. Cambridge/New York/Melbourne/New Delhi: Cambridge University Press.

Parsons, H.L. (1969). "A Philosophy of Wonder", *Philosophy and Phenomenological Research* 30: 84–101.

Politis, V. 2018. "*Aporia* and Sceptical Arguments in Plato's Early Dialogues", in: George Karamanolis and Vasilis Politis (eds.), *The Aporetic Tradition in Ancient Philosophy*: 48–66. Cambridge/New York/Melbourne/New Delhi: Cambridge University Press.
Prier, R.A. 1989. *THAUMA IDESTHAI: The Phenomenology of Sight and Appearance in Archaic Greece*. Thallahassee: Florida State University Press.
Priestley, J. 2014. *Herodotus and Hellenistic Culture: Literary Studies in the Reception of the Histories*. Oxford: Oxford University Press.
Primavesi, O. 2012. "Aristotle's *Metaphysics* A: A New Critical Edition with Introduction", in: Carlos Steel (ed.), *Aristotle's* Metaphysics *Alpha (Symposium Aristotelicum)*, (with a New Critical Edition of the Greek Text by Oliver Primavesi): 385–516. Oxford: Oxford University Press.
Rangos, S. 2005. "On Diotima's Allusions to Earlier Speakers in Plato's *Symposium*", *Skepsis* 16.1: 164–178.
Rapp, C. 2018. "*Aporia* and Dialectical Method in Aristotle", in: George Karamanolis and Vasilis Politis (eds.), *The Aporetic Tradition in Ancient Philosophy*: 112–136. Cambridge/New York/ Melbourne/New Delhi: Cambridge University Press.
Robin, L. ²1989. *Platon: Œuvres complètes, IV.2: Le banquet (notice de Léon Robin, texte établi et traduit par Paul Vicaire)*. Paris: Les Belles Lettres.
Rosen, R.M. 2016. "Towards a Hippocratic Anthropology: *On Ancient Medicine* and the Origins of Humans", in: Lesley Dean-Jones and Ralph M. Rosen (eds.), *Ancient Concepts of the Hippocratic*, 242–257. Leiden/Boston: Brill.
Ross, W.D. 1924. *Aristotle's Metaphysics (A Revised Text with Introduction and Commentary)*. 2 vols. Oxford: Oxford University Press.
Rowe, C.J. 1998. *Plato: Symposium (Edited with an Introduction, Translation and Commentary)*. Oxford: Aris & Phillips.
Rowe, C. 1999. "The Speech of Eryximachus in Plato's *Symposium*", in: John J. Cleary (ed.), *Traditions of Platonism: Essays in Honour of John Dillon*: 53–64. Aldershot/Brookfield/ Singapore/ Sydney: Ashgate.
Sallis, J. 2016. *The Figure of Nature: On Greek Origins*. Bloomington and Indianapolis: Indiana University Press.
Schaefer, D. 1999. "Wisdom and Wonder in *Metaphysics* A: 1–2", *Review of Metaphysics* 52: 641–656.
Schiefsky, M.J. 2005a. *Hippocrates:* On Ancient Medicine *(Translated with Introduction and Commentary)*. Leiden/Boston: Brill.
Schiefsky, M.J. 2005b. "*On Ancient Medicine* on the Nature of Human Beings", in: Philip J. van der Eijk (ed.), *Hippocrates in Context*: 69–85. Leiden/Boston: Brill.
Sherey, P. 2013. "The Varieties of Wonder", *Philosophical Investigations* 36:4: 340–354.
Spatharas, D. 2007. "Gorgias and the Author of the Hippocratic Treatise *De Arte*", *Classica et Mediaevalia* 58: 159–163.
Stern, P. 2008. *Knowledge and Politics in Plato's* Theaetetus. Cambridge/New York/Melbourne/ Madrid/Cape Town/Singapore/São Paulo: Cambridge University Press.
Szaif, J. 2018. "Socrates and the Benefits of Puzzlement", in: George Karamanolis and Vasilis Politis (eds.), *The Aporetic Tradition in Ancient Philosophy*: 29–47. Cambridge/New York/ Melbourne/New Delhi: Cambridge University Press.
van der Eijk, Ph.J. 2005. *Medicine and Philosophy in Classical Antiquity: Doctors and Philosophers on Nature, Soul, Health and Disease*. Cambridge: Cambridge University Press.

Vasalou, S. (ed.) 2012. *Practices of Wonder: Cross-Disciplinary Perspectives.* Cambridge: James Clarke and Co.

West, M.L. 1966. *Hesiod: Theogony (Edited with Prolegomena and Commentary).* Oxford/New York: Oxford University Press.

Part II: **Emotions in the Medical Room**

Elizabeth Craik
The Doctor's Dilemma: Addressing Irrational Fears

Abstract: It is first argued, on the basis both of pragmatic case histories in *Epidemics* and of theoretical observations in *Aphorisms*, that Hippocratic physicians found a correlation between mental and physical conditions. It is seen that, among the former, fear is prominent (as in the list "fear, shame, grief, delight, anger and so on" of *On Humours* 9) and that, among irrational fears, dream terrors or nightmares are most often at issue (as in *On Regimen* 4, where the nature of sleep itself is explored). After a brief treatment of relevant passages in other works, attention is paid to irrational fears in *On the Sacred Disease* and *On Diseases of Girls* with particular regard to the supposed aetiology of, and recommended therapy for, such problems and associated precipitating conditions. In this, attitudes to female physiology and psychology are explored. In conclusion it is contended that there was significant mutual interaction between medical and non-medical writers and further suggested that the author of *On Diseases of Girls* (responsible also for other parts of the Corpus, including the treatise *On Glands*) may have influenced the thought of Aristotle on the emotions. The famous presentation of pity and fear in *Poetics* is viewed as paradigmatic.

In the thriving interdisciplinary fields of affect studies and history of the emotions, medical writing has much to contribute. And in medical writing, the Hippocratic beginnings have a peculiar importance. It is in the Hippocratic *Aphorisms* and the *Epidemics* that general ideas are presented most clearly and it is in these fundamental collections that the essential tenets of Hippocratic medicine emerge. In this paper it is argued, through a close study of these and other Hippocratic texts, and with particular reference to *On Diseases of Girls*, that ancient doctors viewed the physical body as functioning in conjunction with the mental and emotional persona in a system of organic unity. It is seen further that views of the troubled mind are analogous to views of the ailing body; also that therapy based on the principle of *katharsis*, clearance of undesirable matter, is regarded by various writers as appropriate for mental or emotional disturbance in the same way as for somatic malfunction. Finally, it is suggested that Aristotle's celebrated view that tragedy effected *katharsis* of pity and fear arose through familiarity with contemporary medical usage. Physical purgation, achieved by laxatives, emetics, errhines or by other means, was routine. Mental or emotional purgation was recognised as an ideal. While there is clear evidence of this theory in several texts, it is impossible to determine whether it was widely held or confined to a group of medical pioneers.

There is a rich and varied terminology of the mind and the emotions in the Greek language. In this terminology, mental and emotional faculties are mapped on the physical body. In the fluid language of physiology and associated pathology recurrent terms applied to bodily parts regarded as seats of cognition are: *enkefalos*; *phrenes*; *kardia*; *gnômê*; *psuchê*; *thumos*. Different medical authors hold different views of the locality in the body most important in reason and feeling, as do non-medical authors writing under their influence. Some view the head and the brain (*enkefalos*) as fundamental; others centre thought (*gnômê*) and emotion (*pathos*) in areas of the chest, not all easy to translate or equate precisely with bodily organs: midriff, heart (*phrenes*, *kardia*) and the more elusive soul, spirit (*psuchê*; *thumos*). These terms will appear in the ensuing discussion. We may note at this stage that in addition to foregrounding the emotions (*pathê* and *pathêmata*) of pity and fear in *Poetics*, Aristotle in *On Soul* explored the emotions (*pathê*, located in the *psuchê*) of anger, gentleness, fear, pity and boldness, explicitly stating that they are inseparable from doctors' business, the physical matter of beings (403a–b).[1]

We return to *Aphorisms* and *Epidemics*. A clear indication that physical malaise and sensation is allied with mental states is apparent in the aphoristic judgment that "in the case of people who have some bodily ailment and fail in general to recognise it, their mind is troubled" (*Aph.* 2.6 [4. 470 L.]).[2] At the same time, cases of protracted depression are thought to involve black bile, having a (physically) melancholic character (*Aph.* 6.23 [4.568 L.]).[3] As a corollary we may cite the connection regularly posited between *paraphrosynê* mental derangement and *spasmos* physical convulsions (as *Aph.* 7.9 [4.580 L.]). In the case histories of *Epidemics* such precipitating factors as grief and depression are considered crucial determinants of physical illness. Mental, emotional and physical states are thus viewed in conjunction.

The densely challenging work *On Humours* is generally regarded as ancillary to *Epidemics*. In that work, there is a lengthy series of cryptic staccato notes suggesting a correlation between mental and physical conditions (*Hum.* 9 [5. 488,

---

1 τὰ πάθη τῆς ψυχῆς inseparable from φυσικὴ ὕλη τῶν ζῴων.
2 Ὁκόσοι, πονέοντές τι τοῦ σώματος, τὰ πολλὰ τῶν πόνων οὐκ αἰσθάνονται, τουτέοισιν ἡ γνώμη νοσέει.
3 Ἢν φόβος ἢ δυσθυμίη πουλὺν χρόνον διατελέῃ, μελαγχολικὸν τὸ τοιοῦτον.

490 L.]). The former, located in the *psuchê*, appear in personal character traits and affect the *gnômê*. Disorders of the *psuchê* are manifested in disruption of regular eating, drinking and sleeping patterns. Problems in personal character manifest as episodes of grief, of irascibility and of desires. There is a list of appropriate bodily reactions to particular mental stimuli: to fears, shame, grief, anger and similar things;[4] the response is sweats, heart palpitations and so on. Accounts in case histories describe bouts of weeping, shouting and terror (*Epid.* 7.11 [5.384–6 L.]). The prominence of fear in the list of emotions is striking. As seen above, Aristotle too singles out fear for particular emphasis. It appears that in Greek thought generally, fear is paramount in perception of the emotions. Fear may be seen as peculiarly primal: already in infancy ailments are found to include "sleeplessness and fears" (*Aph.* 3.24 [4.496 L.]).[5] Mention of night terrors is particularly prevalent in the literature; in sleep the individual loses consciousness and with it control; nightmares may take over and dominate thought; sleep is a simulacrum of death. In common parlance, fear is generally allied with "chill", trembling and a rush of fluids. Aristotle aptly remarks that both fear and death are chilling (Arist. *Probl.* 877a).

Women are thought to be peculiarly susceptible to fear, anxiety and depression. Among cases described is one that details the salient symptoms of a girl's condition as follows: "being silent, she was totally unresponsive; poor spirits; she despaired of herself" (*Epid.* 3, case 6 [3.50, 52 L.]).[6] Another describes a woman's situation after miscarriage as "she was distraught; terrors and low spirits" (*Epid.* 3, case 11 [3.60, 62 L.]).[7] Men too suffered fears, but in some recorded cases these were more active, or rather less passive: fear of the flute-girl; fear of heights; fear of flashing lights (*Epid.* 5.81, 82, 83 [5.250 L.]). We may see the problem of bipolar disease, or manic depression, in other cases: in one, "there was onset of depression and suicidal thoughts; but sometimes again of good spirits" and in another the sufferer in sleep and dreams "felt unhappy or happy; was fearful or confident" (*Epid*, 5.84 [5.252 L.] and *Epid*. 6.8–9 [5.346 L.].[8] The treatise *On the Sacred Disease* ranges widely over many diseases other than that which is its main subject.

---

4 φόβοι, αἰσχύνη, λύπη, ἡδονή, ὀργή, τἆλλα τοιαῦτα.
5 The terms are ἀγρυπνίαι and φόβοι.
6 σιγῶσα οὐδὲν διελέγετο· δυσθυμίη· ἀνελπίστως ἑαυτῆς εἴχεν.
7 ... παρέκρουσεν· φόβοι, δυσθυμίαι.
8 In the former, ἐνέπιπτον ἀθυμίαι καὶ ἀπαλλαγῆς βίου ἐπιθυμίη, ὁτὲ δὲ πάλιν εὐθυμίη and in the latter, ἄχθεται, καὶ ἥδεται, καὶ φοβεῖται, καὶ θαρσέει.

Among those are night terrors and wild states causing people to rush out of bed and outside. (*Morb. Sacr.* 1 [6.362 L.]. The author is emphatic in asserting that the brain is source of pleasures, joys, laughter and jests as well as of pains, troubles, unhappiness and tears; it is through the brain that "we become mad or deranged, and that fears and terrors approach us, some by night and some by day, also dreams and inappropriate wanderings" (*Morb. Sacr.* 14 [6.386, 388 L.]).⁹ The stress on ineluctable fears is consonant with evidence from other Hippocratic sources. To this may be added disease descriptions from two loosely related nosological works, *On Diseases* 2 and *On Internal Affections*. In the former, the sufferer feels nausea, shuns light and people, seeks the dark, is seized by fear ... feels terror, sees terrible apparitions and has terrifying dreams, sometimes with appearance of the dead (*Morb.* 2. 72 [7.108, 110 L.].¹⁰ In the latter also waking hallucinations as well as terrifying dreams are experienced (*Int.* 48 [7.284 L.]).¹¹

The writer of the treatise *On Regimen* expresses clear views on the conjunction of body and *psuchê* in sickness and in health. The *psuchê* resides in and draws nourishment from the body. In the aetiology and therapy of sickness, body and mind are alike: in both cases, errors in regimen cause trouble; regulation of regimen serves as corrective. In particular, excess causes *plêsmonê* surfeit and requires a regimen of purgation by emetics or similar means. The *psuchê* is centre of *gnômê* thought (*Vict.* 1.21 [6.494 L.]) and may be possessed of differing degrees of *phronêsis* intelligence (*Vict.* 1.35 [6.512L.]).¹² Cases of *mania* are noted, in which people weep when nothing troubles or strikes them, and in which they are afraid of things which are not fearsome. (Vict. 1.35 [6.518 L.]).¹³ Book 4 at the end of the treatise is devoted to dreams.

Although the content is considerably more sophisticated than that of passages from other works already discussed, in that dream interpretation is essayed and therapy for the dreamer prescribed, the nature and purported effect of the dreams remarked is very similar: "when strange bodies are seen in the course of sleep and terrify the person, this indicates a surfeit of unaccustomed

---

9 καὶ μαινόμεθα καὶ παραφρονέομεν, καὶ δείματα καὶ φόβοι παρίστανται ἡμῖν τὰ μὲν νύκτωρ τὰ δὲ μεθ' ἡμέρην, καὶ ἐνύπνια καὶ πλάνοι ἄκαιροι.
10 καὶ φόβος λάζεται ... καὶ φοβεῖται, καὶ δείματα ὁρᾷ καὶ ὀνείρατα φοβερὰ καὶ τοὺς τεθνηκότας ἐνίοτε.
11 παραφρονέει ... ἐνύπνια ...φοβερά.
12 περὶ δὲ φρονήσιος ψυχῆς καὶ ἀφροσύνης ὀνομαζομένης ὧδε ἔχει.
13 οὗτοι κλαίουσί τε οὐθενὸς λυπέοντος ἢ τύπτοντος, δεδίασί τε τὰ μὴ φοβερά.

food ..." (*Vict.* 4.93 [6.660 L.]).¹⁴ This is viewed as a "dangerous disease" in exactly the terms used of physical diseases and the treatment too is the same, with a prescription of emetics followed by particular light foods and limited exercises.¹⁵

In the fragmentary piece *On Diseases of Girls* (*Virg.* [8.466, 468, 470 L.]), the main subject matter is prefaced by comments on the "sacred disease"; that is "on people who are struck down, and on the terrors which people feel so strongly that they are deranged and imagine they see spirits hostile to them, sometimes by night, sometimes by day, and sometimes at both times."¹⁶ A tendency to suicide, especially among women, "as the female sex is weaker and more inclined to despondency", is remarked.¹⁷ So far the matter coincides with that encountered in other texts, especially *On the Sacred Disease*, noted above. The discussion then moves to problems besetting unmarried girls, who are subject to an excess of blood rushing from uterus to heart and diaphragm: the heart is numbed by pressure, there is shivering and young girls become deranged, terrified and suicidal.¹⁸ Here emotional upheaval ensues on bodily disorder. There is no escape until the blood is discharged. The standard therapy is required: fluid accumulating in an excess amount and in the wrong place must be removed by *katharsis*. Aristotle, like our author, surmised that fear caused chill in the region of the heart; similar language is used in both of the bodily *topos* or part affected (Arist. *Probl.* 11.902b).¹⁹

The author of *On Diseases of Girls* was author of a substantial portion of the Hippocratic Corpus: *On Diseases of Women* (in part), *On the Nature of Woman*, *On Generation, On the Nature of the Child*, On *Diseases 4*, *On Glands* and demonstrates connections with Demokritos of Abdera in Thrace. The authors of *Epidemics* practised in North Greece in the late fifth and first half of the fourth century BC. Aristotle, who was the son of a doctor and evinced medical interests throughout his oeuvre, was born at northern Stagira in 384 BC. It may be suggested that the apparently radical views expressed in *Poetics*, on *katharsis* of the

---

14 ὁκόσα δὲ ἀλλόμορφα σώματα φαίνεται ἐν τοῖσιν ὕπνοισι καὶ φοβέει τὸν ἄνθρωπον, σιτίων ἀσυνήθων σημαίνει πλησμονήν.
15 See Bartos 2015: esp. 187, 194–195, 199; also Craik 2015: 266–276; van der Eijk 2005.
16 καὶ περὶ τῶν ἀποπλήκτων, καὶ περὶ τῶν δειμάτων, ὁκόσα φοβεῦνται οἱ ἄνθρωποι ἰσχυρῶς, ὥστε παραφρονέειν καὶ ὁρῆν δοκέειν δαίμονάς τινας ἐφ' ἑωυτῶν δυσμενέας, ὁκότε μὲν νυκτός, ὁκότε δὲ ἡμέρης, ὁκότε δὲ ἀμφοτέρῃσι τῇσιν ὥρῃσιν.
17 ἀθυμοτέρη γὰρ καὶ ὀλιγωτέρη ἡ φύσις ἡ γυναικείη.
18 μαίνεται ... φοβέεται καὶ δέδοικεν ... ὁ θυμὸς κακὸν ἐφέλκεται ... κελεύουσιν ἄλλεσθαι καὶ καταπίπτειν ἐς τὰ φρέατα καὶ ἄγχεσθαι.
19 καταψύχεται ὁ τόπος περὶ τὴν καρδίαν.

emotions of pity and fear, stem from familiarity with medical theory and practice.

Bibliography

Bartos, H. 2015. *Philosophy and Dietetics in the Hippocratic* On Regimen. Leiden/Boston: Brill.
Craik, E.M. 2006. "Tragedy as Treatment: Medical Analogies in Aristotle's *Poetics*", in: D. Cairns and V. Liapis (eds.), *Dionysalexandros*: 283–299. Ceredigion, Wales: The Classical Press of Wales.
Craik, E.M. 2016. "[Hippocrates] *On Glands*", in: L. Dean-Jones and R. Rosen (eds.), *Ancient Concepts of the Hippocratic*: 195–208. Leiden/Boston: Brill.
van der Eijk, P. 2005. *Medicine and Philosophy in Classical Antiquity*. Cambridge: Cambridge University Press.

Jennifer Kosak
Shame and Concealment in the Hippocratic Corpus

Abstract: This paper examines the nexus of emotions and motivations that lie behind veiling and self-covering in the Hippocratic Corpus. The most explicit discussion of the emotions that precipitate veiling occurs in *On the Sacred Disease* 12, where the author states that the mature patient veils himself from shame (*aiskhunê*) and not fear (*phobos*); however, younger patients, who do not yet have understanding of their disease, react with fear since they have not yet learned to feel shame. The Hippocratic Corpus frequently mentions shuddering (*phrikê*) and trembling (*tromos*) as indicators of both emotional and physical suffering, and likewise often notes that patients may suffer fear (*phobos, deima*). However, whereas Hippocratic writers seem to consider fear as both a symptom of disease and a patient reaction to disease, they mention shame much less often and arguably consider shame as an appropriate emotional response to a situation in which a patient has lost self-control. The paper examines a number of instances of veiling in the Hippocratic Corpus in an effort to understand the emotions associated with the gesture and to consider ways in which the meaning of the gesture is differentiated by the age and gender of the patient and by the diagnosis of the disease.

The writer of the Hippocratic treatise *Humors* provides a fairly comprehensive list of everything the good healer ought to consider in treating patients. In section 9, the author gives a list of issues connected to the mind, soul, and behavior that the healer should attend to and eventually turns to a consideration of a patient's character, experiences and behaviors:

> ἐκ τῶν ἠθέων, φιλοπονίη ψυχῆς, ἢ ζητῶν, ἢ μελετῶν, ἢ ὁρῶν, ἢ λέγων, ἢ εἴ τι ἄλλο, οἷον λῦπαι, δυσοργησίαι, ἐπιθυμίαι· ἢ τὰ ἀπὸ συγκυρίης λυπήματα γνώμης, ἢ τὰ διὰ τῶν ὀμμάτων, ἢ ἀκοῆς· οἷα τὰ σώματα, μύλης μὲν τριφθείσης πρὸς ἑωυτήν, ὀδόντες ἡμώδησαν, παρά τε κοῖλον παριόντι σκέλεα τρέμει, ὅταν τε τῇσι χερσί τις, ὧν μὴ δεῖται, αἴρῃ, αὗται τρέμουσιν, ὄφις ἐξαίφνης ὀφθεὶς χλωρότητα ἐποίησεν. οἱ φόβοι, αἰσχύνη, λύπη, ἡδονή, ὀργή, ἄλλα τὰ τοιαῦτα, οὕτως ὑπακούει ἑκάστῳ τὸ προσῆκον τοῦ σώματος τῇ πρήξει, ἐν τούτοισιν ἱδρῶτες, καρδίης παλμός, καὶ τὰ τοιαῦτα.
>
> *Humors* 9 (5.488 L.)

Of moral characteristics: diligence of mind, whether in inquiry or practice or sight or speech; similarly, for example, griefs, passionate outbursts, strong desires. Accidents grieving the mind, either through vision or through hearing. How the body behaves: when a mill grinds the teeth are set on edge; the legs shake when one walks beside a precipice; the hands shake when one lifts a load that one should not lift; the sudden sight of a snake causes pallor. Fears, shame, pain, pleasure, passion and so forth: to each of these the appropriate member of the body responds by its action. Instances are sweats, palpitation of the heart and so forth.

trans. W.H.S. Jones, LCL 150, 81

While the writer urges his readers to note the patient's personal qualities and bodily reactions to external stimuli, he also stresses the importance of paying attention to the patient's emotional responses, grounded within the body and individual constitution, indicated by certain signals such as shaking, sweating, growing pale and experiencing heart palpitations. The passage mentions several emotions specifically: λύπη, 'grief' or 'sadness', is mentioned twice, first in the plural, and thereafter in the singular, along with a variant, λυπήματα;[1] δυσοργησίη, translated here by Jones as 'passionate outbursts', is picked up later by the simpler form ὀργή, often translated as 'anger', but here in Jones' translation, 'passion'; in addition, the passage mentions ἐπιθυμίαι, 'desires', along with φόβοι, 'fears', αἰσχύνη, 'shame', and ἡδονή, 'pleasure' or 'happiness'.

This passage raises a number of questions regarding the relationship between emotions and disease. Is a particular emotion a symptom of a disease, an appropriate or inappropriate reaction to a disease on the part of the patient, a reaction provoked in the doctor or onlookers by the disease, or a combination of all of these at different times? Can an emotion even provoke a disease? The author of *Humors* first suggests that the kind and even more the intensity of some emotional responses depend on an individual's character. In other cases, a random external event (συγκυρίη) provokes distress. And finally, the body responds automatically and with predictable accompanying emotions to certain types of stimuli, such as the sight of a snake.

In a discussion of (often culturally contingent) metaphors that communicate emotions, Douglas Cairns reminds us: "there are substantial aspects of emotional experiences that depend on the biological heritage of our species and are deeply rooted in basic mechanisms of bodily regulation that human beings

---

[1] The full expression, λυπήματα γνώμης, 'accidents grieving the mind' or perhaps 'pains affecting thought', should be noted here, as a contrast to the next segment, which features pains to the body (οἷα τὰ σώματα). Although mind and body may be contrasted to each other, the sources of the pains, λυπήματα, are potentially the same — similar stimuli affecting different parts of the body. For more on the relationship between mind, body, pain and emotion, see Kazantzidis (2019).

share with other animals".² The list of emotions in *Humors* 9 includes several that are arguably universal and basic: anger, fear, happiness, sadness; missing are disgust and surprise (the latter of which is not, however, always included in the *communis opinio*).³ Although research shows that there are certain emotions grounded in human biology, there is less agreement whether the triggers, responses to, and appraisals of, emotions are universal.⁴ That is to say, even if there are some universal human emotions, cultural differences may provoke different emotions in response to similar events.⁵ Anger, fear and sadness are common emotions named in the Hippocratic Corpus; surprise and disgust also occur.⁶ Happiness does not receive frequent mention, as might be expected in such painful contexts, though medical writers do note when patients are able to take pleasure in activities such as eating and drinking. Of the other two emotions named in *Humors* 9, desire (ἐπιθυμία) and shame (αἰσχύνη), the former is well represented in the Hippocratic Corpus — or, perhaps better put, matters of the *thumos* (such as δυσθυμία, ἀθυμία and εὐθυμία) are.⁷ Shame, however, appears to play a relatively small role in the Hippocratic Corpus, at least on a lexical level.⁸ This is perhaps surprising: not only does the author of *Humors* in-

---

2 Cairns (2016) §5.1
3 Sanders 2014: 3; Ekman 2016: 32. For a helpful overview on the state of modern research on emotions, see Lateiner and Sparathas 2017, esp. 6–11, who, as they focus on disgust, also consider distinctions between emotion, reflex, and mood. Kazantzidis (personal communication) suggests that the sudden reaction to the snake in the passage may indicate the presence of disgust, as well — the person may feel a kind of instinctive revulsion when sighting a snake that does not derive from any recognition that the snake should be feared (cf. also Kazantzidis 2019: 141–142).
4 Paul Ekman's survey of emotion researchers reports: "The existence of 'compelling evidence for universals in any aspect of emotion' was endorsed by 88% of the respondents. The evidence supporting universal signals (face or voice) was endorsed by 80%. There was less agreement about whether there is compelling evidence for universals in the events that trigger an emotion (66%), physiology (51%), or appraisal mechanisms (44%)" (2016: 32).
5 As Cairns (2016) himself addresses: in his discussion of garment metaphors, he writes, "While many, most, or all cultures no doubt use dress to express and symbolize emotion, the specific metaphors that Greek culture uses are not universal" (§19).
6 For a rich discussion of emotions in the Hippocratic Corpus, see Thumiger 2017: 335–376, but in many ways *passim*. See also Kazantzidis (2017) for a discussion focused on disgust in the corpus.
7 By contrast, 'erotic desire' (ἔρως) is not an emotion of much interest to the writers of the Hippocratic Corpus, even if they take note of sexual behavior and drive; cf. Thumiger 2017: 374–376. For a discussion of *thumos*-related emotions in the Corpus, see also Thumiger 2017b.
8 A search of the *TLG* (excluding the Hippocratic *Letters*) reveals three results for αἰσχύνη in the Hippocratic Corpus (*Hum.* 9 [5.490 L.], *Fract.* 19 [3.482 L.], *Morb. Sacr.* 12 [6.382 L.]); three

clude it in his list of issues central to the concern of the healer, but shame plays such an essential role in so many classical texts and seems to have been an important factor in social interactions throughout ancient Greece. Furthermore, it is the focus of many articles in current medical literature, where shame is associated with everything from chronic illnesses such as cancer to PTSD to breastfeeding to depression and suicide. Moreover, the healers represented in the Hippocratic Corpus not only frequently call attention to the emotions of their patients, especially fear and distress, but are also attuned to the social dynamics of disease and concerned for the emotional well being both of their patients and themselves. So the fact that words such as αἰσχύνη and αἰσχρός ('shameful') do not appear regularly throughout the Hippocratic Corpus may require some explanation.

1 Shame in the Medical Encounter

The role of shame in the context of the meeting between healers and patients, at least in early modern and modern Western culture, has been subject to increasing scrutiny in the scholarship of the past thirty years, with many scholars pointing to the importance of Aaron Lazare's 1987 article, "Shame and Humiliation in the Medical Encounter" in laying the groundwork for this research.[9] Lazare defined shame as "distress concerning the *state of the self* that the person regards as no good, not good enough, or defective", maintaining that with shame, "we feel or believe that we do not measure up to the ideals or standards that we have set up for ourselves" (1653). He argued that both patients and physicians may experience shame that derives from the interaction of three factors: "(1) the shame-inducing event; (2) the vulnerability of the subject; and (3) the social context, which includes the roles of the people involved" (1654). Lazare discussed how patients may feel shame not only because of the weakness or deficiency they experience from the disease itself but also from the need to communicate the symptoms of disease, which they perceive to be shameful, and to do so in situations where they must often make themselves especially vulner-

---

for αἰσχύνειν (*de Arte* 1[6.2 L.], 3 [6.6 L.]; *Morb. Sacr.* 12 [6.384 L.])); and thirteen for αἰσχρός (*Off.* 3 [3.278 L.], *Fract.* 30 [3.524 L.], *Artic.* 11 [4.106 L.], 13 [4.116 L.], 14 [4.118 L.], 37 [4.166 L.], 44 [4.188 L.], 64 [4.274 L.]; *Morb. Sacr.* 14 [6.386 L.]; *Reg.* 1.24 [6.496 L.]; *Mul.* 1.62 [8.126 L.]; *Medic.* 6 [9.212 L.] and [*de Purg.*] 65). The word αἰδώς, that very complex term that combines modesty, shame and honor, does not occur.

9 Lazare 1987: 1653–1658.

able to the gaze and knowledge of others (1655); doctors, too, he suggested, may feel shame when they fail to diagnose or treat a disease successfully (1656). Moreover, feelings of shame may not be obvious: shame may hinder the patient from seeking medical care at all, or a patient may hide their shame through expressions of anger or by becoming subdued (1655–1656). Lazare argued that every disease, whether physical or psychological, has the potential to cause shame, even if it is not immediately apparent, and that therefore the physician "should assume that any disease (and treatment) can be a shame-inducing event which then interacts with a patient's individual vulnerabilities" (1656).

Lazare's analysis is situated within the context of modern biomedicine, with many examples drawn from the milieu of the clinic and the hospital. Yet he also describes physical responses to feelings of shame that may be more universal:

> Accompanying autonomic reactions may include blushing, fainting, sweating, burning, freezing, and a sense of weakness. On a cognitive level there is a painful awareness of oneself as defeated, deficient, exposed, a failure, inadequate, wanting, worthless, and wounded. The deficiency seems all pervasive. The very essence of the self feels wrong. The person feels alone and estranged from the world; there seems no way to redress the situation. He or she wants to sink through the floor, disappear, or cease to exist. (1654).

Later, Lazare notes that adaptive (or maladaptive) reactions to the experience of shame include laughter, humor, avoidance, lying or hiding. Especially with regard to the hiding response, he writes: "Shame ... acts as an emotional wall or boundary around a person serving as a protection against violations, assaults, or incursions against the self" (1655). Because shame may inhibit successful treatment, Lazare urged doctors to be attentive to feelings of shame in their patients and in themselves, and suggested some ways to manage and ameliorate this emotion.

Lazare's work points to the importance of recognizing the presence of shame even when it is not verbalized. Indeed, research on emotions in recent years has shown the importance of moving beyond the pure lexical approach (that is to say, identifying words for given emotions and examining the contexts in which they are used) and taking up what have been called "scripts" (Kaster 2005: 8–10):[10] with this method, we "read" a scenario and try to understand its

---

[10] And see further especially Chapter 2 in Kaster (2005); cf. also Sanders 2014: especially 4–6 on the benefits and potential limitations of the script-based approach; and Cairns (2008), who demonstrates the value of scripts in trying to understand emotions across cultures and argues that, given that it is through language that we try to discern and understand emotions, "The best we can do is to use our language to interpret theirs, with the fullest possible attention to

emotional underpinnings, the mix of emotions felt and expressed or sometimes suppressed. Sometimes these emotions are named, but they also have to be interpreted based on the gestures and actions of the individuals involved. Furthermore, some gestures have an almost universal meaning (the facial response to disgust, for example, according to Lateiner and Spatharas' work);[11] others are much more culturally contingent. The range of possible emotions communicated by a given gesture provides additional challenges: so, for example, throwing up one's arms can indicate gleeful surprise or shocked anger; turning away can occur out of sadness, anger or disgust; concealing one's face can hide amusement, shame, guilt, or anger. Reading emotions can be all the more challenging when we are attempting to do so not in a living human standing before us but through the medium of literary or visual artifacts of the past.[12] And even within a culture, we may misread the emotion that lies behind a gesture. Indeed, because, as Chiara Thumiger points out, the emotion of shame "has stronger social constructedness than anger and fear," it is necessary to look beyond lexical cues to spot behavioral signs that indicate feelings of shame may be present.[13] In fact, we often see the Greek medical writers themselves doing exactly the same thing: that is to say, while these writers may explicitly mention an emotion like fear in a list of symptoms, and thus interpret the presence of the emotion directly, they also note gestures, actions or speeches that they deem meaningful in some way for understanding the patient's illness and his or her emotional register.[14] The writers in the Hippocratic Corpus do not always say or perhaps even cannot interpret exactly what the gestures portend, just as they do not know what every other symptom they record means in a given case. However, when it comes to shame, as we shall see, these writers are willing to admit to its role as a motivating factor in their own lives, but they are more reticent about reading it into the experiences of their patients.

---

the diversity of the data regarding the scenarios to which the terms of both languages refer" (58).

11 Lateiner and Spatharas 2017: 8.

12 Cf., for example, Gertsman (2010), who argues against Ekman's thesis that facial expressions reliably communicate certain emotions across cultures, maintaining instead that the facial gestures in gothic art are often ambiguous and must be interpreted within the context of the communities that produced them.

13 Thumiger 2017: 359.

14 Thumiger (2017b) discusses how the medical writers intermingle behavioral, psychological, and physiological signs in the course of their observations; thus, emotions are often read by ancient medical observers as one sign among many of some (often mysterious) underlying pathology.

In considering shame in classical Greek medicine, we also have to reckon with the fact that our evidence is largely one-sided and confined by the reporting of the medical authors; thus, much of what we have access to is limited to the medical encounter and the healer's perspective. The behavior of patients prior to or after the meeting with the physician — the symptoms of shame, behaviors of avoidance, reluctant disclosure — are not easy to access. Although the medical writers report what they themselves do not see directly but have been told by the patient or third-parties, such reports typically blend with the healer's own observations and ideas.[15] Thus, while other genres of classical Greek literature can provide a framework for interpretation and help to legitimate certain readings, the medical encounter itself is potentially fraught with shame that will not be articulated. As Luna Dolezal explains, "Revealing that one is experiencing shame, through blushing, trembling, stuttering, etc., is *itself* shameful ... As a result, shame is an emotion that is often fastidiously avoided and if that is not possible, it is to be scrupulously ignored and unacknowledged."[16] An analysis of shame in classical Greek medicine must largely be filtered through the healer's perspective and within the setting of the clinical encounter; nonetheless, given the paucity of direct references to shame in the medical literature, evidence from other genres can also inform the reading of emotional "scripts" in the effort to understand the place of shame in Greek experiences of disease.

2 Patients: Veiling, Wrapping, and Withdrawal

Let us look at the well-known passage in *On the Sacred Disease* that speaks of the shame felt by experienced sufferers of epileptic attacks.

---

15 For a detailed analysis of the complex entanglement of these different perspectives, see Thumiger 2016a.
16 Dolezal 2015: 570.

Ὅσοι δὲ ἤδη ἐθάδες εἰσὶ τῇ νούσῳ, προγινώσκουσιν ὅταν μέλλωσι ληφθήσεσθαι, καὶ φεύγουσιν ἐκ τῶν ἀνθρώπων· ἢν μὲν ἐγγὺς ᾖ αὐτῷ τὰ οἰκία, οἴκαδε, εἰ δὲ μὴ, ἐς τὸ ἐρημότατον, ὅπῃ μέλλουσιν αὐτὸν ἐλάχιστοι ὄψεσθαι πεσόντα, εὐθύς τε ἐγκαλύπτεται. τοῦτο δὲ ποιεῖ ὑπ' αἰσχύνης τοῦ πάθεος, καὶ οὐχ ὑπὸ φόβου, ὡς οἱ πολλοὶ νομίζουσι, τοῦ δαιμονίου. τὰ δὲ παιδάρια τὸ μὲν πρῶτον πίπτουσιν ὅπῃ ἂν τύχωσιν ὑπὸ ἀηθίης· ὅταν δὲ πλεονάκις κατάληπτοι γένωνται, ἐπειδὰν προαίσθωνται, φεύγουσι παρὰ τὰς μητέρας ἢ παρὰ ἄλλον ὅντινα μάλιστα γινώσκουσιν, ὑπὸ δέους καὶ φόβου τῆς πάθης· τὸ γὰρ αἰσχύνεσθαι παῖδες ὄντες οὔπω γινώσκουσιν.

Sacred Disease 12 Jouanna (6.382–384 L.)

Those who are already accustomed to the disease recognize when they are about to be seized, and they flee from their fellow humans; if they are near their home, they flee home, but if not, to the most private place where they are going to be least likely to be seen when they fall, and right away they veil themselves. The patient does this because of shame about the disease, and not from fear of the divine, as many think. Little children initially fall wherever they happen to be out of inexperience; but when they are attacked more times, whenever they have a premonition, they run to their mothers or anyone else whom they know well, out of dread and fear of the disease; for as children they do not yet know the feeling of shame.

my translation

This passage contains, to my knowledge, the most direct statement connecting disease and shame in the Hippocratic Corpus; the shame in this case seems to result from the lack of self-control that forces the sufferer to fall to the ground (no other symptoms are mentioned in this passage). The fact that it is a chronic condition (though of course treatable in the eyes of the treatise's author!) actually enables the patients to manage the feelings of shame, since over time they learn to get out of sight and veil themselves. The degree of shame is apparently so strong that simply seeking privacy is not sufficient: the sufferer must veil him or herself as well. The author's attention to the psychology of shame and fear is noteworthy: he suggests that shame is a learned emotion, dependent on social experience, whereas fear is an emotion naturally felt by both adults and children. Children are initially afraid because of fear of the unknown; later, when they have developed the knowledge to anticipate what is about to happen, they are still afraid of the event itself. Yet older people, the author insists — in contrast to what is apparently the most common interpretation (ὡς οἱ πολλοὶ νομίζουσι) — do not feel fear, but shame. Their experience helps them to avoid fear, but recognize that suffering an attack of the disease is a shameful experience. It is unclear precisely why the attack is shameful, but in the context of this passage, it is likely connected either with the loss of self-control (falling to the ground), since self-control is so privileged in Greek society, or out of a sense that on-lookers may feel the sufferer is being attacked by the gods in response to some improper action or omission. Additional evidence from both this and later authors suggests a further possibility: in *Sacred Disease* 7, the sufferer appears not only out of control (with hands that aren't under control [ἀκρατέες], and involuntary bowel movements) but also grotesque (foam at the mouth, distorted eyes, teeth locked), and it is this latter issue of grotesquerie that draws the particular attention of Aretaeus of Cappadocia, who deplores how the disease, which he endows with a malicious envy, destroys young people by taking away their youthful beauty (ἀπόλλυσι τοὺς παῖδας φθόνῳ τοῦ κάλλεος, ἢ χειρὸς ἀκρασίῃ, ἢ προσώπου διαστροφῇ, ἢ πηρώσει τινὸς αἰσθήσιος, "[the disease] destroys youth in envy of their beauty, either through loss of use of a hand, or the deformity of the face or the disabling of a sense," p. 38 Hude). He later writes that he believes if epileptic sufferers "ever were to look at one another in the midst of the paroxysms, they would not endure to live" (εἴπερ ἐς ἀλλήλους ἐν τοῖσι παροξυσμοῖσι ἐνέβλεπον ... οὐκ ἂν ἔτι ζώειν τλαῖεν ἄν, p. 152 Hude).[17] Aretaeus' emphasis on the ugliness imposed by the disease provides another source of shame for these sufferers. They therefore seek privacy, but even in a private setting, they also veil themselves.

Let us consider the issue of veiling a little more fully. Does the author's insistence that the sufferers veil themselves from shame conflict with the possibility that sufferers, now out of sight, are still concerned with a ritual necessity of veiling, in fact out of fear of the gods? Or does the act suggest that the social identity of the sufferer is threatened even when not seen by others, in an internalization of shame?[18] These adults have interiorized the standards of the community that sees falling to the ground in the absence of obvious external causes as a shameful thing.[19] The author claims that the disease is a disease like any other (*i.e.*, that it is caused by an excess, deficiency or corruption of a given humor), but in his insistence that the sufferers veil themselves from shame, he is acknowledging that the *hierê nosos* still causes social problems even for experienced patients. The gesture of veiling is, as Douglas Cairns has argued, less marked for women, who were typically veiled in Greek societies, than for men, who veiled under exceptional circumstances and signaled thereby feelings of

---

17 I owe thanks to George Kazantzidis for the reference to Aretaeus in demonstrating additional reasons for the shame experienced by sufferers of the sacred disease.
18 Thumiger (2016b) remarks on the different perspectives brought to bear in this passage: the rationalistic optimism of the writer versus the external reader, for whom "the passage speaks equally of the fear that comes with the patient's personal 'prognosis', his or her projection of the attack, and the limitations to what reason can do to master it" (214).
19 On the complex issues of exterior pressure and internalization of *mores*, especially with regard to veiling and shame, see discussion in Llewellyn-Jones 2003: 155–188, who also draws especially upon Cairns (1993) on *aidôs*.

grief, shame or anger.[20] In his discussion of veiling on the tragic stage in particular, Cairns concludes: "Veiling is a remarkably versatile symbolic gesture: it marks a number of transitions and crises, both emotional and ritual. The crucial common ground in its manifestations is the issue of social status and identity; the use of the veil typically constitutes a visible, symbolic marker of a scenario in which a person's social self and public identity are challenged or threatened."[21] Cairns' analysis underscores the need to pay close attention to the use of veiling in *On the Sacred Disease*, and, indeed, throughout the Hippocratic Corpus. For veiling is not only a meaningful gesture, but its meaning is different depending on the individual who veils: Greek women typically wore veils "in public situations or in the presence of men,"[22] whereas men did not. As we have seen, the author connects the veiling with shame, but it should be noted that the sufferers, who are not distinguished by gender, veil themselves even in private. If the sufferers are women, their heads would normally be covered in public, so removing themselves to a private place and veiling in this situation would be more a case of remaining veiled. By contrast, for men, veiling is a marked gesture, and, indeed, as Llewellyn-Jones suggests, occurs "when their masculinity is compromised ... The veil acts as a symbolic barrier and separates the emotional man from the rest of his society; in effect it turns a man into a woman, because it makes him socially invisible".[23] Llewellyn-Jones adds that the response to a veiled man is often to try to persuade him to unveil, thus moving him back into his proper social position.[24] The passage in *On the Sacred Disease* thus prompts a number of questions: is withdrawal or, more explicitly, veiling in the context of illness always triggered by feelings of shame, as the author of *On the Sacred Disease* maintains for the *hierê nosos*? Does the gender of the patient (not distinguished in this passage) make a difference? Or do medical writers connect the gesture of veiling to a wider range of emotions or concerns? Or is the patient's experience sometimes not marked, at least by the observer, by emotion at all?

The lexical issues here are arguably important. In *On the Sacred Disease*, the verb chosen to express the act of covering, ἐγκαλύπτειν, has specific nuances; καλύπτειν and its compounds when used to describe a patient or healer's actions indicate covering the head or face — that is to say, veiling, which is both

---

[20] Cairns 2011: 22.
[21] Cairns 2011: 26.
[22] Llewellyn-Jones 2003: 12.
[23] Llewellyn-Jones 2003: 17.
[24] Llewellyn-Jones 2003: 17.

an act of covering and a display of covering.²⁵ These verbs are not especially common in the Corpus, in comparison to words for covering, wrapping and applying such as κρύπτειν, περιστέλλειν, ἐπιβάλλειν and ἐπιτίθημι.²⁶ Healers recommend wrapping or covering patients in order to facilitate treatments requiring heat or salves.²⁷ However, even self-wrapping or self-covering is unusual; rather, patients are said to throw off their clothes or uncover themselves, often because they are too hot but also as a sign of mental distress.²⁸ But in one case history, a woman is said to have 'kept herself wrapped up' (περιεστέλλετο) in the course of an illness caused by grief: "In Thasos, the wife of Delearces, who lay sick on the plain, was seized after a grief with an acute fever with shivering. From the beginning she would wrap herself up" (ἐν Θάσῳ Δελεάρκεος γυναῖκα, ἣ κατέκειτο ἐπὶ τοῦ λείου, πυρετὸς φρικώδης, ὀξὺς ἐκ λύπης ἔλαβεν. ἐξ ἀρχῆς δὲ περιεστέλλετο, *Epid.* 3.17, case 15 [3.142 L.], trans. Jones). The mention of grief pushes us to attribute the self-wrapping to emotional distress, but the author also discusses the wrapping directly after the symptoms of "acute fever with shivering", so he may be more interested in her chill. In *Epid.* 2.2.22 (5.94 L.), another woman who suffers multiple painful symptoms was 'out of her mind' (παρεφέρετο) and 'kept herself wrapped up' (περιεστέλλετο), but no particular emotion is mentioned. However, *Epidemics* 7 includes two lengthy descriptions of sick women who are specifically said to veil themselves (the chosen verb is ξυνκαλυπτέσθαι). The fascinating details of the sad story of Hermoptolemus' wife (*Epid.* 7.11 [5.382–386 L.]) include unintelligible speech, wild

---

25 Interestingly, when not used for human actions, this word-group is used of the skin — skin covers or conceals the inner parts of the body. One notable example is *Loc. Hom.* 10.1 (6.294 L.), where the author describes the windpipe as especially vulnerable to cold because it is not 'veiled' (τὸ εὔροον γίνεται ἐς τὸν βρόγχον, ὥστε οὐδὲ συγκεκαλυμμένον). The link between vulnerability and the choice of verb for covering is, I think, significant.

26 The *CHC* shows 27 occurrences for all variants of this word: they include ἀμφικαλύπτειν, ἀνακαλύπτειν, ἐγκαλύπτειν, κατακάλυπτειν, περικαλύπτειν, συγκάλυπτειν, along with the nouns κάλυμμα and καλυπτήρ in *Haem.* 4 (6.440 L.), referring to a covering made by the skin and to a kind of medical instrument (a speculum, according to Potter *ad loc.*). It should be noted that the verb ἀποκαλύπτειν, to unveil, so very important in various Greek rituals, does not occur in the Hippocratic Corpus.

27 Wrapping for treatment: e.g., *Acut. Sp.* 8 (2.424 L.); *Acut. Sp.* 8 (2.428 L.); *Morb.* 2.22 (7.36–38 L.); wrapping to induce sweat: *Int. Aff.* 27 (7.236–240 L.); *Morb.* 2.42 (7.58–60 L.); *Morb.* 2.43 (7.60 L.); at *Epid.* 2.6.31 (5.138 L.), the healer is instructed to have his patient "wrap himself" as part of a treatment for fever. The vocabulary of such covering and wrapping includes, for both men and women, active verbs such as περιστέλλειν, ἀμφιβάλλειν, περιβάλλειν, ἀμφιέννυναι, and καταπλάττειν.

28 For a discussion of removing clothes or blankets, see Thumiger 2017: 154–155 and 324.

talk, sometimes throwing off the covering (τὸ ἱμάτιον ἔστιν ὅτε ἀπερρίπτει), weeping like a child, fears (δείματα), frights (ξυγκαλύπτσθαι), anger, 'inappropriate behavior' (τὸ παράκαιρον), and 'drawing her body together and veiling herself' (ξυνάγειν τὸ σῶμα, καὶ ξυγκαλύπτεσθαι); on the very last day, however, the writer notes that she had quiet periods, 'without veiling herself' (ἄνευ τοῦ ξυγκεκαλύφθαι). The wife of Theodorus (*Epid.* 7.25 [5.394–398 L.]) suffered terrible pain in her chest, some delirium and fever; she spoke irrationally on several occasions, and on what appears to have been her final day, she kept reaching her hand toward the wall or towards the blankets; finally, "she plucked at the blankets and veiled her face" (καὶ ἐκροκυδολόγει, καὶ ξυνεκάλυπτε τὸ πρόσωπον) and later that day she died. These two women appear to be observed within the private home setting, and the writer clearly has some of the information provided to him by their respective companions.[29] Hence both the veiling and unveiling are marked gestures, meaningful because they are occurring when atypical. Is it possible to read any emotion in these two scripts? In the case of *Epid.* 7.11, the writer tracks the emotions of the patient, mentioning both fear and anger, but also speaks of inappropriate speech; it is possible the woman is veiling from shame at her behavior, but it is hard to be sure. In *Epid.* 7.25, the writer speaks less clearly of the woman's emotion, but the veiling, so near to her death, may indicate deep sadness or mourning for her own impending death.

While acts of self-covering in the Hippocratic Corpus are rare, self-veiling *per se* is rarer still; and for men, it may not happen (or at least be described) at all. In only one case in the *Epidemics* is there a clear instance where a man has covered his face (and thereafter uncovered it), but, perhaps significantly, no verb is used — there is no explicit veiling involved here:

καὶ ἤδη τι ὑποπαρέκρουε, καὶ νοτὶς ἐπ' ὀλίγον ἔστιν ὅτε περὶ μέτωπον· τὸ ἱμάτιον ἐπὶ τὸ πρόσωπον· τὰ ὄμματα διὰ κενῆς ὡς εἴ τι βλέπων ξυνέστρεφε, καὶ πάλιν κατέμυεν· τὸ ἱμάτιον ἀπέβαλλεν.

Epid. 7.83 (5.440 L.)

At that time he became somewhat delirious, and had dampness briefly sometimes about the forehead. He covered over his face. He moved his eyes about emptily, like one glancing about, and again nodded off. He would throw the bedclothes off.

trans. W.D. Smith, LCL 477, 360–61

---

29 See, for example, in *Epid.* 7.11 (5.382–386 L.), where "they" could not take the drink away from the woman (ἀποσπάσαι οὐκ ἐδύναντο); and in *Epid.* 7.25 (5.394–398 L.), the woman upbraids those present (τοῖσι παροῦσιν ἐλοιδορεῖτο). On the roles of "other people present", see King 1998: 166–168.

Here, as I read it, the covering has more to do with the moisture and sweating that the patient suffers than with his emotional state.[30] Thus, apart from the important case of the *hierê nosos*, self-*veiling* seems largely to be a "women's" issue, and the gesture reveals a woman's emotional condition. Men are socially conditioned not to veil, and so they do not do so, except in very specific circumstances, such as an attack of the sacred disease, with its many cultural and, indeed, mythical resonances.[31]

If veiling is rare, withdrawing or pulling away from company is a little more common. Thus, while the act of patients lying down or becoming bedridden is common and seems largely unmarked emotionally, for a couple men, this act may indeed signify something about their emotional state: in *Epidemics* 7.85 (5.444 L.), Androthales is said to 'take to his bed', for the winter and to have 'lost himself' (τέλος δέ, χειμῶνος κατακλιθείς, ἐξ ἑωυτοῦ ἐγένετο), while in *Epidemics* 7.89 (5.446 L.; cf. *Epid.* 5.84 [5.252 L.]), Parmeniscus, who is clearly described as having depression and desire for death, is also said to have "taken to his bed" and to have become voiceless: "Parmeniscus had previously been affected by depression and desire for death, and then again by optimism. One time in Olynthus in the fall he took to his bed, voiceless" (Παρμενίσκῳ καὶ πρότερον ἐνέπιπτον ἀθυμίαι καὶ ἵμερος ἀπαλλαγῆς βίου,[32] ὁτὲ δὲ πάλιν εὐθυμίη. ἐν Ὀλύνθῳ δέ ποτε φθινοπώρου ἄφωνος κατέκειτο ἡσυχίην ἔχων, trans. Smith, 368–369). If these patients are feeling shame or are withdrawing out of shame, these passages do not draw attention to this emotion; instead the withdrawals

---

30 At *Epid.* 3.1, case 3 (3.42 L.), a man is said 'to have wrapped himself up' (περιεστέλλετο), but the writer mentions this action directly after he observes that the patient 'felt cold in his extremities' (ἄκρεα ψυχρά), so it seems likely that the wrapping is an attempt to feel warm rather than to conceal or express an emotion.

31 On the history and social significance of this disease, see the discussion in Jouanna's introduction to his edition of the text (2003: esp. xxii–xxiv and 1–li); for the connection with Heracles especially, see von Staden 1992 and Holmes 2008.

32 This is an odd use of ἀπαλλαγή for a writer in the Hippocratic Corpus: normally this word and its cognates refer to the escape from or exiting of disease. By contrast, this phrase is remarkably close to one in Euripides' *Hippolytus* that describes the Nurse's desire for death upon hearing of Phaedra's love for Hippolytus: ἀπαλλαχθήσομαι βίου θανοῦσα (356–357; "in death I will have been released from life"). The Nurse also describes Phaedra's efforts to die with a similar phrase, stating that Phaedra is making herself sick "for the purpose of rejecting life" (εἰς ἀπόστασιν βίου, 277). The many connections between the mental illnesses of tragedy and those of the Hippocratic Corpus are beyond the scope of this paper, but this verbal similarity seems very strong to me, and may indicate that the writer is influenced by tragic portrayals of illness in his description of Parmeniscus.

are associated with sadness and loss of self — perhaps the loss of self to a degree that is immune to shame.[33]

3 Shame and the Medical Practitioner

To summarize the analysis thus far, the medical writers arguably accord a diverse set of associations to the actions of withdrawal and veiling in their patients: they do not necessarily signify shame, but may also indicate sadness or despair or despondency. What about the emotions of the healers themselves? As noted earlier, shame on the part of the healer may also play an important role in the clinical encounter. Thus, the treatise *Prorrhetics II* urges the healer not to be surprised or afraid of certain symptoms when treating patients suffering from wounds:

> ἀλλὰ χρὴ μήτε ταῦτα θαυμάζειν, μήτε ὀρρωδέειν κεῖνα, εἰδότα ὅτι αἱ ψυχαί τε καὶ τὰ σώματα πλεῖστον διαφέρουσιν αἱ τῶν ἀνθρώπων, καὶ δύναμιν ἔχουσι μεγίστην. ὅσα μὲν οὖν τῶν τραυμάτων καιροῦ ἔτυχεν, ἢ σώματός τε καὶ γνώμης τοιαύτης, ἢ ὀργῶντος οὕτω τοῦ σώματος, ἢ μέγεθος τοσαῦτα ἦν ὥστε μὴ δύνασθαι καταστῆναι τὸν ἄνθρωπον †εἰς τὴν ἴησιν καταφρονέοντα,† τοῖσι μὲν ἐξίστασθαι χρὴ ὁποῖα ἂν ᾖ, πλὴν τῶν ἐφημέρων λειποθυμιῶν,
>
> *Prorrhetics* 2.12 (9.34–36 L.)

> But you should neither be surprised by the latter nor dread the former, being aware that the minds and the bodies of people differ very greatly, and that these differences have great consequences. Now whenever wounds reach a danger point, when body and mind are in this condition, or if the body is inflamed in the way mentioned, or if in magnitude the wound is such that the person cannot recover ... these you must abandon as they are, except for cases of ephemeral fainting spells.
>
> trans. P. Potter, *LCL* 482, 248–249

We might note, however, that the passage pitches the experience of these emotions in negative terms: that is, the writer urges healers *not* to feel these emotions. Indeed, the idea that healers should train themselves not to feel emotions, despite their involvement in what the author of *Breaths* terms 'distasteful things' (ἀηδέα, 1 [6.90 L.]), is an assumption present throughout much of the Corpus. As Kazantzidis has shown with regard to the emotion of disgust, the

---

[33] For more on the emotional state of Parmeniscus, see Thumiger 2017: 364–365, who argues that his "is the fullest example of a case resembling depression both in its emotional features and for the chronic and resilient character of the ailment".

writers of the Hippocratic Corpus recognize the potential to share emotions with their patients but develop a kind of disembodied stance (as Brooke Holmes puts it) that allows them to treat their patients without expressing their emotions.[34] To be sure, the author of *Prorrhetics II* also suggests that it is acceptable to abandon the patient in incurable cases.[35] At the same time, the writers recognize that the emotional support to patients provided by the doctor can be helpful to the patients' well-being:[36] as the writer of *Precepts* argues when urging his fellow healers to treat patients with kindness and generosity,

> ἔνιοι γὰρ νοσέοντες ᾐσθημένοι τὸ περὶ ἑωυτοὺς πάθος μὴ ἐὸν ἐν ἀσφαλείῃ, καὶ τῇ τοῦ ἰητροῦ ἐπιεικείῃ εὐδοκέουσι, μεταλλάσσοντες ἐς ὑγιείην
>
> 6 (9.258 L.)
>
> For some patients, though conscious that their condition is perilous, recover their health simply through their contentment with the goodness of the physician.
>
> trans. W.H.S. Jones, *LCL* 147, 318–319

Thus, healers pay attention to the emotions of their patients because they understand from their own human vantage point the effects that emotions can have on human illness. Such fellow feeling from doctors on behalf of their patients may explain why we see the most attention to the sense of disgrace — an emotion that attends shame — in the surgical treatises. These treatises are particularly public in their focus: both *Fractures* and *Joints* mention the pressure of the public opinion (even occasionally giving in to public expectations),[37] while *Joints* insists that practicing medicine that makes the patient well is 'more honorable' (ἀνδραγαθικώτερον), even if the measures used are humble (78 [4.312 L.]). Both treatises push for proper treatment over appearances, asserting that poor treatment brings disgrace to the art of medicine. So, for example, the author of *Fractures* writes: "Other mechanisms also should either be well arranged or not used, for it is shameful and contrary to the art to make a machine and get no mechanical effect" (χρὴ δὲ καὶ τὰς ἄλλας μηχανὰς ἢ καλῶς μηχανᾶσθαι, ἢ μὴ μηχανᾶσθαι· αἰσχρὸν γὰρ καὶ ἄτεχνον μηχανοποιέοντα ἀμηχανοποιέεσθαι (30 [3.524 L.], trans. Withington, *LCL* 149, 68–69); and in *Joints*, we are told: "but it is disgraceful in any art, and especially in medicine, to make a parade of much trouble, display and talk, and then do no good" (αἰσχρὸν μέντοι καὶ ἐν πάσῃ

---

34 Kazantzidis 2017: 61; Holmes 2013, esp. 432–433.
35 On this issue, see von Staden 1990.
36 For comparison, see Paez, Dario et al. 1995.
37 For susceptibility (and resistance) to public pressure, see e.g. *Fract.* 16 (3.476 L.) and *Artic.* 1 (4.78–80 L.).

τέχνῃ καὶ οὐχ ἥκιστα ἐν ἰητρικῇ πουλὺν ὄχλον, καὶ πολλὴν ὄψιν, καὶ πουλὺν λόγον παρασχόντα, ἔπειτα μηδὲν ὠφελῆσαι, 44 [4.188 L.], trans. Withington *LCL* 149, 288-289). While such passages indicate sensitivity to the pride of the healer, there are also passages that recognize that some treatments may challenge the patients' sense of pride or propriety: for example, *Joints* 64 (4.274 L.) acknowledges that the necessary avoidance of reduction will result in lameness and concomitantly a σχῆμα αἰσχρόν ('shameful form') for the patient. It should be noted that, amidst all this concern for patients' feelings and proper medical treatment, there is a passage in *Joints* that seems to criticize first the healers and thereafter the patients for avoiding short term pain in order to obtain an aesthetically pleasing result: in a section describing the treatment of a broken nose (37 [4.166 L.]), the author claims that quick, vigorous reconstitution of the nose is best, but apparently some doctors 'hold back' (καταβλακεύσουσιν) and do the procedure 'more gently than necessary' (ἀπαλωτέρως ... ἢ ὡς χρὴ) while some patients resist this treatment, since they care less for their appearance than for avoiding pain: "But while men will give much to avoid being ugly (αἰσχροί), they do not know how to combine care with endurance, unless they suffer pain or fear death" (ἀλλὰ γὰρ οἱ ἄνθρωποι αἰσχροὶ μὲν εἶναι πολλοῦ ἀποτιμῶνται, μελετᾶν δὲ ἅμα μὲν οὐκ ἐπίστανται, ἅμα δὲ οὐ τολμέουσιν, ἢν μὴ ὀδυνέωνται, ἢ θάνατον δεδοίκωσιν, trans. Withington, *LCL* 149, 271). The writer rebukes the patients for not having the hardiness to endure short term pain for the gain of a good-looking nose in the long term; he also implies that the healers are not doing their job since they shrink from causing their patients short-term (and not deathly) pain that will benefit them socially in the long run.

One final passage of special interest appears to combine the shame of the patients with the errors of the healers. This passage, from *Diseases of Women*, has received much attention because of what it may reveal about women's knowledge and women's relationship to healers,[38] but it is also worth reminding ourselves that it discusses women's feelings of shame:

καὶ ἔστιν ὅτε τῇσι μὴ γινωσκούσῃσιν ὑφ' ὅτευ νοσεῦσι φθάνει τὰ νοσήματα ἀνίητα γινόμενα, πρὶν ἂν διδαχθῆναι τὸν ἰητρὸν ὀρθῶς ὑπὸ τῆς νοσεούσης ὑφ' ὅτου νοσέει· καὶ γὰρ αἰδέονται φράζειν, κἢν εἰδῶσι, καὶ σφιν δοκέουσιν αἰσχρὸν εἶναι ὑπὸ ἀπειρίης καὶ ἀνεπιστημοσύνης. ἅμα δὲ καὶ οἱ ἰητροὶ ἁμαρτάνουσιν, οὐκ ἀτρεκέως πυνθανόμενοι τὴν πρόφασιν τῆς νούσου, ἀλλ' ὡς τὰ ἀνδρικὰ νοσήματα ἰώμενοι· καὶ πολλὰς εἶδον διεφθαρμένας ἤδη

---

38 On the complicated interactions between female patients and male doctors, especially with regard to this passage in *Diseases of Women* 1, see, e.g., Lloyd 1983: 70-79; King 1998: 47-49, 138.

ὑπὸ τοιούτων παθημάτων. ἀλλὰ χρὴ ἀνερωτᾶν αὐτίκα ἀτρεκέως τὸ αἴτιον· διαφέρει γὰρ ἡ ἴησις πολλῷ τῶν γυναικηΐων νοσημάτων καὶ τῶν ἀνδρῶν.

Mul. 1.62 [8.126 L.]

Sometimes diseases become incurable for women who do not learn why they are sick before the doctor has been correctly taught by the sick woman why she is sick. For women are ashamed to tell even if they know, and they suppose that it is a disgrace, because of their inexperience and lack of knowledge. At the same time the doctors also make mistakes by not learning the apparent cause through accurate questioning, but they proceed to heal as though they were dealing with men's diseases. I have already seen many women die from just this kind of suffering. But at the outset one must ask accurate questions about the cause. For the healing of the diseases of women differs greatly from the healing of men's diseases.

trans. Ann Hanson [1975], p. 582

There is a noticeable tension in this passage in the allocation of responsibility: the writer states that women are ashamed of what they are suffering because they don't know what is happening to them. The treatise implicates both their misunderstanding of their own bodies, in particular their lack of knowledge about diseases that arise from menstruation, and the shame that arises from that — a shame that perhaps arises from multiple sources: a sense of estrangement from their own bodies in the event of menstruation, the need to conceal the strange event, since they don't realize that it is common to menstruate or common to have problems with menstruation. The fact that we are learning about these issues from the male writer of the treatise also poses problems for interpretation: can we trust him to represent accurately what the women thought or felt? In any case, the situation as described creates considerable tension over the issue of responsibility: if the woman doesn't know what the problem is, then she can hardly be blamed for not communicating the problem to the healer; if, however, she is aware but conceals the truth, then the healer cannot act accordingly. The woman's failure to communicate her symptoms properly causes the healer to fail since he is not acting on the basis of accurate information; however, the writer also assigns responsibility to the healer who makes mistakes by not investigating properly and by making improper assumptions. Are those mistakes also causes for shame? Perhaps so: after all, while the writers of the Hippocratic Corpus do not blame the worthy healer for making small mistakes (cf., e.g. *Vet. Med.* 9 [1.290 L.], 12 [1.596 L.]; *Precepts* 8 [9.262 L.]), they also take pride in their professional practices and standards.[39] If a healer

---

[39] Of course, these practices and standards were hotly debated; ancient medicine was a competitive business. See Lloyd 1979, esp. 37–49 and 89–98; Nutton 1992, esp. 16–29.

makes a mistake based on deeply flawed assumptions, as here, this would be cause for recrimination and resultant feelings of disgrace and shame.

To conclude, then: in the Hippocratic Corpus we see feelings of shame explicitly associated with the patient's loss of self-control and susceptibility to a particular disease (the *hierê nosos*), and permanent disfigurement, as discussed in *Fractures* and *Joints*, and with both healer's and patient's lack of courage and lack of knowledge. Except for the sacred disease (and even in that case, the medical writer seems eager to remove that shame through naturalizing and normalizing the disease), just having a disease or becoming sick does not appear to be a source of shame; even when the medical writers mention patient behavior, such as disobedience or intemperance, that might cause or exacerbate the illness, they do not indicate that the patients feel shame, or should feel shame, because of their actions.[40] The unusual focus on shame in *On the Sacred Disease* helps to underscore the extraordinary role this disease, the *hierê nosos*, played in Greek culture, with its many mythical and religious resonances; it is certainly exceptional.[41] There are passages in the Hippocratic Corpus describing illnesses that, given what we know about the Greek male's desire for self-sufficiency and self-control or the high value accorded to women's privacy and modesty, might well have been quite embarrassing — such as Nicanor's fear of flute girls (*Epid* 7.86 [5.444 L.]; cf. *Epid*. 5.81 [5.250 L.]) or the man from Olynthus who suffered from δεινὴ ἐκλύσις ('terrible bodily disorder', *Epid*. 7.80 [5.436 L.]) or Androthales, who couldn't speak and who had to be brought outside by others to urinate (*Epid*. 7.85 [5.444 L.]; cf. *Epid*. 5.80 [5.248–249 L.]) or Democles, who seemed to 'lose control of his body' (λυσισωματεῖν, *Epid*. 7.87 [5.444 L.]; cf. *Epid*. 5.82 [5.250 L.]),[42] or even the young man who in his delirium used foul language when he wasn't that sort of person (αἰσχρομυθέειν ἰσχυρῶς, οὐ τοιοῦτος ἐών, *Epid*. 4.15 [5.152 L.]); likewise, the myriad observations of the woman's αἰδοῖα ('genitals') in the gynecological texts and elsewhere might have

---

40 They do occasionally indicate their particular approval of patient behavior, by calling a patient *kosmios*; see further Thumiger 2017: 168 with notes 197 and 198.

41 The symptoms accorded to male characters suffering from madness in Greek tragedy, such as Ajax in Sophocles' *Ajax* or Heracles in Euripides' *Heracles*, coincide with many of the symptoms described in *On the Sacred Disease*. However, the tragic characters do have the capacity to speak, which is a significant difference (cf. von Staden 1992); and they also take shame to an extreme, by expressing a desire to die (in the case of Heracles) or by actually committing suicide (in the case of Ajax). Nevertheless, the emphasis on shame experienced by males who suffer any sort of malady in tragic texts contrasts strongly with the absence of shame accorded to patients in most of the treatises of the Hippocratic Corpus.

42 On Nicanor and Democles' social problems, see King 2013.

occasioned shame or at least reticence on the part of the woman (and the term itself, αἰδοῖα, suggests this would be so!).[43] Examples abound — but again, the writers of the Hippocratic Corpus do not appear to read shame in these situations. If such patients felt shame, these writers aren't telling.

Bibliography

Texts and translations for the Hippocratic Corpus:

Hippocrate. *De l'ancienne médecine (Vet. Med.)*. Ed. J. Jouanna. *Collection des Universités de France*, Tome I. Paris: Les Belles Lettres, 1990.
Hippocrate. *De l'art. (de Arte)*. Ed. J. Jouanna. *Collection des Universités de France*, Tome V 1, 165–280. Paris: Les Belles Lettres, 1988.
Hippocrate. *Des vents. (Flat.)* Ed. J. Jouanna. *Collection des Universités de France*, Tome V 1. Paris: Les Belles Lettres, 1988.
Hippocrates. *Epidemics II. (Epid. 2)*. Ed. W.D. Smith. *Loeb Classical Library* 477. Cambridge, Massachusetts: Harvard University Press, 1994.
Hippocrates. *Epidemics IV. (Epid. 4)*. Ed. W.D. Smith. *Loeb Classical Library* 477. Cambridge, Massachusetts: Harvard University Press, 1994.
Hippocrates. *Epidemics V. (Epid. 5)*. Ed. W.D. Smith. *Loeb Classical Library* 477. Cambridge, Massachusetts: Harvard University Press, 1994.
Hippocrates. *Epidemics V. (Epid. 5)*. Ed. J. Jouanna. *Collection des Universités de France*, Tome IV 3, 1–46. Paris: Les Belles Lettres, 2003.
Hippocrates. *Epidemics VII. (Epid. 7)*. Ed. W.D. Smith. *Loeb Classical Library* 477. Cambridge, Massachusetts: Harvard University Press, 1994.
Hippocrates. *Epidemics VII. (Epid. 7)*. Ed. J. Jouanna. *Collection des Universités de France*, Tome IV 3, 47–118. Paris: Les Belle Lettres, 2003.
Hippocrates. *On Fractures. (Fract.)* Ed. E.T. Withington. *Loeb Classical Library* 149. Cambridge, Massachusetts: Harvard University Press, 1948.
Hippocrates. *Haemorrhoids(Haem.)*. Ed. P. Potter. *Loeb Classical Library* 482. Cambridge, Massachusetts: Harvard University Press, 1995.
Hippocrates. *Humours. (Hum.)*. Ed. W.H.S. Jones. *Loeb Classical Library* 150. Cambridge, Massachusetts: Harvard University Press, 1931.
Hippocrates. *Internal Affections. (Int.)*. Ed. P. Potter. *Loeb Classical Library* 473. Cambridge, Massachusetts: Harvard University Press, 1998.
Hippocrates. *Places in Man. (Loc. Hom.)* Ed. E. Craik. Oxford: Clarendon Press, 1998.

---

[43] In contrast to the Hippocratic authors, the 2nd century CE author Soranus does pay attention to the possibility of the healer causing shame during a medical examination, instructing the healer not to look even when touching: Sor. *Gyn.* 2.6.2. so as to avoid causing shame. On this passage, see Porter 2016: 289–291.

Hippocrates. On Joints. (Artic.) Ed. E.T. Withington. *Loeb Classical Library* 149. Cambridge, Massachusetts: Harvard University Press, 1948.

Hippocrate.La maladie sacrée. (Morb. Sacr.). Ed. J. Jouanna. *Collection des Universités de France,* Tome II 3. Paris: Les Belles Lettres, 2003.

Hippocrate. Maladies II. (Morb. II). Ed. J. Jouanna. *Collection des Universités de France*, Tome X 2. Paris: Les Belles Lettres, 1983.

Hippocrate. Les Maladies des Femmes I. (Mul. I). Ed. É. Littré. *Oeuvres complètes d'Hippocrate,* Tome VIII. Paris: Ballière, 1853 (repr. Amsterdam: Hakkert, 1962).

Hippocrate. Les Maladies des Femmes II. (Mul. II). Ed. É. Littré. *Oeuvres complètes d'Hippocrate,* Tome VIII. Paris: Ballière, 1853 (repr. Amsterdam: Hakkert, 1962).

Hippocrates. Precepts. (Praec.). Ed. W.H.S. Jones. *Loeb Classical Library* 147. Cambridge, Massachusetts: Harvard University Press, 1923.

Hippocrates. Prorrhetic II. Ed. P. Potter. *Loeb Classical Library* 482. Cambridge, Massachusetts: Harvard University Press, 1995.

Modern References

Cairns, Douglas L. 1993. *Aidōs: The psychology and ethics of honour and shame in ancient Greek literature.* Clarendon Press: New York and Oxford.

Cairns, Douglas. 2008. "Look both ways: studying emotion in ancient Greek", *Critical Quarterly* 50.4: 43–62.

Cairns, Douglas L. 2011. "Veiling Grief on the Tragic Stage", in: Dana LaCourse Munteanu (ed.), *Emotion, Genre and Gender in Classical Antiquity*, 15–33. Bristol Classical Press: London.

Cairns, Douglas L. 2016. "Mind, Body, and Metaphor in Ancient Greek Concepts of Emotion", *L'Atelier du Centre de recherches historiques* [En ligne] 16, mis en ligne le 26 mai 2016, consulté le 2 juillet 2018. URL: http://journals.openedition.org/acrh/7416 ; DOI: 10.4000/acrh.7416

Dolezal, Luna. 2015. "The phenomenology of shame in the clinical encounter", *Medicine, Health Care and Philosophy* 18.4: 567–76.

Ekman, Paul. 2016. "What Scientists Who Study Emotion Agree about", *Perspectives on Psychological Science* 11.1: 31–34.

Gertsman, Elina. 2010. "The Facial Gesture: (Mis)reading Emotion in Gothic Art", *Journal of Medieval Religious Cultures* 36.1: 28–46.

Hanson, Ann. 1975. "Hippocrates: *Diseases of Women 1*", *Signs* 1.2: 567–584.

Holmes, Brooke. 2008. "Euripides' Heracles in the Flesh", *Classical Antiquity* 27.2: 231–281.

Holmes, Brooke. 2013. "In strange lands: Disembodied Authority and the Role of the Physician in the Hippocratic Corpus and Beyond", in: Markus Asper (ed.), *Writing Science: Medical and Mathematical Authorship in Ancient Greece*, 431–472. Berlin: De Gruyter.

Kaster, Robert. 2005. *Emotion, Restraint and Community in Ancient Rome.* New York: Oxford University Press.

Kazantzidis, George. 2017. "Empathy and the Limits of Disgust in the Hippocratic Corpus", in: Donald Lateiner and Dimos Spatharas (eds.), *The Ancient Emotion of Disgust*, 45–68. Oxford: Oxford University Press.

Kazantzidis, George. 2019. "Cognition, Emotion and the Feeling Body in the Hippocratic Corpus", in: Miranda Anderson, Douglas Cairns, and Mark Sprevak (eds.), *Distributed Cognition in Classical Antiquity*, 132–149. Edinburgh: Edinburgh University Press.

King, Helen. 1998. *Hippocrates' Woman: Reading the Female Body in Ancient Greece*. Routledge: London.

King, Helen. 2013. "Fear of Flute-Girls, Fear of Falling", in: W.V. Harris (ed.), *Mental Disorders in the Classical World*, 265–283. Leiden: Brill.

Lateiner, D. and D. Spatharas (eds.) 2017. *The Ancient Emotion of Disgust*: Oxford: Oxford University Press.

Lazare, Aaron. 1987. "Shame and Humiliation in the Medical Encounter", *Archives of Internal Medicine* 147.9: 1653–1658.

Llewellyn-Jones, Lloyd. 2003. *Aphrodite's Tortoise: The Veiled Woman of Ancient Greece*. Swansea: Classical Press of Wales.

Lloyd, Geoffrey E.R. 1983. *Science, Folklore and Ideology: Studies in the Life Sciences in Ancient Greece*. Cambridge: Cambridge University Press.

Nutton, Vivian. 1992. "Healers in the medical market place: towards a social history of Graeco-Roman medicine", in: Andrew Wear (ed.), *Medicine in Society: Historical Essays*, 15–58. Cambridge: Cambridge University Press.

Paez, Dario, Nekane Basabe, Maite Valdoseda, Carmen Velasco, and Ioseba Iraurgi. 1995. "Confrontation: Inhibition, Alexithymia and Health", in: J. Pennebaker (ed.), *Emotion, Disclosure and Health*, 195–222. Washington, DC: American Psychological Association.

Porter, Amber J. 2016. "Compassion in Soranus' *Gynecology* and Caelius Aurelianus' *On Chronic Diseases*", in: Georgia Petridou and Chiara Thumiger (eds.), *Homo Patiens: Approaches to the Patient in the Ancient World*, 285–303. Leiden: Brill.

Sanders, Ed. 2014. *Envy and Jealousy in Classical Athens: A Socio-Psychological Approach*. Oxford: Oxford University Press.

Thumiger, Chiara. 2016a. "Patient Function and Physician Function in the Hippocratic Cases", in: Georgia Petridou and Chiara Thumiger (eds.), *Homo Patiens: Approaches to the Patient in the Ancient World*, 107–37. Leiden: Brill.

Thumiger, Chiara. 2016b. "Fear, Hope and the Definition of Hippocratic Medicine", in: William V. Harris (ed.), *Popular Medicine in Graeco-Roman Antiquity: Explorations*, 198–214. Leiden: Brill.

Thumiger, Chiara. 2017. *A history of the mind and mental health in classical Greek medical thought*. New York/Cambridge: Cambridge University Press.

Thumiger, Chiara. 2017b. "Grief and Cheerfulness in Early Greek Medical Writings", in: Philip Bosman (ed.), *Ancient Routes to Happiness*, 55–72. Pretoria: Classical Association of South Africa.

von Staden, Heinrich, 1990. "Incurability and Hopelessness in the Hippocratic Corpus", in: P. Potter, G. Maloney and J. Desautels (eds.), *La maladie et les maladies dans la Collection hippocratique*, Actes du VIe Colloque international hippocratique, 75–112. Quebec: Editions du Sphinx.

von Staden, Heinrich. 1992. "The Mind and skin of Heracles: Heroic diseases", in: Danielle Gourevitch (ed.), *Maladie et Maladies: histoire et conceptualisation (Mélanges en l'honneur de Mirko Grmek)*, 131–50. Geneva: Droz.

Chiara Thumiger
The Body to be Hidden: Shame and Ancient Medicine

Abstract: The subjective emotion of shame, "a painful feeling of humiliation or distress caused by the consciousness of wrong or foolish behaviour", as well as its objective correspondent, "a loss of respect or esteem; dishonour", has received more attention than other emotions or psychological experiences in ancient cultural studies, arguably because of its perceived social and political significance, reliance on symbolic and economical manifestations, and intertwinement with ethical ideas; in short, because of its inherent historicity. In this paper, I analyse the restricted sphere of medicine and the subjective experience of patients as they emerge thorough ancient medical texts, with particular attention to "hiding oneself" and "covering one's body" as phenomenological instances of shame.

1 Introduction

The subjective emotion of shame — "a painful feeling of humiliation or distress caused by the consciousness of wrong or foolish behaviour", as well as its objective correspondent, "a loss of respect or esteem; dishonour"[1] has received more attention than other emotions or psychological experiences in ancient cultural studies, arguably because of its perceived social and political significance, reliance on symbolic and economical manifestations, and intertwinement with ethical ideas; in short, because of its inherent historicity. The definition I have quoted above (which is just one of the many alike formulations one may find in contemporary English dictionaries), in fact, with its emphasis on *behaviour* as cause or trigger, and on a social damage as effect, involuntarily betrays an ethical understanding of shame which certainly was at home in ancient cultures (as it is in modern ones), but which only covers a part of the experience, namely the most construed, status-related form. The Greek words usually analyzed in association with this emotional sphere — *aischunê* and *aidôs* (indicating shame, humiliation, modesty, pride), their complementary concepts

---

[1] As per Oxford Living Dictionaries definition (2018), https://en.oxforddictionaries.com [last access date on February 17, 2022].

https://doi.org/10.1515/978311077193-007

timê (the due retribution and the honour it bestows on the receiver) and *nemesis* (conversely, the punishment that follows offence at the expenses of the *timê* of others) — match the spectrum of socio-cultural values and negotiations associated with 'shame' on that reading.

Based on such externalized and interpersonal understanding the opposition, and contrast between a socially understood 'shame' and an internalized psychological counterpart ('guilt') affirmed itself as paramount in ancient cultural history, brings in a stock of implications: suggestions of primitivism, hetero-direction as drive to behaviour and the reliance on an audience of onlookers in a strongly competitive context attributed to the first; and a conscience-based, more sophisticated psychological and ethical quality, instead, attributed to the second. On this view, a sense of 'guilt' is seen to emerge only later in Greece, after the end of the archaic world, and together with notions of individual responsibility, to find its peak in Hellenistic and Christian morality. Several famous scholarly works contributed to this narrative;[2] the classic study by E.R. Dodds, in particular, seminally made a strong claim for employing the anthropological distinction between 'shame culture' and 'guilt culture' for Greek antiquity, firmly identifying the Homeric world as expression of the first.[3]

Many readers have since nuanced this opposition, and the antiquarian simplifications which derived from it have been variously criticized and adjusted by historians.[4] Most valuably, the mutually exclusive understanding of the shame/guilt binary, with its primitivist generalization, has been disputed. A further perspective is essential to the rephrasing of the discussion on this topic, one which — it seems to me — has been less emphasized in the debate, focused as it is *either* on the emotions as internal and subjective, *or* on the social datum as shared and interpersonal: namely, one's body and body-image as seat of the self, to use a contemporary expression, as fundamental (if in more or less direct and literal ways) and universal feature in experiences of shame.[5] It is here helpful to consider William's point, that shame, although usually associated to vision and a transitory 'being seen' (while guilt would be more dependent on the

---

[2] Most famously Snell 1946/1960: 43–70 on the 'rise of the individual' and Adkins 1970; see Gill 1996: 29–41, Williams 1992 for an assessment.
[3] Dodds 1951: 17–18; cf. also Adkins 1960: 48–49; Crisp 2013: 9–12.
[4] See Crisp 2013 for a survey, Cairns 2011c.
[5] Critical approaches to ancient culture shaped by embodied cognitivism have recently made important progresses in this direction (for a recent example of the developing discussions on embodiment, metaphor and ancient emotions see Cairns 2016; Short 2020); shame, however, has received less attention than *erôs* or anger, precisely by virtue of its alleged stronger sociocultural rooting.

sense of hearing as vehicle for lasting opinion)[6] can also be aroused through the evocation of the *"fantasy* of an audience", or of an *"imagined* observer":[7] i.e. shame, however public and social to an irreducible extent, can also occur in the absence of the social trigger, actually preventing the cause of social distress by means of an anticipation of the social exposure and by the enactment of the correspondent physical suffering. All these are rooted in one's (entirely individual, and private) perception of his or her own body as object in the world.[8] In these occasions the distinction between the exteriorly projected shame and an interiorized guilt becomes secondary, as does the ethical (and only ethically relevant) difference between undeserved and deserved suffering as source of shame: the shamed body is left in a medium point in which subjective self-perception, individual and private anguish on the one hand, and the weight of the surrounding world converge at a common point of pressure.

These distinctions might sound like scholarly abstractions or mere psychological labels; on the contrary, the acknowledgement of the embodied, and morally neutral component of shame can very concretely contribute to contain its social and psychological consequence (e.g., the well-known stigma felt by certain categories of victims of violence, such as rape) and, in the medical field, help counteract its effects on patients' health state: shame is an experience of the body and can be curbed by soothing, protecting, respecting, shielding and even dressing the body in certain ways.[9] In cultural-historical terms world, in

---

6 See Barton 2002: 219–220, especially on the link between been seen and honour in Roman society.

7 My emphasis, Williams 1992: 89; Crisp 2013: 10, quoting Ruth Benedict.

8 Scholarship in the medical humanities have contributed the most to this perspective: Lazare (1987: 1653) offers a much richer definition of shame, that accounts for the role played by the body; see also Dolezal (2015a, 2015b, 2016); Dolezal (2017) is grounded precisely on an embodied and phenomenological perspective of shame as experience of the body in the world. For the use of a phenomenological frame as interpretive instrument for representations of medical suffering, see Thumiger (2019) on Sophocles' *Philoctetes* as an example of change in one's 'being-in-the-world'.

9 See Lazare (1987: 1656–1657) on concrete measures to counteract the sense of shame in patients. The discussion has been acquiring importance in the past two decades, as reflections on stigma are being incorporated into the professional concerns of medical practitioners, especially vis-à-vis mental health; notions of disability; addiction; infective conditions such as HIV (see Weiss et al. 2006 for a sociological and culture-specific approach to stigma as a pathogenic factor in current medical practice; Lyons and Dolezal 2017). Two current projects on medical ethics and anthropology exemplify this growing interest: the *Shame and Stigma Network* by Medical Humanities at the university of Sheffield (http://mhs.group.shef.ac.uk/shame-stigma-network-publications-presentations/) and the *Shame and Medicine Project* based at

parallel, a methodology mindful of embodiment as universal human experience grants the possibility for cross-cultural and comparative extensions when it comes to emotion studies.[10]

Let us return to our dichotomy above, for a long time taken as standard in ancient world anthropology, between a shame- and a guilt- culture summing up the archaic world at one extreme of the spectrum, and the Hellenistic/Christian developments in ethics and spirituality at the other end. The general claim of a lesser emphasis on conscience[11] and interiorized regret in earlier Greek culture remains an acceptable narrative that reflects the available sources of the archaic period; still, it should be more convincingly rephrased as emphasis on the emotion expressed and communicated — shame as perceived inadequacy to a shared standard, as public sanction and interpersonal display — as opposed to the hidden, privately experienced feeling of regret explored in personal philosophies. Thus, the shift should be attributed to the preferences and conventions of cultural expression, by no means to an ontological datum — the lack of the experience itself. In this chapter I do not plan to engage extensively with the bulk of scholarship about shame and honour in the Greek world, a huge task that lies with others.[12] The current study aims to focus on shame as embodied experience in medicine as a sphere of life and activity in the ancient world, and to consider ancient medical texts at different stages in the history of Graeco-Roman medicine. This shall add to the existing scholarship the fundamental testimony about one of the most painfully and challenging bodily experiences in human life, that of illness, weakness and disability in their various forms and manifestations. Given their relevance to an emotion in which embodiment is fundamental, it is surprising that medical texts should not have been given primary attention in the analysis of shame and, in parallel, it is surprising and significant for the historian and anthropologist of medicine that discussions of feelings in the sphere of shame should be so scanty and indirect in most of these texts. Both data are meaningful for a cultural historian, the first illustrating the unconscious reluctance to consider the body as fully integrated part of the self

---

Trinity College Dublin (Medical Humanities, http://www.shameandmedicineproject.com, last access date on February 17, 2022).

10 Despite cultural-historical variations, we agree with recognising a basic, universal quality to the experience of shame, in line with Lyons and Dolezal's reminder (quoting Sartre, *Being and Nothingness*), that "in fact, some philosophers argue that shame is inescapable in human experience, a fundamental part of child development that textures personal, social and political aspects of adolescent and adult life".

11 And perhaps lack of a concept thus formulated, as in Sorabji's study (2014).

12 See especially Williams (1992); Cairns (1993); a survey in Crisp (2011).

in history of psychology; and the second showing the importance, in the self-fashioning of our medical tradition, of shunning the burden of weakness, fallibility and fragility that must be at the core of the experience of illness.[13]

2 Medicine and Shame

That medicine, as is also the case with various other aspects of ancient psychology–, has not been interrogated to reconstruct the ancient experience of shame can be explained on various grounds: first, the fact that ancient medicine (especially that of the classical period) avoids details of private psychology as material for case histories;[14] secondly, the fact that medicine in this tradition generally avoids consideration for iatrogenic emotions, unless they can be concretely soothed by the physician's intentions and justified assurance — i.e., unless they are deontologically sound and do not put the reputation of the doctor at risk;[15]

---

13 Iatrogenic shame has not been an easy topic for modern medical thinkers either: Lazare (1987: 1658) proposes as explanation the lack of attention to patient subjectivity in our medical tradition, the physicians' naïve trust in their own good intentions towards patients, and a general unease to discuss shame: "neither patients nor physicians like to acknowledge or discuss their own shame or humiliation". See Lyons and Dolezal (2017) on this void in our own medical culture.
14 See Thumiger 2017: 419–421 and 2018 for a summary of the argument.
15 On deontology in the texts of the *Hippocratic Corpus*, see Leven 2018; Ecca 2018. In fact, a parallel topic whose conspicuous, even programmatic absence deserves attention is the shame of the physician for his mistakes and helplessness, the never-mentioned driving force behind much of ancient deontology and code of practice. Much of the prognostic style of Hippocratic medicine is indeed a reaction, or even a prevention, of the shame brought to the professional doctor by an unexpected death after a positive prognosis, or by the failure to foresee the worst (see Thumiger 2016 for a summary of this well-known feature of classical medicine, with discussions of the key scholarship: Edelstein 1975; Robert 1975: 262–265; Marzullo 1986–87; von Staden 1987; cf. also Nutton 2004; Lloyd 2005: 56–58). The shame of not having succeeded to preserve the body (of others) is close to the shame felt by the patient him — or herself for his or her crippled, suffering body (surely, closer to this very personal pain than to the abstract hurt to one's reputation experienced by any other professional). The failure, or helplessness of a medical authority incarnates most literally the idiomatic 'wounded pride' (*vulnus*), a common embodied metaphor for shame, recognised to affect medical professionals today in similar ways: see Lazare (1987: 1656) for a seminal illustration of the problem (and its unmentioned character); Cunningham and Wilson (2003) for an operational discussion. The only explicit addressing of professional shame in the Hippocratics is of a lighter kind and concerns matters of style only: at *Joints* 42 (L. 4.184), where the physician-author (discussing the use of the harsh, and spectacular method of the 'ladder' to treat hump-backs) frankly admits "for myself,

thirdly, even when later medicine considers human emotions as object of medical attention – as it is notably the case in Galen's ethical writings[16] – it avoids including shame among the objects of a philosophical therapy, which typically includes strong individualistic, ethically reprehensible emotions such as fear, envy and anger. Those are regarded as truly dangerous for the development of the individual, openly associated as they are with the dynamics of social aristocratic competition and its perceived virtues.

There are minor episodes, it is true, in which shame is mentioned as a potentially pathogenic force – famously, in a patient case narrated by Galen in *Comm.Hipp.Epid. VI* shame can cause a psychic distress that can be fatal: the story of the "man who had farted in the presence of other people, and who wasted away and died out of shame".[17] This case is however anecdotal and is to be compared with other calamities or sudden losses of status associated, for instance, to damages to one's patrimony or to the sudden death of a family member which Galen discusses.[18] The example of flatulence in this passage, in fact, is extreme and it is included within a selection of absurd anxieties, from the fear of ghosts, to the phobia of swallowing a snake, to an 'Atlas' complex' – the worry that the world might fall from one's shoulders, as the patient is carrying its weight like the mythical character. Galen, thus, does not focus in depth on the peculiarity of shame *qua* shame, a reasonable, understandable reaction for the suffering patient: the real emotion remains generally relegated to the realm of the implicit. In short, when it comes to pathology, shame remains 'shameful',[19] a core element within the experience of illness unavoidable as much as undeserving of discussion, unrelated to objective guilt or personal responsibility, impossible to fight or prevent, just as in Galen's episode of embarrassment with lethal consequences, which is in this respect a fitting illustration. Medical shame is inherently corporeal, embodied, and as such impossible

---

however, I felt ashamed (κατῃσχύνθην) to treat all such cases in this way, and that because such methods appertain rather to charlatans".

16 On these, see Gill (2010, 2013, 2018); Singer (2013, 2018).

17 *Comm.Hipp.Epid.*VI, 8 (487,3–23 Wenkebach/Pfaff), "die Geschichte von dem Mann, dem in Anwesenheit von Leuten ein Wind entfahren war und der aus Scham darüber hinsiechte und starb", transl. by S. Coughlin).

18 Discussed by Mattern (2015) as examples of *lypê*, 'anxiety', in her interpretation; cf. especially 206 with n. 13.

19 Shame and the socially perceived values of shamefulness and shamelessness are closely related; shame is shameful, an emotion that contains the emotion of the emotion at the same time. 'Shamefulness' and 'shamelessness' are thus an interesting case of two opposite terms which can be used, in the derogatory sense, to convey basically the same meaning.

to master through reason or good will, just as its bodily origin and its urgent nature often escape the control of the individual.

3 Medical Experiences: Shame and the Body

As we have anticipated, one of the most common and direct associations of the emotions of shame is to one's body and body-image, bodily functions and corporeal physiology. The objectification of one's body as observable item, its sudden emergence from the realm of the ordinary and inconspicuous into the spectacularisation through disease are discussed by a phenomenological critique of illness as 'lived experience'.[20] As Carel has explored in her work on the phenomenology of illness, and as Dolezal, more to the point, has remarked in her account of the phenomenology of 'body and shame', society and interrelations are at the centre here too: the 'socially shaped body' is in fact essential to this emotion. Shame, writes Dolezal (with some overstatement of her case perhaps) "is an emotion that is *always manifested* and experienced through the body", and in some cases "it arises explicitly *as a result of the body* (my emphasis)".[21] This is the case (generally and, cross-culturally) in every-day life and social interaction, but even more when illness causes a deviation from one's body's regular functioning and appearance: feelings of degradation and shame are defining experiences of being a medical patient.

Thus, I propose to illustrate the representation of this emotion, or this cluster of emotions as inherent to the condition of the ill in ancient medical writings, on the one hand; on the other, I wish to explore the converse — shamelessness as pathologized item in human psychology — as it emerges as a marker of mental and sexual disturbance in late-antique nosology. These two research topics are not just fortuitously or semantically affiliated: the acknowledgement of shame as part of human psychology under the pressure of disease, in fact, belongs to the same sensibility that values the ability to feel shame as a feature of a wholesome psychological state and sound mind, necessarily implying an ethical perspective on human health. These two form the two faces of the same coin: a kind of shame *felt* and triggered by a dissonance between one's actual bodily state and a perceived idea of its needed adequacy (that I search for, most of all, in the texts of the *Corpus Hippocraticum*); secondly, a sense of

---

20 Carel 2016: 1–7 for a summary.
21 Dolezal 2015: ix.

shame as projected on others by the gaze of an authoritative observer or by society as a collective vehicle of judgment (as we shall see most prominently in late antique nosology). The resulting picture corroborates the fundamental neutrality of classical medicine vis-à-vis questions of value and decorum; the growing intersection between medicine, ethics, and social sensibility in the medicine of our era; finally, the general reluctance, on the part of the ancient physicians, to address aspects belonging to the private sphere of the individual patient's life.

4 Classical Medicine and Tragedy: Hidden and Open Forms of Shame

Several studies have explored in recent times the elision, from the narrative of earlier medicine, of certain emotions that we would naturally imagine to characterize patienthood and the interaction between patient and doctor.[22] Still, as I explored with reference to the emotion of hope, which constitutes, in my opinion, a comparable case,[23] basic strong emotions that concern the survival of one's body and bodily integrity are irreducible part of the experience of being ill — and surely shame, as the strongest, non-negotiable discomfort deriving from the perception of one's bodily flaws being exposed to the outside world belongs to the same discussion. Our task, as readers and historians, is to look for it in the details and clues offered to us indirectly by the clinical observations preserved in medical writings, in the absence of the magniloquent speeches that belong to other genres. This oblique quality to the personal evidence in our sources is in line with the expectations — we might even say conventions — which are commanded by the style and professional agenda one can observe in the medical writings, especially those of the classical era.

One example where shame is centered clarifies this point well. Compare this famous, and explicit first-person celebration of human shame and tainted honour, coeval to the dating of the Hippocratic texts: the lamentation of the hero who awakens to discover he has humiliated himself in front of his peers while

---

[22] Holmes (2013); See also Kazantzidis (2016) on the issue of disgust, identifying a similar lack of emphasis — surprising in medical contexts; and Kosak (2005), who discussed the absence of a thematisation of empathy and compassion in a similar spirit.
[23] As I explore in Thumiger (2016).

under an attack of *mania*, in Sophocles' *Ajax* 356–480.[24] Here too pathology and the shamed body are fundamental, although no medical component is foregrounded.[25] In dialogue with his wife Tecmessa and his Chorus of fellow sailors from Salamis, once he has regained reason and bodily strength after a long sleep, Ajax realizes what he has done and invokes death (361), berating sarcastically his own actions (364–366): "*look at* the bold one, the hero, the one who does not tremble in the mist of the fight!" and again, "alas what a *laughing stock*, what a *shame*!" (Οἴμοι γέλωτος, οἷον ὑβρίσθην ἄρα). The famous, suggestive words at 394–397 emphasize the role of vision in the construction of this emotion, the spectacle Ajax has offered of himself with his own bodily actions: "Darkness, my light! (σκότος, ἐμὸν φάος)", an invocation to hiddenness and — in theatrical terms — to semiotic disappearance.[26] There is an obvious disjunction and fragmentation of the subject through shame and suffering that sees the body and the person becoming painfully self-conscious and conspicuous: Ajax insists visualizing himself in the third person[27] and sees himself as "*exposed to everyone, shamed*" (426–427, τὰ νῦν δ' ἄτιμος / ὧδε πρόκειται). Most eloquently, at 430–480 he speaks in an articulated manner of his own fate: his very name — the first depository of honour in Greek culture — now spells out pain and humiliation (430–431, Αἰαῖ· τίς ἄν ποτ' ᾤεθ' ὧδ' ἐπώνυμον / τοὐμὸν ξυνοίσειν ὄνομα τοῖς ἐμοῖς κακοῖς;); the thought of his illustrious father, the famous Telamon, exacerbates by contrast the agony of the son's disgrace (434–6); he *dies of shame* before the Greeks (440, ἄτιμος Ἀργείοισιν ὧδ' ἀπόλλυμαι); his enemies laugh at him (454, κεῖνοι δ' ἐπεγγελῶσιν ἐκπεφευγότες). At 457–480 he explores "what to do", καὶ νῦν τί χρὴ δρᾶν; (457): having considered all possibilities — to return home alone and meet his father dishonored (460–465) or to assault the Trojan army in a (surely fatal) one-man attack, thus doing a service to his Greek enemies (466–470), he concludes that death is the only option, to take himself out of sight (470–480), the only way to prove to his fa-

---

[24] Ajax has been driven to madness by Athena, in alliance with her protégée Odysseus; during the attack he slaughters the herd of cattle of the Greeks, mistaking them for his human enemies; once his senses are restored, he realizes his own mistake and is devoured by shame at what he perceives to be a most humiliating mistake, an unbearable parody of heroic boldness — the abuse of force against harmless animals (on Ajax and the topic of being exposed to the view of others, see Thumiger, 2013b: 226–227; on Ajax's madness, Thumiger 2017: 189, 267–268; on pitiful Ajax, Johnson and Clapp 2005: 126–129).
[25] However, Israelowich (2017) finds a discussion on illness important in the Sophoclean play.
[26] See Instone (2007) on these words.
[27] This fragmented self and externalized self-perception in the experience of illness is most evident in the Sophoclean *Philoctetes*, as I notice in Thumiger (2019).

ther that he is not "a degenerate, but indeed his son" (470–472). The words Ajax uses to reinforce this glorious familial bond now tainted by shame evokes no patrician lineage nor ethical value, but his very flesh and bones, *his body* in its innermost fibers:

> γέροντι δηλώσω πατρὶ
> μή τοι φύσιν γ' ἄσπλαγχνος ἐκ κείνου γεγώς.
>
> I will show the father,
> that by nature *not without guts* I was born to him.

a clumsy translation for a passage that is impossible to render into English effectively, and can only be understood in the context of its deeply embodied sense of shame and honour.[28]

The text continues with great psychological, ethical, and existential complications. For our purpose, it suffices to notice how the subject Ajax is here perfectly aware about his situation vis-à-vis shame and his own bodily faults; the effects of his 'illness', and the mess caused through it; the judgement of others, the laughter provoked; additionally, the joy of his enemies at his disgrace. At 317–325, we find the description of his shocking realization:

> Ὁ δ' εὐθὺς ἐξῴμωξεν οἰμωγὰς λυγράς,
> ἃς οὔποτ' αὐτοῦ πρόσθεν εἰσήκουσ' ἐγώ·
> πρὸς γὰρ κακοῦτε καὶ βαρυψύχου γόους
> τοιούσδ' ἀεί ποτ' ἀνδρὸς ἐξηγεῖτ' ἔχειν·
> ἀλλ' ἀψόφητος ὀξέων κωκυμάτων
> ὑπεστέναζε, ταῦρος ὣς βρυχώμενος.
> Νῦν δ' ἐν τοιᾷδε κείμενος κακῇ τύχῃ
> ἄσιτος ἀνήρ, ἄποτος, ἐν μέσοις βοτοῖς
> σιδηροκμῆσιν ἥσυχος θακεῖ πεσών.
>
> But he immediately groaned mournful groans, such as I had never heard from him before. For he had always taught that such wailing was for cowardly and low-hearted men. He used to grieve quietly without the sound of loud weeping, but instead moaned low like a bull. And now, prostrate in such miserable fortune, tasting no food, no drink, the man sits idly where he has fallen in the middle of the iron-slain cattle.

There is complete awareness and unbearable pain: he weeps loudly, adding undignified groaning to his actions, and refuses the food he needs to sustain himself.

---

28 On Ajax's body at the centre, see Thumiger (2013), Finglass (2011).

Nowhere in our medical sources can we find a similar awareness of one's corporeal existence — surprising as it sounds — with the shame such awareness of the body during illness may bring. The only mention of patient shame (or, of any body-aware emotion) in classical medicine is a passage from *On the Sacred Disease* which shows well the unsympathetic, almost manipulative approach to human emotional vulnerability in the medical texts of the classical period, in stark contrast with the tragic portrayal.[29] The context is the onset of an epileptic attack and the reaction of the patient (*Morb.Sacr.* 12.1, Jouanna 22,13–23, 5 = L. 6.382,19 – 384,3):

> ὅσοι δὲ ἤδη ἐθάδες εἰσὶ τῇ νούσῳ, προγινώσκουσιν ὅταν μέλλωσι ληφθήσεσθαι, καὶ **φεύγουσιν** ἐκ τῶν ἀνθρώπων· ἢν μὲν ἐγγὺς ᾖ αὐτῷ τὰ οἰκία, οἴκαδε, εἰ δὲ μή, **ἐς τὸ ἐρημότατον**, ὅπῃ **μέλλουσιν αὐτὸν ἐλάχιστοι ὄψεσθαι πεσόντα, εὐθύς τε ἐγκαλύπτεται**. τοῦτο δὲ ποιεῖ **ὑπ' αἰσχύνης τοῦ πάθεος**, καὶ οὐχ ὑπὸ φόβου, ὡς οἱ πολλοὶ νομίζουσι, τοῦ δαιμονίου. τὰ δὲ παιδάρια τὸ μὲν πρῶτον πίπτουσιν ὅπῃ ἂν τύχωσιν ὑπὸ ἀηθίης, ὅταν δὲ πλεονάκις κατάληπτοι γένωνται, ἐπειδὰν προαίσθωνται, φεύγουσι παρὰ τὰς μητέρας ἢ παρὰ ἄλλον ὄντινα μάλιστα γινώσκουσιν, ὑπὸ δέους καὶ φόβου τῆς πάθης· **τὸ γὰρ αἰσχύνεσθαι οὔπω γινώσκουσιν**.

> Those however who are used to the [sacred] disease know beforehand when they are about to be seized and *flee from men*; if their own house be at hand, they run home, but if not, to a *deserted place*, where *as few persons as possible will see them falling*, and they immediately *cover themselves up*. This they do from *shame of the affection*, and not from fear of the divinity, as many suppose. And little children at first fall down wherever they may happen to be, from inexperience. But when they have been often seized, and feel its approach beforehand, they flee to their mothers, or to any other person they are acquainted with, from terror and dread of the affection, *for being still infants they do not know yet what it is to be ashamed*.

This is in many ways an extraordinary passage.[30] First of all, the text is striking for the amount of attention given to emotions as causes of behaviour, especially if we compare it with the absence of any reference in this sense otherwise. In the Hippocratic texts, in fact, the emotions are only analysed physiologically, as is the case with anger (*orgê*, *oxythumia*), or only quickly registered, and not deconstructed or addressed therapeutically, as is the case with fear (*phobos*).[31] Moreover, the passage interests us for the way it distinguishes between two key medical emotions, fear and shame, discussing their anthropology in terms of

---

29 Sophocles' *Philoctetes* would offer, of course, another great contrasting example, as I present it in Thumiger (forthcoming).
30 I already discuss this in Thumiger 2016: 213 and 2017: 360; see Kosak 2015: 252.
31 Thumiger 2017: 352–359.

emotional 'ages of maturity' — the first befalls children, the second is appropriate for adults, who have a developed sense of decorum and as such are capable of feeling shame. In this context, shame is opposed to fear in an intellectualistic critique of popular credence about the sacred disease's supposed supernatural nature. In the case of the epileptic attack, fear is only worthy of small children and, for the purposes of medical discussion, it needs to be eliminated from the spectrum of patient emotions: once someone (an adult person)[32] knows about the disease and its causes, by definition irrational fear is dispelled. What remains, rather, is shame as an adult, socialized reaction to a degrading experience (the falling, foaming, perhaps passing urine and excrements), which causes the patients to flee.

This is a highly unusual digression in psychology in the context of fifth century medicine: among all the testimonies we have, only in this passage is such a complex reflection on patient psychology allowed. The reason behind this exception, I propose, is precisely the desire to dispel the idea of a 'fear of the unknown', rejected by the Hippocratic doctor with particular force and engagement in the anti-irrationalistic treatise *On the sacred disease*, where the crusade against metaphysical terrorism and vulgar forms of religiosity are famously salient.[33] What motivates the analysis of shame here, then, is not an anthropological interest in the emotion as a constituent element of the phenomenology of illness, but a key ideological purpose. Nonetheless, this passage allows us a glimpse on an experience that must have been common — the desire to flee, to hide, to be secluded, to cover oneself up because of disease-caused, body-related shame.[34]

We shall now turn to this experience. In our sources we find staple gestures which point towards an experience of shame combined with grief and refusal to join contact rather than explicitly stated expressions of shame as a felt emotion. This non-directedness of the evidence is pregnant for additional reasons: shame is by its own nature peculiar for being more often than other emotions denied, hidden, left unexpressed: the negotiation of visibility and admission is inherent to it.

---

32 On children patients and their peculiarity, see Graumann and Thumiger (forthcoming).
33 On this, see van der Eijk (2005).
34 And remains common nowadays — arguably, a universal feature of illness and bodily suffering: see Lazare 1987: 1655 on the 'hiding response' in relation to medicalized shame.

5 Symbols and Tokens of Shame: Covering Oneself Up

A recurrent gesture found in our texts can only be understood in connection with the emotionally hidden and unexpressed, and especially in the experience of shame in an embodied perspective: covering and wrapping oneself up with clothing or blankets.

Descriptions of patients hiding their own bodies in various ways at critical points, in fact, are recurrent and noteworthy in the patient cases of the *Epidemics*. I discuss these elsewhere in detail,[35] illustrating the obvious association between these behaviors and contexts of mental disorder. As we shall see, Galen also later interpreted them as mental disturbance.[36] The fact that mental disorder is the dominant pathological context of these gestures does not exclude an interpretation in terms of emotional turmoil – the painful elaboration of one's self-image. In fact, this enhances and refines a mental interpretation by presenting extremes of shameful feelings as belonging to mental disorder, and the reverse.

The gesture of hiding and covering oneself, as Cairns noticed, is a double-edged one.[37] Partly drawing on the work of Ferrari,[38] Cairns analyzed the gesture of veiling in ancient literature and figurative art as token and expression of grief and sorrow as much as interpersonal negotiation of the needs and weaknesses that accompany these emotions. He proposes that these symbolic gestures are peculiar in so far as they have as objective a withholding from sight, on the one hand and, on the other, as they attract attention by their very nature on the withheld scene and on the withholding in itself. The act of veiling and concealing acquires ritual import, inviting reactions of compassion, understanding, and respect. The medical evidence I am going to present reinforces this interpretation of covering as powerfully revealing sign:[39] shame, like grief, is an emotion

---

[35] Thumiger 2017: 153, 260, 559–560.
[36] See below.
[37] Cairns 2009: 52; Cairns himself (2009: 45–46) explains the display (or lack thereof) of grief as related to the intervening αἰδώς, an "emotion about the emotion" making the association between the strong feeling and a related shame obvious; see also Cairns 2016: 22–28 on garments and embodied emotions with reference to shame; in the same spirit, see Cairns (2001) on anger.
[38] Ferrari 1990; see Cairns 2009: 52 n. 24.
[39] Cairns 2011a and 2011b. For a famous parallel to this effect, compare the paradoxical semiotics of the shields which hide and protect the chest while revealing the *ethos* and history of

boiling under the surface, and to it also belong forms of 'emotional performance'.⁴⁰

To illustrate the meaning gained by the actions of "covering oneself" and "wrapping oneself up" in these texts, let us start with a passage from *Epidemics* 6. This is one of the lists of "things the physician should observe" in the state of patients found in various Hippocratic texts; here, among the things that fall under "habit, those things through which we preserve our health" the author lists: "lifestyle, *covering*, exercise, sleep, sexual activity, mental activity" (ἔθος δὲ ἐξ οἵων ὑγιαίνομεν, διαίτῃσι, σκέπῃσι, πόνοισιν, ὕπνοισιν, ἀφροδισίοισι, γνώμῃ).⁴¹ Admittedly, the reference to 'coverings' (σκέπῃσι) here is of ambiguous interpretation: the Greek term σκέπη can indicate a shelter, or a covering for the body, an item of clothing or a blanket; one wonders what it is meant to designate in this context. I suggest that the way one dresses and behaves with coverings such as blankets and clothes is likely to be meant, in its relevance to general health — diet, sleep, and activities like exercise are mentioned together, so the context seems more personal, and definitely body-related than just an indication of the kind of place where one lives.⁴²

Most importantly, the psychological interpretation is in line with the concrete examples offered by patient cases. At *Epid.* 3.1, case 3 (218.6–8 Kühlewein = 3.42.9–11 L.), for example, we have a deranged individual, "the man lying sick in the garden of Delearces", who displays the following symptoms:

Ἕπτα καὶ δεκάτῃ, πρωῒ ἄκρεα ψυχρά· **περιεστέλλετο**· πυρετὸς ὀξύς· ἵδρωσε δι' ὅλου· ἐκουφίσθη· κατενόει μᾶλλον· οὐκ ἄπυρος· διψώδης· ἤμεσε χολώδεα, ξανθά, ὀλίγα· ἀπὸ δὲ κοιλίης κόπρανα διῆλθε, μετ' ὀλίγον δὲ μέλανα, ὀλίγα, λεπτά.

---

each of the heroes in the Aeschylean *Seven at Thebes* (375–654), with an expressionist peak in the case of Amphiaraos, whose shield is blank: "no symbol was fixed to his shield's circle. For he does not wish *to appear* the bravest, but *to be* the bravest" (my emphasis, 593–595).

40 The gendered nature of veiling in tragic examples (where the protagonists are basically female) does not appear to be replicated by the medical instances. Interestingly, this can be interpreted in the light of the well-known metaphorical representation of the sexes in tragedy, where wailing, irrationality, and enclosure are assigned to 'females' and are attributed to a failure of 'maleness' (on Heracles' depiction in the *Trachiniae*, see Thumiger 2013: 35; see also Hall (1997) on the tropes through which social entities (genders, or ethnic identities especially) are represented in tragedy.

41 My translation of *Epid.* 6.8.23 (184.1–2 Manetti-Roselli=5.352.8–9 L.). On these, see Thumiger 2017: 51–52.

42 Although on this specific instance Galen's commentator takes it in the letter sense, and thus translates σκέπη with *Zelte*, 'tents' is the German translation from the Arabic (*Comm.Hipp.Epid.VI*, 484.21–4 Wenkebach-Pfaff).

Seventeenth day. Extremities cold in the early morning; *would wrap himself up*; acute fever; sweated all over; was relieved; more rational; some fever; thirst; vomited bilious matters, yellow and scanty; solid motions from the bowels; after a while they became black, scanty and thin.

trans. W.H.S. Jones

The wrapping accompanies the cold, and, although mental health is considered here (the patient is said to be 'more rational' at some point, κατενόει μᾶλλον), it must, perhaps, be explained by the fever. Another case is the patient at *Epid.* 2.2.22 (38.3–11 Smith = 5.94.1–7 L.), Lyciê, who becomes delirious and 'wraps herself up':

Ἰήθη ἐλλεβόρου πόσει Λυκίη ... παρεφέρετο, **περιεστέλλετο**· φῦσα ἐνεοῦσα· οὐ διῄει κάτω οὐδέν, οὐδὲ οὔρει· ἀπέθανε.

Lycie was treated with a potion of hellebore ... She became delirious. *She was wrapped up/wrapped herself up.* She was full of wind which did not pass. No faeces and no urine. She died.

trans. Smith

Also at *Epid.* 7.25.6 (67.15–68.7 Jouanna = 5.396.14–397.1 L.) we have a patient suffering mentally, who feels weak and downcast. The description runs as follows:

Towards day she answered mostly with nods, her body unmoving, reasonably alert. Again the sweat at the same hour. The eyes similarly downcast, leaning more on the lower lid, staring, torpid, the whites of the eyes yellowish and corpselike. Her whole color yellowish and dark. Mostly reaching with her hand towards the wall or the bedclothes. The gurgling occurred when she drank, and she spurted it out and brought it up through her nose. She plucked at the blankets, *and kept her face covered up* (τῇ χειρὶ τὰ πολλὰ πρὸς τοῖχον ἢ πρὸς ἱμάτιον· οἱ ψόφοι πινούσῃ ἐγίνοντο· ἀπεπύτιζε καὶ ἄνω ἐς τὴν ῥῖνα ἐφόρει· καὶ ἐκροκυδολόγει καὶ **ξυνεκαλύπτετο πρόσωπον**). After the sweats her hands were like ice. Cold sweat persisted. Body cold to the touch. She jumped up, cried out, raved. Breathing very rapid. She developed trembling in the hands. At the point of death she twitched.

trans. W.D. Smith

As she falls into delirium, it seems, with typhoid manifestations such as hand compulsory movement and crocydism,[43] she hides her face from the physician, obviously a sign of distress and emotional disturbance. Other patients suffering

---

43 The compulsive hand movement, sometimes plucking hair or chasing imaginary insects from the wall or the bed's covers, described by the Hippocratics is neurologically associated with ardent fevers.

from derangement offer this sign in this combination: at *Epid.* 3.3.17, case 15 (244.2 Kühlewein = 3.142.7–8 L.), among the typical signs of derangement and discomfort (hand movements, the so-called crocydism, eye behaviours, stillness of the body, raving) the patient περιεστέλλετο, 'wrapped herself up', and did it from the beginning; her entire behaviour belongs to a mentally pathological picture. It is important to highlight that, in her case, a lasting, repeated behaviour is at stake, something that happens "from the start": ἐξ ἀρχῆς δὲ περιεστέλλετο, καὶ διὰ τέλεος αἰεὶ σιγῶσα, ἐψηλάφα, ἔτιλλεν, ἔγλυφεν, ἐτριχολόγει, δάκρυα καὶ πάλιν γέλως, οὐκ ἐκοιμᾶτο ("from the beginning she would wrap herself up, and throughout, without speaking a word, she would fumble, pluck, scratch, pick hairs, weep and then laugh, but she did not sleep"). Shortly after this (244.15 Kühlewein = 3.146.5 L.), we read that "she *constantly* wrapped herself up; either much rambling or silence throughout"; a later hand, interpolating the text, added the psychiatric diagnosis [*phrenitis*], fittingly for our interpretation (αἰεὶ περιεστέλλετο· ἢ λόγοι πολλοὶ ἢ σιγῶσα διὰ τέλεος. [φρενῖτις]).[44]

When we look at these examples, an obvious objection arises: there is always a possibility, one might say (in some cases more than in others), that the gestures of covering up might belong to the physiology of fevers, with their consequent shivering and the felt need to keep oneself warm.[45] The insistence of the Hippocratic physicians on such a contingent and even trivial behavioural detail, however, invites us nonetheless to recognize an additional relevance in it. Galen also later attributes these acts to mental complaints, although he does not explicitly identify shame in those cases: "the excessive talk", he writes, "belongs to *phrenitis*, the fact of being silent is melancholic, *and the wrapping oneself up belongs to both, unless of course one is doing it because of feeling cold*" (my translation: τὸ μὲν γὰρ λόγοι πολλοί φρενιτικόν, τὸ δὲ σιγῶσα μελαγχολικόν, τὸ δὲ περιεστέλλετο κοινὸν ἀμφοῖν, εἰ μή πως ἄρα καὶ διὰ τὴν κατάψυξιν ἐνίοτε περιεστέλλετο, *Comm.Hipp.Epid. III* 90 (186.4–7 Wenkebach = XVII.789 K.)). The physician from Pergamon readily sees the psychological relevance of this gesture (itemized under the heading τὸ δὲ περιεστέλλετο) as he comments on the *Epidemics* case, and differentiates it clearly from the physiology of fevers. In fact, there are cases in which an explanation in terms of fever is much less probable, as at *Epid.* 7,11 (61.13; 19 Jouanna=5.386.13; 18 L.), when again the more emotionally loaded gesture of keeping one's face covered, rather than the body is at stake:

---

44 On these interpolations, see Thumiger 2018c: 53–54.
45 On the relevance of fevers to ancient medical suffering and hypotheses on their incidence, see Hamlin 2014: 17–87.

On the three or four days before the end shivers came on her at times so that *she would draw her body together, cover up* and breathe hard (ὥστε ξυνάγειν τὸ σῶμα καὶ ξυγκαλύπτεσθαί τε καὶ πνευστιᾶν). Cramps in the legs, cold feet. The thirst as before, and mental affection similar ... *She was quiet at times, without huddling under covers or coma* (ἡσυχίην ἔσχεν ἔστιν ὅτε καὶ ἄνευ τοῦ ξυγκεκαλύφθαιτε καὶ κεκωματίσθαι) ... She showed recognition and answered what was asked. Her voice lisping after much talking, and broken and hoarse from the shouting.

The covering of the face belongs to the same category of bodily behaviours as crouching on the bed and other similar cocooning postures,⁴⁶ very clearly signaling a need to protect oneself from sight and interpersonal contact. On the whole, what emerges from these passages is a desire to shield and protect the body in reaction to a state of vulnerability and danger, with the instinct to hide oneself from others, finding shelter under the covers or by fleeing — as in the most explicit case of the patient of *De Morbo Sacro* we mentioned at the start. Even if shame is nowhere explicitly evoked, the analysis of these gestures as symbolic points us in the direction of the unacknowledged, otherwise silent emotions rooted in the suffering body. The striking insistence on wrapping and covering oneself in the texts of classical medicine is a powerful gesture where suffering and grief and a desire to hide the shame of a sick body combine in one evident sign.

6 Late Antique Developments: Pathology-related Shame ...

A picture complementary to the meagerness of explicit discussions of emotions in the classical sources reaches us from the genre of nosological treatises of the imperial era. In these texts, we find a growing medical interest in social values such as decorum, honour, and appropriateness. More generally, a shift in emphasis is made noticeable in the way the medical authors approach their human subjects: while a biological and materialistic interpretation of the emotions was dominant in classical medicine, and personal details were either avoided or reduced to physiology, medical texts now begin to include social and interpersonal concerns as part of the picture, and an ethical project is recognized as part of the territory of medicine.⁴⁷ In parallel, the developments in deontological

---

46 As I discuss in Thumiger 2017: 167–169.
47 On which, Galen is especially central: see Gill 2010; 2013; 2018; Singer 2013; 2018.

literature alongside medical nosology confirm the growing consideration for the feelings of the patients as part of the concerns of the physician.⁴⁸ And so, it does not surprise us to meet again the feelings of shame associated to the epileptic crises in Aretaeus, *Ac.* 1, 5 (5.12–13 Hude): the physician describes those patients who are used to the crises, have prescience of their coming (3.23–4.6 Hude) and are left "*dejected* from the *suffering* and *shame* of the dreadful malady", (κατηφέες καμάτῳ καὶ αἰσχύνῃ τοῦ δεινοῦ). Moreover, at *Ac.* 1, 6 (7.9 Hude), along similar lines, death is clearly seen as deliverance from shame (among other things) for patients labouring under the attacks of *tetanus*: a quick death is "a blessing, to himself as liberation from pains, distortion and shame" (ἀγαθὸν μὲν τῷ νοσέοντι ἐς πόνων καὶ διαστροφῆς καὶ αἰσχύνης ἀπαλλαγήν, 7.8–10 Hude). Again, at *Chron.* 2, 2 (Hude 65.29), the life of the diabetic patients is described as "disgusting and painful" (βίος αἰσχρὸς καὶ ἐπίπονος) due to the excessive urination that comes with the condition. This cannot be helped by restraining oneself from drinking, because "how can shame be stronger than pain?" (ἢ τίς αἰσχύνη πόνου κρέσσων;).

This more personal, private part of the experience of illness is thus now openly recognized and discussed; and it is no coincidence that a failure in this area of morality, the ability to feel the appropriate shame towards certain functions of the body, should in parallel become important. The accent is placed, unsurprisingly, on the sexual sphere. We should then focus our attention on "shamelessness" as the other side of the same coin, the perceived lack of shame towards one's bodily behaviours and appearances from the focalizing point of view of the writing physician and of society at large; shamelessness is pathologized within the medical narrative and brought back to a profile of mental disorder. Diseases connected to the sexual sphere come into play here, with a characteristic prudishness that is nowhere to be found in the Hippocratics.⁴⁹

7 ... and Pathological Shamelessness

The first example I wish to bring into attention is that of the disease *satyriasis*, described in various imperial sources.⁵⁰ Despite differences in etiology and

---

48 See Ecca 2018; Leven (2018) on deontology; Thumiger (2016: 208) on this trajectory.
49 See Thumiger 2017 and 2018 for discussions.
50 The most important discussions are found in Anonymus Parisinus (first-second century AD: '*Satyriasis*', 16 Garofalo); Aretaeus (second century AD; *Ac. Dis* 2.12=34, 11–35, 12 Hude, 'On *Satyriasis*'); Caelius Aurelianus (fifth century AD; *Ac. Dis.* 3, XVIII, 175–187=402 Bendz, '*Satyri-*

pathological details, all authors agree on its core aspect, a deviated sexual behavior unanimously qualified in terms of shamefulness and lack of dignity. *Satyriasis* manifests itself in male patients as a state of painful, uncontrollable erection of the sexual organ, that cannot be relieved through sexual activity. Patients perceive the strong urge to seek relief through intercourse, hence the shameless sexual aggressiveness. In some authors, a female counterpart to the disease is contemplated,[51] in which only the behavioural sexual component is retained, making this an interesting example of "sexual disease" as belonging, at least in part, to a (here disembodied) sphere of psychology and morality.

At *Caus. Ac.* 2.12 (34,15–24 Hude; transl. by F. Adams) Aretaeus describes the psychological manifestation in these patients, emphasising their lack of restraint and inappropriate behaviours towards others. We find again the pathological wrapping oneself up (with shame?), until obscenity takes full control over the person and full-blown indecency appears: "*Wrapped up*, in silent sorrow, they are stupid, as if grievously afflicted with their calamity. But if the affection *overcomes the patient's sense of shame* (ἢν δὲ ὑπερίσχῃ καὶ τὴν αἰδῶ τοῦ ἀνθρώπου τὸ πάθος), he will *lose all restraint of tongue as regards obscenity*, and likewise all restraint in regard to the *open performance of the act*, being *deranged in understanding as to indecency* (παράφοροι τὴν γνώμην ἐς τὸ ἄσχημον); for they cannot restrain themselves, are thirsty, and vomit much phlegm" (περιστελλόμενοι, ἡσυχῇ ἐπίλυποι, κατηφέες, ὥσπερ ἀχθόμενοι τῇ ξυμφορῇ. ἢν δὲ ὑπερίσχῃ καὶ τὴν αἰδῶ τοῦ ἀνθρώπου τὸ πάθος, ἀκρατέες μὲν γλώσσης ἐς τὸ ἄκοσμον, ἀκρατέες δὲ ἐς τὸ ἀμφαδὸν καὶ τῆς τοῦ ἔργου πρήξιος· παράφοροι τὴν γνώμην ἐς τὸ ἄσχημον· κατέχειν γὰρ οὐ δύνανται. διψώδεες· φλέγμα πολλὸν ἐμέουσι). Shortly after, at *Caus. Ac.* 2.12 (35,3–7; transl. by F. Adams), it is evident that a moral evaluation is involved: "of the periods of life, it occurs principally in boys and youths, more especially in such as are naturally prone to sexual intercourse" (ἡλικίῃσι δὲ μειρακίοισι καὶ νέοισι, μάλιστα δὲ ὁκόσοισι ἡ φύσις ἐς ξυνουσίην ἑτοίμη. ὀξύτατον ἠδὲ ἀτερπὲς ἠδὲ ἄκοσμον κακόν). "It is a most *acute, disgusting, and debasing ailment*" (ὀξύτατον ἠδὲ ἀτερπὲς ἠδὲ ἄκοσμον κακόν).

The discussion of this disease has many points of interest for the cultural historian. There is the pathologized *lack of shame*, a sphere of socio-cultural and ethical life which is made the area of health evaluation; there is the anatomical localisation of the trigger, source, and main organic actor of this shame-

---

asis'). Rufus of Ephesus (first century AD), who wrote an entire treatise '*On Satyriasis and Gonorrhea*'.
51 See Gourevitch 1995; 1997; Thumiger 2018: 276–278.

lessness, the male genitalia (with the tension, erection, and pain that prompt the aggressive attempts to find relief).⁵² This entirely novel fact, that a bodily part should be able to become an active ethical agent, its very flesh a catalyser of shame, is most evident with reference to sexual life, and brought to its extreme consequences, with no surprise, in the case of women. In the striking account of clitoridectomy in Philomenus' *Peri Nymphotomias* not pathology, but — it seems — a commonly occurring deformity of the body makes the female external genitalia responsible for individual cases of 'inappropriateness' and 'shamelessness', ἀπρέπεια and αἰσχύνη. The justification (as reported by the sixth century medical compiler Aetius 152,13–153,10) reads as follows:⁵³

> What is called the *nympha* [i.e., the clitoris] is a muscle- or skin-like structure situated at the upper junction of the labia, in the area where the urinary meatus is located. It becomes considerably enlarged in some women when it begins to grow, *and it turns into something indecent and shameful* (εἰς ἀπρέπειαν καὶ αἰσχύνην γίνεται). But also, since it is constantly rubbing against her clothing, it irritates and excites sexual desire, which is why the Egyptians thought the best time to remove it was before it becomes enlarged, when young girls are about to be married.⁵⁴

Paul of Aegina (seventh century) preserves a similar version in his *On clitoridectomy and tail* (Heiberg, CMG IX 2, 112,21–30).

---

52 With a final move, this bodily token is then deprived of its physiological import when the disease is, by way of extension, attributed to women too, "although they lack the organ that can undergo erection"; "it is said (λόγος δὲ) that women also suffer from this affection: that they have the same *impulse* to venery, and the *other symptoms* the same (ἐς τὰ ἀφροδίσια ὁρμὴ ὁμοίη καὶ τὰ λοιπὰ ξύμπαντα τὰ αὐτά). I believe, indeed, that lust (μαχλοσύνην) is engendered in women of a humid temperament, so as to induce a copious discharge of the superfluous humours; but I do not at all believe that they are affected with *satyriasis*, for their nature, being cold, is not adapted to it. But neither, also, has woman the parts necessary for erection" (35, 5–12 Hude). See n. 52 above for references to this discussion about male-female differentiation of sexual diseases.
53 *Aetius Sermo sextidecimus et ultimus erstens aus Handschriften veröffentlicht mit Abbildungen Bemerkungen und Erklärungen* (ed. by Skevos Zervos).
54 Ἡ λεγομένη νύμφη οἷον μυῶδες ἢ δερματῶδες ἐστὶ συγκριμάτιον κείμενον κατὰ τὴν ἄνωθεν τῶν πτερυγωμάτων συμβολήν, καθ' ὃν τόπον ἡ οὐρήθρα τέτακται· μεγεθύνεται δέ τισιν ἐπὶ πλέον τῶν γυναικῶν αὔξησιν λαμβάνον, καὶ εἰς ἀπρέπειαν καὶ αἰσχύνην γίνεται. ἀλλὰ καὶ παρατριβόμενον συνεχῶς ὑπὸ τῶν ἱματίων ἐρεθίζει, καὶ τὴν πρὸς συνουσίαν ὁρμὴν ἐπεγείρει, διόπερ πρὸ τῆς μεγεθοποιήσεως ἔδοξε τοῖς Αἰγυπτίοις ἀφαιρεῖν αὐτὸ τότε μάλιστα, ὁπότε πρὸς γάμον ἄγεσθαι μέλλοιεν αἱ παρθένοι. Here and below, translations from Aetius and Paul are by Sean Coughlin, whom I thank for bringing these passages to my attention.

For some women, the clitoris becomes excessively large *and approaches an indecent shamefulness* (εἰς ἀπρέπειαν αἰσχύνης ἀπαντᾷ). As certain people tell the story, *some women get erections in this part and sexual desire resembling men*. For this reason, when the woman has been placed on her back, with forceps we grasp the excess part of the clitoris and we cut with a scalpel, taking care not to cut it too deep, so that a condition of urinary incontinence does not come about from it. And the 'tail' is a fleshy outgrowth arising from the mouth of the womb and filling the female genitals, sometimes even falling outside like a tail. It is to be removed in the same way as the clitoris.[55]

This bodily localization of shame, combined with its severance from a firm bodily determinism — where there is no natural necessity there is no moral absolution: *satyriasis* involves *some* individuals; the enlarged clitoris is an occurrence in *some* women, not all —, indicates an altogether new way of looking at the body as a complex place of struggle, a landscape with its own moral geography, contradictions, deformities and deceitful lures through which one moves with caution and at the price of great exertion. The most eloquent, and famous example of the complex discussions sexuality and sex originate in this timeframe — admittedly unique in ancient medicine in its richness —, is offered by the discussion of the *Malthacoi* ('passive homosexuals', or 'pathics' at Caelius Aurelianus' *Morb. Chr.* 4.131-2 (848-9 Bendz; transl. by I.E. Drabkin)).[56] Caelius' pathologization of homosexual actions focuses, in the case of the male patients especially, on the shamefulness of operating bodily parts (here: the anus) destined by nature to other use for sexual purposes: "not from nature did this become a human practice, but having lust overcome *modesty* it put to *shameful use* parts intended for other functions" (*non enim hoc humanos ex natura uenit in mores, sed pulso pudore libido etiam in debitas partes obscenis usibus subiugauit*).[57]

---

[55] Ὑπερμεγέθης ἐνίαις γίνεται νύμφη καὶ εἰς ἀπρέπειαν αἰσχύνης ἀπαντᾷ· καθὼς δέ τινες ἱστοροῦσιν, ἔνιαι διὰ τοῦ μέρους καὶ ὀρθιάζουσιν ἀνδράσιν ὁμοίως καὶ πρὸς συνουσίαν ὁρμῶσιν. διόπερ ὑπτίας ἐσχηματισμένης τῆς γυναικὸς μυδίῳ κατασχόντες τὸ περιττὸν τῆς νύμφης ἐκτέμωμεν σμίλῃ φυλαττόμενοι τὸ ἐκ βάθους αὐτὴν ἐκτέμνειν, ἵνα μὴ ῥυαδικὸν ἐκ τούτου γένηται πάθος. καὶ τὴν κέρκωσιν δὲ σαρκώδη ἔκφυσιν οὖσαν ἀπὸ τοῦ στομίου τῆς μήτρας ἀναπληροῦσαν τὸ γυναικεῖον αἰδοῖον, ποτὲ δὲ καὶ εἰς τὰ ἔξω δίκην κέρκου προπίπτουσαν, παραπλησίως ἀφαιρετέον τῇ νύμφῃ.

[56] See my discussion of this text in Thumiger 2018: 277–282.

[57] For a close parallel, see Claudius Ptolemaeus, *Tetrabiblos* III 14 (368–373; trans. by F.E. Robbins), the section *Of the Diseases of the Soul*. Philip van der Eijk was the first to analyse the medicalisation of sexual behaviour in this passage and its points of contact with the text in Caelius Aurelianus: see van der Eijk 2013: 333–335.

8 Conclusion

We have opened this discussion on an essentialist (if a reduced one) claim concerning the emotion of shame, that of the fundamental presence of this emotion and its affiliations (shamefulness, shamelessness) in human medical cultures, basing my analysis on an interpretation of 'illness' as embodied experience, and reading the emotion primarily in terms of self-image, perceived body and bodily exposure. Despite the obvious variables, gradations of shame thus intended seem to belong cross-culturally to human life (and experience of illness). What differs is the narrative mode, and the space allowed to this element within different genres or, in our case, by the different socio-ethical agendas of the medical texts analyzed. Thus, within ancient medicine the authors of the classical period rarely recognize delicacy to pathological experiences and only exceptionally thematize patient shame and the embarrassment of bodily dysfunction.[58] Nonetheless, clinical texts of this period register behaviours which convey this spectrum of emotions, such as hiding and covering oneself; but they do so indirectly, and focusing on the external manifestation of distress. Tragedy is a fit term of comparison: fifth-century drama reaches levels of unique depth in addressing the interlacement of felt embodiment, body-image, and projected visibility to an audience that come together in the experience of being shamed, alongside the ethical and societal consequences a shameful conduct brings. Later medical sources, finally, are both more sensitive to humanistic levels of discourse (ethical, emotional, psychological) and more normative: shame attracts greater attention, and especially in the construction of the idea of mental disorder it becomes important in the evaluation of what is perceived as a 'mental deviance' as much as a physiological defect.

In her exploration of phenomenology, embodiment, and shame, Dolezal stresses how shame is characterized by *visibility* — it is about visibility to others and self-presentation — by being peculiarly "an invisible and silent force, it is unacknowledged, but lurking"[59] — in life, I would add, as much as in a text one analyzes in search for traces of this experience. The analysis of the presence of shame and related emotions in the two phases of medicine I discussed brings out, I hope, the two features that find themselves combined in the experience of

---

58 See Dean-Jones 1995: 48–49 and Leven 2018: 157 on gynecology as a special case; Kosak 2015: 252 on the absence of any mention of shame in male patients in the Hippocratics; Bolton 2015: 278 and Porter 2015: 289–291 on the issue of female shame during visits in Soranus; see also Thumiger 2018: 277–278.
59 Dolezal 2015: xv–xvi.

shame: hiddenness and covering, on the one hand, and external visibility and social judgement, on the other.

Bibliography

Adkins, A.W.H. 1970. *From the Many to the One*. London: Constable.
Barton, C.A. 2002. "*Being in the Eyes*: Shame and Sight in Ancient *Rome*", in: David Fredrick (ed.), *The Roman Gaze. Vision, Power and the Body*. Baltimore/London: Johns Hopkins University Press: 216–236.
Bolton, L. 2015. "Patience for the Little Patient: The Infant in *Soranus' Gynaecia*", in: Georgia Petridou and Chiara Thumiger (eds.), *Homo Patiens. Approaches to the Patient in the Ancient World*. Leiden: Brill: 265–284.
Cairns, D. 1992. *Aidos. The Psychology and Ethics of Honour and Shame in Ancient Greek Literature*. Oxford: Oxford University Press.
Cairns, D. 2001. "Anger and the Veil in Ancient Greek Culture", *Greece & Rome* 48: 18–32.
Cairns, D. 2009. "Weeping and Veiling: Grief, Display, and Concealment in Ancient Greek Culture", in: Thorsten Fögen (ed.), *Tears in the Greco-Roman World*. Berlin: De Gruyter: 37–57.
Cairns, D. 2011a. "Looks of Love and Loathing: cultural models of vision and emotion in ancient Greek culture", *Metis* 9: 37–50.
Cairns, D. 2011b. "Veiling Grief on the Tragic Stage", in: Dana Munteanu (ed.), *Emotion, Genre and Gender in Classical Antiquity*. London: Bloomsbury Academic: 15–33.
Cairns, D. 2011c. "Honour and Shame: modern controversies and ancient values", *Critical Quarterly* 53: 23–41.
Cairns, D. 2016. "Mind, Body, and Metaphor in Ancient Greek Concepts of Emotion", *L'Atelier du centre de recherche historique* 16.
Carel, H. 2016. *Phenomenology of Illness*. Oxford: Oxford University Press.
Crisp, R. 2013. "Homeric Ethics", in: Roger Crisp (ed.), *The Oxford Handbook to the History of Ethics*. Oxford: Oxford University Press.
Cunningham, W. and H. Wilson. 2003. "Shame, Guilt and the Medical Practitioner", *The New Zealand Medical Journal* 116.
Dean-Jones, L. 1995. "Autopsia, Historia and What Women Know: the authority of women in Hippocratic gynaecology", in: Don Bates (ed.), *Knowledge and the Scholarly Medical Traditions: A Comparative Study*. Cambridge: Cambridge University Press: 41–58.
Dean-Jones, L. 1996. *Women's Bodies in Classical Greek Science*. Oxford: Clarendon Press.
Dodds, E.R. 1951. *The Greeks and the Irrational*. Berkeley and Los Angeles: University of California Press.
Dolezal, L. 2015a. "The Phenomenology of Shame in the Clinical Encounter", *Medicine, Health Care and Philosophy* 18(4): 567–576.
Dolezal, L. 2015b. *The Body and Shame: Phenomenology, Feminism, and the Socially Shaped Body*. London: Lexington Books.
Dolezal, L. 2016. "Body Shame and Female Experience", in: Hilge Landweer and Isabella Marcinski (eds.), *Dem Erleben Auf Der Spur: Feminismus und Phänomenologie*. Bielefeld: Transcript Verlag: 45–68.

Dolezal, L. and B. Lyons. 2017. "Health-related Shame: An Affective Determinant of Health?", *Medical Humanities* 43(4): 1–7.

Dolezal, L. 2017. "Shame, Vulnerability and Belonging: Reconsidering Sartre's Account of Shame", *Human Studies* 40(3): 421–438.

Dolezal, L. and B. Lyons (eds.) 2017. *Special Issue of Medical Humanities Journal on Shame, Stigma and Medicine* (*Medical Humanities* 43,4).

Ecca, G. 2018. *Etica medica sulle orme di Ippocrate*. Milan: Editrice Bibiliografica.

Ferrari, C. 1990. "Figures of Speech. The Picture of *Aidos*", *Metis* 5: 185–204.

Van der Eijk, P. 2005. "*The 'theology' of the Hippocratic Treatise On the Sacred Disease*", in: Philip van der Eijk (ed.), *Medicine and Philosophy in Classical Antiquity: Doctors and Philosophers on Nature, Soul, Health and Disease*. Cambridge: Cambridge University Press: 45–73.

Van der Eijk, P. 2013. "Cure and (In)curability of Mental Disorders in Ancient Medical and Philosophical Thought", in: William V. Harris (ed.), *Mental Disorders in the Classical World*. Leiden: Brill: 307–338.

Finglass, P.J. (ed.) 2011. *Sophocles. Ajax: Edited with Introduction, Translation, and Commentary*. Cambridge: Cambridge University Press.

Gill, C. 1996. *Personality in Greek Epic, Tragedy and Philosophy*. Oxford, Clarendon Press.

Gill, C. 2010. *Naturalistic Psychology in Galen and Stoicism*. Oxford: Oxford University Press.

Gill, C. 2013. "Philosophical Therapy as Preventive Psychological Medicine", in: William V. Harris (ed.), *Mental Disorders in the Classical World*, Leiden: Brill: 339–360.

Gill, C. 2018. "Philosophical psychological therapy - did it have any impact on medical practice?", in: Chiara Thumiger and Peter Singer (eds.), *Mental Illness in Ancient Medicine. From Celsus to Paul of Aegina*, Leiden: Brill: 365–380.

Gourevitch, D. 1995. "Une autresatyriasis. Médecine antique, philologie et histoire", *Medicina nei Secoli* 7(2): 273–279.

Gourevitch, D. 1997. "Women Who Suffer from a Man's Disease: the example of satyriasis and the debate on affections specific to the sexes", in: Richard Hawley and Barbara Levick (eds.), *Women in Antiquity. New Assessments*. London: Routledge: 149–165.

Graumann, L. and C. Thumiger. Forthcoming. "Children and the Art of Medical Story-telling: Contemporary Practice and Hippocratic Case-taking Compared," in: Markus Asper (ed.), *Cases and Anecdotes*.

Hall, E. 1997. "The sociology of Athenian tragedy", in: Pat Easterling (ed.), *The Cambridge Companion to Greek Tragedy*. Cambridge: Cambridge University Press: 93–126.

Holmes, B. 2013. "In Strange Lands: Disembodied Authority and the Role of the Physician in the Hippocratic Corpus and Beyond", in: Markus Asper (ed.), *Writing Science. Mathematical and Medical Authorship in Ancient Greece*. Berlin: De Gruyter: 431–472.

Instone, S. 2007. "Darkness my Light: Enigmatic Ajax", in: Patrick Finglass (ed.), *Studies in Ancient Greek Poetry Presented to M. L. West on his Seventieth Birthday*. Oxford: Oxford University Press.

Hamlin, C. 2014. *More Than Hot: A Short History of Fever*. Baltimore: Johns Hopkins University Press.

Israelowich, I. 2017. "The Theme of Illness in Sophocles' *Ajax*", *SCI* 36: 1–16.

Johnson, J.F. and D.C. Clapp. 2005. "Athenian Tragedy: an education in pity", in: Rachel Sternberg (ed.), *Pity and Power in Ancient Athens*. Cambridge: Cambridge University Press: 123–164.

Kazantzidis, G. 2016. "Empathy and the Limits of Disgust in the *Hippocratic Corpus*", in: Donald Lateiner and Dimos Spatharas (eds.), *The Ancient Emotion of Disgust*. Oxford: Oxford University Press: 45–68.
Kosak, J.C. 2005. "A Crying Shame: Pitying the Sick in the Hippocratic Corpus and Greek Tragedy", in: Rachel Sternberg (ed.), *Pity and Power in Ancient Athens*. Cambridge: Cambridge University Press: 253–276.
Kosak, J.C. 2015. "Interpretations of the Healer's Touch in the *Hippocratic Corpus*", in: Georgia Petridou and Chiara Thumiger (eds.), *Homo Patiens. Approaches to the Patient in the Ancient World*. Leiden: Brill: 245–64.
Lazare, A. 1987. "Shame and Humiliation in the Medical Encounter", *Archives of International Medicine* 147: 1653–1658.
Leven, K.-H. 2018. "Ethics and Deontology", in: Peter Pormann (ed.), *The Cambridge Companion to Hippocrates*. Cambridge: Cambridge University Press: 000.
Lyons, B. and L. Dolezal 2017. "Shame, Stigma and Medicine", *Medical Humanities* 43(4): 208–210.
Mattern, S. 2015. "Galen's Anxious Patients: *lype* as anxiety disorder", in: Georgia Petridou and Chiara Thumiger (eds.), *Homo Patiens. Approaches to the Patient in the Ancient World*. Leiden: Brill: 201–223.
Petridou, Georgia and Chiara Thumiger (eds.) 2015. *Homo Patiens. Approaches to the Patient in the Ancient World*. Leiden: Brill.
Porter, A.J. 2015. "Compassion in Soranus' Gynecology and Caelius Aurelianus' On Chronic Diseases", in: Georgia Petridou and Chiara Thumiger (eds.), *Homo Patiens. Approaches to the Patient in the Ancient World*. Leiden: Brill: 285–303.
Short, W. 2020. "'Holism' in Cognitive Approaches to the Ancient Emotions", in: Chiara Thumiger (ed.), *Holism in Ancient Medicine and Its Reception*. Leiden: Brill: 84–110.
Singer, Peter N. 2013. *Galen: Psychological Writings. Avoiding Distress, Character Traits, The Diagnosis and Treatment of the Affections and Errors Peculiar to Each Person's Soul, The Capacities of the Soul Depend on the Mixtures of the Body*. Translated with introduction and notes by V. Nutton, D. Davies and P.N. Singer, with the collaboration of P. Tassinari. Cambridge: Cambridge University Press.
Singer, Peter N. 2018. "Galen's Pathological Soul: Diagnosis and Therapy in Ethical and Medical Texts and Contexts", in: Chiara Thumiger and Peter Singer (eds.), *Mental Illness in Ancient Medicine. From Celsus to Paul of Aegina*. Leiden: Brill: 381–420.
Snell, B. 1960. *The Discovery of the Mind. The Greek Origins of European Thought*. Trans. Thomas G. Rosenmeyer. New York: Torchbooks (*Die Entdeckung des Geistes*. Hamburg 1946).
Sorabji, R. 2014. *Moral Conscience through the Ages: Fifth Century BCE to the Present*. Oxford: Oxford University Press.
Thumiger, C. 2013a. "Mad Eros and Eroticized Madness in Tragedy", in: Ed Sanders, Chiara Thumiger, Christopher Carey, and Nick Lowe (eds.), *Eros in Ancient Greece*. Oxford: Oxford University Press: 27–40.
Thumiger, C. 2013b. "Vision and Knowledge in Greek drama", in: Douglas Cairns, Nancy Rabinowitz, and Sue Blundell (eds.), *Vision and Viewing in Ancient Greece*. Special Issue of *Helios* 40: 223–246.
Thumiger, C. 2016. "Fear, Hope and the Definition of Hippocratic Medicine", in: William V. Harris (ed.), *Popular Medicine in the Graeco-Roman World: Explorations*. Leiden: Brill: 198–214.

Thumiger, C. 2017. *A History of the Mind and Mental Health in Classical Greek Medical Thought.* Cambridge: Cambridge University Press.

Thumiger, C. 2018a. "*A History of the Mind and Mental Health in Classical Greek Medical Thought.* A Resume", *History of Psychiatry* 29: 000.

Thumiger, C. 2018b. "Doctors and Patients", in: Peter Pormann (ed.), *The Cambridge Companion to Hippocrates* Cambridge: Cambridge University Press: 177–194.

Thumiger, C. 2018c. "The Professional Audiences of the Hippocratic *Epidemics*: Patient Cases in Hippocratic Scientific Communication", in: Petros Bouras-Vallianatos and Sophia Xenophontos (eds.), *Greek Medical Literature and its Readers. From Hippocrates to Islam and Byzantium*. London and New York: Routledge: 48–64.

Thumiger, C. Forthcoming. "Animality, Illness and Dehumanisation: The Phenomenology of Illness in Sophocles' *Philoctetes*", in: Giulia Maria Chesi and Francesca Spiegel (eds.), *Undoing the Human: Classical Literature and the Post-Human*. London: Bloomsbury: 000.

Weiss, M.G., J. Ramakrishna, and D. Somma. 2006. "Health-related Stigma: rethinking concepts and interventions", *Psychol. Health Med.* 11: 277–287.

Williams, B. 1992. *Shame and Necessity.* Berkeley: University of California Press.

Yamagata, N. 1994. *Homeric Morality.* Leiden: Brill.

Texts Used

Aetius, ed. Skevos Zervos. 1901. *Aetius Sermo sextidecimus et ultimus. Erstens aus Handschriften veröffentlicht mit Abbildungen Bemerkungen und Erklärungen.* Leipzig: Verlag von Anton Mangkos.

Aretaeus, ed. Karl Hude. 1958. *On the Causes and Indications of Acute Diseases (De Causis et Signis Acut. Morb.), De Causis et Signis Acutorum Morborum;On the Causes and Indications of Chronic Diseases (De Causis et Signis Diut. Morb.), De Causis et Signis Diuturnorum Morborum; On the Therapy of Acute Diseases (Curat. Acut.), De Curatione Acutorum Morborum; On the Therapy of Chronic Diseases (Curat. Diut.), De Curatione Diuturnorum Morborum* (CMG II). Berlin: Akademie-Verlag.

Caelius Aurelianus, ed. Gerhard Bendz. 2002. *On Acute Diseases (Acut.Morb.); On Chronic Diseases (Diut.Morb.), Caelii Aureliani Celerum passionum libri III, Tardarum passionum libri V* (CML VI 1, Editio altera). Berlin: Akademie-Verlag.

Galen, ed. Ernst Wenkebach. 1956. *In Hippocratis Epidemiarum Librum VI Commentaria I–VI* (CMG V 10,2,2, Editio altera). Berlin: Akademie-Verlag.

Hippocrates, ed. Hugo Kühlewein. 1894. *Epidemics I (Epid. I). Hipp. Opera Omnia I.* Leipzig: Teubner: 180–245.

Hippocrates, ed. Hugo Kühlewein. 1894. *Epidemics III (Epid. III). Hipp. Opera Omnia I.* Leipzig: Teubner: 180–245.

Hippocrates, ed. Jacques Jouanna. 2000. *Epidemics V, VII (Epid. V, VII). Epidémies V et VII.* Paris: Les Belles Lettres.

Hippocrates, eds. Daniela Manetti and Amneris Roselli. 1982. *Epidemics VI (Epid. VI). Ippocrate. Epidemie. Libro sesto.* Florence: La nouva Italia editrice.

Hippocrates, ed. Wesley D. Smith. 1994. *Epidemics II, IV (Epid. II, IV) Hippocrates. Volume VII.* Cambridge, MA: Loeb.

Hippocrates, Jacques Jouanna. 2003. *Sacred Disease (Morb.Sacr.). La Maladie Sacrée*. Paris: Les Belles Lettres.
Paul of Aegina, ed. Johannes L. Heiberg. 1924. *Paulus Aegineta, Libri V-VII*, CMG IX 2. Leipzig and Berlin: Teubner.
Sophocles, ed. Hugh Lloyd-Jones and Nigel G. Wilson. 1990. *Sophoclis Fabulae*. Oxford: Oxford University Press.

Translations Used

Aretaeus, trans. Francis Adams. 1856. *The extant works of Aretaeus the Cappadocian*. London: Sydenham Society.

Hippocrates, trans. William H. S. Jones. 1923 *Volume I*. Cambridge, MA: Loeb.
Ancient Medicine
Airs, Waters Places
Epidemics I and III
Oath
Precepts
Nutriment

Hippocrates, trans. Edward T. Withington. 1928. *Volume III* Cambridge, MA: Loeb.
On Wounds in the Head
In the Surgery
Fractures, Joints, Mochlicon
Hippocrates, trans. Wesley D. Smith. 1994. *Volume VII*. Cambridge, MA: Loeb.
Epidemics 2–7
Sophocles, transl. Richard C. Jebb. 1917. *The Tragedies of Sophocles, translated into English prose* Cambridge: Cambridge University Press.

George Kazantzidis
Reading and Misreading Medical Emotions: Some Cases of Female Patients in the Hippocratic *Epidemics*

Abstract: This chapter argues that, while the bodily origin and nature of emotions in early medical literature are indeed incontestable, in some cases a patient's emotional profile reveals more about his or her "psychology" than is usually assumed to do. It shows that emotions in medical records should not be exclusively discussed as though they were merely symptoms of an ailing body. There are cases where the narrative suggests — or, at least, leaves us enough space to assume — that the emotions displayed by a patient are deeply anchored to their behavioral traits; they are manifestations, in other words, of the mood patterns and the emotional make-up that characterize them as individuals. The case studies discussed mainly revolve around female patients. The reason is simple: among the hundreds of cases reported throughout the *Epidemics*, the richest and most distinctively psychological patient-profiles concern women. My reading attempts to use medical emotions as ways of recovering the ancient (female) patient's identity and character — a character that is all too often believed to be suppressed and become obliterated under the sweeping presence of bodily symptoms which constitute the experience of what we call "illness".

Emotions feature time and again in the case histories of the Hippocratic *Epidemics*. The general tendency in scholarship is to discuss them as affective disorders which make their presence felt in the course of, and as an immediate result, of *physical* illness. Unwarranted depression, sudden fits of excessive fear, anger and anxiety — all these conditions are regularly reported by doctors as signs indicating that something is wrong with the patient's *body*. The underlying causes vary: sometimes emotional disturbance is attributed to a radical change of temperature or to humoural imbalance; in other cases, an organ is believed to have been affected, which is taken to be the seat of intelligence, and as a consequence a person's mental functions and her control of emotions become compromised.

The present chapter adopts a different perspective. I argue that, while the bodily origin and nature of emotions in early medical literature are indeed incontestable, in some cases a patient's emotional profile reveals more about his or her "psychology" than is usually assumed to do. What I mean by this is that emotions in medical records should not be exclusively discussed as though they were merely symptoms of an ailing body. There are cases where the narrative suggests — or, at least, leaves us enough space to assume — that the emotions displayed by a patient are deeply anchored to their behavioural traits; they are manifestations, in other words, of the mood patterns and the emotional makeup that characterize them as individuals. My case studies will mainly revolve around female patients. The reason is simple: among the hundreds of cases reported throughout the *Epidemics*, the richest and most distinctively psychological patient-profiles concern women, for reasons that will be explained in detail below. For the time being, suffice it to be noticed that my reading attempts to use medical emotions as ways of recovering the ancient patient's identity and character — a character that is all too often believed to be suppressed and become obliterated under the sweeping presence of bodily symptoms which constitute the experience of what we call "illness".

1 Trapped in her Body: The "Gloomy" Woman of Thasos (*Epidemics* 3.17, case 11)

Let me begin straightaway with a medical report which stands out as perhaps the most unique and puzzling one, when it comes to emotions, in the entire of the *Epidemics* collection:

> Ἐν Θάσῳ γυνὴ δυσάνιος ἐκ λύπης μετὰ προφάσιος ὀρθοστάδην ἐγένετο ἄγρυπνός τε καὶ ἀπόσιτος καὶ διψώδης ἦν καὶ ἀσώδης. ᾤκει δὲ πλησίον τῶν Πυλάδου ἐπὶ τοῦ λείου. τῇ πρώτῃ ἀρχομένης νυκτὸς φόβοι, λόγοι πολλοί, δυσθυμίη, πυρέτιον λεπτόν. πρωὶ σπασμοὶ πολλοί· ὅτε δὲ διαλίποιεν οἱ σπασμοὶ οἱ πολλοί, παρέλεγεν, ᾐσχρομύθει· πολλοὶ πόνοι, μεγάλοι, συνεχέες. δευτέρῃ διὰ τῶν αὐτῶν, οὐδὲν ἐκοιμᾶτο, πυρετὸς ὀξύτερος. τρίτῃ οἱ μὲν σπασμοὶ ἀπέλιπον, κῶμα δὲ καὶ καταφορὴ καὶ πάλιν ἔγερσις· ἀνήϊσσε, κατέχειν οὐκ ἠδύνατο, παρέλεγε πολλά, πυρετὸς ὀξύς, ἐς νύκτα δὲ ταύτην ἵδρωσε πολλῷ θερμῷ δι' ὅλου· ἄπυρος, ὕπνωσε, πάντα κατενόει, ἐκρίθη. περὶ δὲ τρίτην ἡμέρην οὖρα μέλανα λεπτά, ἐναιώρημα δὲ ἐπὶ πολὺ στρογγύλον, οὐχ ἱδρύετο, περὶ δὲ κρίσιν γυναικεῖα πολλὰ κατέβη.[1]

> In Thasos a woman of gloomy temperament, after a grief with a reason for it, without taking to bed lost sleep and appetite, and suffered thirst and nausea. She lived near the place of Pylades on the plain. First day: As night began there were fears, much rambling, de-

---

[1] 3.134 L.

pression and slight feverishness. Early in the morning frequent convulsions; whenever these frequent convulsions intermitted, she wandered and uttered obscenities; many pains, severe and continuous. Second day: Same symptoms; no sleep; fever more acute. Third day: The convulsions ceased, but were succeeded by coma and oppression, followed in turn by wakefulness. She would jump up; could not restrain herself; wandered a great deal; fever acute; on this night a copious, hot sweating all over; no fever; slept, was perfectly rational, and had a crisis. About the third day urine black and thin, with particles mostly round floating in it, which did not settle. Near the crisis copious menstruation.

Text and translation in Jones 1923a: 276–277

On the face of it, there is nothing unusual about this case history. In fact, it is quite common in early medical texts to read about female patients who display *dusthumia*[2] at some point of their illness, along with conditions such as fever, insomnia, restlessness, and anxiety. The Hippocratic physicians find women to have a despondent nature when compared to men;[3] their underlying principle that a woman's body is "colder",[4] in combination with the belief that an excessively low temperature is sometimes enough by itself to trigger a state of depres-

---

[2] The noun — variously translated as "despondency", "dejection" or "depression" — is not found in Homer and Aeschylus, but is attested in Euripides and Sophocles. A quick look at its tragic usage reveals that δυσθυμία describes a psychological state of distress, which is so severe that it can even make someone fall ill (a Sophoclean fragment — fr.663 P. — informs us that: τίκτουσι γάρ τοι καὶ νόσους δυσθυμίαι, "for sicknesses too are caused by depressions", in the translation by Lloyd-Jones 1996: 319); what is more, it seems to affect women, more than men; see e.g. Eur. *Med.* 691, Soph. *Elec.* 218; cf. [Hom.] *In Cererem* 362. The fact that δυσθυμία occurs only a couple of times in Plato (one of them found in the "medical" section of *Timaeus* 87a, the other in *Laws* 666b7) allows us to identify it as an originally poetic word that was picked up, from an early point on, by medical writers who then turned it into a technical term, designating with it a pathological state of sadness; not just sadness, that is, as a normal response to adverse circumstances in a person's life, but the sort of sadness that is symptomatic of an illness and requires further examination; see [Hipp.] *On Ancient Medicine* 10; *Epidemics* 1.2.9, 3.2.6, 3.2.11, 3.3.17; *Aphorisms* 6.23; cf. *On the Diseases of Women* 2.72. Aristotle does not use the noun but has twice the adjective δύσθυμον: the first time it is applied to animals of a generally mild temperament (*Hist. anim.* 488b13); the second time, it identifies a characteristic quality of women (*Hist. anim.* 608b10), when one compares them to men.

[3] As we read in *Diseases of Young Girls*: ἀθυμοτέρη γὰρ καὶ λυπηροτέρη ἡ φύσις ἡ γυναικείη (8.466 L.). Cf. Arist. *Hist. anim.* 608a7–11: Διόπερ γυνὴ ἀνδρὸς ἐλεημονέστερον καὶ ἀρίδακρυ μᾶλλον, ἔτι δὲ φθονερώτερον καὶ μεμψιμοιρότερον, καὶ φιλολοίδορον μᾶλλον καὶ πληκτικώτερον. Ἔστι δὲ καὶ δύσθυμον μᾶλλον τὸ θῆλυ τοῦ ἄρρενος καὶ δύσελπι. For this text, see Mayhew 2004: 9–102; Sissa 2018: 159–160.

[4] See e.g. *Regimen* 1.34 where it is argued that because menstrual blood (which is hot by its nature) becomes evacuated every month, the female body ends up being cold; see Föllinger 1996: 31–32. Hanson 1992 argues that, in *Diseases of Women*, women's heat varies over the month, hottest just before menstruation and coldest at its end. Cf. King 1998: 32–33.

sion,⁵ makes them overall sensitive in noticing the dusthumic symptoms displayed by their female patients. A closer look at *Epid.* 3.17.11 yields more common patterns. *Dusthumia* is often accompanied in Hippocratic writings by φόβος ("fear"):⁶ φόβος conveys a heightened sense of engagement with the external environment (once we see it, we start wondering about the patient's *object* of fear), while *dusthumia* suggests a certain degree of withdrawal into oneself.⁷ We often get to hear of patients who feel despondent "for no apparent reason", the point being that however hard they are pressed to disclose what is troubling them, they will not tell.⁸ Fear and *dusthumia* thus seem to be generally working in complementary ways, and together they are opposed to other symptoms which imply an aggressive behaviour. In our text, such a symptom is indicated by ᾐσχρομύθει (an extremely rare verb in ancient Greek),⁹ which suggests that the patient becomes mentally agitated — perhaps even angry and violent¹⁰ with those around her —, using obscene and foul language. This grouping of emotions into polarized opposites is employed on a standard basis by Hippo-

---

5 See e.g. *Coa Praesagia* 4: Ἐκ καταψύξιος φόβος καὶ ἀθυμίη ἄλογος ἐς σπασμὸν ἀποτελευτᾷ. Cf. [Arist.] *Problemata Physica* 954b35–36 (on black bile): ψυχροτέρα μὲν γὰρ οὖσα τοῦ καιροῦ δυσθυμίας ποιεῖ ἀλόγους, and 955a16–17: διὸ καὶ οἱ μὲν παῖδες εὐθυμότεροι, οἱ δὲ γέροντες δυσθυμότεροι. οἱ μὲν γὰρ θερμοί, οἱ δὲ ψυχροί.
6 E.g. in *Epid.* 1.29, 3.2.11; *Aphorisms* 6.23: ἢν φόβος ἢ δυσθυμίη πολὺν χρόνον ἔχουσα διατελῇ, μελαγχολικὸν τὸ τοιοῦτον.
7 On *dusthumia* and silence, see e.g. *Epid.* 3.2.6: σιγῶσα, οὐδὲν διελέγετο· δυσθυμίη· ἀνελπίστως ἑωυτῆς εἶχεν. Already in tragedy, *dusthumia* comes with a visible degree of introversion and appears to present obstacles to the communication between the one who has been affected and those around him, e.g. in Eur. *Ion* 255: τί χρῆμ' **ἀνερμήνευτα** δυσθυμῆι, γύναι; *Med.* 691: τί φῄς; **σαφῶς** μοι σὰς φράσον δυσθυμίας. Cf. Montiglio 2000: 228–233.
8 See Kazantzidis 2018: 42: "Hippocratic writers are ... aware that, under normal circumstances, a person's emotional state needs to be sufficiently explained by his external environment... Accordingly, when someone is behaving emotionally in ways that lack an identifiable, external stimulus, the suspicion is raised by doctors that a hidden, organic cause is affecting the body's chemistry and causes the patient to behave erratically... *Coa praesagia* 4 (V.588,4–5 L.=108 Potter) speaks of ἄλογος ἀθυμίη, a feeling of 'groundless' despondency, even though it has previously identified excessive coldness in the body as an internal cause".
9 On the use and semantics of obscene language in antiquity, see Halliwell 2004: 117–130.
10 On the only other occasion that the verb is attested in the Hippocratic Corpus, violence is explicitly present (*Epid.* 4.15 = 5.152 L.): Ὁ πρῶτος παρενεχθείς, μειράκιον ... πυρετὸς περικαής, ἄγρυπνος, κοιλίη κυρτή. οὗτος παρέκρουσεν, οἶμαι ὀγδόῃ, τρόπον τὸν ἀκόλαστον, ἀνίστασθαι, μάχεσθαι, αἰσχρομυθεῖν ἰσχυρῶς, οὐ τοιοῦτος ἐών, "The first to have delirium, a young man ... Burning fever, sleepless, belly bulging. He was delirious on the eighth day, I think, in the irrepressible way: leapt up, fought, used very foul language. He wasn't that type" (translation in W.D. Smith 1994, 97).

cratic physicians when they are trying to figure out a patient's profile: thinking in pairs (e.g. fear and sadness), and establishing connections between contrasting states of mind (e.g. mental withdrawal vs. mental agitation) emerge as crucial ways of making sense of the patient's shattered and fragmented world[11] — and in this respect the woman of Thasos presents us with a fairly typical case.

That said, *Epid.* 3.17.11 has a rather unusual detail at its beginning. The medical author (either because he happens to be himself familiar with the patient or because her relatives and friends have informed him so) finds it significant to start by telling us that the woman had by nature a "gloomy temperament". Δυσάνιος is an intriguing word, not very commonly attested in ancient Greek,[12] and, as is to be expected, not a term that would have escaped Galen's linguistic attention. For Galen, the word designates what we would call an "over-sensitive" person, someone who is too easily distressed even by little, insignificant things (ἐπὶ τοῖς μικροῖς ἀνιᾶται), or, when a cause for worry is actually present, becomes upset more deeply and for a longer period of time than other people do (καὶ ἐπὶ τοῖς μεγάλοις μᾶλλον ἢ οἱ ἄλλοι ἄνθρωποι <ἢ> πλείω χρόνον).[13] Precisely because a person of this nature does not always need a specific "reason" to be moody and irritable, the medical author adds the information that, in that particular case, something had actually happened to the woman in Thasos (though what this was precisely, we are never told): γυνὴ δυσάνιος **ἐκ λύπης μετὰ προφάσιος** ὀρθοστάδην ἐγένετο ἄγρυπνός τε καὶ ἀπόσιτος. Πρόφασις, as James Hankinson observes, "is simply the ostensible reason or surface cause for something, as contrasted with its full cause or complete reason (generally denoted in the Hippocratic Corpus by the term *aition*)".[14] This definition seems to work well in our case: we could say that the real cause for the patient's illness is her own disposition and bad temperament, while *prophasis* points in the direction of a painful incident (ἐκ λύπης) which serves as a trigger.

So, in what sense does δυσάνιος stand out as an unusual detail? The reason is that among the hundreds of patient stories reported in the *Epidemics*, this is the only case where a patient's character is so explicitly and so meaningfully highlighted as being directly relevant to the illness that follows. In this respect, it is by no means a coincidence that — once more, quite exceptionally by Hippo-

---

[11] On polarity as a hermeneutic tool in classical Greek medicine and philosophy, see Lloyd 1966.
[12] This is the only time that we find it in the Hippocratic Corpus. See Pigeaud 1981: 394.
[13] Galen, *In Hippocratis librum iii epidemiarum commentarii* 17a.778 K.
[14] Hankinson 1998: 58.

cratic standards — an unpleasant event is said to be the trigger for the illness; consequently, and without stretching things too much, we could speak of a "psychological" origin in this instance.[15] In the vast majority of cases where emotions such as sadness, fear, joy, and anger make their appearance in the Hippocratic Corpus, they are mentioned as *symptoms*: something bodily is always at play, which then affects principally the patient's *sôma*, and *as a result* alters also the patient's mood and emotional patterns. Emotions, in other words, guide us into what is ultimately a bodily — sometimes hidden and sometimes more apparent — origin of illness, usually yielding information about the body's internal temperature, the excess of one humour or the other, or an organ that has been affected.[16] The woman of Thasos is no such case: having a fully-shaped and distinctive emotional profile of her own, she is said to develop bodily symptoms as a *reaction* to a psychologically painful event. The usual order has been reversed here: the patient's emotions are not incidentally mentioned as side-effects of a bodily condition, but lie instead at the very origin of it.

Historians of Greek medicine point out time and again that while some sort of distinction between different "temperaments" is already at play in the Hippocratic Corpus, these temperaments do not yet carry with them any psychological or moral significance, and they are considered exclusively from a physical point of view. For example, the adjective "melancholic", μελαγχολικός, does not mean someone with a "gloomy temperament", but serves simply as an indication that a person's physical constitution is defined and shaped — in ways that are not always fully explained — by the presence of "(black) bile", μέλαινα χολή, in their body.[17] Hippocratic patients are missing the detailed psychological profiling which one finds, for instance, in Aristotle's ethical writings; when visited by the doctor, it is as though they have been stripped from their identities, from all those distinctive qualities that make them different "personalities"

---

15 Cf. *Epid.* 3.17, case 15 (3.142 L.): Ἐν Θάσῳ Δελεάρκεος γυναῖκα, ἣ κατέκειτο ἐπὶ τοῦ λείου, πυρετὸς φρικώδης, ὀξὺς **ἐκ λύπης ἔλαβεν**. ἐξ ἀρχῆς δὲ περιεστέλλετο καὶ διὰ τέλεος αἰεὶ σιγῶσα ἐψηλάφα, ἔτιλλεν, ἔγλυφεν, ἐτριχολόγει, δάκρυα καὶ πάλιν γέλως, οὐκ ἐκοιμᾶτο, "In Thasos the wife of Delearces, who lay sick on the plain, was seized after a grief with an acute fever with shivering. From the beginning she would wrap herself up, and throughout, without speaking a word, she would fumble, pluck, scratch, pick hairs, weep and then laugh, but she did not sleep". As Thumiger 2017: 364 points out, this text and *Epid.* 3.17.11 are the only two cases in the Hippocratic Corpus where we have an *explicit* reference to a psychological origin, or trigger, for a disease. Cf. Lloyd 1995: 70.
16 See Kazantzidis 2019.
17 See Jouanna 2012: 229–236.

from one another, appearing instead as "bodies in need of repair".[18] Precisely because their subjectivity is being downplayed, we hardly ever get to hear of a Hippocratic doctor engaging in dialogue with these patients — trying to make them feel better emotionally, lift their spirits or address their fears — as part of the therapy.[19]

There is an agenda here, which touches directly upon issues of authority, and is also extremely significant for our present discussion. Brooke Holmes has shown how the Hippocratic physician capitalizes on what she calls a "disembodied authority", a subject position, that is, from which he can objectively observe the pain and illness of others, while staying himself immune, as it were, to the perils of embodiment.[20] This near-total invisibility of the physician's *body* translates, I would argue, also to the physician's silence when it comes to expressing his *emotions*. The medical scene is one full of tragic suffering and pain, yet doctors avoid mentioning their emotional involvement.[21] Inevitably this physical and emotional distancing on the doctor's part reflects also on the patient's own de-emotionalization: what is at stake here, in other words, is an attempt to stop seeing the patient as an emotive subject, and turn him instead into an affected and ailing body: this guarantees both a frame in which authority can be more easily exerted (since the patient becomes "silenced") but also, in theory, an environment of clinical detachment that can yield better and more effective therapeutic results since all medical attention is focused on the body — which is all that should matter.

---

18 This is not to say of course that the Hippocratic physicians are entirely blind to the individual habits and character of the patient (see Gundert 2000: 34–35); still, they do not seem to invest in it too much when it comes to the diagnosis and therapy of illness. Cf. Holmes 2013a on the limited attention paid by Hippocratic physicians on their patients *qua* agents: "Even when the Hippocratic writers are implicating the springs of our actions in physical conditions, they are doing so as part of a larger project to account for all of human nature within a limited set of causal terms, rather than addressing patients as agents with a critical role to play in health and disease" (2013: 18).
19 See Thumiger 2020: 4 (on the conspicuous absence of the so-called "therapy of the word" in the Hippocratic Corpus): "The impression is that the medicine of this early period programmatically excluded from its domain any aspect that might have to do with the emotions, with subjectivity, with the ethical and private — in short, whatever belongs to the personal sphere and comes to the fore in psychotherapy". Cf. Thumiger 2017: 335–345; Graumann-Thumiger 2019: 43.
20 Holmes 2013b.
21 See e.g. Kazantzidis 2016, on the doctors' systematic avoidance to express disgust at what they touch and see during medical practice.

In this context, we often find cases where emotions hardly register as being categorically different from other, bodily, symptoms. Take, for instance, the cluster of symptoms listed in *Epid.* 1.2.9, where we read that in those affected "right from the beginning there was acute fever with slight rigors, sleeplessness, thirst, nausea, slight sweats about the forehead and collar-bones ... much delirium, fears, depression, very cold extremities, toes and hands, especially the latter" (φόβοι, δυσθυμίαι, ἄκρεα περίψυχρα, πόδες ἄκροι, μᾶλλον δὲ τὰ περὶ χεῖρας).[22] "Fears" and "depression", in Jones' Loeb translation, have been squeezed by the medical author between thirst and nausea, sweats in the forehead and coldness in the hands. It is, of course, significant that terms which involve the patient's psychology make their presence felt in the text; however, it is equally noteworthy that the medical author is not willing to isolate them and discuss them independently. Fear and sadness seem to be simply mentioned in order to confirm the fact that the body's temperature has gone low (cf. ἄκρεα περίψυχρα).

Against this background, the woman of Thasos presents us with a unique, psychologically nuanced and poignant case history. This psychologizing attitude is precisely what Galen finds puzzling in his comments on the text (*In Hippocratis librum iii epidemiarum commentarii* 17a.778 K.):

> Θαυμάζω γε μήν, πῶς οὐ προσέγραψεν ἐπὶ τῆς γυναικὸς ταύτης ἤτοι γε ἐπεσχῆσθαι τὰ καταμήνια παντάπασιν ἢ μὴ τελέως γεγονέναι. φαίνεται γὰρ ὀξέως τε ἅμα καὶ πληθωρικῶς νοσῆσαι καὶ τῇ τρίτῃ τῶν ἡμερῶν εἰς νύκτα δι' ἱδρώτων τε κριθῆναι καὶ καταμηνίων ἐκκρίσεως. ἀλλὰ καὶ μετὰ τὴν κρίσιν ἐκκενωθέντα πολλὰ βέβαιον εἰργάσατο τὴν γενομένην ἀπαλλαγὴν τοῦ νοσήματος. ἡ δὲ τῶν οὔρων χροιὰ καίτοι μέλαινα γενομένη χαλεπὸν οὐδὲν εἰργάσατο, διότι καταμηνίων ἐπίσχεσις ἦν μελαγχολικωτέρων, ἐφ' οἷς εἰκότως ἡ γυνὴ δυσάνιος ἐγένετο καὶ φοβερὰ καὶ παρέκρουσεν ἐν μέρει ποτὲ καὶ κωματώδης γενομένη.

I am surprised by the fact that the author did not add for this woman that she must have suffered either from a complete retention of the menses or because she did not menstruate normally. For, it is clear that her illness was both acute and full, and on the night of the third day she had a *crisis* through sweating and the secretion of menses. And even after the crisis, her copious menstruation made it certain that she had a full recovery from the illness. The fact that her urine was black did not cause any trouble, because the menses that had been retained inside her body were of a melancholic nature; and it was because of this that she naturally became gloomy and scared, and she lost her wits and, at some point, she even fell into a coma.[23]

---

22 Translation in Jones 1923a: 173.
23 My translation.

And yet, this is not exactly what the Hippocratic text is telling us. Galen explains *Epid*. 3.17(11) in light of other Hippocratic parallels which make it clear that *dusthumia* in women is most often connected to an excess of black bile in their uterus. As we read in *Diseases of Women* 2.72 (8.364–66 L.), "When a woman has a headache and pain in her bregma and throat, sees things spinning before her eyes, becomes sullen and afraid, passes dark urines and the same kind of fluid from her uterus, has nausea, and feels depressed (καὶ ἄση ἔχῃ καὶ δυσθυμέῃ), then there is dark bile in her uterus".[24] The fact that the woman of Thasos displays similar symptoms is enough to make Galen suspect that something must have gone wrong with her menstruation too, and then to wonder why this crucial detail has been omitted from the text. However, the story in *Epid*. 3.17(11) is a different one: whatever the condition of the patient might have been, it started — as we are explicitly told — because of an incident that made her very distressed (ἐκ λύπης μετὰ προφάσιος), and it was certainly related to the fact that this particular woman was, by nature, *dusanios* — a word that is supposed to introduce a trait of her character, and not, as Galen would have it, an incidental side-effect of her retained menses (διότι καταμηνίων ἐπίσχεσις ἦν μελαγχολικωτέρων, ἐφ' οἷς εἰκότως ἡ γυνὴ δυσάνιος ἐγένετο). Whether deliberately or not, Galen is misreading at this point the Hippocratic passage and, by doing so, he almost deprives us of a wonderfully nuanced character who enters the pathological landscape of the *Epidemics* not because of her body but because of her moody temperament.

2 *Mis*understanding Emotions in the Hippocratic Corpus

Galen's reading illustrates, I suggest, how emotions in a clinical context are often liable to misconstructions and misunderstandings. In fact, such misunderstandings are already deeply ingrained in the Hippocratic texts, in the sense that physicians there record emotional symptoms primarily as signs of an ailing body; this means that they do not subject them to further scrutiny and they do not use them as tools that would help them understand better how, for instance, their patients might be responding emotionally to their illness, how the feelings

---

[24] Translation in Potter 2018: 403–405.

that affect them, in the course of the illness, may be related to their established mood patterns and whether they are generally acting out of character or not.[25]

Assessing a patient's emotions in a clinical context is not, of course, an easy thing to do. Using Fricker's notion of "epistemic injustice", Havi Carel observes that:

> Ill people are more vulnerable to testimonial injustice, because they are often regarded as cognitively unreliable, *emotionally compromised* (emphasis added), or existentially unstable in ways that render their testimonies and interpretations suspect. Ill people are also more vulnerable to hermeneutical injustice, because the kind of experiences illness affords are often difficult to make sense of and communicate. Perhaps certain extreme and unique experiences cannot be communicated in any direct, propositional manner, and so are only shareable with persons with whom one shares a standpoint or a sense of solidarity.[26]

Carel's point is that there are serious limits on the quality and amount of information that a patient can communicate to a doctor. This is particularly relevant to the texts which I am examining here, especially if we consider the fact that when some sort of emotional trouble makes its appearance in the *Epidemics*, this happens in close association with the patient's mental and cognitive impairment. Thus, when the woman of Thasos begins to display symptoms of "fear" and "depression", the author links them to delirious talk: νυκτὸς φόβοι, **λόγοι πολλοί**, δυσθυμίη, πυρέτιον λεπτόν. πρωὶ σπασμοὶ πολλοί· ὅτε δὲ διαλίποιεν οἱ σπασμοὶ οἱ πολλοί, **παρέλεγεν**, ᾐσχρομύθει. The terms highlighted in this passage occur on a regular basis throughout the *Epidemics*; they are taken to suggest a (temporary) loss of capacity to think and talk in a way that is comprehensible to others.[27] Accordingly, just as words fail to make sense and turn into "an irredeemable babble",[28] so do the patient's emotions become compromised, and they turn to incoherent and disjointed affective manifestations that can only reveal so much about how the patient interacts emotionally with his or her environment; what they are believed to do instead is point to an unbalanced humoural chemistry, or to a sudden change in the body's temperature, or to an internal organ whose function has been compromised, and so on. In this context, it is often difficult to tell whether certain terms should be trans-

---

25 See the exceptional reference in *Epid.* 4.15 (cited in n. 11 above): Ὁ πρῶτος παρενεχθείς, μειράκιον ... πυρετὸς περικαής ... τρόπον τὸν ἀκόλαστον, ἀνίστασθαι, μάχεσθαι, αἰσχρομυθεῖν ἰσχυρῶς, **οὐ τοιοῦτος ἐών**. This is an extremely rare occurrence where a Hippocratic physician observes that the patient suffering from delirium "was not his usual self".
26 Carel 2016: 182.
27 See Thumiger 2017: 388–389. Cf. Kidd 2014: 4–5.
28 Porter 2002: 156.

lated as referring to what we would call an "emotion" or whether they simply designate a bodily symptom.[29]

While all this is to be expected in the context of Hippocratic medicine — where, according to Peter Singer, a body and mind dualism does not yet exist, and the body accounts for the totality of experience —,[30] it also has certain consequences: first and foremost, that of turning the patient into a silent, non-active participant, a body to be deciphered but not a "person" to converse with and read in his/her emotions something deeper than a simple physiological reaction. This reductive approach can prove particularly misleading when it comes to female patients, who are constantly exposed to a number of psychologically demanding and extremely testing experiences, such as menstruation, defloration, pregnancy, birth and abortion. In what follows, I will look briefly at some such cases, and I will try to illustrate how women's emotions can be often gravely *mis*read by their doctors. But let me start first with an unsettling sepulchral epigram by Antiphanes (3 G-P), written for Petal who died a virgin at the night of her marriage:

Δυσμοίρων θαλάμων ἐπὶ παστάσιν οὐχ Ὑμέναιος,
Ἀίδης ἔστη πικρογάμου Πετάλης.
δείματι γὰρ μούνην πρωτόζυγα Κύπριν ἀν' ὄρφνην
φεύγουσαν, ξυνὸν παρθενικαῖσι φόβον,
φρουροδόμοι νηλεῖς κύνες ἔκτανον· ἣν δὲ γυναῖκα
ἐλπὶς ἰδεῖν, ἄφνως ἔσχομεν οὐδὲ νέκυν.

At the doors of the ill-fated chamber of Petal, bride of sorrow,
There stood not Hymen but Hades.
As she fled in terror, alone through the darkness, away from
Aphrodite's first yoking — a shared fear of maidens —
She was killed by the pitiless, house-guarding dogs. Our hope was
To see a wife; suddenly we had not even a corpse.[31]

In Simon Goldhill's words, "the poem ... deploys a set of standard motifs: the fear of virgins ... the woman who flees ... the worry of penetration, leading to the dismemberment of the body, so that the moment of transition does not merely confuse the *telos* of marriage and the *telos* of death, but also violently distorts the standard idea of the wedding-night as a specifically *bodily* transfor-

---

[29] See Kazantzidis 2021. Cf. Cairns 2015.
[30] Singer 1992.
[31] Translation by Goldhill 1995: 37.

mation."³² That the transition from girlhood to womanhood can be rather painful and emotionally testing for a young *parthenos* is also observed by Hippocratic physicians — only in that case the whole situation is interpreted in a radically different way. The Hippocratic Περί παρθενίων is full of emotional vocabulary. Young girls at the age of marriage (ὁκόσῃσιν ὥρη γάμου) are observed by the author to exhibit all sorts of erratic behaviour: they become frightened and terrified because they think they see malevolent spirits; they throw themselves down the wells or hang themselves; they become infatuated with the idea of death and they desire it as if it were a good thing. These observations could have been a wonderfully nuanced comment on the tremendous pressures exerted on a young woman at the age of marriage, and on the responses this pressure might elicit, had it not been for the medical author's blunt statement, at the beginning of the text, that all this comes down to a single *bodily* cause: because too much blood is trapped in the young girl's body, it flows upwards and floods the area around the heart — which is taken to be the seat of cognition. The patient thus becomes deranged, hence her erratic mental and emotional behaviour. One could not have come up with a more narrowly focused and reductive explanation. We can think here of how often a Hippocratic physician must have come across an emotionally troubled and stressed young girl;³³ and how often, instead of inquiring into what might be troubling her, he simply recommended marriage (and sex) as the only solution — the idea being that defloration will remove some kind of impediment —,³⁴ and then the trapped blood will flow out easily. Rather than look at each female patient individually, Hippocratic physicians operate on the basis of pre-established patterns and cultural stereotypes: this is just the way women are — we read at a point of the Περί παρθενίων —, 'fainthearted' and 'sorrowful' (ἀθυμοτέρη γὰρ καὶ λυπηροτέρη ἡ φύσις ἡ γυναικείη), hence their extreme reactions and suicidal behaviour when their blood circulation has been compromised. What is striking is that in a text which is entirely devoted to the emotional troubles of young girls, there is not even a point where the possibility is entertained that other, more "psychological", causes may be involved.

---

32 Goldhill 1995: 37.
33 Sometimes possibly in love. McNamara 2016: 319–320 aptly observes that many of the symptoms reported in the *Diseases of Young Girls* recall the symptomatology of lovesickness in literary sources.
34 The medical author makes no explicit mention of a virginal hymen. See the discussion in Sissa 2013: 91–92; cf. Sissa 1990.

Misunderstandings persist even when the girls make the transition and become mothers. Often the medical texts speak of women who have just had a miscarriage, and suffer from severe complications.[35] Among the latter, "fear" and "sadness" make their appearance, as for instance in *Epidemics* 3.1.11 (3.62 L.):

> Ἑτέρην ἐξ **ἀποφθορῆς** περὶ πεντάμηνον, Ἰκέτεω γυναῖκα, πῦρ ἔλαβεν. ἀρχομένη κωματώδης ἦν, καὶ πάλιν ἄγρυπνος, ὀσφύος ὀδύνη, κεφαλῆς βάρος. δευτέρῃ κοιλίη ἐπεταράχθη ὀλίγοισι, λεπτοῖσιν, ἀκρήτοισι τὸ πρῶτον. τρίτῃ πλείω, χείρω· νυκτὸς οὐδὲν ἐκοιμήθη. τετάρτῃ παρέκρουσε, **φόβοι, δυσθυμίαι**. δεξιῷ ἴλλαινε, ἴδρωσε περὶ κεφαλὴν ὀλίγῳ ψυχρῷ, ἄκρεα ψυχρά.

> Another woman, after a miscarriage about the fifth month, the wife of Hicetas, was seized with fever. At the beginning she had alternations of coma and sleeplessness; pain in the loins; heaviness in the head. Second day. Bowels disordered with scanty, thin stools, which at first were uncompounded. Third day. Stools more copious and worse; no sleep at night. Fourth day. Delirium; fears; depression. Squinting of the right eye; slight cold sweat about the head; extremities cold.[36]

A miscarriage is by itself a profoundly traumatic event, all the more so — we may add — in the ancient world[37] considering the sheer violence used by medical practitioners for the extraction of the dead fetus. Consider, for instance, the advice given in *The Diseases of Women* 1.70 (8.148 L.): when you are trying to pull it out of the woman, and the fetus is "at the level of its shoulders, cut the two arms at their shoulder joints. After you have removed these, if it is possible to dislodge it, simply draw the rest out. But if it does not respond to your traction, sever the whole chest up as far as the jugulars, being careful not to cut into the belly or strip off any part of the fetus, since the belly, intestine and feces would then come out, and if any of these do the case becomes more troublesome. Also break up the sides and bring the shoulder blades together so that the rest of the fetus will pass more easily".[38] Factual though it is aimed to be, the text ends up describing a horrific scene of mutilation that must have left the mother in shock. And yet, although we read of many miscarriages throughout the Hippocratic Corpus, nowhere do the emotions of fear and despondency become explicitly linked to the mother's mourning and her response to the loss

---

35 Cf. Demand 1994: 44: "One of the more striking aspects of the childbirth cases in [*Epidemics*] I and III is the relatively high mortality rate for these patients ... In Book I, three of the five patients died, while in Book III, all five cases proved fatal. Taking the two books together, this gives a mortality rate of 80 percent for cases associated with pregnancy".
36 Translation in Jones 1923a: 235.
37 For abortion in antiquity, see the book-length study by Kapparis 2002.
38 Translation in Potter 2018: 155.

of her child. *Phobos* and *dusthumia* are linked in these cases to the patient's delirium, her ensuing fever and the *cold* sweating that affects her body (cf. *Epidemics* 3.1.11 above: φόβοι, δυσθυμίαι ... ἵδρωσε περὶ κεφαλὴν ὀλίγῳ ψυχρῷ, ἄκρεα ψυχρά). Although Chiara Thumiger is right to note that these terms point to recognizable patterns of "psychological distress",[39] this distress is only circumstantially appended to what is principally construed as a list of *physical* symptoms.

The fact that Hippocratic physicians show no interest in exploring further their patients' feelings does not mean of course that we, as readers, should do the same. In the same way that bodily signs are not always conclusive and they are liable to misinterpretation,[40] emotional symptoms can be equally misguiding. This is the lesson that Galen wants to teach us when in *On Prognosis* 6 (14.630–33 K.), he tells us the story of Justus' wife whom he visits after her relatives inform him that she suffers from insomnia. Galen questions the patient, but she remains unresponsive, wrapping herself in her veiling and staying in bed. Having found no sign of fever, Galen leaves the scene declaring that the patient's depressed mood (*dusthumia*) originates *either* from black bile *or* from some external cause that the patient is not willing to disclose. When the chambermaid eventually informs him, on the fourth day, that her mistress is troubled by some sort of "anxiety" (λύπη), Galen becomes more suspicious. At this point, someone happens to enter the house and, coming from the theater, says that Pylades was dancing that day. Galen observes that Justus' wife immediately becomes agitated: her colour changes, and her pulse becomes suddenly irregular. Upon testing his hypothesis over the course of the next few days (by putting each day a slave announce the name of a different dancer, and observing that the patient is not affected in any way whatsoever), Galen reaches the conclusion that the woman does not suffer from a melancholic illness; she just has a crush on Pylades.[41]

As it happens, another man of the same name makes his appearance already in *Epidemics* 3.17.11: the woman of Thasos, we are informed, "lived near the place of Pylades in the plain" (ᾤκει δὲ πλησίον τῶν Πυλάδου ἐπὶ τοῦ λείου). The information is typical of the tendency in the *Epidemics* to mention patients by locating them geographically in relation to other names and places, thus

---

[39] Thumiger 2017: 354.
[40] For diseases, in general, hiding in the unseen cavities of the Hippocratic body, see Holmes 2010: 121–122.
[41] For the story of Justus' wife, see Mattern 2013: 250–251. For Galen's case histories, see Lloyd 2009.

establishing a sense of community of people. That said, we cannot help wondering whether Pylades in that case had something to do with that incident which caused grief to the woman of Thasos, for which no more information is divulged. For, just as Galen's patient, this woman too remains silent throughout, keeping to herself and posing obstacles to a conclusive diagnosis.[42] The striking difference is that Galen — as would seem natural to us — remains alert to the fact that, precisely because patients do not always tell the truth,[43] their emotions are liable to be misinterpreted; and that a patient's dejection or fear might not just be a sign of black bile having gone awry, but can have other, more "psychological" explanations.[44] This hermeneutic openness when it comes to diagnosing emotions is a quality which Hippocratic physicians are lacking to an upsetting degree.

3 Putting the Emotion back into Medical Literature

Many of the issues I have been exploring in the previous sections continue to be a matter of debate in the medical field today. Oliver Sacks in the 1980s and 1990s was the one to draw attention to the fact that diseases cannot be reduced to "pathological facts"; instead, they constitute "other worlds". For a better grasp of these worlds to be attained and for better therapies to be found, Sacks insisted that the doctor-patient relationship had to reclaim its lost energy and vitality: rather than turn the patient into a silent character in the drama of sickness — reduced, as it were, to a "body" that is lost in dehumanizing diagnostic machines and technical procedures —, the doctor had to provide him with space

---

[42] The epidemics do not explain theories etc.
[43] This is something that Hippocratic physicians know very well. For the presentation of patients as consistently unreliable partners in dialogue (especially in *Epidemics* 1), see Webster 2015: 167. Special obstacles are presented when the male doctor is invading a woman's female privacy by inspecting her body. As Kosak 2004: 57–58 points out: "It is unclear to what extent, if any, women were unclothed by a healer. Whether or not she was seen nude or even touched by the *iatros*, the introduction of this exceptional, unrelated male into the women's quarters was occasioned only by the intrusion of disease into the woman's body'. For the knotty subject of the interaction between male healers and female patients, see Lloyd 1983: 70–76; Dean-Jones 1995; King 1998: 44–49.
[44] That said, Galen's reading of the woman of Thasos is quite reductive, as we have seen: according to his interpretation, the patient's affected mood should be explained — exclusively — through her retained menses.

to assume his voice again.⁴⁵ In this context, the "story" becomes important. Patients with severe neurological and psychological disorders are given ample space in Sacks' therapy room and writings to convey their own experience of their condition, and, by expressing their feelings and thoughts, to help define and shape it. The narrative space provided to the patients consequently allows the doctor to become a story-teller himself: virtually every single one of Sacks' case histories reads like a short piece of fiction, co-authored by the patient and his doctor. This is not just a fanciful way of speaking about illness. On the contrary: the very idea that the patient can assume control as a narrator makes the gap between "normal" and "pathological" easier to bridge somehow. Illness turns, in this process, from a pathological fact to be isolated and shunned, into a series of experiences — some painful, others weirdly funny, but all of them engaging and empathy-inducing — from which a meaningful story can be created; once turned into a narrative, disease can become more easily accommodated in the greater scheme of events in the patient's life. According to Sacks, "a disease is never a mere loss or excess… There is always a reaction, on the part of the affected organism or individual, to restore, to replace, to compensate for and to preserve its identity". Accordingly, "the physician is concerned not, like the naturalist, with a wide range of different organisms theoretically adapted in an average way to an average environment, but with a single organism, the human subject" striving to preserve that identity.⁴⁶

Emotions in this context become extremely important. Today's "narrative medicine" relies heavily on the idea that doctors should be more attentive to the emotional undercurrents of a patient's (hi)story while allowing themselves at the same time to become emotionally engaged with it. As Rita Charon points out:

> In order to do all these things at once, I had to do what all doctors — ideally — do, whether they realize it or not. I had to follow the patient's narrative thread, identify the metaphors or images used in the telling, tolerate ambiguity and uncertainty as the story unfolded, identify the unspoken subtexts, and hear one story in light of others told by this teller. Like the reader of a novel or the witness of a drama — who naturally do all these things seamlessly — I also had to be aware of my own response to what I heard, allowing myself to be personally moved to action on behalf of the patient. I was the interpreter of these accounts of events of illness that are, by definition, unruly and elusive. I saw that, while I had very demanding "listening" tasks, the patient's "telling" tasks were even more de-

---

45 Cf. Porter 1985.
46 Sacks 1986: 3.

manding, because pain, suffering, worry, anguish, and the sense of something not being right are conditions very difficult, if not impossible, to put into words.⁴⁷

Hippocratic physicians are firmly aware of the fact that illness is a shattering experience, full of anguish and suffering. It is like watching a tragedy — one of them tells us —, only worse: for while the audience "sees" terrible things taking place on stage, the doctor has to get close and "touch" them.⁴⁸ And yet, for all the clarity of this statement, these physicians consistently avoid expressing their emotions, while at the same time "silencing" their patients. As Brooke Holmes argues, despite tacitly acknowledging the patient's agency as a force that cannot be simply reduced to the automatic behaviour of the body, the Hippocratics are content with seeing themselves as experts who are primarily preoccupied with and act over *physical* forces. This means that the patient's ethical qualities, his emotional make-up and character are largely left out from medical diagnosis and therapy.⁴⁹ Inevitably, this leaves little space for the patient to talk and give her own version of the story. Her voice becomes suppressed, and can only be indirectly reconstructed on the basis of implicit textual indications that afford us little insight into her feelings.⁵⁰ The opening section of the *Regimen in Acute Diseases* (ch. 1, 2.224 L.) shows that this silencing of the patient is part of an agenda:

> Οἱ συγγράψαντες τὰς Κνιδίας καλεομένας γνώμας ὁποῖα μὲν πάσχουσιν οἱ κάμνοντες ἐν ἑκάστοισι τῶν νοσημάτων ὀρθῶς ἔγραψαν καὶ ὁποίως ἔνια ἀπέβαινεν· καὶ ἄχρι μὲν τούτων, καὶ ὁ μὴ ἰητρὸς δύναιτ' ἂν ὀρθῶς συγγράψαι, εἰ εὖ παρὰ τῶν καμνόντων ἑκάστου πύθοιτο, ὁποῖα πάσχουσιν· ὁπόσα δὲ προσκαταμαθεῖν δεῖ τὸν ἰητρὸν μὴ λέγοντος τοῦ κάμνοντος, τούτων πολλὰ παρεῖται, ἀλλ' ἐν ἄλλοισιν καὶ ἐπίκαιρα ἔνια ἐόντα ἐς τέκμαρσιν.

> The authors of the work entitled *Cnidian Sentences* have correctly described the experiences of patients in individual diseases and the issues of some of them. So much even a

---

47 Charon 2006: 4.
48 [Hipp.] *On Breaths* 1 (6.90 L.): Εἰσί τινες τῶν τεχνέων, αἳ τοῖσι μὲν κεκτημένοις εἰσὶν ἐπίπονοι, τοῖσι δὲ χρεωμένοις ὀνήισται, καὶ τοῖσι μὲν δημότῃσι κοινὸν ἀγαθόν, τοῖσι δὲ μεταχειριζομένοις σφᾶς λυπηραί. τῶν δὴ τοιούτων ἐστὶ τεχνέων ἣν οἱ Ἕλληνες καλέουσιν ἰητρικήν· ὁ μὲν γὰρ ἰητρὸς ὁρῇ τε δεινά, θιγγάνει τε ἀηδέων, ἐπ' ἀλλοτρίῃσί τε συμφορῇσιν ἰδίας καρποῦται λύπας, "There are some arts which to those that possess them are painful, but to those that use them are helpful, a common good to laymen, but to those that practise them grievous. Of such arts there is one which the Greeks call medicine. For the medical man sees terrible sights, touches unpleasant things, and the misfortunes of others bring a harvest of sorrows that are peculiarly his" (translation in Jones 1923b: 227).
49 Holmes 2013b.
50 For the ways in which such reconstruction can be attempted, see Thumiger 2015.

layman could correctly describe by carefully inquiring from each patient the nature of his experiences. But much of what the physician should know besides, without the patient's telling him, they have omitted; this knowledge varies in varying circumstances, and in some cases is important for the interpretation of symptoms.[51]

Melinda Letts observes that the critique against the authors of the now lost *Cnidian Maxims* has precisely to do with the fact that they are believed to have paid way too much attention to patients' experiences and words, at the expense of medical observation, calculated inference and "professional" diagnosis.[52] As the author of *Epidemics* 6.8.17 notes, a doctor should primarily busy himself with bringing the patient's "*body* under investigation", employing the full arsenal of his senses and reasoning to understand what is going on: τὸ σῶμα ἔργον ἐς τὴν σκέψιν ἄγειν, ὄψις, ἀκοή, ῥίς, ἀφή, γλῶσσα, λογισμὸς καταμανθάνει (5.350 L.).[53] The statement, formulated in an authoritatively aphoristic tone, sets up a contrast that is hard to miss: on the one hand, the doctor is highlighted as an astute observer, engaging in a multi-sensory way with his object on inquiry; on the other hand, the patient is overshadowed, entering the scene simply as σῶμα ("body").

And yet, not all patients in our early medical sources are merely bodies. I submit that more can be done in the direction of unearthing their lost subjectivity and identity, as long as we are willing to stop seeing the *Epidemics* simply as lists of dry clinical notes, and leave the possibility open that at least some of these micro-narratives might have been composed with a more literary touch. Little can be said about the intended audience of the Hippocratic treatises: while some of them appear to have been written for groups of specialized medical professionals, others are more open, and it is even assumed that they were delivered orally in front of extended mixed audiences including experts and laymen alike. Chiara Thumiger has recently argued that the *Epidemics* were "firmly delimited as professional" texts; "no literary pretence, nor broader intellectual appeal of the kind shown by Galen is on the horizon of these writers, nor any explicit attempt to win over lay audiences".[54] The notion of "pretence" here can be slightly misleading; for, whereas it is true that the authors of the *Epidemics* are never led astray and they remain focused on keeping their notes meticu-

---

51 Translation in Jones 1923b: 63.
52 Letts 2014: 7.
53 For this text, see Holmes 2013a: 444–445.
54 Thumiger 2018: 58. See, though, the different approach by Demand 1994: 38: some parts of the *Epidemics* read as "carefully crafted literary pieces, which suggests that they were intended for publication, either to students or to the general public".

lously, in some cases the details included engage us emotionally by putting before our eyes little dramas of sickness that are played out usually with a bad ending.⁵⁵ Consider, for instance, the touching case of the daughter of Nerius in *Epidemics* 5.50 (5.236 L.):

> Ἡ παρθένος ἡ καλὴ ἡ τοῦ Νερίου ἦν μὲν εἰκοσαέτης, ὑπὸ δὲ γυναίου φίλης παιζούσης πλατέῃ τῇ χειρὶ ἐπλήγη κατὰ τὸ βρέγμα. καὶ τότε μὲν ἐσκοτώθη καὶ ἄπνοος ἐγένετο, καὶ ὅτε ἐς οἶκον ἦλθεν αὐτίκα τὸ πῦρ εἶχε, καὶ ἤλγει τὴν κεφαλήν, καὶ ἔρευθος ἀμφὶ τὸ πρόσωπον ἦν. ἑβδόμῃ ἐούσῃ, ἀμφὶ τὸ οὖς τὸ δεξιὸν πύον ἐχώρησε δυσῶδες, ὑπέρυθρον, πλεῖον κυάθου, καὶ ἔδοξεν ἄμεινον ἔχειν, καὶ ἐκουφίσθη. πάλιν ἐπετείνετο τῷ πυρετῷ, καὶ κατεφέρετο, καὶ ἄναυδος ἦν, καὶ τοῦ προσώπου τὸ δεξιὸν μέρος εἵλκετο, καὶ δύσπνοος ἦν, καὶ σπασμὸς τρομώδης ἦν. καὶ γλῶσσα εἴχετο, ὀφθαλμὸς καταπλήξ· ἐνάτῃ ἔθανεν.

> The pretty virgin daughter of Nerius was twenty years old. She was struck on the bregma (front of the head) by the flat of the hand of a young woman friend in play. At the time she became blind and breathless, and when she went home fever seized her immediately, her head ached, and there was redness about her face. On the seventh day foul-smelling pus came out around the right ear, reddish, more than a cyathus (one-fifth of a cup). She seemed better, and was relieved. Again she was prostrated by the fever; she was depressed, speechless; the right side of her face was drawn up; she had difficulty breathing; there was a spasmodic trembling. Her tongue was paralyzed, her eye stricken. On the ninth day she died.⁵⁶

The text starts as though we were reading a stylized funerary epigram.⁵⁷ The young daughter of Nerius is curiously identified as ἡ καλή, the "pretty" one — a unique and, from a strictly medical perspective, irrelevant detail which, however, adds pathos to the scene especially when we juxtapose it with what happens next (the right side of her beautiful face is drawn up, foul-smelling pus comes out from her ear, and so on). Equally striking is the information that the unfortunate girl had her accident while she was "playing" (παιζούσης), and that the one who inflicted the wound, by mistake, was one of her friends (ὑπὸ δὲ γυναίου φίλης). Παίζειν here is a hapax in the Hippocratic Corpus. The verb brings to mind instances from literature and mythology where scenes centered on a

---

55 For the high proportion of cases ending in the death of the patient in the *Epidemics* (some 60 per cent), see Lloyd 2009: 124.
56 Translation in Smith 1994: 199.
57 I am thinking specifically of the first sentence: Ἡ παρθένος ἡ καλὴ ἡ τοῦ Νερίου ἦν μὲν εἰκοσαέτης, ὑπὸ δὲ γυναίου φίλης παιζούσης πλατέῃ τῇ χειρὶ ἐπλήγη κατὰ τὸ βρέγμα. The text here features several characteristics which are well known from funerary epigrams, e.g.: the designation of the deceased as παρθένος, the emphasis placed on her "beauty", the specification of her age (and the implicit idea of a *mors immatura*) and the detailed reference to the circumstances of her death. See Wypustek 2013: 187–188 and González González 2019: 41–42.

young girl playing with her friends foretell an unfortunate twist of events, and sometimes death (cf. the case of Persephone who is abducted by Hades under similar circumstances). What is more, the designation of the patient as παρ-θένος sets up a scene of transition which in the end goes awry: several of the symptoms she displays in the course of her illness — breathlessness, loss of voice, redness about her face — could have been used, in a different context, to indicate a person who is falling in love.[58] But just as in funerary epigrams we often get to hear about desirable young girls who are suddenly snatched away by death, thus missing the chance to turn into "women",[59] in a similar way, the daughter of Nerius dies a *parthenos*.

This is not just a dry list of symptoms recorded day by day (a practice commonly attested elsewhere in the case histories of the *Epidemics*). What we witness instead is the emergence of a "plot", in the sense that the medical author — to use Hayden White's formulation — has imposed upon the processes of disease "the formal coherency that only stories possess". White observes that any account of events in an order of narrative "makes them, at one and the same time, questionable as to their authenticity and susceptible to being considered as tokens of reality. In order to qualify as historical, an event must be susceptible to at least two narrations of its occurrence". Narrativity, for White, blurs the boundaries between "reality" and "fiction" — and it is precisely this blurring that gives the opportunity to the historian "to take upon himself the authority of giving the true account of what really happened".[60] Many of these insights can be creatively applied to the question of the markedly different and varying generic modes on which case histories throughout the *Epidemics* operate.[61] For what concerns our discussion, I would suggest that a higher degree of narrativity in a medical case history usually involves the category of "emotion" more energetically — be it the patient's own emotions or our own.

---

58 Cf. McNamara 2016.
59 For the motif of the virgin for whom death replaces marriage, see e.g. Antip. Thess. *AP* 7.185 and Phil. *AP* 7.186.
60 White 1987: 20. Cf. Pearcy 1992: 605: "No one will maintain that *Epidemics* 1 and 3 rank with the *Odyssey* or *War and Peace* as narrative. I do, however, wish to emphasize the choices made by the Hippocratic author in telling his stories and so to suggest that ancient accounts of disease often appear in the form of a narrative, that they are shaped by the constraints and impulses that govern all narrative as well as by the particular rhetorics of narrative in Greek and Roman culture, and that paying attention to their universal and Greco-Roman narrativity can help us to understand some of the important differences between ancient medicine and our own".
61 See Smith 1990.

4 Conclusion

I have started my discussion with the woman of Thasos, arguing that when emotions are mentioned as symptoms in the Hippocratic *Epidemics*, they often involve the patient's personality and psychology more actively than we usually assume they do. I have then ended up by discussing the daughter of Nerius, using her story to illustrate that acknowledging the role of emotion in early medical narratives depends also on how we, as readers, respond to these texts and engage with them emotionally. A more empathetic reading of these narratives, I argue, can be a useful way of cracking them open interpretively and rediscovering the lost subjectivity of the patient that lies hidden beneath the cold surface of clinical lists of symptoms.

So, by way of conclusion, let us return briefly to the "gloomy" woman of Thasos. In his *Glossary on Hippocrates* (19.94 K.), Galen explains the adjective in question as follows: δυσάνιος — he tells us — can mean either someone "who is grieved beyond measure" (μὴ εὐκόλως ἀνιώμενος), or someone who is "hard to manage/disobedient" (δυσχαλίνωτος).[62] The second interpretation is striking: it brings out a controlling environment of medical surveillance that is shaped directly by the doctor's male gaze. Illness, in this case, seems to be posing a threat not only for the patient's health but, crucially, also for the underlying system of male domination, which is dictating that women are in constant need of being "tamed"[63] — for their own benefit (cf. the *Diseases of Young Girls*). The woman of Thasos, as I have been suggesting throughout, is an incredibly rich psychological character[64] — on a par with other memorable figures such as Mnesianax (*Epid.* 7.45, 5.414 L.), Nicanor (*Epid.* 7.86, 5.444) and Parmeniscus (*Epid.* 7.89, 5.446 L.). Despite Galen's attempt to play down that crucial aspect of her case history (the problem is only her retained menses, and nothing else — he tells us), she remains one of the first patients to enter the pathological landscape of the *Epidemics* as a fully-formed individual, with her own distinctive psychological profile and with a subjectivity that is usually missing from other patients. There is one last detail that is significant, and deserves our attention. When Galen is glossing δυσάνιος, he is quoting from Critias (fr. 88 B 42 D.-K): Τί ἡ δυσάνιος φωνὴ σημαίνει, Κριτίας ἐδήλωσε γράψας ὧδε· "δυσάνιος δ' ἐστίν,

---

62 Cf. *Epid.* 3.17, case 14 (3.140–42 L.): another female patient, a woman in Cyzicus, is said to be "silent", "sad" and "disobedient", σιγῶσα δὲ καὶ σκυθρωπὴ καὶ οὐ πειθομένη.
63 On women and taming, see Calame 2001: 239–240.
64 This should explain why she keeps being quoted so often by psychiatrists today as an important case study; see Healy 2008: 3.

ὅστις καὶ ἐπὶ τοῖς μικροῖς ἀνιᾶται καὶ ἐπὶ τοῖς μεγάλοις μᾶλλον ἢ οἱ ἄλλοι ἄνθρωποι <ἢ> πλείω χρόνον". The quotation is the only textual evidence that survives from Critias' *Περὶ φύσεως ἔρωτος ἢ ἀρετῆς*. The title of the treatise is intriguing, and it makes us think twice of that painful incident, ἐκ λύπης μετὰ προφάσιος, which is mentioned at the beginning of *Epid.* 3.17(11), but for which no more information is provided. Could that incident have been somehow related with that man, Pylades, who is said to live in close proximity to the woman of Thasos?

To ask such a question would be characteristic of a "bad" commentator, according to Galen. In his commentary on *Epidemics* 3, Galen reserves some space to provide a brief overview of the previous exegetical tradition, and to attack all those who, before him, approached from a wrong angle the text whose meaning is now his turn (and responsibility) to elucidate.[65] What annoys Galen, more than anything else, is over-interpretation — the tendency to read too much into details that should not even bother a commentator. One time, Galen reports, he happened to be in Alexandria, attending someone's lectures on *Epidemics* 1. At some point, reference was made to a patient by the name of Silenus whose case is reported in *Epid.* 1.26(2) (2.684 L.):

> Ἐν γὰρ τῷ διηγεῖσθαι τὰ συμβάντα τούτῳ καὶ τοιαύτην τινὰ ῥῆσιν ἔγραψεν ὁ Ἱπποκράτης· "νυκτὸς οὐδὲν ἐκοιμήθη, λόγοι πολλοί, γέλως, ᾠδή". τούτοις οὖν ἐπεφώνησεν "ἰού" ὁ ἐξηγούμενος τὸ σύγγραμμα, "Σιληνὸς γὰρ ἦν." οἱ μαθηταὶ δ' ἀναπηδήσαντες ἐκεκράγεσαν ὑπερθαυμάζοντες. ἔνιοι δὲ τῶν ἐξηγουμένων εἰς τοσοῦτον ἥκουσι περιεργίας, ὥστε ζητοῦσι, πότερον ἐπὶ τοῦ πλαταμῶνος <ἢ τοῦ πλατανῶνος> ὁ Σιληνὸς ᾤκει, τινὲς μὲν διὰ τοῦ μῦ "πλαταμῶνος" ἀξιοῦντες γράφειν, ἔνιοι δὲ διὰ τοῦ νῦ "πλατανῶνος". (17a.500 K.).

> In the course of narrating what happened to that patient, Hippocrates added the following remark: "no sleep at night, much rambling, laughter, singing". When he read this, the person explaining the text let out a loud cry, saying: "No wonder! After all his name was Silenus!" The students listening to him jumped up and shouted in huge admiration. Some of the commentators become so curious with the text that they even ask whether Silenus lived ἐπὶ τοῦ πλαταμῶνος (on the Broadway) or ἐπὶ τοῦ πλατανῶνος (near the plane trees). Some of them prefer to write the word with μ, while others with ν.[66]

Galen's story documents a brilliantly open and playful reading community which is more than willing to tease out allusions and implications from a medical text that is otherwise written in a dry, clinical tone. The name of the patient,

---

65 See Smith 1979: 162–163. For Galen's work as a commentator and his (critical) stance towards the earlier exegetical tradition, see von Staden 2009. Cf. Hanson 1998 and van der Eijk 2012.

66 My translation.

on the Alexandrian's interpretation, brings to mind the reveling companion of Dionysus, and this should be something to think about when we consequently read that Silenus displays symptoms of incontinent laughter and singing. Some of these observations must have been made in a jocular spirit. At any rate, what we should keep from Galen's testimony is the fact that the *Epidemics* — composed, as they were, in that distinctive style and format of individual case histories — must have excited the readers' interest and intellectual curiosity (cf. εἰς τοσοῦτον ἥκουσι περιεργίας)[67] in ways that extended far beyond the strictly medical information that was conveyed in the text. Medical emotions, I submit, provide promising ground for us to keep engaging with these patients in a creative fashion: they allow us to delve a bit deeper on their psychology and to turn them, effectively, from suffering, silent bodies to worrying, tense, hopeful, unhappy or relieved individuals in battle for survival.

Bibliography

Cairns, D.L. 2015. "The Horror and the Pity: *Phrike* as a Tragic Emotion", *Psychoanalytic Inquiry* 34: 75–94.

Calame, C. 2001. *Choruses of Young Women in Ancient Greece: Their Morphology, Religious Role, and Social Functions* (translated by D. Collins/J. Orion). Lanham: Rowman and Littlefield.

Carel, H. 2016. *Phenomenology of Illness*. Oxford: Oxford University Press.

Charon, R. 2006. *Narrative Medicine: Honoring the Stories of Illness*. Oxford: Oxford University Press.

Dean-Jones, L. 1995. "Autopsia, Historia and What Women Know: The Authority of Women in Hippocratic Gynecology", in: D. Bates (ed.), *Knowledge and the Scholarly Medical Traditions*. Cambridge: Cambridge University Press: 41–58.

Demand, N. 1994. *Birth, Death, and Motherhood in Classical Greece*. Baltimore: The Johns Hopkins University Press.

Föllinger, S. 1996. *Differenz und Gleichheit: Das Geschlechterverhältnis in der Sicht griechischer Philosophen des 4, bis 1. Jahrhunderts v. Chr.* Stuttgart: F. Steiner.

Goldhill, S. 1995. *Foucault's Virginity: Ancient Erotic Fiction and the History of Sexuality*. Cambridge: Cambridge University Press.

González González, M. 2019. *Funerary Epigrams of Ancient Greece: Reflections on Literature, Society and Religion*. London/New York: Bloomsbury.

Graumann, L.A./Thumiger, C. 2019. "Children and the Art of Medical Storytelling: Contemporary Practice and Hippocratic Case-taking Compared", in: M. Asper (ed.), *Thinking in Cas-*

---

[67] For περιέργεια as a distinctive quality of ancient grammarians in Hellenistic Alexandria, see Leigh 2013: 161–163.

es: *Ancient Greek and Imperial Chinese Case Narratives*. Berlin/Boston: De Gruyter: 31–48.

Gundert, B. 2000. "Soma and Psyche in Hippocratic Medicine", in: J. Wright/P. Potter (eds.), *Psyche and Soma: Physicians and Metaphysicians on the Mind-Body Problem from Antiquity to Enlightenment*. Oxford: Oxford University Press: 13–36.

Halliwell, S. 2004. "Aischrology, Shame, and Comedy", in: I. Sluiter and R. Rosen (eds.), *Free Speech in Classical Antiquity*. Leiden: Brill: 115–143.

Hankinson, R.J. 1998. *Cause and Explanation in Ancient Greek Thought*. Oxford: Oxford University Press.

Hanson, A.E. 1992. "The Origin of Female Nature", *Helios* 19: 31–71.

Hanson, A.E. 1998. "Galen: Author and Critic", in: G. Most (ed.), *Editing Texts/Texte edieren*, Aporemata 2. Göttingen: 22–53.

Healy, D. 2008. *Mania: A Short History of Bipolar Disorder*. Baltimore: Johns Hopkins University Press.

Holmes, B. 2010. *The Symptom and the Subject: The Emergence of the Physical Body in Ancient Greece*. Princeton/Oxford: Princeton University Press.

Holmes, B. 2013a. "Causality, Agency, and the Limits of Medicine", *Apeiron* 46: 1–25.

Holmes, B. 2013b. "In Strange Lands: Disembodied Authority and the Physician Role in the Hippocratic Corpus and Beyond", in: M. Asper (ed.), *Writing Science: Medical and Mathematical Authorship in Ancient Greece*. Berlin: de Gruyter: 431–472.

Jones, W.H.S. 1923a. *Hippocrates: Vol. I*. Cambridge, Mass.: Harvard University Press (Loeb Classical Library).

Jones, W.H.S. 1923b. *Hippocrates: Vol. II*, Cambridge. Mass.: Harvard University Press (Loeb Classical Library).

Jouanna, J. 2012. *Greek Medicine from Hippocrates to Galen: Selected Papers*. Leiden/Boston: Brill.

Kapparis, K.A. 2002. *Abortion in the Ancient World*. London: Duckworth.

Kazantzidis, G. 2016. "Empathy and the Limits of Disgust in the Hippocratic Corpus", in: D. Lateiner and D. Spatharas (eds.), *The Ancient Emotion of Disgust*. Oxford: Oxford University Press: 45–68.

Kazantzidis, G. 2018. "Between Insanity and Wisdom: Perceptions of Melancholy in the Ps.-Hippocratic *Letters* 10–17", in: C. Thumiger and P.N. Singer (eds.), *Mental Illness in Ancient Medicine: From Celsus to Paul of Aegina*. Leiden/Boston: Brill: 35–78.

Kazantzidis, G. 2019. "Cognition, Emotions and the Feeling Body in the Hippocratic Corpus", in: M. Anderson, D. Cairns, and M. Sprevak (eds.), *Distributed Cognition in Classical Antiquity*. Edinburgh: Edinburgh University Press: 136–153.

Kazantzidis, G. 2021. "Medical and Scientific Understandings", in: D. Cairns (ed.), *A Cultural History of the Emotions in Antiquity*. London/New York: Bloomsbury: 17–34.

Kidd, S.E. 2014. *Nonsense and Meaning in Ancient Greek Comedy*. Cambridge: Cambridge University Press.

King, H. 1998. *Hippocrates' Woman: Reading the Female Body in Ancient Greece*. Routledge: London.

Kosak, J. 2004. *Heroic Measures: Hippocratic Medicine in the Making of Euripidean Tragedy*. Brill: Leiden.

Leigh, M. 2013. *From Polypragmon to Curiosus: Ancient Concepts of Curious and Meddlesome Behaviour*. Oxford: Oxford University Press.

Letts, M. 2014. "Rufus of Ephesus and the Patient's Perspective in Medicine", *British Journal for the History of Philosophy* 22: 996–1020.

Lloyd, G.E.R. 1966. *Polarity and Analogy: Two Types of Argumentation in Early Greek Thought*. Cambridge: Cambridge University Press.

Lloyd, G.E.R. 1983. *Science, Folklore and Ideology: Studies in the Life Sciences in Ancient Greece*. Cambridge: Cambridge University Press.

Lloyd, G.E.R. 1995. *The Revolutions of Wisdom: Studies in the Claims and Practice of Ancient Greek Science*. Berkeley/Los Angeles: University of California Press.

Lloyd, G.E.R. 2009. "Galen's Un-Hippocratic Case-histories", in: C. Gill, T. Whitmarsh, and J. Wilkins (eds.), *Galen and the World of Knowledge*. Cambridge: Cambridge University Press: 115–131.

Lloyd-Jones, H. 1996. *Sophocles: Fragments*. Cambridge, Mass.: Harvard University Press (Loeb Classical Library).

Mattern, S.P. 2013. *The Prince of Medicine: Galen in the Roman Empire*. Oxford: Oxford University Press.

Mayhew, R. 2004. *The Female in Aristotle's Biology: Reason or Rationalization*. Chicago/London: University of Chicago Press.

McNamara, L. 2016. "Hippocratic and Non-Hippocratic Approaches to Lovesickness", in: L. Dean-Jones and R.M. Rosen (eds.), *Ancient Concepts of the Hippocratic*. Leiden/Boston: Brill: 308–327.

Montiglio, S. 2000. *Silence in the Land of Logos*. Princeton (NJ): Princeton University Press.

Pearcy, L.T. 1992. "Diagnosis as Narrative in Ancient Literature", *AJPh* 113: 595–616.

Pigeaud, J. 1981. *La Maladie de l'âme: Étude sur la Relation de l'Âme et du Corps dans la Tradition Medico-Philosophique Antique*. Paris: Les Belles Lettres.

Porter, R. 1985. "The Patient's View: Doing Medical History from Below", *Theory and Society* 14: 175–198.

Porter, R. 2002. *Madness: A Brief History*. Oxford: Oxford University Press.

Potter, P. 2018. *Hippocrates: Diseases of Women 1–2* (Loeb Classical Library). Cambridge (MA): Harvard University Press.

Sacks, O. 1986. *The Man Who Mistook his Wife for a Hat*. London: Picador.

Singer, P.N. 1992. "Some Hippocratic Mind–Body Problems", in: J. Lopez Ferez, (ed.), *Tratados Hipocraticos*: 131–143. Madrid.

Sissa, G. 1990. "Maidenhood without Maidenhead: The Female Body in Ancient Greece", in: D.M. Halperin, J.J. Winkler, and F.I. Zeitlin (eds.), *Before Sexuality: The Construction of Erotic Experience in the Ancient Greek World*. Princeton: 339–364.

Sissa, G. 2013. "The Hymen is a Problem, still. Virginity, Imperforation, and Contraception, from Greece to Rome", *EuGeStA* 3: 67–123.

Sissa, G. 2018. "Bulls and Deer, Women and Warriors: Aristotle's Physics of Morals", in: M. Formisano and C. Shuttleworth (eds.), *Marginality, Canonicity, Passion*. Oxford: Oxford University Press: 141–176.

Smith, W.D. 1979. *The Hippocratic Tradition*. Ithaca: Cornell University Press.

Smith, W.D. 1990. "Generic Form in *Epidemics* I to VII," in: G. Baader and R. Winau (eds.), *Die hippokratischen Epidemien: Theorie, Praxis, Tradition. Verhandlungen des Ve Colloque international hippocratique*, Sudhoffs Archiv, Beiheft 27. Stuttgart: 144–158.

Smith, W.D. 1994. *Hippocrates: Vol. VII*. Cambridge (MA): Harvard University Press (Loeb Classical Library).

Thumiger, C. 2015. "Patient Function and Physician Function in the *Epidemics* Cases", in: G. Petridou and C. Thumiger (eds.), *Homo Patiens: Approaches to the Patient in the Ancient World*. Leiden: Brill: 107–137.

Thumiger, C. 2017. *A History of the Mind and Mental Health in Classical Greek Medical Thought*. Cambridge: Cambridge University Press.

Thumiger, C. 2018. "The Professional Audiences of the Hippocratic *Epidemics*: Patient Cases in Hippocratic Scientific Communication", in: P. Bouras-Vallianatos and S. Xenophontos (eds.), *Greek Medical Literature and its Readers: From Hippocrates to Islam and Byzantium*. Routledge: London: 48–64.

Thumiger, C. 2020. "Therapy of the Word and Other Psychotherapeutic Approaches in Ancient Greek Medicine", in: R. White and S. Xenophontos, et al. (eds.), *"Other Psychotherapies": Healing Interactions across Time, Geographies, and Cultures*. Special issue of the journal *Transcultural Psychiatry*: 1–21.

van der Eijk, P.J. 2012. "Exegesis, Explanation and Epistemology in Galen's Commentaries on *Epidemics* I–II", in: P.E. Pormann (ed.), *Epidemics in Context: Greek Commentaries on Hippocrates in the Arabic Tradition*. Berlin: De Gruyter: 25–47.

Von Staden, H. 2009. "Staging the Past, Staging Oneself: Galen on Hellenistic Exegetical Traditions", in: C. Gill, T. Whitmarsh, and J. Wilkins (eds.), *Galen and the World of Knowledge*. Cambridge: Cambridge University Press: 132–156.

Webster, C. 2015. "Voice Pathologies and the 'Hippocratic Triangle'", in: G. Petridou and C. Thumiger (eds.), *Homo Patiens: Approaches to the Patient in the Ancient World*. Leiden: Brill: 166–199.

White, H. 1987. *The Content of the Form: Narrative Discourse and Historical Representation*. Baltimore/London: The Johns Hopkins University Press.

Wypustek, A. 2013. *Beauty in Funerary Verse Inscriptions of the Hellenistic and Greco-Roman Periods*. Leiden: Brill.

Part III: Medico-philosophical Treatments of Emotion

Teun Tieleman
Posidonius and the Pneumatists: The Aetiology of Emotions and Diseases

Abstract: Evidence from Galen and other sources permits us to explain the origins of the medical school of the Pneumatists against a Stoic, and in particular Posidonian, backdrop. Galen's report at *On Cohesive Causes* that the school's founder, Athenaeus of Attalia, studied with Posidonius, is reliable. Athenaeus found in Posidonius already a well-developed interest in medical issues. There is a clear connection between Athenaeus and Posidonius where the aetiology of disease is concerned. Here, as elsewhere, the information taken from Galen is indispensable as it throws light on Posidonius' notion of predisposing cause in his analysis of the soul's affections, or emotions. Evidence from Plutarch (*Life of Marius* 45.3–7) reflects Posidonius' interest in the soul's interaction with the body. Posidonius developed his analysis following Chrysippus who had already drawn an extensive analogy between mental and bodily states and presented philosophy as the medicine of the soul. Here Posidonius followed him to a greater extent than has so far been assumed. But in fact, his concern with medical matters reflects a more general feature of the work of this wide-ranging and scientifically minded Stoic. This makes him both a witness to and (in the case of Pneumatism) contributor to Graeco-Roman medicine.

1 Introduction

A crucial piece of evidence concerning the Pneumatist school of medicine is the testimony from Galen, *On Cohesive Causes* (hereafter *CC*) 1–2, that its founder, Athenaeus of Attalia (first half of first century BCE),[1] based himself on Stoic elemental and pneumatic theory. Athenaeus, Galen tells us, studied with the Stoic philosopher-cum-scientist Posidonius of Apamea (c. 130–c. 51 BCE), taking over his causal theory. Thus he distinguished between three types of cause: the cohesive, the prior (or predisposing), and the immediate. Earlier studies have shown that Galen's report can be paralleled from Stoic texts, in particular in

---

[1] This rough dating is solely (and necessarily) based on Galen's testimony about his connection with Posidonius, which, as I will argue below, should be accepted.

regard to the cohesive and immediate causes.[2] The origin and role of the predisposing cause seem less clear, which raises historical questions about the interaction between the philosophical (Stoic) and medical traditions. Answers to these questions have been sought mainly in Stoic (non-Posidonian) texts dealing with human responsibility and determinism. In what follows, I will take a different approach by focusing upon medical and medically relevant texts attributed to Posidonius. First (§1) I will subject the key text from Galen (*CC* 1–2) to close scrutiny with the aim of establishing the precise relation between Posidonius and Athenaeus. Included in this section is a discussion of Posidonius' engagement with medicine in general. Posidonius' interest in medicine, I will argue, was stronger than it would appear at first blush and is often supposed.[3] If so, interaction between Posidonius and Athenaeus also becomes more probable.[4] In addition, I will discuss evidence from Plutarch's *Life of Marius* and *Desire and Grief*. Next (§ 2) I will proceed to consider further evidence relating to Posidonius and in particular a few neglected fragments regarding medical issues and the aetiology of disease from his *On Affections* (or *On Emotions*: Περὶ παθῶν) as well as Seneca (*Letter* 87). As we shall see, these fragments treat mental, or moral, disease in a way that within the Stoic corporealist context involves pneumatic and elemental theory and an explicit analogy between disease of the soul and that of body.

---

[2] *SVF* 2.974, 3.346–356. See Frede 1980; Görler 1987; Schröder 1989; 1990a; 1990b; Hankinson 2003.

[3] That there is nothing implausible about such an interest is indicated by Kidd in his comments on Galen's testimony about Posidonius and Athenaeus (F 190 EK): "Posidonius, with his attested involvement in the sciences, should also have had a philosophical interest (cf. F18) in such a major science as medicine with its long historical connection and parallels with philosophy," Kidd 1988: 692.

[4] Cf. also Coughlin 2018, who discusses fragments from Athenaeus dealing with body-soul interactions and their consequences for therapy and regimen and shows that Athenaeus held that mental states and habits, both emotional and intellectual, influence bodily health and so also fall within the province of the doctor, not just the philosopher. Athenaeus, then, shared with Posidonius an interest in the interaction between soul and body but may also reflect the influence of particular ideas held by Posidonius (e.g. as expounded in his *On Affections*): see Coughlin 2018: 21, 29.

2 Posidonius and Athenaeus

In the introductory chapter of his *On Cohesive Causes*[5] Galen tells us that the Stoics were the first to speak of the "cohesive" or "containing" cause.[6] The Stoics, he goes on to explain, took it to refer to the breath or 'spirit' (πνεῦμα), which consists of the two active elements, viz. air and fire. When the elements are intermingled, air and fire, having fine parts, totally penetrate the material or passive elements, earth and water. Further, air is cold and fire is hot; the natural tendency of air is to contract and consolidate, whereas fire by nature expands.[7] Breath, being compounded of these two, thus lends cohesion (*continere*) to natural animate bodies (1.1–3, p.53.1–17 Lyons).[8] At this point Galen includes an intriguing report about the founder of the Pneumatist school of medicine, Athenaeus of Attaleia. Lyons' translation of the extant Arabic version runs as follows:

> As for Athenaeus the Attalean, he founded the medical school known as that of the Animists.[9] It suits his doctrine to speak of a cohesive cause in illness since he bases himself upon the Stoics and he was a pupil and disciple of Posidonius.[10] But it does not suit the

---

[5] This treatise is extant in an Arabic translation by (probably) Hunain ibn Ishāq (d. 873) preserved in a single 11th cent. MS and a Latin one (from the Arabic) by Niccolò da Reggio (active 1304–1350), both included in *CMG Suppl. Or.* II (Berlin 1969): see further Bibliography, Lyons 1969.

[6] The expression 'cohesive cause' (αἴτιον συνεκτικόν) came to be applied not merely to the necessary and sufficient conditions for object persistence, but also to conditions of events and processes. See Gal. *Against Julian* XVIIIA, pp. 278–279 K. with Hankinson 2003: 301–302.

[7] These opposing tendencies cause 'tension' (τόνος), a key concept of Stoic physics, which is left implicit here: see *SVF* 2.447–457. Athenaeus and the Pneumatists also employed this Stoic concept: see Gal. *Diff. puls.* VIII, 646, 652 K. (explaining a vehement pulse). For the doctrine as applied to emotion see *SVF* 3.278, 473 Tieleman 1999; 2003: 112–113, 238; on traditional notions concerning the hot and the cold in mental life see Zink 1962. See further *infra*, n.62 and text thereto.

[8] This report of Stoic doctrine is not included in Von Arnim's *Stoicorum Veterum Fragmenta*, still the standard edition of (early) Stoic fragments. The volume containing the physical fragments (II) appeared in 1902, two years before Kalbfleisch's edition of the Latin translation. However, in the relevant section of his collection Von Arnim presents a considerable number of parallel passages drawn from Galen and other sources (*SVF* 2.432–462). The report in *CC* is peculiar only in referring to air and fire as being of fine *parts* (*leptomerea* in the Latin version).

[9] i.e. Pneumatists. The Latin version gives *spiritualem nominatam heresim*, p. 134.3–4 Kalbfleisch *et al*.

[10] G. Strohmaier as cited by Kudlien 1962: 420 n. 1 translates this crucial phrase "er war ein Schüler des Poseidonios und lernte von ihm."

theories of those other doctors who hold different views to look for a cohesive cause in every illness nor to try to find it in the homoiomeries in their natural state and they cannot say, as Athenaeus did, that there are three types of primary cause that are ultimate in their class. Athenaeus' three types are as follows: first that of the cohesive causes, then that of the prior causes while the third type is comprised of the matter of the immediate causes. This latter term is applied to externals whose function it is to produce some change in the body, whatever this change may be. If what is thus produced in the body belongs to the class of what causes disease, then, while it has not yet actually given rise to a disease, it is known as a prior cause. Alterations are produced in the natural spirit by these causes together with those that are external, leading to moisture, dryness, heat or cold, and these are known as the cohesive causes of disease. For, in Athenaeus' view, the spirit, having penetrated the homoiomerous parts of the body, changes them through its own change and assimilates them to itself (*CC* 2.1–3, p. 45.4–24 Lyons).[11]

Galen next expounds, on Athenaeus' behalf, how this threefold distinction can be used to explain the occurrence of disease. For instance, when a man is affected by the sun's heat, this produces a change in his natural spirit, disturbing its hot/cold or dry/moist balance. Here the sun's heat is the immediate or initiatory cause of the disease, the unbalanced spirit its cohesive cause. In other cases, disease is not directly triggered but manifests itself only after some time, through the medium of the prior (or predisposing) cause, which Athenaeus and his Pneumatist followers locate in the body's humours. Here, too, the equilibrium, or right mixture, between the elementary qualities may be upset and this will affect the primary parts but the alteration will be gradual, not immediate. This mediated type of causation is illustrated by the gradual effect of certain poisons and drugs, or by an abundance of blood (4, p.54.25–p.56.6 Lyons).[12]

We need not doubt that the reference is to Posidonius of Apamea, the leading Stoic philosopher of the first half of the first century BCE, whom Galen mentions more often, albeit almost exclusively in books 4 and 5 of his *On the Doc-*

---

[11] The first two sections of the Latin version (of a Greek *Vorlage*: cf. Kollesch *et al.* 1969: 115–116) have been printed by Kidd-Edelstein as Posidonius F 190 (cf. T51). Kidd's (slightly modified) translation runs: "It is therefore appropriate that Athenaeus of Attaleia, the founder of the Pneumatist medical school, speaks of a cohesive cause of diseases, as he based himself on the Stoic school (after all he had studied with Posidonius); but it does not suit the theories of those other physicians, who hold different tenets, to look for a cohesive cause in every illness, nor in the homoiomerous bodies in their natural state; nor can they say, as Athenaeus did, that there are three types of primary and most general cause. The different kinds, which Athenaeus said were three, are the following: (1) cohesive [*coniuncta*/συνεκτικόν]; (2) predisposing [*antecedens*/προηγούμενον]; (3) initiatory [*procatarctica*/προκαταρκτικόν]" (p.134.3–13 Kalbfleisch=Posid. T 26a Theiler).

[12] For the role of *pneuma* in explaining diseases according to Pneumatist pathology, see also Coughlin and Lewis 2020: 218–219.

trines of Hippocrates and Plato. Here Galen draws rather extensively[13] on Posidonius' treatise *On Affections* (or: *On Emotions*, Περὶ παθῶν) in discussing whether the soul has different powers and, if so, how many.[14] The information about Posidonius' connection with Athenaeus probably reached Galen in another way. His report gives the impression that he was well-informed. On the most natural reading, Athenaeus' dependence upon Posidonius should be taken to pertain not only to the cohesive cause but to include the distinction between the three types of cause mentioned in passage quoted above (p. 206) and explained in the ensuing context.

That we are dealing with an authentically Stoic, and indeed Posidonian, distinction is further borne out by the textual evidence concerning Stoic causal theory. The Stoics referred to the active principle, i.e. the πνεῦμα/λόγος, as *the* Cause: it determined each object's being, behaviour and characteristics. This is the cohesive cause, the αἴτιον συνεκτικόν. So they could, and did, say that there is *one* cause only.[15] But causal analysis did not stop there. In the debate on human agency and determinism the Stoics elaborated further distinctions. Thus Chrysippus distinguished between two types: the 'complete' (αὐτοτελής) cause and the 'initiatory' (προκαταρκτική) one.[16] This distinction permitted the Stoics to apportion responsibility and freedom (in the Stoic 'compatibilist' sense) to the (moral condition of the) human soul (the principal cause of action) as opposed to the mental presentation of an external object (the initiatory or immediate cause). A well-known example preserved by Cicero is that of the cylinder which on being pushed rolls down from a hill: the cylinder would not have moved without the push but the main cause of its movement is its cylindrical shape; the push counts as its immediate or initiatory cause.[17]

---

13 Though probably not as extensively as has often been supposed: see *infra*, n.23.
14 *Pace* Nutton 2004: 202 we need not doubt that 'Posidonius' refers to the well-known Stoic philosopher of that name. Galen refers to the Stoic school and we do not know of any other Stoic of that name. Whether or not Athenaeus actually sat at the feet of Posidonius of Apamea is another matter: see further *infra*, p. 211.
15 Sen. *Ep.* 65.4, 12 (*SVF* 2.346a), Ar. Did. fr. 18 Diels (*SVF* 1.89, 2.336, Posid. F 95 EK). See Frede 1980: 243–249; Kidd *ad* F 190 (p. 692).
16 Plut. *SR* 1056B-C (*SVF* 2.997). Similarly, Cic. *Fat.* 41–44 (*SVF* 2.974) presents Chrysippus' analysis of human agency in terms of 'complete and principal' (*perfectae et principales*) causes as distinguished from 'auxiliary and proximate' (*adiuvantes et proximae*) ones. The relatively extensive account in Cicero is the starting point for the interpretations by Görler (1987) and (also with reference to Pneumatism) Schröder (1989), (1990a), (1990b); Hankinson 2003: 301–306.
17 See *supra*, n.11 with text thereto. Harig (1988: 222) suggests that Chrysippus borrowed his distinction between causes from Hellenistic medicine instead of the other way round.

The complete or sufficient cause is said to be synonymous with the cohesive cause by one of our sources, in an account that reflects Stoic school definitions and should be accepted as reliable.[18] The complete or cohesive cause does not admit of further elaboration, whereas the secondary cause does. Thus, one comes across two tripartite classifications, one of which runs parallel to the one ascribed by Galen to Posidonius and his follower Athenaeus. The pseudo-Galenic *Medical Definitions*, XIX, pp. 392–393 K. distinguishes between initiatory, 'predisposing' and 'cohesive causes' (αἴτια προκαταρκτικά / προηγούμενα / συνεκτικά) in a way that invites comparison with Galen, *CC* 2.1–3, p. 45.4–24 Lyons, from which we started.[19] It is worth noting that the *Medical Definitions* has been traditionally considered to be a product of the Pneumatist school of medicine.[20]

Posidonius stood out among the Stoics for his predilection for causal explanation. This point is made for instance by the geographer Strabo:

> there is much enquiry into causes in him, that is, 'Aristotelizing', a thing which our school[21] sheers off from because of the concealment of causes (Strabo II. 3. 8=T85 EK; trans. I.G. Kidd).[22]

That Strabo points to a real difference between Posidonius and the other Stoics, notably Chrysippus, is borne out by some of the fragments from his *On Emotions*

---

18 Clem. Al. *Strom.* VIII.9 (*SVF* 2.346, 351).
19 As pointed out by Kidd *ad* Posid. F190. It should be noted that in the same context (XIX, p. 392 K.) Athenaeus is credited with the following explanation: αἴτιόν ἐστι τὸ ποιοῦν, τοῦτο δὲ ἐστι προκαταρκτικόν (printed by Theiler as Posidonius T26b, no doubt in view of Gal. *CC* 2). While echoing Stoic and indeed Posidonian doctrine (i.e. cause as that which acts upon something else: see Ar. Did. fr. 18 Diels = *SVF* 1.89, 2.336, Posid. F 95 EK), the limitation to the initiatory cause is misleading, at least from the Stoic point of view. But Athenaeus' presence in this lemma may certainly be taken as another piece of evidence for the Stoic-Pneumatist continuity in causal theory. Note however that although the initiatory cause is explained in a way that runs parallel to that provided by Galen on behalf of Athenaeus (including the example of the impact of the sun's heat), the account of the predisposing causes is markedly different.
20 More sceptical however Kollesch 1973.
21 Here, as elsewhere, Strabo presents himself as a Stoic.
22 It is worth comparing the relatively extensive section from Geminus' epitome of Posidonius' *Meteorology*, which, via Alexander of Aphrodisias, found its way into Simplicius' extant commentary on the Aristotelian *Physics* (II,2, pp. 291,21–292,31 Diels=Posid. F 18 EK). Here Posidonius explains that the natural philosopher, as opposed to the astronomist, is typically concerned with the *causes* of the phenomena studied. His view of the relation between philosophy and (other) arts is said to have taken its starting points from Aristotle; cf. Strabo's observations as cited in the text and see further Kidd 1978.

(Περὶ παθῶν) preserved by Galen. Posidonius took up certain questions which had been noted but, he felt, were inadequately addressed by Chrysippus in his work of the same title, viz. how to account for phenomena such as weeping or laughing against one's will. Chrysippus, it seems, had felt the very irrationality of these phenomena meant they were beyond causal explanation, even if one might try preventively to strengthen one's mind against such occurrences.[23]

Posidonius' concern with causal explanation is related to his interest in the special sciences, in which he immersed himself to a greater degree than his fellow-Stoics found necessary for underpinning Stoic philosophy with a respectable and scientifically up-to-date account of the natural world.[24] Among Posidonius' many fields of interest were geography, anthropology, history, astronomy, meteorology, geometry. Medicine seems to have engaged his attention to a much lesser degree. But it is worth noting a few passages that point to a distinct interest in illness and health, starting with Galen's report on Posidonius and what appears to have been his influence on Athenaeus in *CC* 2.1–3. Let us take a closer look at it and ask first of all what exactly it permits us to conclude regarding the relation between Posidonius and Athenaeus.

We need not doubt that Galen means to say that Athenaeus had met Posidonius in person. The Arabic version refers to his having been a pupil or student of the Stoic philosopher. The same is implied in the Latin translation (*conversatus ... cum Posidonio fuit*).[25] If so, given Posidonius' dates (130–c.51 BCE), Athenaeus has to be dated to the first half of the first century BCE. This dating, however, is controversial. Kalbfleisch's edition of the Latin translation of *On Cohesive Causes* (1904) came too late for Wellmann to take Galen's testimony

---

[23] Chrysippus *ap*. Gal. *PHP* IV, 7.12–17 (*SVF* 3.466), 26–27, 30–31 (*SVF* 3.467). These passages have been taken by Galen from Posidonius' discussion of Chrysippus. They form part of a very large chunk of Galenic text — constituting almost an entire chapter of *PHP* IV, five pages in De Lacy's *CMG* edition — printed by Edelstein-Kidd as Posidonius F 165 (*PHP* IV, 7,1–45, pp. 280.19–290.22 De Lacy). This is in line with Edelstein-Kidd's criterion for inclusion, viz. explicit attribution, since Posidonius is referred to throughout this passage. But presenting as a long Posidonian "fragment" what is really a paraphrase by Galen is questionable. In fact, we are dealing with not just a paraphrase, but a polemic mounted by Galen against Chrysippus, which may have led him to exaggerate the disagreement between the latter and his fellow-Stoic Posidonius. On these Chrysippean passages as used by Posidonius and Galen, see Tieleman 2003: 122–132.
[24] On Posidonius on causal explanation, see *supra*, n. 22 and text thereto.
[25] This phrase may render Greek συγγίγνεσθαι, which is used in the Platonic dialogues with reference to the personal and educational relationship between Socrates and the young men around him and later on became a technical term for the relation between disciple and master. But cf. Kudlien 1962: 420 n. 1 for a few different suggestions.

into account in his monograph on the Pneumatist school, and in his subsequent RE-article on Athenaeus.[26] Wellmann dated the beginnings of the Pneumatist school to the first century CE, when Athenaeus founded the school in Rome, or so he assumed. This dating is based on another assumption, viz. that the Pneumatist Agathinus of Sparta, who was in Rome in the first century CE,[27] was a pupil of Athenaeus.[28] It is of course possible that Athenaeus too was in Rome but there is simply no evidence for this, nor for his association with Agathinus.[29] But scholars have adduced further reasons for rejecting the first century BCE dating. Using an argument from silence they point to the fact that Celsus (whose *On Medicine* is traditionally dated to the reign of Tiberius, 13–37 CE) and Pliny the Elder (23/4–79 CE) do not refer to Athenaeus (but this may simply mean he was not known in Rome, where he may not have lived and worked at all).[30] Also, the first Pneumatists after Athenaeus we hear of date from the middle or second half of the first century CE. But they are never referred to as Athenaeus' own pupils.[31] So while we can see where the doubts about Galen's testimony come

---

26 Wellmann 1895 and 1896.

27 In an earlier stage of his career, Agathinus lived for some time in the house of the Roman Stoic L. Annaeus Cornutus: see Suet. *Vita Persii*, p. 74.1–3 Reifferscheid (taking the doctor from Sparta referred to be 'Agathinus' instead of mss. 'Agaturinus', as first convincingly proposed by Friedrich Osann in his 1844 ed. of Cornutus' theological treatise [p. XVIII**]). Cornutus lived in Rome in the 50s and early 60s until he was exiled (in either 63 or 64 or 65); whether he ever returned is a moot point. Cf. also Wellmann 1895: 9. Of course, this report has been taken as further proof of the close ties between Stoicism and Pneumatism.

28 Wellmann (1895: 8) inferred this from Galen's designation of Agathinus as ἀπ' Ἀθηναίου τοῦ Ἀτταλέως (VIII, p. 787), which would make it impossible to date Athenaeus to the first half of the first century BCE. But, as has been pointed out by Kudlien 1968: col. 1098, this type of phrase is a normal way of describing someone as a member of a particular school, as in this case Agathinus as belonging to the *school founded by* Athenaeus.

29 Wellmann 1895: 9. In a more recent study Arena (2007) (*non vidi*) points to epigraphic evidence for the presence of Pamphylian doctors in Rome and postulates a local school of medicine in Pamphylia, to which Athenaeus had also belonged before coming to Rome (according to the summary in Marouzeau's *L'année philologique*).

30 Cf. Kudlien 1968: cols. 1097–1098. Yet the reticence of these two Roman authors induces Nutton (2004: 202–203) to question the first century BCE dating and to stick to Wellmann's, explaining Galen's testimony as a reflection of doctrinal influence. Similarly, Smith 1979: 230 n. 72. Coughlin and Lewis (2020: 226–228) take the Stoic backdrop of Pneumatist physiology (including causal theory) to be clear from the consensus of our sources, although Pneumatist authors themselves seem to have been rather silent on their intellectual debt to the Stoics and Posidonius. For an earlier, more sceptical view, see Harig 1988.

31 Diog. Laert. 2.103 mentions one Theodorus as a physician who was pupil of Athenaeus, i.e. probably our Pneumatist. But we know nothing more about him. Cf. Wellmann 1895: 13 n. 3.

from (a gap of one century may seem a lot) there is really no good reason to brush aside Galen's testimony. In his *Differences of Pulses*, too, Galen associates Athenaeus' Pneumatist school with Stoicism, calling the great Stoic scholarch Chrysippus (c. 280–204 BC) the "grandfather" of Pneumatist medicine.[32] In calling Chrysippus its grandfather Galen may be thinking of Posidonius as its father, given the direct connection between the latter and the founder of the Pneumatist school Galen speaks about in *CC* 2.1–3. But there are even more passages where Galen links Athenaeus to Stoicism or Chrysippus.[33]

If we accept Galen's testimony, as I think we should, the question arises what can be said about the time Athenaeus spent with the great Stoic. Again, our documented evidence permits little more than sketching a possible scenario. About Athenaeus' biography we know next to nothing. Attaleia is usually taken to be the town of that name in Pamphylia. There are two other less important Attaleias in Asia Minor, but nothing important depends on which Attaleia was his native town. The place where he met and studied with Posidonius must have been Rhodes, where the latter had taken up residence. Posidonius is on record as having obtained Rhodian citizenship and fulfilled civic duties such as the high office of the prytany and taking part in a Rhodian embassy to Rome.[34] In the 90s BCE Posidonius was often away from Rhodes, travelling to many parts of the Mediterranean world. But, it seems, he spent most of his career teaching and writing in Rhodes, where he attracted many people from various backgrounds and places, the most illustrious examples being Pompey and Cicero.[35] Some visitors (including these Roman statesmen) wanted to meet the

---

[32] πρόπαππος τῆς αἱρέσεως αὐτῶν [scil. τῶν Πνευματικῶν], *Diff. puls.* VIII, p. 631 K. Cf. Kudlien 1962: 424.
[33] See esp. *Diff. puls.* VIII, p. 642, *Hipp. Elem.* I, 486–488, *Temp.* I, 523 K. Our passage from *CC* is unique is linking Athenaeus to Posidonius in particular.
[34] The evidence for Posidonius' offices is assembled by Edelstein-Kidd TT 27, 28. At an early stage of his career Posidonius left Rome for his extensive travels in the western parts of the Mediterranean, an experience on which drew for the rest of his career as a philosopher and scientist: see the evidence assembled as TT 14–26 EK; cf. Laffranque 1964: 77–85.
[35] Posidonius received Cicero in 77 and Pompey in both 66 and 62 BCE while acting in a teaching capacity: TT 29–39 EK. Our sources name a mere handful of "pupils", none of whom appears to have distinguished himself in philosophy (with the possible exception of Apollodorus of Tarsus, also called Apollodorus Calvus): TT 40–44; cf. 45 with Kidd *ad loc.* One Phanias, called an acquaintance of Posidonius, published *Lectures of Posidonius:* T 43). Jason, son of Menecrates, grandson and pupil of Posidonius, is on record as having succeeded him as head of the school in Rhodes (which apparently did not survive Jason). On Posidonius' life, see further Reinhardt 1954: cols. 562–567; Laffranque 1964: ch. 2 (esp. 86–98 on his activities in Rhodes).

great man and hear him speak but did not stay long, while others did spend a longer time studying with him.³⁶ We do not know in which category Athenaeus belonged. But, as we have noticed, both the Latin and the Arabic version of the crucial passage from *CC* make him Posidonius' pupil, which suggest a period of some length.

Athenaeus may have taken an interest in Stoic natural philosophy, with its pivotal concept of *pneuma*, and from *CC* 2.1–3 we know that he took an interest in Stoic causal theory. There may have been more facets of Stoicism that attracted him to Posidonius, with or even without immediate relevance to medicine. For all we know, he may have studied with Posidonius before he turned to medicine. Posidonius for his part was more interested than most other Stoics in 'special' sciences. This included medicine. Thus he is on record as having attended a surgery performed by a renowned physician, Zopyrus, in Alexandria, however, appears to emerge from an intriguing passage from the commentary on the Hippocratic *On Joints* by Apollonius of Citium, who was active in Alexandria around the middle of the first century BCE:

> [...] on the reduction of limbs, some I set myself, others I observed when I attended Zopyrus,³⁷ in Alexandria. And that he in the case of fractures and the surgery of dislocations for the most part followed the treatment of Hippocrates, Posidonius, who had spent time (συνδιατετριφώς) with this same doctor, can bear witness for us.
> (*CMG* XI.1.1, p. 12.1–5=T112 EK; transl. Kidd, slightly modified)

We need not doubt that Apollonius knew, and here refers to, Posidonius of Apamea, in Kidd's words, "the outstanding intellectual figure of the previous generation."³⁸ Hence there is no need for Apollonius to add any specification as

---

36 One may compare the admittedly later school of the Stoic Epictetus (50–135 CE) at Nicopolis in Epirus — at some distance from Rome but not a big detour for those travelling from Rome east or in the opposite direction — which had serious, long-term students but also received visitors who limited themselves to one lecture.
37 Zopyrus was famed for pharmacology as well as surgery: see further *RE*² XA (1972) (15).
38 Kidd (1988) *ad loc.* (p. 93). I do not wish to suggest that the question of identity should not be raised. This is certainly necessary in regard to the texts assembled as "medical references" in the Edelstein-Kidd collection (TT 112–115). Thus the texts presented as TT 114–115 certainly refer to other persons of the same name, as is acknowledged by Kidd: in the text printed T 114a, as elsewhere, Aetius of Amida (fl. 530 CE) must be taken to refer to the physician Posidonius who lived in the second half of the 4th cent. CE, not our Stoic philosopher-cum-scientist. T 114b is from a famous 13th c. CE Arabic dictionary on famous physicians referring to 'Posidonius' as the author of a treatise entitled *Delicious Potions for Healthy Persons*. In T 115 'Posidonius' refers to a minor Latin poet. T113 (from Oribasius of Pergamum [c. 325–400] via Rufus of Ephesus, active in the time of the Emperor Trajan) is a debatable case. It refers to Dioscorides and

to his identity. This reference occurs in the introduction of his commentary, dedicated to king Ptolemy (Auletes?). Apollonius gives his credentials and Posidonius is a great reference to use. There is nothing improbable about Posidonius visiting Alexandria or attending a surgical demonstration by Zopyrus, a distinguished physician of the Empiricist school, whose activity is dated to around 100 BCE.[39] That Posidonius spent more time with this doctor is indicated through the participle συνδιατετριφώς 'having spent time with', a verb also and more specifically used for studying with someone (see *LSJ* s.v.). But given Apollonius' purpose in writing his introduction he may have been induced to exaggerate the latter's association with Zopyrus (whereas one cannot see what Galen had to gain from exaggerating Posidonius' association with Athenaeus).[40] For our purposes, the testimony may stand as a reminder of Posidonius' interest in medicine, both contemporary and Hippocratic, including, as this testimony suggests, human anatomy.

No less intriguing is a fragment concerned with the illness and death of the Roman Marius, whom Posidonius met when he took part in the Rhodian embassy to Rome in January 86 BCE. The fragment has been preserved by Plutarch in his *Life of Marius*:

(3) Marius was elected consul for the seventh time [...] (4) Worn out now with his exertions, awash as it were with anxieties, he could not lift his mind, which was already quivering from his past experience of horror and weariness, in the face once again of the overwhelming thought of a new war and fresh combats and terrors; reckoning that the dangers

---

Posidonius as having provided the "most detailed discussion" of the plague that occurred in Libya in their time. The identity of Dioscurides is uncertain too, but he may be the esteemed physician Dioscurides Phakas, who was active in Alexandria under Ptolemy Auletes and Cleopatra and Marc Antony and authored twenty-four books on medicine: see Kudlien 1962: 427–428. If this is correct, his coupling with Posidonius makes it more likely that his contemporary Posidonius of Apamea is meant. In this case the report would suit his anthropological and historical interests; cf. Thucydides' famous account (II, 7) of the plague that struck Athens at the beginning of the Peloponnesian war (430 BCE). but his association with a medical author with respect to the "most detailed" treatment of a particular epidemic is striking. Against Kuldien 1962 and 1968, Harig (1988: 220–223) plays down Posidonius' concern with medicine, arguing that some of the references to Posidonius from late antiquity do not refer to the Stoic. This is no doubt correct, but the remaining evidence indicates that Posidonius may have been keenly interested in medical matters.

39 On the likelihood that Posidonius included Alexandria, the great centre of culture, among his extensive travels (though without reference to the testimony from Apollonius), see Laffranque 1964: 57, 60, 72–74 (on the close cultural ties between Rhodes and Alexandria), 80, 183.

40 Kudlien 1962: 427–428; Kidd (1988) *ad* T 112, with whom I find myself in basic agreement as to the significance of this testimony.

he was to face was not an Octavius or Merula as generals in charge of a flotsam band or seditious rabble, but it was Sulla that comes against him, the man who earlier had driven him from his country, and now had Mithridates penned in the Black Sea. (5) Broken by such calculations, and continually fastening on visions before his eyes of his long wanderings, his flights and dangers, as he was driven through land and sea, he fell into terrible distress with fears in the night and troubling dreams, for ever imagining he heard a voice saying: 'Dread is the lair, though the lion is gone.' (6) As more than anything he was afraid of insomnia, he threw himself into drinking bouts, a drunkenness at all hours that fitted ill with his years, in an attempt to induce sleep as a kind of escape from his worries. (7) And finally, when a messenger came from the sea, new fears attacked him, partly apprehension for the future, partly because he could take no more of the burden of the present that weighed upon him, a little swing on top of the rest to tip the scale, and he sank into an illness, pleurisy, as Posidonius the philosopher recounts, saying that he went in personally and conversed with him on the topics of his embassy, with Marius already ill

(Plutarch, *Life of Marius* 45.3–7=Posid. F 255 EK; cf. T 28. Transl. Kidd, modified).[41]

Kidd in his commentary on this passage argues that the only secure evidence for Posidonius is limited to the last sentence. Even so, he prints the entire passage, thus inviting further study of this issue.[42] It does indeed seem unduly restrictive not to consider seriously Posidonian provenance for the description of Marius' deteriorating condition preceding the final sentence. The entire text printed by Kidd (3–7) forms a coherent whole: the pleurisy is presented as the direct outcome of the physical and mental afflictions suffered by Marius. Moreover, Plutarch proceeds to give rival accounts of Marius' death in what follows (8–9,

---

41 (3) ὕπατος μὲν οὖν ἀπεδείχθη τὸ ἕβδομον Μάριος [...] (4) αὐτὸς δ' ἤδη τοῖς τε πόνοις ἀπειρηκὼς καὶ ταῖς φροντίσιν οἷον δ' ἤδη τοῖς τε πόνοις ἀπειρηκὼς καὶ ταῖς φροντίσιν οἷον ὑπέραντλος ὢν καὶ κατάπονος, τὴν ψυχὴν πρὸς τοσαύτην αὖθις ἐπίνοιαν νέου πολέμου καὶ καινῶν ἀγώνων καὶ φόβων ὑπ' ἐμπειρίας δεινῶν καὶ καμάτου τρέμουσαν οὐκ ἀνέφερε, λογιζόμενος ὡς οὐ πρὸς Ὀκτάβιον οὐδὲ Μερούλαν σύγκλυδος ὁμίλου καὶ στασιώδους ὄχλου στρατηγοὺς ὁ κίνδυνος ἔσοιτο, Σύλλας δ' ἐκεῖνος ἔπεισιν ὁ τῆς πατρίδος αὐτὸν ἐξελάσας πάλαι, νῦν δὲ Μιθριδάτην συνεσταλκὼς (5) εἰς τὸν Εὔξεινον Πόντον. ὑπὸ τοιούτων θραυόμενος λογισμῶν, καὶ τὴν μακρὰν ἄλην αὐτοῦ καὶ φυγὰς καὶ κινδύνους διὰ γῆς καὶ θαλάττης ἐλαυνομένου λαμβάνων πρὸ ὀφθαλμῶν, εἰς ἀπορίας ἐνέπιπτε δεινὰς καὶ νυκτερινὰ δείματα καὶ ταραχώδεις ὀνείρους, ἀεί τινος ἀκούειν φθεγγομένου δοκῶν· δειναὶ γὰρ κοῖται καὶ ἀποιχομένοιο λέοντος. (6) μάλιστα δὲ πάντων φοβούμενος τὰς ἀγρυπνίας, ἐνέβαλεν εἰς πότους ἑαυτὸν καὶ μέθας ἀώρους καὶ παρ' ἡλικίαν, ὥσπερ ἀπόδρασιν τῶν φροντίδων τὸν ὕπνον μηχανώμενος. (7) τέλος δ' ὡς ἧκέ τις ἀπαγγέλλων ἀπὸ θαλάσσης, νέοι προσπίπτοντες αὐτῷ φόβοι, τὰ μὲν δέει τοῦ μέλλοντος, τὰ δ' ὥσπερ ἄχθει καὶ κόρῳ τῶν παρόντων, ῥοπῆς βραχείας ἐπιγενομένης, εἰς νόσον κατηνέχθη πλευρῖτιν, ὡς ἱστορεῖ Ποσειδώνιος ὁ φιλόσοφος, αὐτὸς εἰσελθεῖν καὶ διαλεχθῆναι περὶ ὧν ἐπρέσβευεν ἤδη (8) νοσοῦντι φάσκων αὐτῷ. (ed. K. Ziegler, Teubner 1971)

42 See Kidd (1988) *ad loc.* (p. 890). Cf. his comment on the same passage in his 1999 translation: "But of course elements from the preceding description could have derived from him [scil. Posidonius]".

attributed to "the historian Gaius Piso" and § 10–12, derived from unidentified sources: "but some say ..."). This strengthens the impression that Plutarch is concerned to make clear that he gives three different accounts from different sources. We are supposed to understand, then, that not only the final sentence of the account at § 3–7 derives from Posidonius but the preceding report as well.

Let us now turn to the account itself. This may have been drawn from Posidonius' *History,* or to a more strictly philosophical work such as *On Affections* (or *On Emotions*).[43] The fact that Plutarch refers to "Posidonius the philosopher" may perhaps tell in favour of the latter option. But nothing much depends on this, since Posidonius may be expected to describe the figures and events in his historical work in light of his psychological theory. His account of Marius' physical and mental decline contains no theorizing or technical terminology, while at the same time being rather detailed. It seems to be designed to show a succession of stages involving both mental and bodily factors in a downward spiral towards illness and death: Marius' fatigue makes it impossible for him to lift his mind and he succumbs to mental troubles (worries, fear, frightening dreams), which cause insomnia, from which he seeks escape through heavy drinking. David Hahm, discussing the passage in a study of historical causation in Posidonius, has argued that there is a perfect match between the account of Marius' physical and mental decline and Posidonius' emotion theory as presented by Galen in *PHP* books IV–V in particular.[44] Since Hahm accepts Galen's attribution of the Platonic tripartite psychology to Posidonius, he explains the report on Marius' demise accordingly: Marius' fear of Sulla coming against him is caused by the spirited part of his soul, which is the part desirous of honour, status and victory — in which Marius despairs. This soul-part impedes his rational part in thinking rationally about his situation: instead of ways of organizing the defense of Rome or seeking a peaceful solution by retiring from political life Marius remains caught in worried visions.[45] When he then seeks relief in

---

[43] The latter possibility is considered but rejected by Hahm (1989: 1355 n. 49) on the grounds that the *History* is Plutarch's source elsewhere in his *Lives* (cf. F256, F257, where however no title is given). At the same time Hahm believes that Plutarch knew Posidonius' *On Affections* (or *On Emotions*, Περὶ παθῶν) on the basis of the Posidonian fragment found at Plutarch, *Desire and Grief: Psychical or Bodily Phenomena?* (usually referred to under the Latin title *De libidine et aegritudine*), ch. 6 (4–6= Posidonius F154 EK), on which see *infra*, n. **46** with text thereto.

[44] Hahm 1989: 1353–1357; cf. 1332–1334. A modern medical reading is offered by Carney (1958).

[45] Hahm (1989: 1355) argues that the reference to the frightening dream in which Marius heard a voice saying "Dread is the lair, though the lion is gone" (with the lair standing for Rome and the lion for Sulla, Plut. *Mar.* 45.5=Posid. F255.13–15) confirms that this passage is firmly based

alcohol, this is another irrational response caused by the lowest, appetitive part of the soul, which after all is the part that direct us towards food and drink.

A Platonizing reading along such lines is perhaps possible but hardly compelling. What seems to underlie this account is not so much the conflict between psychic powers or parts, each marked by its own type of desire. In fact, there is no inkling to be found here that what really lies behind his fear is Marius' harking after victory or political status. It all starts from his physical exhaustion. Moreover, Marius' heavy drinking is explained by reference to his wish to end his insomnia not by a positive desire for drinking, sleep being an escape from his worries. What seems central to this account is rather the interplay between mental and physical factors. On the mental side we have Marius' fears and worries, which are described in cognitivist terms as turning on mental impressions (i.e. thoughts) and calculations. There is no separate role for reason alongside emotion but rather an explanation in terms of rational thought becoming perverted, feverish and going against optimal rationality. This reading finds support from the fragment preserved by Plutarch,[46] *Desire and Grief: Psychical or Bodily Phenomena?* 6 (4–6=Posidonius F154 EK):[47]

> Posidonius divides them [*scil.* the affections, πάθη] into (1) those of the soul; (2) those of the body; (3) <those of the body> and involving, although not being of, the soul; (4) <those of the soul and involving, although not being of, the body. Of the soul>without qualification he calls those which consist of (1) judgements and assumptions, e.g. desires, fears, fits of anger; (2) of the body without qualification are fevers, chills, contractions and opening up of the pores; (3) of the body but involving the soul are cases of lethargy, derange-

---

on Posidonius' psychological theory, given Posidonius' example of thinking of a lion as inducing the emotion of fear at Posid. *ap.* Gal. *PHP* V 6.26 (F162.10–11 EK). But we cannot be sure whether Posidonius in the latter passage must be thinking of Marius' dream. In addition Hahm (1989: 1353) notes that the verb ἐμπίπτω as used at § 4 (F255.12–13EK: εἰς ἀπορίας ἐνέπιπτε δεινὰς καὶ νυκτερινὰ δείματα καὶ ταραχώδεις ὀνείρους) can be paralleled from Posid. *ap.* Gal. *PHP* IV 5,31 (F164.36–37 EK), Gal. *PHP* V 6.26 (F162.10 EK, where note that Edelstein and Kidd, followed by De Lacy, read ἐκπίπτουσι). But this verb in the sense of falling or plunging into something such as an emotional state of mind is not a technical let alone peculiarly Posidonian term. However, that the whole of Plut. *Marius* 45.3–7 derives from or at least reflects the influence of Posidonius is probable for the reasons indicated in the text above.

46 This text, a part or draft rather than a complete treatise, is one of the so-called 'Tyrwhitt's Fragments' published by Tyrwhitt in 1773 from MS Harleianus 5612. Its authorship has long been questioned but is now widely accepted: see Kidd 1988: 206 for a survey of the debate.

47 Referred to by Kidd (1988: 890) and Hahm (1989: 1355 n. 49 –but in the context of the discussion on the authorship of the *Lib. et aegrit*). On this fragment in relation to Posidonius' conception of the soul, see Tieleman 2003: 278–283 (where, however, it is labelled as "certainly spurious").

ments deriving from black bile, mental pangs, mental impressions and feelings of relaxation; (4) of the soul but involving the body are tremors, pallors and other changes of appearance related to fear or distress (trans. mine).⁴⁸

The context is a discussion of the question whether it is the body or the soul which causes affections (πάθη). According to Posidonius, then, the "affections of the soul without qualification", i.e. emotions such as desires, fears and fits of anger are essentially (mistaken) judgements and assumptions, which was the distinctive Stoic position since Zeno, Cleanthes, and Chrysippus.⁴⁹ If Posidonius, as Galen tells us, had really abandoned the theory of emotion of his predecessors in favour of an account in terms of the Platonic tripartition, it is strange that it is absent from this classification of kinds of affection. In fact, it points the other way, viz. to an explanation in terms of the interplay between body and soul, not between soul-parts. This is confirmed by what follows. Plutarch next presents the view of one Diodotus,⁵⁰ who did offer a classification between rational and non-rational elements in the soul. Clearly, then, Posidonius represents here the general Stoic "monistic" doctrine.

---

48 Ὅ γέ τοι Ποσειδώνιος τὰ μὲν εἶναι ψυχικά, τὰ δὲ σωματικά, καὶ τὰ μὲν οὐ ψυχῆς, περὶ ψυχὴν δὲ <σωματικά, τὰ δ' οὐ σώματος, περὶ σῶμα δὲ ψυχικά φησι, ψυχικὰ μὲν> ἁπλῶς τὰ ἐν κρίσεσι καὶ ὑπολήψεσιν οἷον ἐπιθυμίας λέγων, φόβους, ὀργάς, σωματικὰ δ' ἁπλῶς πυρετούς, περιψύξεις, πυκνώσεις, ἀραιώσεις, περὶ ψυχὴν δὲ σωματικὰ ληθάργους, μελαγχολίας, δηγμούς, φαντασίας, διαχύσεις, ἀνάπαλιν δὲ περὶ σῶμα ψυχικὰ τρόμους καὶ ὠχριάσεις καὶ μεταβολὰς τοῦ εἴδους κατὰ φόβον ἢ λύπην. Text from the edition by M. Pohlenz and K. Ziegler, *Plutarchi moralia*, vol. 6.3 (3rd ed. Leipzig: Teubner, 1966) 51–59.
49 D.L. 7.111 (*SVF* 3.456), Plut. *Virt. Mor.* 3, 441C (*SVF* 3.459), Gal. *PHP* IV 3,1; V 1,4 (*SVF* 3.461), where note that Galen says that this definition goes back to Chrysippus not Zeno, who held that the emotions *supervene on* judgements. Kidd (1988: 562), who accepts Galen's attribution of the Platonic tripartition, notes the discrepancy between the two sources but attempts to reconcile them by saying that Posidonius believed that judgements and assumptions were involved in πάθη. In his 1999 translation he also tries to do this: psychic affections without qualification "are those *having something to do with* rational decisions and suppositions" (italics mine). But this certainly blurs the distinction between categories (1) and (3) and (4). The classification is designed precisely to make clear which affections belong to the soul and which involve or affect the soul without being affections *of* the soul. Non-rational soul-parts appear not to have any function in this account.
50 It is unclear who is meant. Strabo, XVI.2.24 mentions a Diodotus of Sidon, brother of the Peripatetic philosopher Boethus, with whom Strabo (64/3 BCE-21+? CE) studied. If this Diodotus was a Peripatetic too (as Strabo seems to imply) the recorded doctrine fits him. Cicero's house-philosopher (d. 60 BCE) was called Diodotus, too, but he was a Stoic, so he can be safely excluded: Posidonius represents here the Stoic position, whereas Diodotus represents a school, or even schools, which explained affection with reference to a non-rational part of the soul.

The division of kinds of affection is developed on the basis of the different ways that body and soul interact. Of particular interest for our present purposes is the third category, viz. affections of the body which are also manifested in the soul, among which certain mental disorders but also the neutral notion of mental impressions or appearances, that is to say, thoughts (Greek φαντασίαι). Just as black bile may cause psychic disorders (i.e. melancholia), the body may suffer affections that come with particular impressions. This may refer not just to disturbances of sense-perception due to physical ailments but to bodily conditions in general. A similar picture arises from Posidonius' account of Marius' demise preserved by Plutarch. Marius' physical exhaustion expresses itself through depressing mental images. These in turn lead to emotions, especially fear, marked by a failure to respond rationally to his situation.[51] We should not take this classification as implying that one can only suffer from one of these four at the same time. Fear in the first sense of a judgement is regularly perhaps even typically accompanied by the physical effects (the fourth sense), which is explicitly stated in the final sentence. The judgement may be the core part of an emotion, but, as the Stoics were fully aware, it is really a complex phenomenon. Like most of his predecessors within the Stoic school, Posidonius took an interest in the interplay between body and soul. But he went further than his predecessors did in looking for exact causes and how they were related. Kidd aptly refers to the fragment preserved at Gal. *PHP* V 5.22–25 (Posid. F164.84–99 EK), in which Posidonius argues that character is determined by our physical make-up, which therefore explains differences in both individual and, through the impact of the physical environment, national character. The notion of character is closely linked to that of emotion because character is the underlying state or disposition which explains what kind of emotions an individual or nation typically has. Posidonius assumed that "the affective movements of the soul always follow the state of the body" (τῶν παθητικῶν κινήσεων τῆς ψυχῆς ἑπομένων ἀεὶ τῇ διαθέσει τοῦ σώματος, Gal. *PHP* V 5.23, p.322.3–4 De Lacy). We also learn here that Posidonius operated with the notion of mixture and attributed a special significance to the composition of the blood in animals, which, he said, differs in warmth and coldness, thickness and thinness and in many properties. Galen wholeheartedly agrees with Posidonius, saying that he could easily quote passages from Hippocrates and Plato showing that Posidonius followed them in these matters Gal. *PHP* V 5.25, p. 322.8–10).

---

51 Hahm (1989: 1353–1357) is no doubt right to point to this aspect of Marius' behaviour; cf. *supra*, p. 215.

To conclude this section, we have seen that Galen's report on the relation between Posidonius and the founder of the medical school of the Pneumatists, Athenaeus of Attaleia, becomes less surprising or unlikely when seen in light of further fragments and testimonies about the interest taken in medicine by the great Stoic. It was greater than has often been supposed. Moreover, part of the evidence suggests that this interest was stimulated by Posidonius' related concern with the interplay between body and soul and the causal explanation of mental phenomena such as the emotions. In the next section, I will take a closer look at some relevant pieces of evidence that may supplement our picture of the medical background to Posidonius' thought and his interest in causal theory. For this we will have to turn to his theory of emotion.

3 Emotion and Causes

Posidonius' distinction between three causes in Galen's *On Cohesive Causes* (*CC* 2.1–3=F190 EK, above, pp. 205–206) invites comparison with another fragment that is "medical" in the sense that it deals with the disease and therapy of the *soul*: Seneca, *Moral Letters* 87.31. This passage is itself part of a much longer section (31–40=F170 EK) in which Seneca draws on Posidonius (no treatise mentioned) in dealing with the question of the value and status of wealth.[52] The Stoics maintain that wealth is not good (since it may be used badly) but may count as one of what the Stoics technically classed as preferred "indifferents". When confronted with objections, certain Stoics argue that it is wrong to blame wealth itself for disadvantageous things that may happen to its possessor: riches harm no one; it is human folly that harms, just as it is not the sword that kills but the killer using it (§ 30). Yet Seneca is not satisfied by this riposte and appeals to Posidonius:

> Posidonius, to my mind, is better [scil. than the Stoics mentioned in § 30]; he says that riches are a cause of evil, not because they themselves do anything, but because they rouse men to do evil. For there is a distinction between efficient cause (*causa efficiens*), which necessarily harms straight off, and antecedent cause (*praecedens, scil. causa*). It is as this antecedent cause that riches act: they swell the temper, beget pride, arouse envy,

---

[52] For what follows see, in addition to Kidd (1988: 628–638), the interpretation offered by Kidd (1985, esp. 9–21), who carefully disentangles Posidonius' position from Seneca's argument, concluding that in regard to the relationship of virtue (or happiness) and external goods such as wealth Posidonius remained within the Chrysippean framework but developed a causal analysis of the effects of wealth that is very typical of him as an individual philosopher.

and so derange the mind that a reputation for having money, even when it is harmful, delights us.

Sen. *Ep.* 87.31=Posidonius F 170 EK

Posidonius, then, defends the Stoic position that wealth is not a good but is not evil either. Even so, it can harm us by acting on the soul *as an antecedent cause*. As an antecedent cause, it may stimulate passions and so corrupt the soul. But the (bad) antecedent cause does not necessarily harm us; it is the *efficient* cause which necessarily harms us. So riches are not evil in themselves. We may infer that the soul itself is the efficient cause of moral corruption and that "evil" (and so "good") strictly refers to the soul alone. This is standard Stoic axiology. Being neither good nor evil wealth is indifferent. Although it is not spelled out here, this evaluation of wealth makes it possible even to treat it as a morally neutral advantage for those with a mind strong enough not to be corrupted by it. But in this context Seneca wishes to stress the corrupting impact of wealth upon all those who cannot handle it properly (which, one may assume, holds for the non-virtuous majority).

In sum, Posidonius justifies the Stoic view of the moral status of wealth in relation to evil through the distinction between efficient and antecedent causes. Posidonius may have been the first to use this distinction in this axiological context. In Seneca's letter, at any rate, it constitutes a refinement to the argument employed by the anonymous Stoics, who bluntly said that riches do not harm. Even so, Posidonius and these Stoics agree on the main point, viz. that the cause of evil in the strictest sense is to be located in the human mind. The distinction itself, moreover, can be paralleled from other Stoic texts. First, there is the testimony from which we started: Galen, *CC* 2.1–3 (Posid. F190 EK). The distinction between efficient and antecedent causes in Seneca runs parallel with what there are called (in Lyon's translation of the Arabic version) cohesive and immediate causes. Here, as we have seen, their combined effect is instantiated in the case of disease by the example of the sun's heat affecting the *pneuma*. There is a further refinement through a third type of cause, viz. the prior or predisposing cause used to explain indirect and gradual forms of causation. But clearly the main distinction is the internal/external one (with the predisposing cause being on the internal side).[53] As we have also noticed, this basic distinction could be made more precise through further distinctions within the external and auxiliary type of cause. However, the distinction applied by Posidonius to explain the cause of moral corruption by wealth coincides with that between

---

53 Cf. Hahm 1989: 1352.

the 'perfect' (or 'complete') and 'antecedent' (or 'initiating') causes (αἰτία αὐτοτελής and προκαταρκτική) drawn by Chrysippus.⁵⁴ Posidonius' application to how we respond to wealth, it turns out, is just an instance of how the causal scheme works in the Stoic explanation of human action in general. In this case the mind decides the outcome when it is confronted with a potentially corrupting impression; if it is diseased already, it is *predisposed* to respond emotionally, and through this response it weakens itself further. This may be illustrated by some further evidence.

Posidonius wrote extensively about these things in his *On Affections* (or *Emotions*, Περὶ παθῶν), with a constant eye on Chrysippus' work of the same title and occasional criticisms of his great predecessor, which our source, Galen, uses to play off the two Stoics against one another. We find the fragments and paraphrases relevant to our present purposes at Galen, *PHP* V (1.3–2.12, pp. 294.32–296.36 De Lacy=Posidonius F 163 EK; *SVF* 3.465 [Chrysippus]).⁵⁵ Posidonius described the souls of imperfect persons (φαῦλοι), viz. as marked by a *proneness* (εὐεμπτωσία, τὸ εὐέμπτωτον) to affections or emotions (πάθη), comparing the state of their souls to that of a body that is either healthy but prone to disease or in a sense diseased already. The crucial piece of evidence reads:

> Therefore, the disease of the soul does not resemble, as Chrysippus had supposed, the sickly constitution (τῇ νοσώδει καχεξίᾳ) of the body, whereby it is carried off in such a way as to fall into irregular, non-periodic fevers; rather disease of the soul resembles either physical health with a proneness to disease (τὸ εὐέμπτωτον εἰς νόσον), or the disease itself. For disease of the body is a state already diseased, but what Chrysippus calls disease resembles rather a proneness (εὐεμπτωσία) to fever.
>
> *PHP* V, 2.7=Posid. F163 EK; transl. De Lacy

Like Chrysippus, Posidonius described the condition of the mind of imperfect people as sick; the emotions are like temporary outbursts of fever supervening on the underlying diseased condition, in this case not the body but a weak character. Given its proneness to affection, it will be triggered by an external cause whether big or small (viz. the particular situation in which one finds oneself and which causes an impression). People differ among themselves by being more or less prone to be affected.

---

54 See esp. Cic. *Fat.* 41–44; Plut. *SR* 1056B, cited *supra*, n.16. Note that Seneca translates *praecedens* (*causa*) whereas Cicero (*Fat.* 41) has *antecedens*. On the passage in Seneca (*Ep.* 87.30) as part of F 170 EK, see further the comments by Kidd 1988: 628–629.
55 The relevant pages in Galen and what they permit us to infer about Posidonius' position are lucidly discussed by Kidd 1988: 580–587. See also Kidd 1983.

In the first six books of *PHP* Galen is eager to play off Posidonius against Chrysippus, presenting the former as a full-blown dissident among the Stoic ranks, an intellectual hero who valued truth more highly than the dogmas of his own school.[56] A closer reading of these pages suggests that Galen inflates certain minor points on which Posidonius felt induced to improve upon Chrysippus. Thus he insisted on causal explanation in regard to irrational phenomena such as weeping or laughing against one's will where Chrysippus had felt this to be impossible and presumably unnecessary.[57] Here and there Posidonius placed a different emphasis and introduced new terminology. Thus he followed Chrysippus in describing the emotions and the underlying diseased or weak character on the analogy of bodily ailments. The notion of proneness to emotion employed by Posidonius in this connection may not be original with him either. Yet the evidence strongly indicates that he emphasized this idea to a far greater extent than did Chrysippus and other predecessors. Indeed, the relatively extensive quotations and paraphrases provided by Galen from the two treatises *On Affections* written by Chrysippus and Posidonius respectively suggest that it was the latter who gave the concept (for which he coined the term εὐεμπτωσία) a definite and more prominent place in the Stoic theory of emotion.[58] Insofar as

---

56 Gal. *QAM*, c.11, pp. 85.12–86.2 Bazou, pp. 77.17–78.2 Müller (Posid. T58 EK. Cf. F35).
57 See esp. the discussion conducted by Galen in ch. 7 of *PHP* IV, with Tieleman 2003: 122–132. So when Chrysippus at one point said that he the cause of certain phenomena of this type is difficult to reason out, Galen tells us that this is because Chrysippus, unlike Posidonius, had abandoned the account of the ancients, meaning that such phenomena cannot properly be explained with reference to non-rational soul-parts (*PHP* IV 7.18–23). Chrysippus was sensitive to the limits of knowledge, whereas Posidonius felt he could and should go beyond the point where Chrysippus stopped. For Posidonius' fondness for exploring causes, cf. the observation by Strabo quoted *supra*, p. 208. On Chrysippus and the limits of knowledge and using insights from the sciences, see Tieleman 1996: 189–195. Galen's presentation of Posidonius' response to Chrysippus has been studied anew by Gill 2006: 266–290 and Long 2017.
58 Cicero, *Tusc.* 4.27 gives a brief explanation of being prone (*proclivus*) to a particular emotion in his account of the Stoic theory of emotion (4.11–33), which is based on (an epitome of parts of) Chrysippus' *On Affections*: see Tieleman 2003: 296–306. But cf. Kidd 1983: 108, pointing to Galen's remark at *PHP* IV, 2.5, p. 296.6 De Lacy that the expression τὸ εὐέμπτωτον εἰς νόσον ("being prone to disease") is Posidonius' phrase. Kidd seems right as far as terminology is concerned. In the preceding context, he cites the sentence from Chrysippus to which Posidonius responds and where a different term is used for the same idea, i.e. being prone: "Chrysippus says that their [scil. the inferior people's] soul is analogous to a body which is apt (ἐπιτηδείοις) to fall into fever or diarrhoea or something else of that kind from a small and chance cause" (*PHP* IV, 2.3, p. 294.34–36 = *SVF* 3.465; transl. De Lacy). Note here also the reference to the immediate or external cause, for which Chrysippus uses προφάσει, a term with a distinctly Hippocratic ring. The term εὐέμπτωσία seems to have become common from the 1st cent. BCE

Posidonius criticized Chrysippus, his point appears to have been that Chrysippus was not explicit enough: the mind's proneness refers to a third cause, viz. the preceding one.

The aspect of the soul's proneness to a particular emotion invites comparison with the third cause (which is actually distinguished as second) in Galen's testimony from *On Cohesive Causes*, viz. the prior or predisposing cause. Here too it marks the stage preceding the outbreak of the affection, the stage of latency. In fact, Posidonius employs the verb used by our other sources for the predisposing cause in a relevant way:

> Posidonius ... tries to show that the causes of all false suppositions arise < in the theoretical sphere through ignorance, but in the practical >[59] through the affective pull (παθητικῆς ὁλκῆς) but that false opinions take the lead (or 'precede', προηγεῖσθαι) when the rational faculty has become weak in regard to judgement.
>
> Gal. *PHP* V, 5.21 = F169 EK, ll. 78–82; trans. De Lacy, slightly modified

This passage is not a verbatim quotation but it may be taken to preserve Posidonius' original wording including the expression "affective pull". Here we see the same causal schema all over again: an emotion occurs when one experiences an impulse (the "affective pull") upon perceiving something desirable or repulsive (i.e. the immediate cause).[60] The view of affection, or emotion, as an impulse,

---

onwards: see Kidd 2003: 108, with examples. It is also used in the relevant sections of Arius Didymus (ap. Stob. *Ecl.* II, 93.1=*SVF* 3.421) and Diog. Laert. 7.115 (*SVF* 3.422) illustrating the proneness to mental affection by character traits such as irascibility and enviousness. Diogenes Laertius has preserved the analogy with bodily ailments (note the echo of the Chrysippean passage just quoted). Both sources distinguish proneness to affection from 'disease' (νόσημα), i.e. the state (ἕξις) in which the affection has become deep-seated, inveterate and intense. This is the state of intense and constant desire or repulsion typically expressed by the nouns with the prefixes φιλ- and μισ- respectively, e.g. φιλογυνία and μισανθρωπία. On anticipations of the Posidonian concept of proneness see further Graver 2007: 142–144; Ranocchia 2012.

59 This addition to the text by De Lacy has been generally accepted.

60 On this passage see further Tieleman 2003: 231–242; Long 2017: 39–40; Lorenz 2011: 191–192, who takes it to imply an affective *soul-part* on the basis of *Galen's* ensuing paraphrase (τῇ κινήσει τοῦ παθητικοῦ, *PHP* V, 5.22, p. 320.28 De Lacy), Here Galen speaks of impulse as often resulting from the παθητικόν in the 'animal' (ζῴῳ). This broader term may be taken to reflect Posidonius' discussion of non-rational animals, including children, in the original context, viz. the causal explanation of vice: see Kidd 1988: 622–623 (who however follows Galen's ascription to Posidonius of the Platonic tripartition). Galen may blur the distinction made by Posidonius between rational and non-rational animals, in line with his general habit of reading Platonic-style soul-parts into Posidonius' account, a possibility overlooked by Lorenz. Another (non-Stoic) source, Plutarch, says that Posidonius identified emotions with judgements: see *supra*, p. 216. Better on this passage Long 2017: 40: "Galen ... glosses Posidonius' point as if it were

viz. an excessive, unnatural one, is traditionally Stoic. This impulse presupposes assent, which will be given if, Posidonius explains, we are predisposed to do so on account of reason' weakness, i.e. its entertaining false opinions — the preceding cause.

Further, the soul–body analogy calls for some comments. In fact, the term 'analogy' is potentially misleading here. We are not dealing with an analogy in the more common sense of a comparison of certain structural characteristics between two things made for the sake of explanation or clarification. In the context of Stoic corporealism, there exists an actual, physical correspondence between psychic and bodily disease. Thus, the psychology of emotion can also be described in purely physical terms. The mental impression of an external object is a qualitative change in the psychic *pneuma*. Under its impact the psychic *pneuma* may be thrown off balance, that is to say, its blend or proportion of hot and cold may be disturbed, which causes the soul to flutter, i.e. suffer an emotion — a typical result of the soul's lack of tension. This is itself caused by an imperfect mixture of elementary qualities.[61] The physical effects of emotion are due either to the soul's contraction in cold emotions (distress and fear) or expansion in hot emotions (lust and desire).[62] That hot or cold sensations ac-

---

about impulse, but his comment has a poor fit with the rest of the passage. In any case, Posidonius shows retrospectively that false suppositions have a rather elaborate chain of causes within the human mind". Unfortunately, Long goes on to say that this resembles Posidonius' substitution, elsewhere, of Chrysippus' explanation for his own as turning on involuntary responses. However, Posidonius' elaborate chain of causes seems to be characterized more adequately as an elaboration within the Chrysippean framework. On the context in Posidonius and Galen's polemical strategy, see further Tieleman 2003: 132–139; cf. 240–241; Gill 2006: 266–290.

61 According to Stoic physical doctrine the psychic *pneuma* itself is fed from both the exhalation of blood in the heart and respiration: see Diogenes of Babylon ap. Gal. *PHP* II 8.40, 44 (*SVF* 3 Diogenes Bab. 30), making the soul receptive to the influence of the constitution of both the body and the environment including climatic factors, an idea to which Posidonius subscribed, see further below in text.

62 On the soul's health and strength (i.e. tension) as residing in the 'symmetry' (συμμετρία) or right blend (εὐκρασία) of elements just like that of the body see *SVF* 3.471, 472, 473, 2.787, all fragments from Chrysippus' *On Affections* (Chrysippus in his turn took his starting point from what Zeno had written: *ib.* 471). On these fragments, see Tieleman 2003: 147–150. On psychic illness as most similar to a feverish state of the body marked by irregular fevers and cold shivers see from the same work *SVF* 3.465. On the emotional soul's fluttering and random movements: *ib.* 476. On hot and cold determining the degree of tension see also *supra*, n. **7** with text thereto.

company emotions was in fact a widespread idea which can be paralleled from Hippocratic literature, tragedy and poetry.[63]

The relation between soul and body is not merely one of correspondence between their elemental composition and hence similarity of functioning but lies also in their being closely interwoven and interacting. This emerges clearly from another fragment preserved by Galen in the fifth book of *PHP*. The context is the explanation offered by Chrysippus and Posidonius of the causes of evil, i.e. moral corruption as expressed in emotional behaviour. Galen praises Posidonius:

> Posidonius reasonably attaches to this discussion [scil. on the causes of evil] the phenomena from physiognomy: all broad-chested and warmer creatures and humans are more spirited in nature, the broad-hipped and colder, more cowardly. And environment contributes to considerable differences in human character with regard to cowardice, daring, love of pleasure or toil; the grounds for this are that the emotional movements of the soul follow always the state of the body, which is altered in no small degree from the temperature (or mixture, κράσεως) in the environment. For he also says that even the blood in animals differs in warmth and coldness, thickness and thinness, and in a considerable number of other different ways, a topic which Aristotle developed at length.
>
> *PHP* V, 5.22–29, pp. 320.29–322.26 De Lacy = F 169, ll. 84–96 EK[64]

Character expresses itself in bodily features but this also works in the opposite way, i.e. the bodily state determines the soul's emotional movements and hence character. The state of the body is in its turn conditioned by the physical environment, i.e. the particular mixture of physical elements that makes up a climate. Theory is again built on key notions such as the mixture of the four elements, with the hot and the cold playing the more active role (a fact which is here illustrated by the association of the hot with a more angry or assertive character and the cold with a timid one). Here too, the predisposition, or proneness, toward a particular emotion is constitutive of a particular character. One would assume that the environment, i.e. the quality of the air, also directly impacts the soul through respiration, as is suggested by other Stoic texts.[65] But in

---

63 See Tieleman 1999: 414–415; 2003: 192–193; cf. Zink 1962.
64 Kidd aptly refers to *PA* 647b, 650b, *Pol.* VII.6, 1327b.
65 Cf. Chrysippus *ap.* Cic. *Fat.* 7–9 (*SVF* 2.950–951, where also note the reference to antecedent causes, *Fat.* 8) relating intelligence and character to climatic condition; cf. Cic. *ND* 2.17 (referring to the quality of the air); Sedley 1993, esp. 319, 331; Tieleman 2003: 194–195. There can be no doubt about the importance of respiration for our psychic condition. At the first inhalation after birth natural *pneuma* turns into psychic *pneuma* under the impact of the cold solidifying air, i.e. the *pneuma* acquires the necessary tension: see *SVF* 2.804–808, Aet. *Plac.* V, 15.4; see *supra*, p. 205. The inhaled air is one of the sources of nourishment: see Diogenes of Seleucia (or

the passage above Posidonius, as paraphrased by Galen, seems to have spoken of an indirect causation: environmental factors impact the soul via the body. At any rate, our physical state as impacted by the wider environment *predisposes* us to particular emotions and hence to a particular character. Since people living in a particular part of the world share this climatic environment they develop a national character. It is hard not to be reminded of such works as the Hippocratic *Airs, Waters and Places*.[66] But in fact the sun as impacting the *pneuma* in the human body in Galen *CC* 4 is a case in point as well (see above, p. 206). In line with his predecessors in the Stoic school Posidonius saw human beings as particles of a greater whole, taking this to apply in a literal and physical sense. The *pneuma* as the stuff of both the cosmic and the human soul functions as the lynchpin of this corporealist, or materialist, world-view. It is within this doctrinal framework that we have to study his ideas on causality.

4 Conclusion

The excesses of so-called 'Panposidonianism'[67] stand as a warning against ascribing a great deal to the influence of Posidonius in cases where he is not explicitly mentioned. The documented evidence from Galen and other sources I have been reviewing, however, permits us to consider the medical thought of the Pneumatists against a Stoic and in particular Posidonian background. There is no good reason to brush aside Galen's report that the school's founder, Athe-

---

Babylon) *ap*. Gal. *PHP* II, 8.40, 44 (*SVF* 3 Diog. 30). For discussion and further references see Tieleman 1996: 79–101; cf. 66.

66 See esp. *Aer*. 16.1, 24.3, pp. 62.1–5, 78, 17–23 Diller (where note the hot/cold ratios).

67 i.e. the tendency to postulate Posidonius as the source of a great many later authors (e.g. Cicero, Seneca) and to reconstruct his philosophy on the basis of their works, eliciting A.E. Housman's sarcastic observation: "Omnia a Posidonio sumpta esse Germanorum nemo ignorat, apud quos iam dudum constat Romanos praeter Posidonium nihil legisse," Housman (1903–1930) *ad* II. V. 93. Panposidonianism was marked by a variety of interpretations of the philosopher, ranging from the empirically minded scientist to the religiously inspired mystic. A more sceptical attitude was advocated by Bréhier 1914; Dobson 1918; and Edelstein 1936. The fragment-collection begun by Edelstein on the basis of this principle was completed by I.G. Kidd: Edelstein-Kidd 1972. Theiler (1982) is based on broader principles of inclusion inspired by the works of Karl Reinhardt in particular. Vimercati (2004) strikes a precarious compromise between the two principles; cf. Algra 2014. On the course taken by Posidonian studies until the 1970s and methodological issues, see further Edelstein-Kidd 1972: xiii–xxii; Laffranque 1964: ch. 1; Reinhardt 1954: cols. 570–624.

naeus of Attalia, studied with Posidonius. Athenaeus found in Posidonius already a well-developed interest in medical issues. In particular, there is a clear connection between Athenaeus and Posidonius where the aetiology of disease is concerned. Here, as elsewhere, the information to be gleaned, with due caution, from Galen, has proved indispensable. In particular, it has thrown light on Posidonius' introduction of the notion of predisposing cause in his causal analysis of the soul's affections, or emotions. But this is not just about the soul. The evidence from Plutarch (both *Marius* and *Desire and Grief*) shows that Posidonius' analysis of emotion reflects a keen interest in the soul's interaction with the body. Posidonius developed this analysis in the light of that of Chrysippus, the greatest among his predecessors in the Stoic school, who had already drawn an extensive analogy between mental and bodily states and presented philosophy as the medicine of the soul. His interest in medicine was continued by Posidonius to a greater extent than has so far been assumed. But in fact, it reflects a more general feature of the work of this wide-ranging Stoic. This makes him both a witness to and (in the case of Pneumatism) contributor to Graeco-Roman medicine.

Bibliography

Algra, K.A. 2014. Review of Vimercati (2004). *Gnomon* 86: 300–307.
Arena, G. 2007. "Il sapere al centro del potere: medici di Panfilia nella Roma imperiale", *QCSAM* n.s. 6: 195–213.
Bréhier, E. 1914. "Posidonius d'Apamée théoricien de la géometrie", *REG* 27: 44–58.
Carney, T.F. 1958. "The Death of Marius", *Acta Classica* I: 117–122.
Coughlin, S. 2018. "Athenaeus of Attalia on the Psychological Causes of Bodily Health", in: C. Thumiger and P. Singer (eds.), *Mental Illness in Ancient Medicine*. Leiden: Brill: 109–142.
Coughlin, S. and O. Lewis 2020. "Pneuma and the Pneumatist School of Medicine", in: S. Coughlin, D. Leith, and O. Lewis (eds.), *The Concept of Pneuma after Aristotle. Berlin Studies of the Ancient World* 61: 201–234.
Diller, H. 1936. "Eine stoisch-pneumatische Schrift im Corpus Hippocraticum", *Sudhoffs Arch. Gesch. Med. Naturw.* 29: 178–195; repr. in *Kleine Schriften zur antiken Medizin*, Hrsg. G. Baader & H. Grensemann (Berlin: De Gruyter 1973): 17–30.
Dobson, J.F. 1918. "The Posidonius Myth", *CQ* 12: 179–195.
Edelstein, L. 1936. "The Philosophical System of Posidonius", *AJPh* 57, 286–325.
Edelstein, E. & I.G. Kidd (eds.) 1972. *Posidonius. Vol. I. The Fragments.* Cambridge: Cambridge University Press.
Frede, M. 1980. "The Original Notion of Cause", in: M. Schofield et al. (eds.), *Doubt and Dogmatism. Studies in Hellenistic Epistemology.* Oxford: Oxford University Press: 217–249; repr. in: M. Frede (1987) *Essays in Ancient Philosophy.* Oxford: Clarendon Press: 125–150.

Gill, C.J. 2006. *The Structured Self in Hellenistic and Roman Thought*. Oxford: Oxford University Press.

Görler, W. 1987. "Hauptursachen bei Cicero und Chrysipp? Philologischen Marginalien zu einen vieldiskutierten Gleichnis", *Rheinisches Museum* 130: 254–274.

Graver, M. 2007. *Stoicism and Emotion*. Chicago: University of Chicago Press.

Hahm, D.E. 1989. "Posidonius' Theory of Historical Causation", *ANRW* II 36.3: 1325–1363.

Hankinson, R.J. 2001. *Cause and Explanation in Ancient Greek Thought*. Oxford: Oxford University Press.

Hankinson, R.J. 2003. "Stoicism and Medicine", in: B. Inwood (ed.), *The Cambridge Companion to the Stoics*. Cambridge: Cambridge University Press: 295–309.

Harig, G. 1988. "Die Entstehung der pneumatischen Schule und Poseidonios von Apamea", in: H. Schadewaldt and K.-H. Leven (eds.), *Actes. XXX Congrès international d'histoire de la médicine*. Düsseldorf: 220–226.

Housman, A.E. (ed.) (1903–1930), *M. Manilii, Astronomicon*. Five vols. Cambridge. 2nd ed. 1937.

Kidd, I.G. 1978. "Philosophy and Science in Posidonius", *Antike und Abendland* 24: 7–15.

Kidd, I.G. 1983. "Euemptosia - proneness to disease", in: W.W. Fortenbaugh (ed.), *On Stoic and Peripatetic Ethics: The Work of Arius Didymus*. Rutgers Univ. Studies in Classical Humanities, vol. 1, New Brunswick/London: 107–113.

Kidd, I.G. 1985. "Posidonian methodology and the self-sufficiency of virtue", in: H. Flashar and O. Gigon (eds.), *Aspects de la philosophie hellénistique: Entretiens sur l'Antiquité classique XXXII, Vandœuvres-Genève 26-31 août 1985*. Vandœuvres-Genève: Fondation Hardt: 1–28.

Kidd, I.G. 1988. *Posidonius. Vol II. The Commentary:* (i) *Testimonia and Fragments 1–149;* (ii) *Fragments 150–293*. Cambridge: Cambridge University Press.

Kidd, I.G. 1999. *Posidonius. Vol. III. The Translation of the Fragments*. Cambridge: Cambridge University Press.

Kollesch, J. 1973. *Untersuchungen zu den peudogalenischen Definitiones Medicae*. Berlin.

Kudlien, F. 1962. "Poseidonios und die Ärzteschule der Pneumatiker", *Hermes* 90: 419–429.

Kudlien, F. 1968. "Pneumatische Ärzte", *RE* Suppl. XI: cols. 1097–1108.

Laffranque, M. 1964. *Poseidonios d'Apamée. Essai de mise au point*. Paris.

Long, A.G. 2017. "Plato, Chrysippus and Posidonius' Theory of Affective Movements", in: T. Engberg-Pedersen (ed.), *From Stoicism to Platonism. The Development of Philosophy 100 BCE–100 CE*. Cambridge: 27–46.

Lorenz, H. 2011. "Posidonius on the Nature and Treatment of the Emotions", *Oxford Studies in Ancient Philosophy* 40: 189–209.

Mansfeld, J. 2001. "Chrysippus' Definition of Cause in Arius Didymus", *Elenchos* 22.1: 99–110.

Lyons, M. 1969. *Galen On the Parts of Medicine, On Cohesive Causes On Regimen in Acute Diseases in Accordance with the Theories of Hippocrates*, first edition of the Arabic version with English translation. The Latin version of *On the Parts of Medicine* ed. by H. Schöne and *On Cohesive Causes* ed. by K. Kalbfleisch, reedited by J. Kollesch, D. Nickel, G. Strohmaier, *Corpus Medicorum Graecorum, Supplementum Orientale* II (Berlin: Akademie-Verlag 1969).

Kollesch, J. *et alii* 1969, see Lyons 1969.

Nutton, V. 2004. *Ancient Medicine*. London: Routledge.

Ranocchia, Graziano. 2012. "The Stoic concept of proneness to emotion and vice", *Archiv für Geschichte der Philosophie* 94.1: 74–92.

Reinhardt, K. 1954. *Poseidonios*. Frankfurt: Druckenmüller. Repr. of *RE* XXII.1, 557–826 (1953).
Schröder, S. 1989. "Philosophische und medizinische Ursachensystematik und der stoische Determinismus (1. Teil)", *Prometheus* XV: 209–239.
Schröder, S. 1990a. "Philosophische und medizinische Ursachensystematik und der stoische Determinismus (2. Teil)", *Prometheus* XVI: 5–26.
Schröder, S. 1990b. "Philosophische und medizinische Ursachensystematik und der stoische Determinismus (3. Teil und Schluß)", *Prometheus* XVI: 136–154.
Sedley, D.N. 1993. "Chrysippus on Psychophysical Causality", in: J. Brunschwig/M. Nussbaum (eds.), *Passions and Perceptions. Studies in Hellenistic Philosophy of Mind*. Proceedings of the 5th Symposium Hellenisticum. Paris/Cambridge: 313–331.
Smith, W.D. 1979. *The Hippocratic Tradition*. Ithaca: Cornell University Press: 230–233.
Theiler, W. (ed.) 1982. *Poseidonios. Die Fragmente*. I. *Texte*. II. *Erlaüterungen*. Texte und Kommentare Bd. 10. Berlin: De Gruyter.
Tieleman, T.L. 1996. *Galen and Chrysippus on the Soul*. Leiden/Boston: Brill.
Tieleman, T.L. 1999. "Chrysippus' Therapeutikon and the Corpus Hippocraticum. Some Preliminary Observations", in: I. Garofalo/D. Manetti/A. Roselli (eds.), *Aspetti della terapia nel Corpus Hippocraticum. Actes du IXe Colloque Hippocratique*. Firenze: Olschki: 405–418.
Tieleman, T.L. 2003. *Chrysippus' On Affections. Reconstruction and Interpretation*. Leiden/Boston: Brill.
Tieleman, T.L. 2005. "Pneuma", in: K.-H. Leven (ed.), *Antieke Medizin. Ein Lexikon*. München: C.H. Beck: 718–719.
Vimercati, E. 2004. *Posidonio. Testimonianze e Frammenti*. Testo latino [sic] a fronte. Introduzione, traduzione, commentario e apparati di E.V.; presentazione di Roberto Radice. Bompiani, collana *Il pensiero occidentale*. Milano.
Wellmann, M. 1895. *Die pneumatische Schule bis auf Archigenes in ihrer Entwicklung dargestellt*. Philologische Untersuchungen 14. Berlin: Weidmann.
Wellmann, M. 1896. "Athenaios aus Attalia", *RE* II: cols. 2034–2036.
Zink, N. 1962. *Griechische Ausdrucksweisen für Warm und Kalt im seelischen Bereich*. diss. Mainz.

David Kaufman
Galen on Non-Rational Motivation and the Freedom from Emotions: A Reading of *Affections of the Soul*

Abstract: In this chapter, I explore Galen's complex view of the role that non-rational motivation and emotions play in a virtuous and fulfilling life. As has often been commented, Galen's position is, at first sight, rather puzzling: on the one hand, he argues that appropriate non-rational motivation plays an ineliminable and valuable role in a virtuous life; on the other hand, he also argues in favor of the ideal of *apatheia*, the complete freedom from emotions, and develops a detailed method of moral education intended to cultivate it. Although previous scholarship has found Galen's claim that we ought to free ourselves completely from the emotions to sit uneasily with his view that the non-rational parts of the soul have a fundamental role to play in virtuous motivation, I argue that his considered position, developed most fully in *Affections of the Soul*, makes a cogent and innovative contribution to the postclassical *apatheia/metriopatheia* debate. I also discuss some implications of Galen's position for his more general theory of emotions and philosophical psychology.

Among the most popular topics of interschool debate in Hellenistic and Imperial philosophy was the question of what role, if any, ordinary emotions such as love, anger, and the like play in a virtuous and fulfilling life. In this chapter, I wish to explore Galen's view on this issue and its relationship to the two most famous positions in this debate: the Stoic view that ordinary emotions contribute nothing at all to a virtuous life; and the Peripatetic view that such emotions, at least if they are suitably moderate and concordant with the agent's practical reasoning, play a crucial role in virtuous action.[1] As we will see, Galen's position in this debate is rather puzzling: on the one hand, he argues that appropriate non-rational motivation plays an ineliminable and valuable role in a virtuous life; on the other hand, he also argues in favor of the ideal of *apatheia*, the complete freedom from emotions, and develops a detailed method of moral educa-

---

[1] For recent discussion of the postclassical Peripatetic ideal of *metriopatheia* see Inwood 2014 and Sorabji 2007. For an overview of the postclassical *apatheia/metriopatheia* debate, see, e.g., Dillon 1983.

tion intended to cultivate it. Although previous scholarship has found Galen's claim that we ought to free ourselves from the emotions to sit uneasily with his view that the non-rational parts of the soul have a fundamental role to play in virtuous motivation,[2] I argue that his considered position, developed most fully in *Affections of the Soul*, makes a cogent and sophisticated contribution to the *apatheia/metriopatheia* debate, which differs from both Stoic *apatheia* and Peripatetic *metriopatheia*. I also discuss some implications of Galen's position for his more general theory of emotions and philosophical psychology.

1 Galenic Psychology and the Ideal of *Apatheia*

Among Galen's most firmly held philosophical commitments is his support for a tripartite Platonic model of the soul, according to which the soul includes appetite and spirit, in addition to reason.[3] For instance, in his *On the Doctrines of Plato and Hippocrates* he even claims to have provided 'scientific proofs' (ἀποδείξεις ἐπιστημονικαί, *PHP* 9.1.7–8 De Lacy) that the three parts of the soul are located in the liver, heart, and brain respectively. Moreover, there is strong reason to think that Galen not only supports tripartition, but endorses a particularly robust version of it. In particular, he argues in a number of works that we are simply *incapable* of engaging in a wide range of ordinary and essential human activity on the basis of reason alone, without the contribution of spirit and appetite. For example, according to the substantial Arabic epitome of his *On Character Traits*, Galen argues that someone who was missing the appetitive part of the soul would *never* engage in sexual intercourse, whatever the situation, because, in his words, "the rational soul can understand nothing of it and can discover nothing of it" (*Mor.* 27.7–9 Kr.).[4] Along similar lines, he also claims that a person in such a condition would *choose* to die rather than to eat (*Mor.* 27.5–7 Kraus), and argues a bit later that even if they managed to eat something solely

---

[2] For critical discussion of the tension between Galen's ideal of *apatheia* and its relationship to his psychological theory see Donini 2008: 193–194; Gill 2010: 244 and 258–260; Hankinson 1993: 198–204; and Singer 2013: 22–23 and 208–210.

[3] For discussion of Galen's innovative adaptation of Platonic psychology, see De Lacy 1986, Donini 2008, Hankinson 1991 and 1993, Kaufman 2017, Schiefsky 2012, Singer 1991, Tieleman 2003a, and Trompeter 2018.

[4] I print Daniel Davies' recent translation of *On Character Traits*, with minor alterations. My citations of the extent Arabic Epitome of *On Character Traits* follow the numbering in Davies' translation, which is based on Kraus 1939, the standard edition of the Arabic text.

on the basis of their considered view that doing so was right or good for them, they would have difficulty digesting it or even keeping it down without the co-operation of the vegetative or appetitive part of their soul (*Mor.* 41.18–19 Kraus).[5]

Galen argues to similar effect in his other psychological and ethical works. For instance, in his treatise *The Capacities of the Soul Depend on the Mixtures of the Body*, he writes that "neither is the appetitive part of the soul capable of desiring noble things nor is the rational part of the soul capable of desiring sex, food or drink, just as it is also incapable of desiring victory, rule, reputation or honor" (*QAM* 36.3–6 Müller).[6] Again, in *On the Doctrines of Plato and Hippocrates*, he claims to have shown 'indisputably' (ἀναμφισβητήτως) that "*the same power* does not both reason and also desire food, drink, and sex" (*PHP* 5.7.42 De Lacy).[7] There is thus quite strong textual evidence throughout his psychological works that Galen takes people to be simply incapable of pursuing appetitive goods such as food, drink, and sex, or even spirited goods such as victory or reputation, in an effective way on the basis of reason alone. Rather, according to him, every effective human impulse for such things must, at the least, involve the appetitive or spirited part of the soul. According to Galen, then, appetite and spirit are not only an *ineliminable* part of human psychology, but also play a *crucial* and *essential* role in human motivation and survival.[8]

It may seem surprising, then, when in his *Affections of the Soul* Galen insists that a fully virtuous person would not experience any emotions at all. For instance, in the programmatic beginning of Chapter Three, he makes the striking claim that his addressee should first "free himself from the emotions" (ἑαυτὸν

---

[5] As he explains, 'when food is not pleasant the vegetative part of the soul rejects it, digests it badly; and sometimes vomits it out; when it is pleasant it accepts it and digests it well' (*Mor.* 41.18–19 Kraus). In *On Character Traits*, as in many other works, Galen argues that the same part of the soul is responsible for both appetitive desires and appetitive functions, such as the digestion of food and drink. Thus, according to him, the 'appetitive' and 'vegetative' parts of the soul are in fact one and the same; see, e.g., *Mor.* 35.2–5 Kraus, *PHP* 6.3.7 De Lacy, *MM* 10.635 Kühn, and *QAM* 44.9–12 Müller. For critical discussion of Galen's broad conception of the appetitive part of the soul see, e.g., De Lacy 1986; Hankinson 1991: 229–231; and Von Staden 2000.

[6] *QAM* 36.3–6 Müller: οὔτε τῆς ἐπιθυμητικῆς ψυχῆς ὄρεξιν τῶν καλῶν ἔχειν δυναμένης οὔτε τῆς λογιστικῆς ἀφροδισίων ἢ βρωμάτων ἢ πομάτων ὥσπερ οὐδὲ νίκης ἢ ἀρχῆς ἢ δόξης ἢ τιμῆς.

[7] *PHP* 5.7.42 De Lacy: ἀλλ' εἴς γε τὸ προκείμενον ἀπόχρη τὸ περαινόμενον ἀναμφισβητήτως, ὅτι μὴ **τῆς αὐτῆς** ἐστι **δυνάμεως** τό τε λογίζεσθαι καὶ τὸ σιτίων ἢ ποτῶν ἢ ἀφροδισίων ἐπιθυμεῖν, ὅπερ οὐκ οἶδ' ὅπως ὁ Χρύσιππος ἅμα πολλοῖς Στωϊκοῖς ἠγνόησεν.

[8] My account here is based on the discussion in Kaufman 2017: 371–372. For more detailed discussion both of this point and of its implications for Galen's psychological theory see Kaufman 2017.

ἐλευθερῶσι τῶν παθῶν) before turning to errors of reasoning, which are the subject of the companion work *Errors of the Soul* (*Aff. Dig.* 6,25–7,1 De Boer). As Galen makes clear in the following lines and indeed, throughout the work, he is not speaking loosely here, but really does hold that we should aim to eliminate our emotions altogether. For instance, after arguing that someone who hopes to make ethical progress should enlist an expert external observer to watch over and assess their behavior to see if they ever act emotionally, Galen cautions his addressee against readily believing their expert observer should he report that they have not acted emotionally over a span of a couple of days on the grounds that "it is impossible that you committed no error at all" (ἀδύνατον γὰρ εἶναι τὸ μηδὲν ἡμαρτῆσθαί σοι, *Aff. Dig.* 8,17–20 De Boer). The strong implication here is that emotional behavior is a kind of error, which, like errors more generally, we should endeavor to avoid altogether.[9]

Galen asserts the ideal of *apatheia* more explicitly a few lines later, in further defending the view that his readers should distrust an expert observer who reports that he has not observed them acting emotionally (*Aff. Dig.* 9,12–15 De Boer):

> For if people who have cultivated *apatheia* throughout their whole lives are not confident that they have perfectly attained it, how much more will that be true of you, who have never done so? Do not, then, trust someone who says that he has not seen you perform any act on the basis of emotion.[10]

In these passages, as throughout *Affections of the Soul*, Galen is adamant both that we should endeavor to free ourselves from emotions and that doing so is difficult, if not impossible.

Along similar lines, in the course of his extended critique of Chrysippus' theory of the emotions in Books Four and Five of *On the Doctrines of Plato and Hippocrates*, Galen makes the surprising claim that 'the ancients' (οἱ παλαιοί) — by whom he means especially Plato and Aristotle — agreed with Chrysippus that

---

9 Although Galen holds that, in the technical sense of the terms, emotions (πάθη) and errors of reasoning (ἁμαρτήματα) are quite different from one another — according to him, emotions are activities of the non-rational parts of the soul, while errors of reasoning are activities of reason — he also explicitly notes a broader use of the term 'error' (ἁμάρτημα) to encompass *both* emotions *and* errors of reasoning, which he uses here; see *Aff. Dig.* 4,2–7 De Boer, cf. 9,17–20.
10 *Aff. Dig.* 9,12–15 De Boer: ὅπου γὰρ οἱ δι' ὅλου τοῦ βίου <τὴν> ἀπάθειαν ἀσκήσαντες οὐ πιστεύονται τελέως αὐτὴν ἐσχηκέναι, πολὺ δήπου μᾶλλον ὁ μηδέποτ' ἀσκήσας σύ· μὴ τοίνυν πιστεύσῃς τῷ λέγοντι μηδὲν ἑωρακέναι κατὰ πάθος ὑπὸ σοῦ πραττόμενον. Here and elsewhere in the chapter, I print the recent translation of *Affections of the Soul* by Peter Singer, with slight modifications. Unless otherwise noted, all other translations are my own.

a virtuous person would *not* experience any emotions at all, but disagreed with his analysis of emotions.[11] As he writes (*PHP* 5.2.2–3 De Lacy):

> Not only do the ancients agree that emotion is an unnatural and irrational motion of the soul, but so does Chrysippus. And, in fact, it is agreed by both that this motion does not arise in the souls of decent people. But when they come to describe the soul of inferior people both in the grip of emotions and before emotions, their accounts are no longer the same.[12]

According to Galen, the mainstream philosophical tradition, extending from Plato through the Stoics, agrees that emotions are both "unnatural and irrational" and, accordingly, are not experienced by "decent people". Thus, far from being a distinctive feature of Stoic theory, the ideal of *apatheia* is rather, in Galen's view, the standard position in the Greek philosophical tradition.[13] His criticism of the Stoic theory of the emotions, as he represents it, therefore centers not on their ideal of *apatheia*, which he explicitly endorses, but instead on their particular analysis of emotions.

Although Galen is, as we have seen, quite forthcoming about his commitment to the ideal of *apatheia*, he says less about how this view fits together with his tripartite psychological theory. In particular, given his view that appetite and spirit are parts of the adult human soul and play a crucial and ineliminable role in effective human motivation, it might seem difficult to see *why* he would urge us to eliminate our emotions or even, were we persuaded, *how* we could do so on his account. Nevertheless, although Galen's endorsement of the ideal of *apatheia* might seem to fit poorly with his psychological account, I believe that upon closer examination his position makes good sense on the basis of his tripartite psychology, and also helps to elucidate his conception of the complex relationship between reason and the non-rational parts of the soul. In the next

---

11 Galen's use of the phrase 'the ancients' (οἱ παλαιοί) here finds a close parallel in *PHP* 4.7.39 De Lacy, where he uses it to refer collectively to Pythagoras, Plato, and Aristotle; see too, *PHP* 5.1.6 De Lacy and *Mor.* 26.1–5 Kraus.
12 *PHP* 5.2.2–3 De Lacy: τὸ πάθος τῆς ψυχῆς κίνησίν τινα παρὰ φύσιν ἄλογον ὑπάρχειν οὐχ οἱ παλαιοὶ μόνον, ἀλλὰ καὶ Χρύσιππος ὁμολογεῖ. καὶ μὲν δὴ καὶ ὡς ἡ κίνησις αὕτη ταῖς τῶν ἀστείων οὐκ ἐγγίνεται ψυχαῖς, ὡμολόγηται παρ' ἀμφοῖν. ὁποία δέ τίς ἐστιν ἡ τῶν φαύλων ψυχὴ κατά τε τὰ πάθη καὶ πρὸ τῶν παθῶν οὐκ ἔθ' ὁμοίως ἐξηγοῦνται.
13 While it is surprising to read that Plato and Aristotle favored the ideal of *apatheia*, this fits well with the popular tendency in late Hellenistic and Imperial philosophy to read Plato and Aristotle both as being largely in agreement with one another and also as anticipating many of the important developments in Stoic theory. For discussion of this trend see, especially, Karamanolis 2006.

two sections, I will focus, first, on the positive role that Galen ascribes to non-rational motivation, if not to emotions, in virtuous action, and then, on the relationship of his account of *apatheia* to the main positions in the Hellenistic and Imperial *apatheia/metriopatheia* debate.

2 Galen on Emotions, Non-Rational Motivation, and Unemotional Action

Although, as we have seen, Galen argues in *Affections of the Soul* that we should aim to extirpate the emotions altogether, he also argues in the same work, as elsewhere in his corpus, that the non-rational parts of the soul play an important role in human motivation. His most detailed discussion of the positive role of the non-rational parts of the soul in virtuous human motivation is found in Chapter Six of the work. While we might expect Galen, given his endorsement a few pages earlier of the ideal of *apatheia*, to urge us to eliminate or, at the very least, to minimize both spirit and appetite, he instead argues that far from weakening the spirited part of the soul we should aim to cultivate it properly. As he writes (*Aff. Dig.* 19,8–15 De Boer):

> We have discussed more fully in our notes on *On Character Traits*, how one may improve the spirited power to the greatest extent possible; that one must not break its strength, any more than one should that of the horses and dogs that we use, but — as with these animals — one should cultivate its quality of obedience. It has also been shown to you in those notes in particular how you will use the spirited power itself as an ally against the other power.[14]

According to Galen, in educating the spirited part of our soul we should be careful not to break its 'strength' (ἰσχύς), so that it can play its proper role as an 'ally' (σύμμαχος) of reason against appetite.[15] Thus, although Galen insists a few lines later that we should aim at the stable state of 'freedom from anger' (ἀοργησία), he also encourages us to strengthen and shape the spirited part of our

---

[14] *Aff. Dig.* 19,8–15 De Boer: Λέλεκται <δ'> ἐπὶ πλέον ἐν τοῖς Περὶ ἠθῶν ὑπομνήμασιν, ὅπως <ἂν> ἀρίστην τις αὐτὴν [sc. τὴν τοῦ θυμοειδοῦς δύναμιν] ἐργάσαιτο καὶ ὡς τὴν μὲν ἰσχὺν οὐ χρὴ καταβαλεῖν αὐτῆς, ὥσπερ οὐδὲ τῶν ἵππων τε καὶ κυνῶν, οἷς χρώμεθα, τὴν δ' εὐπείθειαν ὡς ἐκείνων οὕτω καὶ ταύτης ἀσκεῖν. ἐπιδέδεικται δέ σοι [καὶ] δι' ἐκείνων τῶν ὑπομνημάτων οὐχ ἥκιστα καὶ ὅπως αὐτῇ πάλιν τῇ τοῦ θυμοειδοῦς δυνάμεις συμμάχῳ χρήσῃ κατὰ τῆς ἑτέρας.

[15] Galen's language here is deeply indebted to Plato's account of psychology in the *Republic*: see, e.g., Pl. *Rep.* 440a9–b7 and 441e3–5; cf. Gal. *PHP* 5.7.53–6.

soul (*Aff. Dig.* 21,11–12 De Boer). Presumably then, if Galen is not simply contradicting himself, he distinguishes between the *emotion* of anger, which he recommends eliminating, and the *appropriate* and *valuable* instances of spirited motivation that he encourages us to cultivate.

Although Galen argues that appetite is less malleable than spirit (*Aff. Dig.* 19,20–5 De Boer), the cultivation of appetite for the right objects is also part of his program of moral education. For instance, later in Chapter Six, in the context of describing how to avoid greedy and unseemly behavior at symposia, he argues that by habitually practicing self-restraint in our use of food and drink, by, say, avoiding rich and luxurious foods, we will ultimately find it both *easy* and *pleasant* to limit ourselves to the healthiest foods (Gal. *Aff. Dig.* 22,21–4 De Boer). Thus, according to Galen, good habits of eating and drinking not only limit our appetites, by, as it were, starving the beast, but also alter the *content* of what we find appetizing and repellent. For example, while in our present depraved states, the idea of eating, let alone limiting ourselves to, kale salads might seem markedly unappetizing, if we habituated ourselves to doing so, we would at some point, Galen predicts, come to anticipate unseasoned kale with something resembling the gusto with which we currently look forward to pastries. According to Galen, then, beyond simply not hindering our virtuous activity, both appetite and spirit may also, if properly habituated, make a significant positive contribution to virtuous action, by helping to stimulate and support impulses for healthy food and noble action. While this is a familiar feature of Platonic and Aristotelian accounts of virtuous motivation, it raises a puzzle for Galen's ideal of *apatheia*.[16] In particular, we might wonder, in what sense a virtuous person who orders and eats a kale salad on the basis of both appetitive and rational motivation is eating the salad in an *unemotional* way.

In order to answer this, it will prove useful to look more closely at Galen's examples both of emotional and unemotional activity. The first thing to call attention to is that when Galen discusses emotions in *Affections of the Soul* he focuses on cases where non-rational motivation is not merely *involved* in an impulse or activity, but where it *guides* our behavior. For instance, when in Chapter Three of the work he proposes that his addressee set a virtuous elderly observer over himself to examine and correct his behavior from an impartial perspective, the elderly observer's task is, in Galen's words, "to indicate straightaway whatever he sees being done by you *on the basis of emotion* (κατὰ

---

[16] For the role of non-rational motivation in Platonic and Aristotelian accounts of virtuous action see, e.g., Cooper 1999 and Sherman 1989.

πάθος πραττόμενον, *Aff. Dig.* 8,7–9 De Boer)".[17] Again, a couple of lines later, he warns his addressee against readily accepting the observer's claim that he has not witnessed him acting badly over the span of a few days on the grounds that "all men err and *act on the basis of emotion* countless time each day (κατὰ πάθος πράττοντας, *Aff. Dig.* 8,17–21 De Boer)".[18] We might wonder, however, what range of actions Galen has in mind when he writes of people acting on the basis of emotion. His clearest examples are cases where the non-rational parts of the soul guide our behavior *independently of* and even *in opposition to* reason, as in cases of, say, involuntary fear or akratic action, respectively.[19] However, there is strong reason to think that, in Galen's view, someone may also act on the basis of an emotion even in cases where they rationally endorse their course of behavior.

To see this, it is worth turning to Chapter Five of *Affections of the Soul*, where Galen discusses his distinction between emotionally motivated and unemotional episodes of reasoning most fully. Galen begins Chapter Five by endorsing a position he attributes to Plato, that we should *never* punish anyone while in the grip of anger, but should instead do so, if at all, only after our rage has subsided. As he explains: "Once your rage has subsided you will consider in a more self-controlled way how many blows are to be inflicted on the person who deserves the punishment" (*Aff. Dig.* 15,24–16,1 De Boer).[20] Beyond urging us to postpone acting, so far as we can, when we are in the grip of emotions, Galen's counsel that we should "consider in a more self-controlled way" (σωφρονέστερον ἐπισκέψῃ) how to respond strongly suggests that even people in the grip of anger may engage in reasoning, albeit of an uncontrolled and emotionally motivated kind.

This is confirmed by Galen's account a few sentences later of the proper role of reason in each of our actions. In particular, after contrasting the run of the

---

[17] *Aff. Dig.* 8,7–9 De Boer: αὖθίς τε παρακάλεσον ἔτι λιπαρέστερον ἢ ὡς πρόσθεν, ὅτι ἂν ὑπὸ σοῦ βλέπῃ **κατὰ πάθος πραττόμενον**, εὐθέως μηνύειν.

[18] *Aff. Dig.* 8,18–20 De Boer: ἅπαντας ἀνθρώπους καθ' ἑκάστην ἡμέραν μυρία μὲν ἁμαρτάνοντας καὶ **κατὰ πάθος πράττοντας**.

[19] See, e.g., *Mor.* 25.5–7 Kraus and *PHP* 4.6.19–28 De Lacy. It is worth noting that, according to the ancient medical tradition, involuntary emotional responses such as episodes of involuntary crying or laughter may also indicate mental illness or delirium; see, e.g., Hipp. *Epid.* 3.17, p. 110 and 5.95, p. 42=7.121, p. 116–7 Jouanna and Hipp. *Reg.* 1.35, p. 154 Joly. I am grateful to George Kazantzidis for emphasizing this point in written correspondence.

[20] *Aff. Dig.* 15,24–16,1 De Boer: καταστάντος γάρ τοι τοῦ θυμοῦ σωφρονέστερον ἐπισκέψῃ, πόσας χρὴ πληγὰς ἐντεῖναι τῷ τῆς κολάσεως ἀξίῳ. Galen's story of Plato and the whip occurs *mutatis mutandis* in a number of Hellenistic and Imperial texts; see, e.g., D.L. 3.38–39; with Socrates as the protagonist, see Sen. *De Ira* 1.15.3; and with Archytas as the protagonist, see *Tusc.* 4.78.

mill senselessness and irrationality that characterizes most human action with the rationally controlled behavior of the morally decent person, he argues that his addressee will achieve the latter, virtuous state if, in his words (*Aff. Dig.* 16,25–17,1 De Boer):

> You are never a slave to rage, but always perform, on the basis of consideration, all those actions which appear to you best on the basis of examination conducted when you are outside the influence of the emotion.[21]

It is worth noting that Galen does not argue here that virtuous *action* must be carried out outside the influence of emotion, even though, as we will see, that is his view, but instead emphasizes that the *reasoning* underlying virtuous action must be undertaken outside the influence of emotion. That is, according to him, a central feature of virtuous behavior is that it is performed on the basis of *unemotional* reasoning. By contrast, according to his theory, more ordinary and unrestrained behavior presumably also often involves reasoning, but of an uncontrolled and emotional kind.

We are now in position to see how, in outline, Galen is able to argue for the ideal of the complete freedom from emotions without abandoning his commitment to tripartite psychology. For, as we have seen, according to his account, the key factor in determining whether an action is performed in an emotional or unemotional way is not whether non-rational motivation happens to be involved in it, but instead whether the action is performed on the basis of cool, unemotional reason or on the basis of one of the non-rational parts of the soul. Thus, if someone orders and eats a kale salad on the basis of their considered view that kale is especially healthy, then whether or not they also experience an appetitive desire for it, they order it *unemotionally* in Galen's sense of the term. I submit, then, that, according to Galen, someone would achieve *apatheia* if they performed all of their actions on the basis of cool, unemotional reasoning, whether or not many or all of their actions also involved non-rational motivation.

---

21 *Aff. Dig.* 16,25–17,1 De Boer: ἔσῃ δὲ τοιοῦτος, ἐὰν μηδέποτε θυμῷ δουλεύων, ἀλλ' ἀεὶ [δια]λογιζόμενος ἅπαντα πράττῃς ἃ [παντα] σοι χωρὶς τοῦ πάθους σκεπτομένῳ φαίνεται κράτιστα.

3 Galen on the *Apatheia*/*Metriopatheia* Debate and Cognitive Therapy

Now that it has been established that Galen endorses a version of *apatheia* in his *Affections of the Soul*, it might seem a rather easy task to position him in the postclassical *apatheia/metriopatheia* debate. After all, if the fundamental issue at stake in the debate is whether one accepts the ideal of *apatheia* or not, then it might seem that Galen belongs in the *apatheia* camp without further discussion. As we will see, however, matters are not nearly so straightforward.

For one thing, Galen's notion of an emotion, or *pathos*, in the relevant sense of the term[22] is more restrictive than the common notion at play in the debate. For instance, as we have seen, in *Affections of the Soul* he distinguishes between the emotion of anger, on the one hand, and appropriate and valuable instances of spirited motivation, on the other, suggesting that he does not take all instances of non-rational motivation to be emotions. Galen expands on his distinction between emotion and non-rational motivation more generally in his more technical discussion of the different senses of the term *pathos* in Book Six of *On the Doctrines of Plato and Hippocrates* (*PHP* 6.1.5–23 De Lacy).[23] In particular, he distinguishes between two senses of the term, which I will refer to for convenience as the *other-caused* sense and the *unnatural* sense of the term. In the other-caused sense of the term, a *pathos* is, in Galen's words, "a movement in one thing that comes from another thing" (τὸ δὲ πάθος ἐν ἑτέρῳ κίνησίς ἐστιν ἐξ ἑτέρου, *PHP* 6.1.5 De Lacy). For example, if a strong gust of wind carries me across the street, then my movement is a *pathos* in the other-caused sense because I am moved by the wind and not by my own agency. By contrast, in the unnatural sense of the term, a *pathos* of something is 'an unnatural movement' of it (παρὰ φύσιν [sc. κίνησιν], *PHP* 6.1.8 De Lacy). So, to use Galen's example, even though a heart palpitation has its origin in the heart itself, and so is not a *pathos* in the other-caused sense of the term, it is a *pathos* of the heart in the unnatural sense of the term because it is an unnatural movement of the heart (*PHP* 6.1.10–13 De Lacy).

Although, as Galen notes, the other-caused and unnatural senses of the term *pathos* often come apart, he is emphatic that the strong emotions he is interested in are *pathē* in *both* senses of the term. In particular, not only are they excessive and unnatural movements of either appetite or spirit, but they also

---

22 On *pathos* as 'emotion', see Singer in this volume.
23 For detailed discussion of this passage see Hankinson 1993: 196–197.

overpower and guide the other parts of the soul by force. For instance, as Galen describes in the case of anger, while it is an activity (*energeia*) of the spirited part of the soul, it is "a *pathēma* of the other two parts, and of our whole body besides, when our body is forcibly driven to its actions by anger" (*PHP* 6.1.7–8 De Lacy).[24] By contrast, Galen is emphatic that most non-rational motivation is not emotional in his sense of the term. Indeed, as he comments, not all movements of the non-rational parts of the soul are excessive and unnatural, but *only* those that are, in his words, 'runaway and immoderate' (ἔκφοροί τε καὶ ἄμετροι, *PHP* 6.1.14 De Lacy), and so also forcibly direct the other soul-parts and the body as a whole. According to the account Galen develops in *PHP*, emotions are, therefore, excessive and runaway movements of either appetite or spirit that are sufficiently strong to overpower the other soul-parts and to control the person's behavior.

It is not too surprising, then, that Galen does not follow the postclassical Peripatetics in endorsing an ideal of *metriopatheia*. On the contrary, when, in *Affections of the Soul*, he writes of 'moderate emotions' (μέτρια πάθη) he means something quite different in accordance with his own use of the term *pathos*. For instance, after remarking on how few of the people he has counseled on how best to avoid distress gained any long-term benefit from his remarks,[25] Galen comments (*Aff. Dig.* 35,7–15 De Boer):

> For most people have already increased the emotions of their soul over such a long period that they are incurable. But if someone is enslaved to *emotions that are still moderate* and is thus able to grasp something of the things said above, and if, as I have previously said, he appoints a monitor and tutor for himself ... he will be able to make his soul free and noble by these arguments.[26]

---

24 *PHP* 6.1.7–8 De Lacy: οὕτως οὖν καὶ ὁ θυμὸς ἐνέργεια μέν ἐστι τοῦ θυμοειδοῦς, **πάθημα δὲ τῶν λοιπῶν τῆς ψυχῆς δύο μερῶν καὶ προσέτι τοῦ σώματος ἡμῶν παντός, ὅταν ὑπὸ τοῦ θυμοῦ βιαίως ἄγηται πρὸς τὰς πράξεις**. It is worth noting that here, as elsewhere in the *PHP*, Galen seems to use the terms πάθος and πάθημα interchangeably; cf. his use of the term πάθημα at *PHP* 4.1.14, 4.2.29, and, citing Plato's *Timaeus*, *PHP* 6.2.9=Pl. *Tim.* 69c7–d1.
25 There is likely an allusion to the Platonic Corpus here and, especially, to Socrates' famous inability to alter the lives of most of his interlocutors, many of whom were persuaded during their discussions with him, but did not alter their behavior at all afterwards: see, e.g., *Symp.* 216b–c. For Galen's use of the character of Socrates in *Affections of the Soul* see Rosen 2009.
26 *Aff. Dig.* 35,7–15 De Boer: τηλικαῦτα γὰρ ἤδη τὰ πάθη τῆς ψυχῆς ηὐξήκασιν οἱ πολλοὶ τῶν ἀνθρώπων ὡς ἀνίατα ὑπάρχειν. ἐὰν δέ τις **ἔτι μετρίοις** δουλεύῃ **πάθεσι** γνῶναί τ' [ἂν] οὕτως δύνηταί τι τῶν πρότερον εἰρημένων, ἐπιστήσας ἑαυτῷ, καθάπερ ἔμπροσθεν εἶπον, ἐπόπτην τινὰ καὶ παιδαγωγόν ... δυνήσεται κατασκευάσαι λόγοις ἐλευθέραν τε καὶ καλὴν τὴν ψυχήν.

Galen strongly distinguishes here between people whose emotions have become so inured that they are incurable and those who are 'enslaved to emotions that are still moderate' (ἔτι μετρίοις δουλεύῃ πάθεσι), and so are still capable of being corrected. Thus, by 'moderate emotions' (μέτρια πάθη) he does not mean appropriate and fitting emotions, but rather emotions that are 'moderate' only in the sense that they still admit treatment, just as one might speak of a 'moderate' case of the flu.[27] Galen, therefore, is hardly sympathetic to the view that fitting and appropriate, moderate *emotions* contribute to a virtuous life. It is worth noting, however, that although Galen denies that even 'moderate emotions' play a role in a virtuous life, he is quite clear both in this work and elsewhere that appropriate and measured spirited and appetitive desires play a crucial role in virtuous motivation.

For instance, as we have seen, in *Affections of the Soul* he argues that spirit plays an important role in virtuous action as an 'ally' (σύμμαχος) to reason, especially in restraining excessive appetitive desires and aversions. He also refers his addressee to his four-book treatise on moral psychology, *On Character Traits*, for more detailed discussion both of how to condition the spirited part of the soul in the best possible way and of the contribution of spirited motivation to virtuous activity (*Aff. Dig.* 19,8–10 De Boer). While the Greek text of *On Character Traits* is no longer extant, we do have a substantial Arabic epitome of the work, which includes material that helps to fill in the details of Galen's account.[28] In particular, as he explains in *On Character Traits*, spirit's assistance is crucial in virtuous action because reason is simply incapable of restraining vehement appetitive desires without spirit's aid.[29] For instance, according to Galen's account, it is by no means a sufficient condition of acting courageously

---

[27] Along similar lines, earlier in the text, Galen notes the difficulty of recognizing cases where the agent is only 'moderately disturbed in their soul' (μετρίως ταραχθῆναι τὴν ψυχὴν) over, say, a great loss of money or some other significant emotionally salient event (*Aff. Dig.* 5,12–13 De Lacy). As in the passage under discussion, Galen argues that even moderate disturbance in such cases is evidence of a moral deficit, albeit one that is less severe than most and which still admits treatment.

[28] The Arabic epitome is based on a no longer extant, complete Arabic translation of Galen's *On Character Traits* by Ḥunayn ibn Isḥāq, the famous 9th Century Arab translator. For recent discussion of Ḥunayn's working methods and reliability as a translator see Overwien 2012 and Cooper 2016, as well as the references collected in Singer 2013: 110 n. 6. Further quotations and paraphrases from Ḥunayn's translation are collected and translated in Davies 2013.

[29] See, especially, *Mor.* 27,10–13 Kraus: "Reason cannot, however, restrain the appetitive soul from excessive movement without calling upon the spirited soul for help, for a person cannot prevent his appetitive soul moving at the wrong time or without due moderation unless there is strength and endurance in his spirited soul, which is his animal soul".

that one comes to believe that she ought to act in a certain way, say, to endure torture rather than to betray her friends or to prefer death in battle to retreat, if she does not also form a corresponding and vigorous spirited desire to do so.[30] For, in such cases, acting courageously involves some degree of psychic conflict between the agent's rational and spirited desire for the good, on the one hand, and her appetitive aversion to pain, on the other.[31] According to Galen, then, not only is non-rational motivation often involved in virtuous reason-guided activity, but the active cooperation of the non-rational parts of the soul is even a necessary condition of consistently and reliably acting on the basis of our rational decisions.[32]

This aspect of Galen's theory is strikingly similar to the postclassical Peripatetic account of *metriopatheia*, which maintained that merely recognizing that one ought to act in a certain way is often motivationally ineffective without the added spur of emotion, especially in cases where so acting involves enduring pain or hardship. For instance, in Book One of *On Anger*, Seneca describes the Peripatetic view of the value of appropriate instances of anger in the following terms: 'Anger raises our spirit and spurs us on; without it courage accomplishes nothing splendid in warfare: it needs that flame set to the kindling, that goad to stir the bold and send them into harm's way' (Sen. *De ira* 1.7.1).[33] According to Seneca's report, as confirmed as well by similar accounts in Cicero and Philodemus, the postclassical Peripatetics held that experiencing anger and other emotions in the appropriate contexts is a necessary condition of virtuous action, without which, even if we recognize how we ought to act, we will often prove incapable of doing so.[34] By contrast, the most famous proponents of the ideal of *apatheia*, the Stoics, argue that reason is perfectly capable not only of *determining* how best to act in a given situation, but also of *motivating* us to act accord-

---

30 I borrow these examples of courageous behavior from *Mor.* 33,6–7 Kraus.
31 To be sure, Galen might allow that courage may also be used in a wider sense to describe, say, choosing the moral good at the cost of one's reputation, but his discussion and examples strongly suggest that he takes courageous action, at least in its primary sense, to be action that one undertakes for the sake of the moral good in spite of the imminent prospect of severe physical pain or death. For a similarly restrictive account of courage, see Arist. *EN* 1115^{a}24–1115^{b}6.
32 For further discussion of Galen's view of spirit's contribution to virtuous action, as well as the more general moral psychology he develops in *On Character Traits*, see Kaufman 2017, esp. 378–82.
33 Sen. *De ira* 1.7.1: *Extollit animos et incitat, necquicquam sine illa magnificum in bello fortitude gerit, nisi hinc flamma subdita est et hic stimulus peragitavit misitque in pericula audaces.* I print the recent translation by R.A. Kaster.
34 See, esp., Cic. *Tusc.* 4.43–46, esp. 43 and Phld. *Ir.* 31,24–32,35. See too, the useful collection of texts in translation in Sharples 2010: 134–149.

ingly, independently of any additional non-rational sources of motivation. In this respect, then, Galen's ideal of freedom from emotions has far more in common with Peripatetic *metriopatheia* than with Stoic *apatheia*.

Nevertheless, if Galen's account of *apatheia* is more similar to Peripatetic *metriopatheia* than to Stoic theory, the method of emotional therapy and moral development he proposes in *Affections of the Soul* has more affinity with Stoic theory.[35] In particular, as has often been commented, a striking feature of Galen's method of moral development in *Affections of the Soul* is his emphasis on belief-based methods of therapy rather than, as might have been expected, methods of therapy aimed at habituating the non-rational parts of the soul.[36] For instance, in Chapter Seven, in advising a young friend on how to remain self-controlled in conventionally distressing situations, Galen gives him the following counsel (*Aff. Dig.* 33,29–34,5 De Boer):

> If you took the function of your possessions as your yardstick of what constitutes moderation, you would already have counted yourself among the rich, or at least among the well-off. I certainly count myself in this category, although I have less than you do. If you convince yourself of this, then you will no longer suffer grief over any of your losses, and you will be blessed in this, that you no longer become distressed over financial affairs.[37]

According to Galen, his friend will effectively eliminate grief, distress, and other related emotions concerning financial affairs if he is fully persuaded that his possessions are of value only insofar as they allow him to provide for his basic and immediate physical needs, apparently independently of the condition of the non-rational parts of his soul. The strong implication is that people who experience distress more often in such cases, including presumably most of his readers, do so *because* they hold false beliefs, exaggerating the value of wealth, reputation, and other merely conventional goods. Galen argues to similar effect in a passage from *On Freedom from Distress* (Gal. *Indol.* 65–66 BJP):

---

35 For Galen's complex relationship to Stoic philosophy more generally see Gill 2007 and 2010 and Tieleman 2009. For analysis of the affinities between Stoic theory and Galen's method of emotional therapy as it is developed in *Affections of the Soul* see Gill 2010: 260–261.

36 For discussion of Galen's use of belief-based therapy, see Gill 2010: 260–261 and 276–278; Hankinson 1993: 201–203; Singer 2013: 22–23; and Singer 2018: 294–299.

37 *Aff. Dig.* 33,29–34,5 De Boer: εἰ δέ γε τῇ χρείᾳ τῶν κτημάτων ἐμέτρεις σαυτῷ τὸ σύμμετρον, ἐκτῶν πλουσίων ἂν ἤδη σαυτὸν ἠριθμήκεις, ἢ πάντως γε τῶν εὐπόρων. ἐγὼ γοῦν ἐμαυτὸν ἐκ τούτων ἀριθμῶ, καίτοι γ' ἐλάττω σοῦ κεκτημένος. ἐὰν οὖν τοῦτο πείσῃς σαυτόν, οὐκέτ' ἀνιάσεισε τῶν ἀπολλυμένων οὐδέν, ἔσῃ τε μακάριος, ὅσον ἐπὶ τῷ μὴ λυπεῖσθαι διὰ χρήματα.

> And since I have always been raised in this way of thinking, I consider all these things to be insignificant. And how could I suppose that leisure activities (σχολάς)[38] and surgical instruments and potions and books and reputation and wealth are worthy of concern? And for someone who considers all these things to be trivial, what anxiety would there be for the presence or absence of them? For it follows that someone who believes that he has been deprived of 'great things' (μεγαλεῖα) 'will always be distressed and worried' (λυπεῖσθαι τε καὶ φροντίζειν ἀεί); but someone who always looks down on such things completely will never be distressed.[39]

Galen argues here that people who believe that they have lost or been deprived of something important will '*always*' (ἀεί) be emotionally affected by its loss. Thus, as he describes it, believing that possessions are of great value is a *sufficient* condition of forming the emotion of distress when one takes their possessions to be either lost or damaged. Therefore, despite Galen's emphasis on the primary role of the non-rational parts of the soul in emotional behavior, he insists that the particular beliefs a person holds are a crucial factor both in their overall susceptibility to emotions and in the particular emotions that they experience. It thus makes a great deal of sense that cognitive therapy plays an important role in Galen's method of emotional therapy in addition to non-rational habituation and training.

Galen's extensive use of belief-based therapy has, I think, at least two implications for understanding his account of the emotions. First, it shows that he recognizes a rather complex relationship between our beliefs and our emotions. For while, as we have seen, Galen holds that emotions can influence and shape our reasoning, he maintains that our beliefs can *also* prompt us to experience strong emotions. For instance, in his view, someone who believes that maintaining a strong reputation is important to the overall quality of their life can hardly help being frightened should they take their reputation to be threatened. Secondly, Galen's use of belief-based therapy also suggests that, in his view, reforming the non-rational parts of our soul is a necessary, but insufficient, condition of establishing rational control over our behavior. Rather, as he argues in *Affections of the Soul*, we must also strengthen our reason, presumably by im-

---

[38] I follow the manuscripts in printing σχολάς rather than σχολάν, which is printed in the edition by Boudon-Millot, Jouanna, and Pietrobelli.

[39] Gal. *Indol.* 65–66 BJP: ἐν τούτῳ τρεφόμενος ἀεὶ τῷ λογισμῷ μικρὰ πάντα εἶναι νομίζω. καὶ σχολὰς καὶ ἄρμενα καὶ φάρμακα καὶ βιβλία καὶ δόξαν καὶ πλοῦτον <πῶς ἄν> ἄξια σπουδῆς ὑπολάβοιμι; τῷ δ' ἡγουμένῳ μικρὰ πάντα εἶναι, τί ἂν ἐπὶ τούτοις ἀπό τε αὐτῶν εἴη φροντίς; ἀκόλουθον γάρ ἐστι τῷ μὲν ὑπολαβόντι μεγαλεῖα ἐστερῆσθαι, λυπεῖσθαι τε καὶ φροντίζειν ἀεί, τῷ δὲ σμικρῶν ἀεὶ διὰ τέλους καταφρονοῦντι, <μηδέ ποτε λυπεῖσθαι>.

proving the content and overall coherence of our evaluative beliefs.⁴⁰ While Galen does not explicitly attribute either of these positions to the Stoics, they both play important roles in Stoic therapy and seem likely to reflect Stoic influence on Galen's account.⁴¹

4 Conclusion

In this chapter, I have argued that although recent scholarship has tended to be rather skeptical about whether Galen's ideal of *apatheia*, as he develops it in *Affections of the Soul*, is compatible with his tripartite psychological theory, his argument fits consistently and coherently with his psychological theory. In particular, as we have seen, when Galen urges us to extirpate the emotions, he is not recommending that we eliminate all non-rational motivation, but instead that we eliminate excessive and inappropriate instances of it. Indeed, far from urging us to eliminate non-rational motivation altogether, Galen takes spirit and appetite to play crucial roles in virtuous motivation. Moreover, since several other postclassical philosophers sympathetic to Platonic psychology, including most notably the 1st century BCE philosopher, Antiochus of Ascalon, also seem to have argued in favor of the ideal of *apatheia*, Galen's account is also helpful as a model of how an author might develop an ideal of *apatheia* while maintaining their commitment to Platonic psychology.⁴² In sum, I hope to have shown that in his *Affections of the Soul* Galen develops a cogent and sophisticated theory of emotions and emotional therapy that incorporates aspects of Platonic, Peripatetic and Stoic theory into a distinctive account of his own.

---

40 Especially relevant here is Galen's exhortation to his addressee at the very conclusion of *Affections of the Soul*, where he argues that his addressee should not lose heart if he does not improve quickly, since as his reason is 'augmented' (αὔξηται) and 'trained' (ἐγυμνάσατο) it will become ever more capable of 'overpowering' (κρατήσει) the emotions and guiding his actions (*Aff. Dig.* 37,10–16 De Boer).
41 For the Stoics' thesis that we form emotions in virtue of holding certain (false) evaluative beliefs see, e.g. Cic. *Tusc.* 4.14–5, DL 7.111, Epict. *Ench.* 5, and Stob. 2.7.10b, p. 90 Wachsmuth. For their view that we become less prone to ordinary emotions as our overall set of beliefs becomes more coherent, culminating in the limit case of the wise man, who is perfectly *apathes*, see, e.g., Sen. Ep. 71.27–37 and 75.8–18. For critical discussion of the Stoic theory of emotions and Stoic therapy see Brennan 1998; Graver 2007; Kaufman 2014; and Tieleman 2003b.
42 For Antiochus' ideal of *apatheia* see Cic. *Acad.* 2.135–136. For discussion of Antiochus' theory of emotions see Bonazzi 2009: 44–50; Gill 2006: 172–173; Gill 2010: 248–249; and Karamanolis 2006: 79–80.

Bibliography

Bonazzi, M. 2009. "Antiochus' Ethics and the Subordination of Stoicism", in: M. Bonazzi and J. Opsomer (eds.), *The Origins of the Platonic System: Platonisms of the Early Empire*. Paris: 33–54.

Boudon-Millot, V./J. Jouanna/A. Pietrobelli (eds.) 2010. *Galien: Ne pas se chagriner*. Paris.

Brennan, T. 1998. "The Old Stoic Theory of Emotions", in: T. Engberg-Pedersen and J. Sihvola (eds.), *The Emotions in Hellenistic Philosophy*. Dordrecht: 21–70.

Cooper, G. 2016. "Ḥunayn ibn Isḥāq's Galen Translations and Greco-Arabic Philology: Some Observations from the *Crises* (*De crisibus*) and the *Critical Days* (*De diebusdecretoriis*)", *Oriens* 44: 1–43.

Cooper, J.M. 1999. "Plato on Human Motivation", in: J.M. Cooper (ed.), *Reason and Emotion*. Princeton: 118–149.

Davies, D. 2013. "Translation of *On Character Traits*", in: Singer 2013: 135–201.

De Boer, W. (ed.) 1937. *Galeni De propriorum animi cuiuslibetaffectuumdignotione etcuratione; De animi cuius libet peccatorum di gnotione et curatione; De atra bile*, Berlin.

De Lacy, P. (ed.) 1978–1984. *Galeni De placitis Hippocratis et Platonis*, 3 vols. Berlin.

De Lacy, P. 1986. "The Third Part of the Soul", in: P. Manuli and M. Vegetti (eds.), *Le opere psicologiche di Galeno*. Napoli: 43–63.

Dillon, J.M. 1983. "*Metriopatheia* and *Apatheia*: Some Reflections on a Controversy in Later Greek Ethics", in: J.P. Anton and A. Preus (eds.), *Essays in Ancient Greek Philosophy*. Albany: 2.508–17.

Donini, P. 1974. *Tre studi sull'aristotelismo nel II secolo d. C.* Turin.

Donini, P. 2008. "Psychology", in: J. Hankinson (ed.), *The Cambridge Companion to Galen*. Cambridge: 184–209.

Gill, C. 2006. *The Structured Self in Hellenistic and Roman Thought*. Oxford.

Gill, C. 2007. "Galen and the Stoics: Mortal Enemies or Blood Brothers?", *Phronesis* 52.1: 88–120.

Gill, C. 2010. *Naturalistic Psychology in Galen and Stoicism*. Oxford.

Graver, M. 2007. *Stoicism and the Emotions*. Chicago.

Hankinson, R.J. 1991. "Galen's Anatomy of the Soul", *Phronesis* 36.2: 197–233.

Hankinson, R.J. 1993. "Actions and Passions: Affection, Emotion, and Moral Self-Management in Galen's Philosophical Psychology", in: J. Brunschwig and M. Nussbaum (eds.), *Passions and Perceptions*. Cambridge: 184–222.

Inwood, B. 1985. *The Early Stoic Theory of Human Action*. Oxford.

Inwood, B. 2014. *Ethics After Aristotle*. Oxford.

Joly, R. (ed.) 1967. *Hippocrate: Du Régime*. Paris.

Kaster, R.A. (trans.) 2010. *Lucius Annaeus Seneca: Anger, Mercy, Revenge*. Chicago.

Kaufman, D.H. 2014. "Seneca on the Analysis and Therapy of Occurrent Emotions", in: M. Colish and J. Wildberger (eds.), *Seneca Philosophus*. Berlin: 111–133.

Kaufman, D.H. 2017. "Galen on Reason and Appetite: A Study of the *De moribus*", *Apeiron* 50.3: 367–392.

Karamanolis, G. 2006. *Plato and Aristotle in Agreement? Platonists on Aristotle from Antiochus to Porphyry*. Oxford.

Kraus, P. (ed.) 1939. "Kitāb al-Akhlāq li-Jālīnus", *Bulletin of the Faculty of Arts of the Egyptian University* 5.1: 1–51.

Kühn, C.G. (ed.) 1821–1833. *Claudii Galeni Opera Omnia*, 22 vols. Leipzig.
Jouanna, J. (ed.) 2000. *Hippocrate: Épidémies V et VII*. Paris.
Jouanna, J. (ed.) 2016. *Hippocrate: Épidémies I et III*. Paris.
Müller, I. (ed.) 1891. *Claudii Galeni Pergameni Scripta Minora*, vol. 2. Leipzig.
Nutton, V./G. Bos (eds.) 2011. *Galen on Problematical Movements*. Cambridge.
Overwien, O. 2012. "The Art of the Translator, or: How Did Ḥunayn ibn Isḥāq and his School Translate?", in: P. Pormann (ed.), *Epidemics in Context: Greek Commentaries on Hippocrates in the Arabic Tradition*. Berlin: 151–170.
Schiefsky, M. 2012. "Galen and the Tripartite Soul", in: R. Barney, T. Brennan, and C. Brittain 2012: 331–349.
Sharples, R. 2010. *Peripatetic Philosophy 200 BC to AD 200: An Introduction and Collection of Sources in Translation*. Cambridge.
Sherman, N. 1991. *The Fabric of Character: Aristotle's Theory of Virtue*. Oxford.
Singer, P.N. 1991. "Aspects of Galen's Platonism", in: J. López Férez (ed.), *Galeno. Obra, Pensamento e Influencia*. Madrid: 41–55.
Singer, P.N. (ed.) 2013. *Galen's Psychological Writings*. Cambridge.
Singer, P.N. 2018. "Galen's Pathological Soul: Diagnosis and Therapy in Ethical and Medical Texts and Contexts", in: P.N. Singer and C. Thumiger (eds.), *Mental Illness in Ancient Medicine: From Celsus to Paul of Aegina*. Leiden: 381–420.
Sorabji, R. 2007. "Peripatetics on Emotion after 100 BC", in: R. Sorabji and R. Sharples (eds.), *Greek and Roman Philosophy 100 BC–200 AD*, 2 vols. London: 2.621–6.
Tieleman, T. 2003a. "Galen's Psychology", in: J. Barnes and J. Jouanna (eds.), *Galien et la philosophie. Entretiens sur l'antiquité classique XLIX*. Geneva: 131–161.
Tieleman, T. 2003b. *Chrysippus' On Affections: Reconstruction and Interpretation*. Leiden.
Tieleman, T. 2009. "Galen and the Stoics, or: The Art of Not Naming", in: C. Gill, T. Whitmarshand, and J. Wilkins (eds.), *Galen and the World of Knowledge*. Cambridge: 282–299.
Totelin, L. 2018. "Gone with the Wind: Laughter and the Audience of the Hippocratic Treatises", in: P. Bouras-Vallianatos and S. Xenophontos (eds.), *Greek Medical Literature and its Readers: From Hippocrates to Islam and Byzantium*. London: 30–47.
Trompeter, J. 2018. "The Actions of Spirit and Appetite: Voluntary Motion in Galen", *Phronesis* 63.2: 176–207.
von Staden, H. 2000. "Body, Soul and Nerves: Epicurus, Herophilus, Erasistratus, the Stoics, and Galen", in: J.N. Wright and P. Potter (eds.), *Psyche and Soma*. Oxford: 79–116.

Julien Devinant
Disorders of the Soul: Emotions and Clinical Conditions in Galen

Abstract: This paper explores Galen's view on the relationship between emotions (such as fear, anger, or sadness) and clinical conditions (such as *phrenitis*, *mania*, or melancholy) and its significance in the ancient medical-philosophical discourse. It points out that for Galen, emotions and mental disorders do not belong to the same category of phenomena but imply two distinct understandings of the phrase "psychic affections". The paper first stresses that the association of passion with madness and disease, taken from the philosophical tradition, functions as an analogy. It then proceeds to explain the emphasis placed on the brain in Galen's psychopathology; the case of melancholia is discussed to show that emotions do play a significant role in brain disorders, but as causes and symptoms. The overall aim of this paper is to challenge the idea of a tension between a Platonic tripartite concept of the soul and a brain-centered treatment of mental disorders in Galen. It does, however, highlight some difficulties, and indicates how ambiguous formulations and the use of traditional, albeit inaccurate, distinctions may have obscured his view, further muddying the issue for subsequent generations.

1 Introduction

The modern Western idea of mental illness is a vague concept but not necessarily an ill-defined notion; that is, its validity depends on how we account for its indeterminacy. There is indeed a strong folk intuition by which people separate mental disorders from other undesirable psychological conditions. Whether it comes down to drawing a line within a continuum or assigning different causes to similar effects, however, often remains unclear. This is well illustrated in intense emotional reactions accompanied by uncontrolled or inappropriate thoughts, feelings, and behaviours. There is some controversy as to when they should be considered a medical problem; for what qualifies them as pathological may involve a difference either of kind or of degree. In this case, the ambiguity comes in part from a long tradition of associating passion with madness and disease, and this paper intends to make clear what role Galen, the second-century C.E. physician and philosopher, has played in it.

By the time Galen was writing, a connection was already well established between clinical disorders of the soul and emotions — that is, illnesses such as *phrenitis*, *mania*, or melancholy, and *pathê* such as fear, anger, or sorrow. By contrast, the nature of this connection was neither consensual nor plainly spelt out. It is therefore not always easy to tell whether our sources take all these conditions as sorts, stages, or aspects of one and the same phenomenon, or even as distinct experiences bearing mere resemblance to each other.[1] This is not only a theoretical or classificatory issue, but also a practical one: if patients suffering from mental disorders are simply some sort of highly emotional people, then ordinary fears and fits of melancholy, for instance, should be open to similar treatment, albeit more or less strong or long. Galen's own position on the subject is however far from clear. One might indeed wonder what distinguishes the phrenetic patient shouting at his physician and assaulting him[2] from the Cretan friend beating his slaves in a burst of rage.[3] And yet Galen approaches those cases with entirely different methods. Moreover, the issue is further complicated by the way we read his work as a whole. Recent scholarship has highlighted a possibly unresolved tension between the ethical treatises, relying on a platonic tripartite conception of the soul, and the medical writings, presenting a brain-centred treatment of mental conditions. A disorder such as melancholy is indeed characterised primarily by strong emotional disturbances, but diagnosis and treatment focus on the head, not the heart: finding out how Galen's aetiological principles are supposed to account for the appearance of emotional symptoms in brain disorders will therefore also help to shed light on the overall coherence of his doctrines.

In what follows, I argue that our puzzlement is based on a confusion between two sets of "psychic affections". As far as Galen is concerned, emotions and medical affections of the soul, albeit strongly interrelated, are categorically distinct: they are neither "psychic" nor "affections" in the exact same sense. While it can be shown that the discourses on both subjects are consistent with one another, I will also try to pinpoint the ambiguities surrounding each subject. This paper will first present the distinction (section 1) and the different dividing lines drawn between the two types of affections (sections 2 and 3) be-

---

[1] Insanity thus often takes the form of an extreme version of our natural psychological makeup: see, e.g. Hippocrates, *Vict.* 1.35–6 (VI.512–24 L. = 150, 29–26, 32 Joly), Prodicus fr. B7 DK. (= Stobæus, *Flor.* 4.20.65 (IV.468 Hense)), Ps.-Aristotle, *Pr.* 30, 954a26–38, Aretæus, *Chr. Dis.* 1.6.3 (41.27–30 Hude).
[2] *Hipp. Epid. VI* 8 (461, 36–62, 10 Pfaff). A 'brutish' (θηριώδης) delirium is indeed generally associated with *phrenitis* and fever — though not always: see *Loc. aff.* 3.9 (VIII.177, 17–8, 7 K.).
[3] *Aff. dig.* 4.9–13 (V.18–20 K.=13, 19–15, 5 de Boer).

fore examining how emotions are involved in some brain-related disorders (section 4).

2 Two Sets of Psychic Affections

Despite the scholarly interest in Galen's views on the soul in the past decades, there are still a number of grey areas, especially regarding its diseases.[4] One particular concern is the existence of two different sets of soul's affections, namely emotional disturbances and psychic diseases. The idea that they are both similar and distinct phenomena has clear antecedents. Plato already hinted at something similar in the *Laws* when he distinguished among the "many ways" of 'being mad' (μαίνεσθαι), be it due to a disease or to innate or acquired traits of character.[5] In Aristotle's view, 'insanity' (μανία) ranks among peculiar behaviours that elude deliberate control and fall outside of the scope of ethics.[6] But, probably because the topic of medical illnesses of the soul gained importance over time, the most pertinent parallel is with the Stoics. As has recently been argued, the well-known ascription of insanity to all humankind does not rule out the notion of madness as an illness. The paradox would not be that striking otherwise.[7] This shows, at least, that there existed a need for differentiation between insanity and moral failure. And the idea that emotional manifestations take on a special meaning when associated with madness seems to have been a widely held opinion. However, such surface agreement does not imply a

---

4 Great progress has been made on the topic since the early studies of García Ballester 1974 and 1988, or Pigeaud 1981: esp. 47–70 and 1988. See also: Jackson 1969; Siegel 1973; Manuli 1988; Hankinson 1993; Dols 1992: 17–37; Stok 1996: 2371–2375. A large number of articles have been published on the subject in the last years: see Gill 2010: esp. 243–329; 2013; and 2018; Singer 2013: esp. 18–33; 2017; and 2018, Jouanna 2009 and 2013; von Staden 2012; Nutton 2013; van der Eijk 2013: 327–332; Boudon-Millot 2013; Holmes 2013; King 2013; Hankinson 2014; Mattern 2016.
5 See *Leg.* IX, 934d5–e2. On that particular point, the text is much clearer than *Tim.* 86b–7b (see esp. 86b2–4). Galen comments on the latter: *QAM* 6, (IV.789–91 = 34, 6–8, 4 Bazou) and 10 (IV.812–13 K.=74, 11–75, 11 Bazou); see Gill 2000: 65–70. But Galen is not interested in subtleties there.
6 See *Eth. Nic.* 7.5–6, 1148b25–7, 1149a4–15 and 1149b29–50a1. But one should note that 'brutish' (θηριώδης) and 'morbid' (νοσηματώδης) conditions are on the same footing as life-long habits.
7 See esp. Diogenes Laertius, 7.118 (542, 6–11 Dorandi) = *SVF* 3.644, ascribed to Chrysippus; Cicero, *Tusc.* 3.11 (321, 22–2, 13 Pohlenz) and 4.30 (376, 7–9 Pohlenz); Seneca, *Epist.* 94.17 (20, 24–2, 10 Gummere). On that distinction, see now Graver 2003, 2007: 109–132 and Ahonen 2018.

consensus on the substance, and its reasons were certainly practical rather than theoretical, with the legal issue of the accountability for our actions lying in the background. The more important question, then, is how that distinction was accounted for.

As far as Galen is concerned, one can start by pointing out a lexical difficulty. In his view, emotions and clinical disorders both involve an impairment or an alteration of psychic capacities. They are called 'affections' (πάθη) at least in virtue of the fact that the soul undergoes some kind of change.[8] But Galen notes an ambiguity in the meaning of *pathos* in his days: the core of the notion had by then shifted from passivity to negativity, from a change merely received to an unfavourable one. This development explains why it has become a term of the art for any type of 'unnatural' (παρὰ φύσιν) condition requiring medical care.[9] Galen himself considers it a rather loose use of the word, that ought to be resorted to with care; but in keeping with medical habits, he commonly refers to 'diseases' (νοσήματα) as *pathê*, especially when he focuses on the dysfunction that they cause. On certain occasions, he even agrees that it matters little if one uses one or the other term.[10] His use of *pathê* to designate mental disorders such as melancholy, *phrenitis*, *mania*, epilepsy, *môrôsis*, lethargy, or paralysis is therefore not surprising.[11] But at the same time, it had also become customary to speak of 'psychic affections' (πάθη ψυχῆς) for what we term 'emotions', especially harmful ones, that is fear, anger, sorrow, anxiety, or shame. And Galen adopts this terminology on many occasions as well, even in medical contexts.[12] This leaves us with the impression that these emotions share common characteristics with the clinical conditions, or, to put it another way, that they are both psychopathological disorders of the same type. But this might be an ill-conceived categorisation, for one feature of Galen's language shows his intention to keep things separated. Emotions are indeed the only 'affections' (πάθη)

---

[8] See *PHP* 6.1 (V.506–7 K.=360, 22–2, 2 De Lacy). On this, see also Singer in this volume.

[9] See *Meth. med.* 2.3 (X.89, 5–17 K.): the meaning evolved from "received movement" to "unnatural movement" and finally to "unnatural state". See also *Loc. aff.* 1.3 (VIII.31–2 K.=262, 6–17 Gärtner).

[10] See, e.g. *Const. art. med.* 14.4 (I.273 K.=98, 12–13 Fortuna).

[11] See i.a. *Loc. aff.* 3.11 (VIII.200, 5–18 K.) and 4.1 (VIII.217, 3–13 K.), *Hipp. Aph.* 6.47 (XVIIIA.79 K.=168.1–3 Savino), *Hipp. Prorrh.* 1.1 (XVI.497 K.=7,3–12 Diels).

[12] See, e.g.: *Ars med.* 24.8 (I.371 K.=351, 3–4 Boudon-Millot), *Cris.* 2.13 (IX.696 K.=161, 13–15 and 162.4–7 Alexanderson), *Præs. puls.* 3.7 (IX.382, 2–3 K.). These texts give lists that are quite unstable but always about emotions: see Manuli 1988: 194; Singer 2013: 220–223. The concept and its extension are indeed a matter of 'public knowledge' (ἅπερ ἅπαντες γινώσκουσι): *Aff. dig.* 3.1 (V.7–8 K.=6, 25–7, 6 de Boer).

that he is willing to call 'psychic' (ψυχῆς or ψυχικά).¹³ This is not the case with the former group of morbid conditions, even though he describes them as affections of 'psychic' *functions* (ἐνέργειαι) or *faculties* (δυνάμεις).¹⁴ As a matter of fact, he provides several examples of lists for each group, which never overlap.¹⁵ This raises the question of what is the difference between them. As I will proceed to illustrate, the answer is twofold, since in each case both the word "affection" and the word "psychic" should be taken in a different sense.

3 Emotions as Diseases?

Some of Galen's claims certainly lead us to believe that he sees no difference between runaway emotions and the psychic disorders addressed by medicine. Most notably, in *Aff. dig.*, he appears to agree with the saying that anger is a mild form of madness,¹⁶ and goes so far as to claim that emotions are indeed diseases and that this is what the word *pathê* means in *pathê psuchês*:

> Ἦ οὐχ ἡγεῖ νόσημα ψυχῆς εἶναι τὸν θυμόν; ἢ μάτην ὑπὸ τῶν παλαιῶν ὀνομάζεσθαι νομίζεις πάθη ψυχῆς πάντα ταῦτα, λύπην ὀργὴν θυμὸν ἐπιθυμίαν φόβον;

> Do you not think that rage is a disease of the soul? Or do you think that the Ancients had no point in calling 'affections of the soul' all these: distress, anger, rage, desire, and fear?¹⁷

But one should not read too much into this passage. Not to mention the motivational rhetoric behind the remark, Galen's identification of emotions as diseases

---

13 See Devinant (2018: 202–205), here further developed. For ψυχικὰ πάθη see, e.g. *PHP* 9.7 (V.781 K.=588, 25–7 De Lacy), *Symp. Caus.* 2.5 (VII.181, 2 and 191, 16–6, 7 K.), *Dig. Puls.* 2.2 (VIII.858, 3–6, παθήματα). The phrase πάθη (τῆς) ψυχῆς has a Stoic colour: e.g. *PHP* 5.2 (esp. V.437 K.=298, 25–7 De Lacy). But the two expressions are equally frequent and semantically coextensive: see *Loc. aff.* 5.2 (VIII.301, 11–2, 5 K.). See also *Mot. musc.* 2.6 (IV.445–6 K.=35, 13–20 Rosa, παθήματα τῆς ψυχῆς).
14 See, e.g. *Loc. aff.* 3.6 (VIII.160, 8–4, 14 K.) or 3.14 (VIII.210, 17–19 K.) for functions, and 1.6 (VIII.53, 10–4, 1 K.) for faculties.
15 Compare the *pathê* from the texts cited n. 12 above with, e.g. *Loc. aff.* 3.5 (VIII.156, 11–7, 3 K.) and 4.1 (VIII.216, 1–17, 13 K.), *MM* 13.21 (X.932,8–17 K.), *Symp. diff.* 3.9–13 (VII.60–62 K.=224,9–226,2 Gundert), *Symp. caus.* 2.7 (VII.200, 9–4, 4 K.).
16 "Rage," he says, "does not fall short of madness (ὁ θυμὸς οὐδὲν ἀποδεῖ μανίας)" and compares it with 'light cases of madness' (μικραὶ μανίαι): *Aff. dig.* 5.5 (V.22 K.=16, 6 and 15 de Boer). Cf. Seneca's *brevis insania* at *De ira* 1.2 (39, 9–10 Reynolds).
17 *Aff. dig.* 5.5 (V.24 K.=17, 8–10 de Boer). All translations are mine.

does not go without qualification. For in other passages, on the contrary, emotions are *contrasted* with *nosêmata*, and especially when Galen takes them as unnatural sources of physiological perturbations. In the case of the pulse, for instance, he explains at *Puls.* 11 (VIII.471, 2–5 K.), that, in addition to malnutrition, severe or long-lasting pains, and immoderate evacuations, disturbance factors include diseases when they are exacerbated (νοσημάτων κακοήθεια) on the one hand, and emotions when they are violent (ψυχικῶν παθῶν ἰσχύς) on the other hand. Given the didactic context, if emotions were diseases strictly speaking, this would be a rather unfortunate repetition.[18] Conversely, a non-literal reading of *Aff. dig.* makes excellent sense. *Nosêma psuchês* is indeed a philosophical turn of phrase in Galen's view and is best understood against the background of the medical analogy, as developed by the Stoics.[19] In a long passage of *PHP* 5.2–3 (V.432–54 K.=294–312 De Lacy), Galen discusses Chrysippus' parallelism between the philosophical therapy of the soul and the medical therapy of the body. He finds fault with him on two grounds.[20] By matching illnesses of the soul with precarious bodily *health* rather than actual illnesses, Chrysippus fails to build a well-balanced parallelism.[21] More fundamentally, he does not provide a definition of health and disease that suits both sides of the analogy. Elaborating on this last point, Galen specifies the conditions under which *he* believes that speaking of "diseases of the soul" is justified. Indeed, he suggests following Plato and understanding disease as the result of a *stasis*: there is a disease when an entity gets disrupted because its components diverge.[22] This, however, is the most inclusive definition possible, and if the term "disease," which typically describes affections such as fever, can also be applied to out-of-

---

18 See also *Symp. caus.* 2.2 (VII.157, 10–8, 6 K.): tremor is due to some weakness (ἀρρωστία) caused either by emotion (ψυχικὸν πάθος) or by bodily diseases (τοῦ σώματος νοσήματα).

19 Therapy of the soul is a *topos* that runs through the whole philosophical tradition for Galen: see *Aff. dig.* 1.4 (V.3 K.=4, 8–12 de Boer). But, as he acknowledges, Chrysippus' *On Affections* has been particularly influential: see Gill 2010: 295–297. On the Stoic analogy in general see Pigeaud 1981: 245–371 and Nussbaum 1994: esp. 13–47.

20 See *PHP* 5.2 (V.442–3 K.=302, 31–4, 1 De Lacy). On the analogy, see viz. *PHP* 5.2 (V. 437–8 K.= 298, 25–39 De Lacy): ἀναλογία τῶν ἐν τῇ ψυχῇ τοῖς κατὰ τὸ σῶμα; Fillion-Lahille 1984: 98–101.

21 On this, see Singer in this volume, Kidd 1983. It has an impact on the association of *pathos* with *nosêma* in Stoic doctrine and hence on the correctness of its translation into *morbus* by Cicero: *Tusc.* 3.22–3 (328, 7–9, 6 Pohlenz) and *Fin.* 3.35 (112 Reynolds). See Graver 2007: 141–145.

22 See *PHP* 5.2 (441–2 K.=302, 8–30 De Lacy) and *PHP* 5.3 (450–1 K.=310, 3–20 De Lacy), with reference to Plato, *Soph.* 228a7–d4 defining disease as "the destruction brought about by some dissension in what is naturally compatible" (ἡ τοῦ φύσει συγγενοῦς ἔκ τινος διαφορᾶς διαφθορά) – see also Plato *Rep.* 8, 556e.

control emotions such as rage, it is in this broader sense of the term only. A structure is no longer operational, having lost its inner balance, but the comparison ends here: for neither the structure nor the balance it needs are of the same type. Ordinary diseases are indeed most often traced back to a qualitative imbalance in the homeomeric bodies, whereas what is at issue with a diseased soul is improper coordination between its *archai*. In his polemic against Chrysippus in the *PHP*, Galen indeed grants a crucial role to the idea that the soul is composed of parts located in different places of the body (brain, heart, and lower body). They are the sources of motivation behind our behaviours, what make us judge that something is worth pursuing, show enthusiasm about it, and desire it. By nature, the soul operates hierarchically, so that rational thinking should dominate and channel the last two types of irrational drives. But when our emotions take over, this natural structure breaks down. This is what a disease of the soul consists in: the reason losing control over the lower impulses.[23] So it is indeed an *analogy* and one that makes sense only with a partitioned soul of the kind postulated by Plato. In other words, Galen endorses it, but in a general metaphorical sense.[24]

When applied to the soul, 'diseases' (νόσημα) and 'affections' (πάθη) are thus most certainly not used by him as distinctly medical notions. This has implications on how to read the contrast that he draws between affections of the soul and affections of the body.[25] Indeed, it is not a question of distinguishing, among medical conditions, those with psychological symptoms from those with physical ones, but of indicating what aspect of ourselves is out of balance and no longer able to function properly. And depending on whether it is the soul or the body, the issues that arise and the method of addressing them are quite different. Now, finding out which category a given complaint falls into is not that straightforward. For a disease is properly speaking a bodily malfunction, but may very well have psychological consequences; and by contrast, a disturbance in our psychic life is only a disease in name, but often results in physical disorders. In fact, there seems to have been a growing concern for such matters

---

[23] Here it matters little whether the soul is actually a body or not because the hierarchy of its parts is not a bodily property.

[24] That may not have been how the Stoics intended it (see Tieleman 2003: 142–157; *contra* Gill 2010: 308–313 and 229–241), but it certainly explains Galen's engagement with the genre of ethical therapy as developed by Plutarch, Marcus Aurelius, or Epictetus (see Singer 2013: 214–16).

[25] See, e.g. *Parv. pil.* 1 (V.900 K.=258, 17–19 Wenkebach) contrasting κατὰ τὸ σῶμα and περὶ τὴν ψυχὴν παθήματα; see also *Caus. puls.* 4.1 (IX.157, 7–13 K.) and *Cons.* 1 (14, 8–9 Schmutte) where the distinction is between ψυχικά and σωματικά πάθη.

from the Hellenistic period onwards. A need was felt to clarify what was falling within the scope of bodily or of psychic affections (i.e. within the competence area of medicine or of philosophy).[26] Probably because the Stoic analogy with madness had become a standard way of describing moral failure, psychopathological disorders took a prominent place in this debate.[27] Although the use of the body-soul polarity itself remained undisputed, they at least demonstrated the importance of going beyond the simple dichotomy. Such considerations are also present in Galen. Thus, in *Præn.*, he discusses several cases of psychic affections mistaken for bodily disorders. For instance, he shows that Justus' wife, who is afflicted with insomnia and has lost interest in the outside world, suffers from love, *not* melancholy.[28] These cases are meant to illustrate "what often affects the body because of psychic affections" (ἃ τὸ σῶμα διὰ τῆς ψυχῆς πάθη πάσχειν εἰώθει), as with anxiety or fear. Galen insists on the idea that there are no bodily affections (κατὰ τὸ σῶμα πάθος, σωματικὸν πάθημα) there; what is at issue is a *pathos* in the philosophical sense of the term (i.e. an emotion), but involving bodily disturbances like sweat and tremors, sometimes as strong as in medical conditions. His way of putting things here comes very close to a typology ascribed to Posidonius by Ps.-Plutarch, according to which, besides affections which are simply of the body or of the soul, there are mixed types of *pathê* that belong to the one but find expression in the other.[29] In this context, melancholy and hallucinations are set in diametrical opposition to the psychosomatic

---

26 See, e.g. Anon. Lond. 1.16–39 and 40 sqq. (1–2 Ricciardetto); Ptolemy, *Tetrabiblos* 3.15.2 (275, 13–276, 6 Hübner) distinguishes among bodily disorders, character flaws (*pathê*), and extreme and so to say pathological (ὥσπερ νοσηματώδη) affections such as epilepsy, *mania*, or possession — on this see van der Eijk 2013: 333–337. A whole book from the Methodist Julian may have had that subject: *Adv. Jul.* 3.7 (XVIIIA.257 K.=42, 1–2 Wenkebach).
27 See Polito (2016) commenting on Caelius Aurelianus, *Acut. morb.* 3.13.109–11 (356,21–358,17 Bendz) on hydrophobia, and *Chron. Morb.* 1.5.154 (522,2–5 Bendz) on *mania*. See also Pigeaud (1981: esp. 112–120).
28 See *Præn.* 6.4 (XIV.631 K.=100, 22–2, 3 Nutton) and 6.7 (XIV.632 K.=102, 10–12 Nutton). See also the case of the anxious slave steward who mismanaged his master's money: *Præn.* 6.10–13 (XIV.633–4 K.=102, 27–104, 8 Nutton) and Boethus' son getting sick from concealed gluttony: *Præn.* 7.1–18 (XIV.635–41 K.=104, 24–10, 12 Nutton). See esp. *Præn.* 7.15 (XIV.640 K.=108, 29–31 Nutton), bringing all three cases together.
29 See Ps.-Plutarch, *Libid. et ægr.*fr. 1.6 = Posidonius, fr. 154 (140, 5–12 Edelstein-Kidd): some *pathê* are (1) psychic (ψυχικά), such as anger and fear, others (2) bodily (σωματικά), such as fevers, yet others (3) not of the soul but bodily with psychic effects (οὐ ψυχῆς, περὶ ψυχὴν σωματικά), such as lethargy, melancholy, or hallucinations, and finally others (4) not of the body but psychic with bodily effects (οὐ σώματος, περὶ σῶμα δὲ ψυχικά), such as tremors or other visible effects of fear and distress. See Tieleman 2003: 278–283.

disorders highlighted by Galen: the former are bodily ailments with psychological manifestations and the latter the physical repercussions of emotional disturbances.

Such a clear distinction is not found in Galen,[30] but it is consistent with the role he gives to emotions in medicine. This topic has received great attention in recent research, which has emphasised how important Galen thinks it is for the physician to give emotions careful consideration.[31] As already noted, the ability to detect emotional disturbances is essential for the differential diagnosis of bodily disorders. But apart from that, two points are worth noting. First, it is in the hygienic part of medicine that the idea of taking care of the patient's mental life comes into play. Indeed, all psychic events coincide with bodily motions in Galen's view; but he regularly describes desires and emotions as being a more direct reflection of the body's condition and of its needs.[32] For that reason, adjusting one's regimen and adopting good lifestyle habits helps bring the non-rational impulses to a more manageable intensity. The physician, therefore, has the ability to regulate affects by means of body-oriented techniques; and, quite remarkably, this is conceived as an integral part of his practice.[33] But this is because emotions have an impact on physical health. Indeed, the second point is that, when it comes to *pathology*, Galen is interested in emotions as possible causes of diseases. As he explains at *Ars med.* 24.8 (I.371 K.=351, 2–7 Boudon-Millot):

> Ἀπέχεσθαι δὲ δηλον ὅτι τῆς ἀμετρίας αὐτοὺς χρὴ ἁπάντων τῶν ψυχικῶν παθῶν, ὀργῆς καὶ λύπης <*et gaudium*> καὶ θυμοῦ καὶ φόβου καὶ φθόνου. Ἐξίστησι γὰρ καὶ ταῦτα, καὶ ἀλλοιοῖ τὸ σῶμα τῆς κατὰ φύσιν συστάσεως.
>
> One must obviously refrain from the imbalance brought about by all the affections of the soul: anger, distress, joy, rage, fear, and envy; for they also upset the body and change its natural constitution.[34]

This idea occurs often in Galen's writings.[35] Galen attaches great importance to the triggering role of emotions, positive or negative, in pathological situations.

---

30 Note, however, that melancholy, *phrenitis* and *mania* are conceived as 'ills of the body' (τοῦ σώματος κακά) that overcome the soul at *QAM* 5 (V.49 K.=33, 12–14 Bazou).
31 See Staden 2012 and Singer 2017.
32 See *PHP* 5.5 (V.465 K.=322, 17–26 De Lacy), *Mor.* 2 (39, 20–40, 10 Kraus); Singer 2013: 130–131.
33 See *San. tu.* 1.8 (VI.39–43 K.=19, 14–21, 3 Koch); and Gill 2013 and 2018 on "preventive medicine". See also *Hipp. Epid. VI* 8 (487,18–23 Pfaff) with Devinant 2018: 205–206.
34 These emotional disturbances have the effect of drying out or moistening the organs: *Ars med.* 25.5 (I.373 K.=353, 17–19 Boudon-Millot).

If 'violent' (ἰσχυρά), they bring about diseases,[36] and sometimes even death.[37] Anger, for instance, acts on innate heat in the heart and increases the temperature throughout the entire body. This in turn affects the physiology of other organs, such as the liver which begins to produce too much yellow bile, thus causing yet more disorders.[38] But again, emotions are not described as medical affections in themselves but as disease factors.[39] On that account, they are part of what Medieval Galenism came to call the "six non-naturals."[40] This ambivalent situation may indeed have led to some confusions or hesitations in the textual tradition.[41] However, as far as pathology is concerned, emotions clearly differ from clinical psychic disorders: for they are not diseases in the same sense, and the physician only seeks to fight them for the adverse consequences they may have.

---

35 See *Hipp. Epid.VI* 8 (485, 17–19 Pfaff), showing that "the mental activity (*Geistestätigkeit*, i.e. γνώμη) itself is the *cause* of health or disease." For other similar examples, see Singer 2017: 190–193.
36 See *Ars. med.* 23.8 (I.367 K.=347, 1 Boudon-Millot); *San. tu.* 4.6 (VI.277–8 K.=122, 17–3, 1 Koch); *Meth. med.* 10.5 (X.685, 4–17 K.); *Cris.* 2.13 (IX.697–8 K.=162,4–3, 10 Alexanderson): see Roselli 2008.
37 As in the case of the grammarian Callistos (or Philippides): *Hipp. Epid.VI* 8 (486, 19–24 Pfaff) and *Indol.* 7 (4, 6–10 Boudon-Millot–Jouanna). See also *Loc. aff.* 5.1 (VIII.301, 5–2, 5 K.).
38 See *Temp.* 2.6 (I.633 K.=78, 7–11 Helmreich). On heating and cooling effects of emotions see esp. *Symp. caus.* 2.5 (VII.191, 4–4, 18 K.) on which see also Singer 2017: 171–172.
39 See von Staden (2012: 80–82) on *Præs. puls.* 3.7 (IX.381, 17, 2–6 K.); see also *Hipp. Prog.* 1.4 (XVIIIB.18–19 K.=207, 2–6 Heeg): they are "procatarctic" as the ancients said. On procatarctic causes, see *Caus. cont.* 2.1–6 (134, 3–36 Kalbfleisch≈54, 3–6, 5 Lyons) Hankinson 2003, Tieleman in this volume.
40 Those are ambient air, movement and rest of the body, sleep and wakefulness, ingested foods, evacuations, and psychic affections. See the source text at *Ars med.* 23.8 (I.367 K.=346, 10–7, 1) and Boudon-Millot (1996: 134–139) for a summary of the scholarly debate; see also von Staden 2012: 82.
41 Thus at *Mot. musc.* 2.6 (IV.445–6 K.=35, 13–20 Rosa), φρενῖτις was listed alongside θυμός and φροντίς among the 'strong affections of the soul' (ἰσχυρὰ τῆς ψυχῆς παθήματα) in Kühn's text. Even though Galen does bring up *phrenitis* in that context (see *Mot. musc.* 2.6 (IV.446–47 K.=35, 29–36, 13 Rosa)), Rosa's correction (keeping only φροντίς) is philologically sound and more in line with what is found elsewhere in the Galenic corpus.

4 Clinical Conditions as "Psychic" Disorders

Not only are emotions and psychic disorders not affections on the same terms, but they also involve different ways of looking at the soul. To put it briefly, when considering a case of *phrenitis*, Galen is not concerned with the structure of the patient's mind (which part of his soul dominates), as is the case with emotional disorders, but with its embodiment (how disturbances in the organs of thought affect the patient's ability to perform mental operations). The approach is, therefore, more physiological than psychological. Curiously enough, however, Galen gives the impression that he is not simply changing perspective, but that he is using a different concept of the soul. Indeed, he makes it perfectly clear that the rather stable group of affections ranging from *môrôsis* to headaches, delirium, convulsions, or *kôma*, are affections of the head,[42] that is of the brain.[43] Yet, as has already been said, he is also used to calling them directly affections of the "psychic" faculties, as if the soul and the brain were one and the same thing. This is especially often the case in *Loc. aff.*, where most of his remarks on the subject are to be found. The fact, for instance, that apoplexy "damages *all* psychic functions" is seen as a clear proof that it is an affection of the brain.[44] At *Loc. aff.* 3.5 (VIII.156, 11–8, 6 K.), he even goes so far as to designate psychic disorders with the phrase ψυχικὰ πάθη, which he usually applies to emotions only. Admittedly, this is an exception to the rule which is rather easily explained. At that point, indeed, Galen is criticising not only Archigenes but all those who support cardiocentrism, and certainly the Stoics in particular.[45] Now, for them, cognitive disturbances and emotions belong to the same category of affections of the soul and are attributed to the same governing centre, located in the heart. In this passage, Galen is interested in challenging this localisation by showing that when hegemonic functions are affected, even cardiocentrists apply the treatment to the head. It is therefore likely that in designating medical conditions impacting cognition as "psychic affections", he is simply using a term that his opponents would have used. This slip of tongue nonetheless shows that Galen is evolving in another framework where it seems

---

42 See, e.g. *Loc. aff.* 3.11 (VIII.193, 7–9 K.).
43 See, e.g. *Loc. aff.* 3.14 (VIII.209, 15–10, 2 K.) and 5.6 (VIII.340, 1–6 K.), and *Loc. aff.* 2.10 (VIII.314, 1–2 K.) for an explicit equation.
44 See *Loc. aff.* 3.14 (VIII.210, 17–19 K.): ἡ τοίνυν ἀποπληξία πάσας ὁμοῦ τὰς ψυχικὰς ἐνεργείας βλάπτουσα, σαφῶς ἡμῖν ἐνδείκνυται τὸν ἐγκέφαλον αὐτὸν πάσχειν.
45 See *Meth. med.* 13.21 (X.928, 2–32, 17 K.) and Tieleman (2003: 62–63) on the dialectical debate behind this. See also Lewis (2018) as to whether his criticisms of Archigenes are valid.

perfectly appropriate to circumscribe the sphere of "psychic" activity to that of cerebral functions. Problem is that some of the psychic disorders that he attributes to the brain involve various forms of emotional outbreaks such as anger, fear, sadness, or excitement, that he himself usually connects with the heart; in other words, one may wonder whether he is not giving up the idea of a tripartite soul.

However, there is no doubt that Galen himself sees no gap between his philosophical and medical works. The tripartition of the soul advocated in the *PHP* indeed provides the setting for the clinical investigations conducted on mental disorders.[46] On one occasion, at *Loc. aff.* 3.6 (VIII.162, 19–3, 5 K.), Galen even writes:

> ποικιλία πολυειδὴς γίνεται τῶν βλαπτόντων τὰς ψυχικὰς ἐνεργείας αἰτίων. Ἕνεκα δὲ σαφοῦς διδασκαλίας αἱ μὲν τοῦ λογιστικοῦ τῆς ψυχῆς ἐνέργειαι καλείσθωσαν ἡγεμονικαί, αἱ δὲ τῶν ἀλόγων ἠθικαί, περὶ ὧν οὐ πρόκειται λέγειν, ὅτι μηδὲ περὶ τῶν τῆς καρδίας, ἢ τοῦ ἥπατος παθῶν.

> Causes of damage to the psychic functions form a complex mosaic. For the sake of clear teaching, let us call 'governing' the functions of the rational element of the soul, and 'ethical' those of the non-rational ones; these are not the question here, nor, indeed, the affections of the heart or the liver.[47]

The remark is made in passing, interrupting a development on the various dyscrasias responsible for encephalic affections, which resumes immediately after. Galen's objective here is not obvious, but the meaning of the term "psychic", as he uses it just here and in the rest of the treatise, is probably what is at issue. The idea is to remove a possible ambiguity since according to him, that term could rightly be used for any function of each of the three parts of the soul. He therefore explains that the disorders of the psychic functions he has in mind are not those affecting the lower organs of the soul. But his point is more specific. In this context, indeed, he is more inclined to call 'natural' (φυσικός) the vital and metabolic activity of the heart and liver.[48] Therefore, he does not say he is removing disorders of physical functions from the discussion; in fact, syncope,

---

[46] See *Loc. aff.* 1.1 (VIII.19, 5–17 K.) or 2.10 (VIII.129, 1–4 K.).
[47] See also Singer (2018: 386) on that text.
[48] It is simply a matter of vocabulary for him: see *Nat. fac.* 1.1 (II.1–2 K.=101, 1–15 Helmreich) or *Prop. plac.* 3 (62 Nutton=174, 16–19 Boudon-Millot–Pietrobelli). The distinction is explained by the way these different functions are performed: the organs of the body draw to them the faculties of the heart and liver, while the brain actively sends (διαπέμπειν) its faculty to them: see *Loc. aff.* 1.7 (VIII.66–7 K.=302, 17–4, 5 Gärtner).

palpitations, jaundice and other hematopoietic disturbances are taken in consideration later in the book.[49] Rather, he says that the psychic disorders at issue should not be confused with the affections of other cardiac and hepatic functions, that he calls 'ethical' (ἠθικαί) here — in other words desires and emotions. Incidentally, the use of the term *êthikos*, otherwise quite rare, may be taken as a sign that it is as moral problems that emotions are put aside, since, as will be shown, they do play a part in brain disorders.[50] At any rate, such a reading seems to be supported by a similar statement made at *Glauc. meth. med.* 1.15 (XI.60, 12–1, 4 K.), where Galen observes that one of the three faculties that 'control' (διοικεῖν) the body is 'specifically' (ἐξαιρέτως) picked out by the term "psychic", that "of the brain".

But even so, not all brain disorders seem to be "psychic" to the same extent. It is indeed worth noting that in the text of *Loc. aff.* 3.6 Galen does not take into account the full range of functions ascribed to the brain; he only acknowledges the existence of the higher 'governing' (ἡγεμονικαί) ones, that is, 'representation' (φαντασία), memory, and 'thought' (διάνοια). He thus leaves aside sensation and movement,[51] even though they are in fact also affected in illnesses such as epilepsy or paralysis. But such emphasis on cognitive functions is not entirely accidental. Indeed, while in a medical context "psychic" disorders clearly mean diseases affecting the brain in general, cognitive disorders seem to occupy a special place in the category, as if they were the very core of it. As a matter of fact, Galen regularly describes the whole group of psychic disorders simply as affections of the *hêgemonikon*.[52] For he holds that the governing part of the soul is the subject of the action in all activities involving the brain, that is both cognitive and sensory-motor activities. The difference is that in the former, the *hêgemonikon* performs its 'proper' (ἴδιαι) functions and operates almost as a standalone entity, whereas it must rely on other organs to execute the latter.[53]

In addition to this distinction, it is also essential to take into account the modalities in which psychic affections take place. Broadly speaking, they can occur in one of two ways: either there is a qualitative change directly in the

---

49 See *Loc. aff.* 5.0–3 (VIII.297, 1–327, 12 K.) and 5.6–8 (VIII.344, 16–72, 11 K.).
50 Put differently, the whole reference to rationality is put aside: the failures of psychic capacities described here are indeed not 'errors' (ἁμαρτήματα) either. On *êthikos*, see Singer 2013: 119–123.
51 See *Symp. diff.* 1.3 (VII.55–6 K.=216, 15–218, 9 Gundert), where all three types of brain function are presented.
52 See *Loc. aff.* 3.7 (VIII.166, 18–8, 14 K.) or 4.1 (VIII.216, 9–17, 13 K.).
53 See *Loc. aff.* 2.10 (VIII.127 K.=372, 29–4, 5 Gärtner); cf. *Hipp. Prog.* 2.6 (XVIIIB.123 K.=266, 11–15 Heeg).

substance of the brain, or, in a more mechanical manner, the flow of faculties connecting it to the other organs is blocked or dissipated, either upstream or downstream.[54] In the first case, the brain is said to be affected 'as a homeomeric part' (ὡς ὁμοιομερεῖ), in the second, as an 'organic part' (ὡς ὀργανικῷ μορίῳ).[55] Cognitive disturbances, especially when there is a distortion of cognition, indicate a "homeomeric" disorder since nothing more than a healthy brain is required for its proper functions to be carried out correctly. By contrast, sensory and motor disturbances are often "organic", meaning that the conditions for a good connection of the brain with the rest of the body are not fulfilled. This is what explains Galen's commentary on the Hippocratic principle of mutual substitutions between epilepsy and melancholy.[56] They can turn into each other, says Hippocrates, depending on how the illness progresses: "if it is towards the body people become epileptics; if it is towards the mind (διάνοια), they become melancholics."[57] Galen simply indicates that not all cases of epilepsy allow for such an evolution and he says nothing of the mind-body distinction. Yet melancholy is no less a bodily disorder according to him. But as a cognitive derangement, it is directly due to an alteration of the organ of thought,[58] whereas epilepsy, affecting motor functions, comes from a blockage of the neural network, which extends throughout the body.[59]

5 The Place of Emotions in Clinical Disorders

Despite appearances, then, the brain does not take the place of the soul in the context of medical pathology. Galen simply uses the term "psychic" in a narrow sense, to refer to the functions of the brain, as opposed to those of the heart and liver, and especially the functions that the brain performs on its own without directly involving its connection with the rest of the body. But to remove any doubt as to whether medical theory conforms to the principles expounded in

---

54 See *Præs. puls.* 4.11 (IX.419, 19–20, 9 K.), *Loc. aff.* 3.3 (VIII.139, 6–9 K.), *QAM* 5 (IV.787–8 K.=32, 18–3, 7 Bazou).
55 See *Loc. aff.* 1.3 (VIII.30 K.=260, 9–15 Gärtner), *Symp. caus.* 3.1 (VII.207, 3–17 K.).
56 See *Loc. aff.* 3.10 (VIII.179, 18–81, 7 K.); see also *Hipp. Epid. VI* (505, 15–6, 20 Pfaff).
57 Hippocrates, *Epid. VI* 8.31 (V.354–6 L.=288, 15–19 Smith): ἢν μὲν ἐς τὸ σῶμα ἐπίληπτοι· ἢν δὲ ἐπὶ τὴν διάνοιαν μελαγχολικοί.
58 See *Loc. aff.* 3.9–10 (VIII.175, 11–93, 6 K.); *Symp. caus.* 2.7 (VII.200, 9–4, 4 K.); *Us. resp.* 5 (IV.506–7 K.=126, 18–8, 11 Furley).
59 See *Loc. aff.* 3.9 (VIII.173, 5–9, 17 K.) and 3.11 (VIII.193, 7–200, 5 K.).

philosophical texts, one still needs to explain how emotions relate to disorders ascribed to the brain.

First of all, as we have seen, it is essentially as causes of diseases that emotions come into play. As regards "organic" disorders of the brain, in most cases, emotions have the effect of cutting off the supply of psychic faculty to the organs, leading to disturbances in wakefulness, sensitivity and movement. Thus, at *Meth. med.* 12.5 (X.841, 16–2, 2 K.), Galen explains why 'strong emotions' (σφοδρά, μεγάλα), such as fear, joy, or anxiety, cause loss of consciousness or even death. The rationale for this is the same as for over-exercising:

> ἐν μὲν δὴ τούτοις ἅπασιν αὐτὴ καθ' ἑαυτὴν ἡ ψυχὴ κινεῖται, κατὰ δὲ τὰς πρακτικὰς ἐνεργείας τὸ σῶμα κινεῖ· καταλύει δὲ αὐτῆς τὸν τόνον ἑκάτερα τὰ γένη τῶν οἰκείων κινήσεων εἰς ἀμετρίαν ἐκταθέντα.
>
> In all these [sc. emotions] the soul itself moves itself, whereas, in action-related functions, it moves the body. But when they exceed measure, both of these [sc. otherwise] adequate types of movements drain its strength.

Here, emotions are harmful simply because of their intensity.[60] They consume too much energy, so to speak. Admittedly, the syncopes discussed in this text are not psychic disorders in the sense of affections of the cerebral faculties, but rather disturbances of the vital faculty, which is maintained by the heart.[61] However, Galen uses the exact same model to explain why fear makes legs tremble in front of a precipice.[62] And he does conceive tremor as an impairment of the psychic motor faculty itself.[63] His reasoning is presumably as follows: the psychic pneuma conveying this faculty is elaborated from the vital pneuma that the brain receives from the heart; when the vital pneuma runs out as a result of strong emotions or violent physical efforts, the whole system collapses, and the psychic faculty also wears off.[64] In this case, emotions are a direct and co-temporal cause of perturbation. Seizures provide another example of how they

---

[60] See also *Loc. aff.* 5.1 (VIII.301, 5–2, 5 K.); King 2013: 265–256; Trompeter 2016. This is why moral education can act as a preventive therapeutic measure.
[61] See *Symp. caus.* 2.5 (VII.191, 16–6, 7 K.), *Glauc. meth. med.* 1.15 (XI.48, 16–50, 4 K.), *Loc. aff.* 5.1 (VIII.298, 11–302, 5 K.).
[62] See *Tremor.* (VII.586, 18–7, 10 K.), *Symp. caus.* 2.2 (VII.157, 10–8, 6 K.). This is presumably a direct comment on Hippocrates, *Humor.* 9 (V.490 L.=168, 7–13 Overwien).
[63] See also *Symp. caus.* 2.1–2 (VII.149, 6–50, 11 K.): it is one of the lesions of 'voluntary' (προαιρετικαί) functions.
[64] See *Tremor.* (VII.601, 8–18 K.); *Hipp. Epid. III* 1.4 (XVIIA.510–11 K.=19, 10–21 Wenkebach). Note that tremor also follows upon direct affections of the organs of the will.

can affect the execution of brain activity. But there is a more indirect mechanism at work: obstruction of the psychic faculty comes indeed from an inflow of sticky substances in the neural network, themselves produced by a qualitative change generated somewhere in the body. And such a change is a possible consequence of emotions in the chest area, and the probable explanation for the grammarian Diodorus suffering from epileptic fits when he fasts for too long, works too late, or gets angry or anxious.[65]

Now, emotions are not only causes but also symptoms of brain disorders. At least, this is so with certain "homeomeric" affections, in which the hegemonic faculties are impaired; the best illustration of this is maybe also the most difficult to interpret, namely the case of melancholy. Sometimes, Galen says, an ordinary emotional reaction is the beginning of this illness.[66] But this is not the typical situation, and it is likely that an indirect mechanism of causation similar to that of epilepsy discussed above is involved. Wherever they are initially produced, black substances that circulate between organs and eventually come into contact with the brain or its psychic pneuma will indeed bring about melancholic symptoms.[67] Again, some emotional outbursts in the heart region may very well, among other things, have this effect.

Much more disconcerting, however, is the fact that emotions are the main symptoms of a brain disorder such as melancholy. 'Fear' (φόβος) and 'despondency' (δυσθυμία) are indeed proper to it.[68] Not only is it the traditional view,[69] but Galen insists on that point: he blames Diocles for not having included these 'proper' (ἰδία) symptoms of the disease in his discussion of its epigas-

---

[65] See *San. tu.* 6.14 (VI.448–9, K.=196, 27–7, 2 Koch); *Loc. aff.* 5.7 (VIII.340, 1–1, 3 K.); *Ven. sect. Er.* 2.9 (XI.241, 16–2, 14 K.).
[66] See *Hipp. Aph.* 6.23 (XVIIIA.35–6 K.=118, 6–14 Savino). Intensity is not the issue here, but duration: Galen explains that when they are without reasons, fear and despondency should be seen as symptoms of melancholy, even when they have not yet become chronic (because they are without reasons); conversely, even if they are triggered for a good reason, their unexpected persistence is a sign of melancholy. The idea is probably that they *become* emotions that are without reason. Compare to ephemeral fevers arising from exhaustion, anger, or sunstroke: persistence of the symptoms after the triggering cause has disappeared points to the onset of *another* type of fever: see *Meth. med.* 9.1 (X.602, 12–3, 9 K.), *Feb. diff.* 1.8 (VII.301, 1–4, 2 K.).
[67] See esp. *Loc. aff.* 3.9–10 (VIII.175, 11–93, 6 K.).
[68] See esp. *Loc. aff.* 3.10 (VIII.189, 19–92, 1 K.): "*all* melancholics have fear and are despondent: they have lost taste for life and hate people"; *Symp. caus.* 2.7 (VII.200, 9–4, 4 K.).
[69] See *Aph.* 6.23, (IV.568 L. = 184, 9–10 Jones). At *Hipp. Epid. VI* 3.12 (XVIIB.30 K.=139, 5–10 Wenkebach) Galen notes that Rufus' reading of the Hippocratic text (φόβος rather than ψόφος) was based on the traditional association of fear with melancholy. See also Ps.-Galen *Def. med.* 247 (XIX.416, 9–13 K.).

tric type.⁷⁰ And when describing them, he clearly claims that they come from the brain.⁷¹ Fear, he writes, arrives as a result of "some sort of darkness enveloping the rational part of the soul".⁷² Put otherwise, Galen seems to have abandoned entirely his views on the cardiac origin of emotions. However, one can certainly resolve the tension by first noticing that in several places, Galen takes up the common idea presenting the emotions of the insane as 'unfounded' (ἄνευ λόγου), but not without explanation.⁷³ As he puts it at *Symp. caus.* 2.7 (VII.203, 14–15 K.), indeed, someone affected by melancholy is

> ἀεὶ φοβεῖσθαι τὸν ἄνθρωπον, ὡς ἂν ἀεὶ τὴν αἰτίαν τοῦ φόβου συμπεριφέροντα τῷ σώματι.
>
> always in fear, because he is always bringing along with him, in his body, the reason for his fear.⁷⁴

Now, melancholy is conceived as a 'delirious disorder' (παραφροσύνη).⁷⁵ And it may be suggested that, as such, it *always* implies some sort of 'visions' (φαντασίαι).⁷⁶ Some of these visions should be simply explained by a disturbance of the sense organs.⁷⁷ Yet others are due to an impairment of the 'faculty' of representation (φανταστικόν) as opposed to that of 'understanding' (διανοητικόν, λογι-

---

70 See *Loc. aff.* 3.10 (VIII.187, 18–8, 18 K.).

71 See, e.g. *Hipp. Aph.* 4.67 (XVIIB748, 1–9, 9 K.); *Hipp. Epid. I* 2.77 (XVIIA.179 K.=90, 21–3 Wenkebach).

72 *Symp. caus.* 2.7 (VII.203, 13–14 K.): οἷον σκότος τι περιχυθῇ τῷ λογιστικῷ μορίῳ τῆς ψυχῆς. Compare to *Loc. aff.* 3.10 (VIII.191,6–7 K.): τῆς μελαίνης χολῆς τὸ χρῶμα παραπλησίως σκότῳ τὸν φρονοῦντα τόπον ἐπισκιάζον.

73 See, e.g. *Plen.* 11.21 (VII.576 K.=74, 7–8 Otte); *Loc. aff.* 6.5 (VIII.418, 8–15 K.); *Hipp. Prorrh.* 1.27 (XVI.565 K.=40,16–21 Diels). Compare Ps.-Aristotle, *Pr.* 30 954b16–18. See Devinant 2018: 217–219.

74 See also *Hipp. Prorrh.* 1.25 (XVI.562 K.=39, 5–7 Diels) about 'brutish' (θηριώδεις) deliria in which the patients "stamp their feet, kick and bite and rage *because they think that anyone approaching is an enemy*."

75 See *Meth. med.* 2.2 (X.81, 17–2, 17 K.).

76 Note that the Stoic technical distinction between φαντασία and φάντασμα (mental images with or without external support) does not apply in Galen. Cf. Aetius. 4.12.1–5 (401–2 Diels), Sextus Empiricus, *Adv. dogm.* 1.162–3 and 247–8 (39, 24–40, 10 and 58, 9–13 Mutschmann); see Lories 2003: 59–69.

77 Something in the eye is obstructing the view: see esp. *Loc. aff.* 4.2 (VIII.227, 11–8, 2 K.). This explanation is based on the model of vitreous detachments (floaters): see *Loc. aff.* 1.1 (VIII.17, 5–17 K.).

στική δύναμις): those are hallucinations proper.[78] Admittedly, to Galen, melancholy is more of an "intellectual" disorder,[79] but even so, one can assume that it involves mental images. Indeed, it is possible that some wrong *phantasia* is produced, that would be the source of undue emotional reactions. For Galen's psychology explicitly adopts a distinctive feature of Posidonius' doctrine, according to which the rational faculty communicates with the non-rational by way of images (for the non-rational part cannot understand anything else). In other words, the rational part is itself a source of *phantasiai* and naturally gives rise to emotions.[80] It can, therefore, be thought that when it is damaged, it produces distorted representations and thus triggers undue emotional reactions. As can be seen, Galen seems to have been well enough equipped to explain why emotional symptoms can be ascribed to a malfunctioning of the intellectual faculties. But nowhere does he venture to explain it clearly. For all his insistence on the truth and merits of tripartition, details of the physiology of the soul are largely left in the shadows.[81]

6 Conclusion

It has been long recognised how difficult it is to approach Galen's views of the various psychic disorders with the modern notions of "psychopathology".[82] Indeed, it is striking that the therapy of the word, well-illustrated in the philo-

---

78 *Symp. Diff.* 3.9–13 (VII.60–62 K. = 224,9–226,2 Gundert); *Loc. aff.* 4.2 (VIII.225,10–228,2 K.). *Ars. med.* 20.1–2 (I.355 K.=333, 5–10 Boudon-Millot) seems to contrast 'delirium' (παραφροσύνη) with affections of the sense *and* of the *phantasia*.
79 Actually, the attribution of melancholy to 'the rational part of the soul', (τὸ λογιστικὸν μόριον τῆς ψυχῆς) or to 'intelligence' (διάνοια) (see above n.72) is not without ambiguity. Quite naturally, this seems to indicate that melancholy affects *reasoning*. But this could be a loose way of referring to the hegemonic faculties more generally: see Jouanna 2009: 194 and *Hipp. Off. med.* 1.3 (XVIIIB.649, 13–57, 10 K.). See also the definitions of the hegemonic faculties at *Loc. aff.* 2.10 (VIII.126–8 K.=372, 21–4, 12 Gärtner): "science, opinion, thought in general" (ἐπιστήμη τε καὶ δόξη ἅπασα τε διανόησις), "understanding, remembering, reasoning, and deciding" (ἐννοεῖν καὶ μεμνῆσθαι καὶ λογίζεσθαι καὶ προαιρεῖσθαι). In fact, in such context "all the affections of the rational [sc. part]" (πάντα τὰ τοῦ λογιστικοῦ πάθη) and "all the affections of the governing functions" (πάντα ... τὰ τῶν ἡγεμονικῶν ἐνεργειῶν πάθη) seem to be used interchangeably: compare *Loc. aff.* 3.6 (VIII.160, 9–12 K.) to *Loc. aff.* 3.7 (VIII.166, 18–7, 8 K.).
80 See *PHP* 5.6 (V.473–4 K.=330, 24–32 De Lacy). This may have been of importance for Seneca's pre-emotions: see Fillion-Lahille 1984: 163–169.
81 See Schiefsky 2012: 345–346.
82 See García Ballester 1974.

sophical treatises, is missing from the medical discourse. It has thus been suggested that a relational therapy of clinical conditions such as that prescribed by Cælius Aurelianus for *mania* could fill the gap.⁸³ This, I believe, would amount to making a category mistake. For ethics and medicine, according to Galen, address different *types* of issues: the former is concerned with misuses of an otherwise functional soul, while the latter takes care of patients whose souls are themselves unable to function correctly. Moral exhortation in philosophical therapy only has a chance of success if the rational soul is able to regain the upper hand, something that medical disorders simply preclude from happening. If emotions do sometimes lead to a corruption of the soul's underlying mechanism, by contrast words are ineffective to remedy that situation.⁸⁴

As I have illustrated in this chapter, distinguishing between emotions and psychic disorders makes it possible to restore some coherence in Galen's views on the soul's affections. But it still requires considerable effort on the part of the interpreter, who gets the impression of being faced with a fragmented and *ad hoc* approach to the subject. Why, then, is the question of the soul's disorders so unclear? Several possible explanations can be suggested. Perhaps Galen was not quite sure whether he was right, and perhaps he did not, even at the end of his life, have a clearly settled opinion on these matters. After all, even in the *QAM*, he admitted to being unsure why melancholy and *phrenitis* had mental symptoms.⁸⁵ An evolution of his thought, a disagreement between diverse disciplinary backgrounds, or a conflict between models of the mind have also been proposed as likely answers by scholars.⁸⁶ However, in this particular case of the soul's *pathê*, the lexical issue probably provides the best explanation.⁸⁷ As argued here, Galen uses a broader concept of disease when he includes emotions

---

83 Gill 2018: 376; see also Singer 2018: 400–401 and Gill 2010: 350–354. On Cælius Aurelianus see Pigeaud 1987: 147–162.
84 As George Kazantzidis rightly pointed out to me, for Galen, Rufus of Ephesus is an authority on melancholy; and he does clearly combine body-oriented therapy (drugs, purges and venesection) with mood-lifting techniques (wine, sex, music and entertainment) for his melancholic patients (see esp. fr 67.16–22 (68 Pormann)). Certainly, Galen owes much to Rufus when it comes to psychopathology, but it is not clear that this aspect of the therapy also meets with his approval. On the one hand, it should indeed be noted that, in its context, Galen's praise of Rufus (see *At. bil.* 1.3 (V.105 K.=71.12–20 De Boer)) concerns much more his humoral aetiology (psychological questions are in fact almost totally left aside in the treatise). On the other hand, while Galen undoubtedly acknowledges a pathological role for emotions, he does not seem to attach importance to the *positive* effects that in theory they can have on the body.
85 See *QAM* 3 (IV.776–7 K.=18, 8–14 Bazou).
86 See, e.g. Manuli 1988 Mansfeld 1991, von Staden 2000.
87 See Singer 2017: esp. 182–183.

in it and a narrower concept of the soul for medical "psychic" conditions. This allows him to borrow arguments from various sources to make his point. The problem is that he does not systematically rephrase them. His use of the common distinction between diseases of the body and of the soul, for example, is particularly confusing: for he apparently does not see that disorders such as melancholy appear on one side or the other of this distinction. Galen keeps saying that words have no importance, as long as people agree on things.[88] But his inattention to terminology is not without consequences; indeed, if he sometimes uses a notion of psychic affection that is vague to the point of being misleading, maybe the concept itself is not the problem so much as the terms in which it is framed.

Bibliography

Ahonen, M. 2018. "Making the Distinction. The Stoic View of Mental Illness", in: C. Thumiger and P.N. Singer (eds.), *Mental Illness in Ancient Medicine. From Celsus to Paul of Aegina*, 343–364: Leiden: Brill.

Boudon-Millot, V. 1996. "L'*Ars Medica* de Galien est-il un traité authentique ?", *Revue des Études Grecques* 109 (1): 111–156.

Boudon-Millot, V. 2013. "What Is a Mental Illness, and How Can It Be Treated? Galen's Reply as a Doctor and Philosopher", in: W.V. Harris (ed.), *Mental Disorders in the Classical World*, 129–145: Leiden: Brill.

Devinant, J. 2018. "Mental Disorders and Psychological Suffering in Galen's Cases", in: C. Thumiger and P.N. Singer (eds.), *Mental Illness in Ancient Medicine. From Celsus to Paul of Aegina*: 198–221, Leiden: Brill.

Dols, M.W. 1992 †, *Majnūn. The Madman in Medieval Islamic Society*, Oxford: Clarendon Press.

Fillion-Lahille, J. 1984. *Le "De Ira" de Sénèque et la philosophie stoïcienne des passions*, Paris: Klincksieck.

García Ballester, L. 1974. "Diseases of the Soul (*Nosēmata tēs Psychēs*) in Galen: the Impossibility of a Galenic Psychotherapy", *Clio Medica. Acta academiae Internationalis Historiae Medicinae* 9 (1): 35–43.

García Ballester, L. 1988. "Soul and Body. Disease of the Soul and Disease of the Body in Galen's Medical Thought", in: P.E. Manuli and M. Vegetti (eds.), *Le opera psicologiche di Galeno*: 117–152. Naples: Bibliopolis.

Gill, C. 2000. "The Body's Fault: Plato's *Timaeus* on Psychic Illness", in: M.R. Wright (ed.), *Reason and Necessity: Essays on Plato's* Timaeus: 59–84. London: Duckworth.

Gill, C. 2010. *Naturalistic Psychology in Galen and Stoicism*. Oxford: Oxford University Press.

---

[88] See *Nom. med.* (8.23–31 Meyerhof-Schacht); *Puls. diff.* 1.2 (VIII.496, 2–7, 12 K.); *Libr. prop.* 19.20 (XIX.44 K.=168, 7–8 Boudon-Millot).

Gill, C. 2013. "Philosophical Therapy as Preventive Psychological Medicine", in: W.V. Harris (ed.), *Mental Disorders in the Classical World*: 339–360. Leiden: Brill.

Gill, C. 2018. "Philosophical Psychological Therapy. Did It Have Any Impact on Medical Practice?", in: C. Thumiger and P.N. Singer (eds.), *Mental Illness in Ancient Medicine. From Celsus to Paul of Aegina*: 365–380. Leiden: Brill.

Graver, M. 2003. "Mania and Melancholy. Some Stoic Texts on Insanity", in: G.W. Bakewell and J.P. Sickinger (eds.), *Gestures. Essays on Ancient Greek History, Literature, and Philosophy*: 40–54. Oxford: Oxbow Books.

Graver, M. 2007. *Stoicism & Emotion*. Chicago: University of Chicago Press.

Hankinson, R.J. 1991. "Galen's Anatomy of the soul", *Phronesis* 36 (2): 197–233.

Hankinson, R.J. 1993. "Actions and Passions: Affection, Emotion and Moral Self-Management in Galen's Philosophical Psychology", in: J. Brunschwig and M. Nussbaum (eds.), *Passion and Perceptions: Studies in Hellenistic Philosophy of Mind*: 184–222. Cambridge: Cambridge University Press.

Hankinson, R.J. 2003. "Causation in Galen", in: J. Barnes and J. Jouanna (eds.), *Galien et la philosophie*: 131–169. Genève.

Hankinson, R.J. 2006. "Body and Soul in Galen", in: R.A.H. King (ed.), *Common to Body and Soul. Philosophical Approaches to Explaining Living Behaviour in Greco-Roman Antiquity*: 232–258. Berlin: de Gruyter.

Hankinson, R.J. 2014. "Partitioning the Soul. Galen on the Anatomy of the Psychic Functions and Mental Illness", in: K. Corcilius and D. Perler (eds.), *Partitioning the Soul. Debates from Plato to Leibniz*: 85–106. Berlin: de Gruyter.

Holmes, B. 2013. "Disturbing Connections: Sympathetic Affections, Mental Disorder, and the Elusive Soul in Galen", in: W.V. Harris (ed.), *Mental Disorders in the Classical World*: 147–176. Leiden: Brill.

Jackson, S.W. 1969. "Galen — On Mental Disorders." *Journal of the History of the Behavioral Sciences* 5 (4): 365–384.

Jouanna, J. 2009. "Does Galen have a medical programme for intellectuals and the faculties of the intellect?", in: C. Gill, T. Whitmarsh, and J. Wilkins (eds.), *Galen and the World of Knowledge*: 190–205. Cambridge: Cambridge University Press.

Jouanna, J. 2013. "The Typology and Aetiology of Madness in Ancient Greek Medical and Philosophical Writing", in: W.V. Harris (ed.), *Mental Disorders in the Classical World*: 97–118. Leiden: Brill.

Kazantzidis, G. 2013. "'Quemnosfurorem, μελαγχολίαν illivocant'. Cicero on Melancholy", in: W.V. Harris (ed.), *Mental Disorders in the Classical World*: 245–264. Leiden: Brill.

Kidd, I.G. 1983. "*Euemptōsia*— Proneness to Disease", in: W.W. Fortenbaugh (ed.), *On Stoic and Peripatetic Ethics. The Work of Arius Didymus*: 107–117. New Brunswick: Transaction Publishers.

King, D.A. 2013. "Galen and Grief. The Construction of Grief in Galen's Clinical Work", in: A. Chaniotis and P. Ducrey (eds.), *Unveiling Emotions II. Emotions in Greece and Rome. Texts, Images, Material Culture*: 251–272. Stuttgart: Franz Steiner Verlag.

Lewis, O. 2018. "Archigenes of Apamea's Treatment of Mental Diseases", in: C. Thumiger and P.N. Singer (eds.), *Mental Illness in Ancient Medicine. From Celsus to Paul of Aegina*: 143–175. Leiden: Brill.

Lories, D. 2003. "*Phantasia*. Aperçu sur le stoïcisme ancien", in: D. Lories and L. Rizziero (eds.), *De la phantasia à l'imagination*: 47–77. Louvain: Peeters.

Mansfeld, J. 1991. "The Idea of the Will in Chrysippus, Posidonius and Galen", *Proceedings of the Boston Area Colloquium in Ancient Philosophy* 7 (1): 107–157.
Manuli, P.E. 1988. "La passione nel *De Placitis Hippocratis et Platonis*", in: P.E. Manuli and M. Vegetti (eds.), *Le opera psicologiche di Galeno*: 185–214. Naples: Bibliopolis.
Mattern, S.P. 2016. "Galen's Anxious Patients. *Lypē* as Anxiety Disorder", in: G. Petridou and C. Thumiger (eds.), *Homo Patiens. Approaches to the Patient in the Ancient World*: 203–223. Leiden: Brill.
Nussbaum, M. 1994. *The Therapy of Desire. Theory and Practice in Hellenistic Ethics*. Princeton (NJ): Princeton University Press.
Nutton, V. 2013. "Galenic Madness", in: W.V. Harris (ed.), *Mental Disorders in the Classical World*: 119–127. Leiden: Brill.
Pigeaud, J. 1981. *La maladie de l'âme, Étude sur la relation de l'âme et du corps dans la tradition médico-philosophique antique*. Paris: Les Belles Lettres.
Pigeaud, J. 1987. *Folie et cures de la folie chez les médecins de l'Antiquité gréco-romaine. La manie*. Paris: Les Belles Lettres.
Pigeaud, J. 1988. "La Psychopathologie de Galien", in: P.E. Manuli and M. Vegetti (eds.), *Le opere psicologiche di Galeno*: 153–183. Naples: Bibliopolis.
Polito, R. 2016. "Competence Conflicts between Philosophy and Medicine. Caelius Aurelianus and the Stoics on Mental Diseases", *Classical Quarterly* 66 (1): 358–369.
Roselli, A. 2008. "*Suntonos phrontis* e malattia d'amore nei testi medici greci da Galeno agli Ephodia", in: P. Heuzé, Y. Hersant, and É. van der Schueren (eds.), *Une traversée des savoirs*, 391–404. Québec: Presses de l'Université Laval.
Schiefsky, M.J. 2012. "Galen and the Tripartite Soul", in: R. Barney, T. Brennan, and C. Brittain (eds.), *Plato and the Divided Self*: 331–349. Cambridge: Cambridge University Press.
Siegel, R.E. 1973. *Galen on Psychology, Psychopathology and Function and Diseases of the Nervous System. An Analysis of his Doctrines, Observations and Experiments*. Bâle: S. Karger.
Singer, P.N. (ed.) 2013. *Galen, Psychological Writings*. Cambridge: Cambridge University Press.
Singer, P.N. 2017. "The Essence of Rage. Galen on Emotional Disturbances and Their Physical Correlates", in: R. Seaford, J. Wilkins, and M. Wright (eds.), *Selfhood and Soul. Essays on Ancient Thought and Literature*: 161–196. Oxford: Oxford University Press.
Singer, P.N. 2018. "Galen's Pathological Soul. Diagnosis and Therapy in Ethical and Medical Texts and Contexts", in: C. Thumiger and P.N. Singer (eds.), *Mental Illness in Ancient Medicine. From Celsus to Paul of Aegina*: 381–420. Leiden: Brill.
Stok, F. 1996. "Follia e malattie mentali nella medicina dell' età romana", *Aufstieg und Niedergang der römischen Welt* II 37 (3): 2282–2410.
Tieleman, T.L. 2003. *Chrysippus' On affections. Reconstruction and Interpretations*. Leiden: Brill.
Trompeter, J. 2016. "Die gespannte Seele. Tonos bei Galen", *Phronesis* 61 (1): 82–109.
van der Eijk, P.J. 2013. "Cure and (In)curability of Mental Disorders in Ancient Medical and Philosophical Thought", in: W.V. Harris (ed.), *Mental Disorders in the Classical World*: 307–338. Leiden: Brill.
von Staden, H. 2000. "Body, Soul, and Nerves: Epicurus, Herophilus, Erasistratus, the Stoics, and Galen", in: J.P. Wright and P. Potter (eds.), *Pyche and Soma. Physicians and Metaphysicians on the Mind-Body Problem from Antiquity to Enlightenment*: 79–116. Oxford: Oxford University Press.

von Staden, H. 2012. "The Physiology and Therapy of Anger. Galen on Medicine, the Soul, and Nature", in: F.M.M. Opwis and D.C. Reisman (†) (eds.), *Islamic Philosophy, Science, Culture, and Religion*: 63–87. Leiden: Brill.

Susan P. Mattern
The Atlas Patient: Galen on Melancholia and Psychosis

Abstract: Galen describes a patient suffering from a pathological anxiety that Atlas will drop the world. His diagnosis is melancholia. A similar story appears in an obscure fragment of Rufus of Ephesus' work on melancholia. Analysis along with similar examples of borrowing in Alexander of Tralles and Aëtius of Amida suggests that physicians recycled stories from older sources when they saw something similar, making changes to adapt the story to the patient they observed. Galen's story about the Atlas patient illustrates the tradition connecting the disease of melancholia with the emotion of fear and with symptoms now called psychotic — frightening hallucinations and delusions. Ancient melancholia deserves a place in the cross-cultural study of schizophrenia.

One of the most interesting of Galen's patients is the man who is worried about Atlas. He is mentioned either two or three times, depending on how one counts, as a textbook example of the potential psychiatric consequences of the condition Galen calls *melancholia*, attributable to an excess of black bile. Black bile could do lots of things to a body; but it had especially interesting effects when it reached the brain.[1]

The first part of this chapter will address the story itself, as its transmission raises unique questions about medical narrative in antiquity; the second part will analyze what the story tells us about psychosis in cross-cultural context.

1 Transmission

One of Galen's stories about the Atlas patient comes from his commentary on the first book of Hippocrates' *Epidemics*, as a gloss on a specific word having to do with deduction by 'symptoms' (*tekmêria*), in which he makes a distinction roughly equivalent to the distinction in modern medicine between a sign and a symptom:

---

[1] Scholarship on melancholia in antiquity is substantial. Fundamental are Flashar 1966; Jackson 1986; Pigeaud 2008; Pormann 2008; Bell 2014.

> The symptom is what the patients clearly express as their opinion and what they do. For when someone was with us in the morning, as usual, he said in response to a question that he had lain awake the whole night, considering what would happen if it should come about that Atlas, being sick, could no longer hold up the sky. And when he said this, we deduced that this was the beginning of a melancholy.
>
> *In Hipp. Epid. 1 comm.* 3.1, 17A.213–214K

He mentions the same story in another passage surviving only in Arabic, in his commentary on the sixth book of *Epidemics*; here it is one of many stories about emotional disturbance and fear of death.

> I know a man from Cappadocia, who had got a nonsensical thing into his head and because of that declined into melancholy. The idea that he had got into his head was completely ridiculous. That is, his friends saw him weeping and asked him about his grief (Kummer). At that he sighed deeply and answered, saying, that he was worried (in Angst) that the whole world would collapse. His worry was that the king, about whom the poets relate that he carries the world and is called Atlas, would become tired because of the long time for which he had carried it. Therefore there was a danger that the sky would fall on the earth and smash it.
>
> *In Hipp. 6 Epid. comm.*, 487 Wenkebach and Pfaff

Galen uses the first person and the aorist tense in both stories. Passage 1 unambiguously indicates something he saw himself — "when someone was with us in the morning" — whereas in passage 2 he uses the introductory phrase "I know a man." In Greek the word "I know" does not always imply autopsy; but in Galen's case histories, it usually does.[2]

The third relevant passage both is and is not a reference to this story. It occurs in a part of Galen's treatise *On the affected parts* (3.9–10, 8.176–193K, Appendix I Pormann), written late in life, in which he discusses the effects of pathological excess of black bile. Galen, drawing on Diocles of Carystus and other predecessors, but especially Rufus of Ephesus, thought black bile could affect the stomach, or the brain, or it could translate from the stomach to the brain. Some of the effects of black bile on the brain result from the dark shadow it casts over a patient's psyche, that makes the patient afraid. The main symptom of melancholia is what Galen calls "bestial hallucinations" and delirium, occurring either with or without fever. Describing some of the delusions that patients with melancholia might experience, he writes:

> They believe they are a piece of pottery and become afraid that they might be broken if they do not flee from everyone they meet; some think they are roosters and imitate them;

---

[2] See Mattern 2008: 39–40.

some fear, that somehow Atlas, who holds up the world, having become tired will shrug it off, and thus he would be smashed himself and we all would perish with him.

De locis affect. 3.10, 8.190K

This last passage is echoed much later, in the sixth century, in Alexander of Tralles' medical encyclopedia in Greek. In his chapter on melancholy, discussing the symptoms melancholia proper — the condition caused by black bile, rather than similar conditions caused by other humoral imbalances that he also recognized — we find the ceramic, the chicken, and the Atlas patient, with a couple of divergences from Galen's passage. Alexander's chicken is a hen rather than a rooster, and the Atlas patient thinks he himself is Atlas. Alexander also writes that,

> I myself saw a woman who had this delusion, and she kept the middle finger of her had wrapped, as she was holding up the whole world on it. She also proclaimed that she was afraid lest, if she curved the finger somehow, the whole cosmos would fall down and all would be instantly destroyed.
>
> Therapeutica 1.17, 605 Puschmann

Scholars have long believed or assumed that Galen took his ideas about melancholia mostly from Rufus of Ephesus, who wrote a lost book on melancholy probably a generation or two before Galen.[3] The evidence for this has never been strong until recently. A passage very similar to the one about the pottery, the rooster, and Atlas appears in two medieval sources that attribute it to Rufus of Ephesus. Both sources are very obscure and the fragment was only recently published by Klaus-Dietrich Fischer.[4] The earlier testimonium is from the sixth-century author Agnellus of Ravenna, among whose surviving works is a commentary on Galen's treatise *On sects for beginners*. In that commentary he writes, in Latin,

> Rufus of Ephesus discussed the differences in melancholia, as some suffering from melancholia think that they are roosters and crow, and others think that they are a vase of pottery, and cry out and say 'stop, don't break me'! And an astronomer with melancholia said: 'Let Atlas never remove himself, who carries the sky on his shoulders, so that it falls on us.' This indeed was the form of his melancholy, and he subsequently died of a seizure.
>
> Westerink 1981: 118

---

3 Pormann 2008.
4 Fischer 2010.

A few other testimonia to this passage also survive,⁵ and it was apparently a popular one, just as Rufus' treatise as a whole was influential and very popular. It seems likely that Alexander of Tralles and Agnellus of Ravenna worked directly from Rufus' lost treatise rather than, for example, from Galen's discussion in *On the affected parts*; both include details not transmitted in Galen.

Given that Rufus had also described an Atlas patient, is Galen's Atlas patient real, or is he lying when he says he saw this patient? Is he appropriating a folktale, or another physician's case history, as his own?

Scholars have made broad claims about the literary license taken by ancient medical authors, and Galen in particular, with case histories claims that they often invent stories or transmit old stories as their own.⁶ The most commonly cited example, first noticed and discussed by Armelle Debru in a 1992 publication, may, in fact, more plausibly prove the opposite. This example is from Aëtius of Amida, writing in the early sixth century CE.⁷ He tells a story about a patient suffering from *hysterikê pnix*, uterine suffocation:

> I myself know, for I once observed, a woman who was suffering from this condition, and when the midwife used a relaxing and sweet-smelling remedy, and rubbing it on her innermost genitals with her fingers, because of the heat from the medicines and the contact of the fingers, spasms occurred with pain together with pleasure, by means of which, after a thick and abundant and sticky seed was expelled, the woman was delivered of her burdensome condition.
>
> Aëtius 16.70

Galen tells a similar story in *On the affected parts* (6.5, 8.420K), which is Aetius' main source for this section on hysterical suffocation; he refers to this same story in *On semen* (8.420, 4.599K) but doesn't include as many details. Galen's relationship to this story is unclear: in neither version does he say he saw it himself. In *On semen* he writes "as was observed even now" and in *On the affected parts* he writes that the story 'appeared' (ἐφάνη); both are unusual constructions for him and very different from how he introduces stories he claims to have seen himself.⁸

Aëtius' language as he tells the story is very close to Galen's version in *On the affected parts*. Thus Debru argues that Aëtius lifted the story from Galen and said that he saw it himself.

---

5 Constantine the African, *Libri duo de melancholia*, 123 Garbers 1977; Johannes of Alexandria, 73 Pritchet 1982 (see Fischer 2010: 182).
6 E.g. Debru 1992; Harris 2001: 12.
7 On this story, besides Debru 1992, see also King 2011.
8 On Galen's language when introducing case histories, see Mattern 2008: 37–40.

One reason to suspect that the story of the widow isn't true is that, like the Atlas story, it sounds like a folktale that is normally transmitted orally. Other examples of folksy stories are common in ancient literature about psychopathology, and indeed in premodern literature more generally on that subject.[9] The famous Erasistratus cured a woman who believed she had swallowed a snake by making her throw up and then putting a snake in the vomit. Rufus told a story about a man who thought he had no head until his doctor gave him a lead crown to wear. Galen tells the story of an augur who scared himself to death.[10] All of these sound like folktales and some recur in multiple sources with variations. Folklore clearly plays a prominent role in how ancient physicians understood mental illness, and it still does for example, in folklore and storytelling about addiction in western culture today.

But why does Aëtius add a first-person interjection to Galen's story about the widow: "I myself know, for I once observed … "?[11] The most natural way to read this phrase is as an apostrophe — Aëtius steps away from the text he is closely paraphrasing to comment that he has seen this case himself, meaning *this type of case*. He observed something similar to what Galen recounts. That Aëtius nowhere calls this patient a widow lends support to this theory; probably he omits this detail because the patient he saw was not a widow.

Something similar may explain the recurrence and variations of the Atlas story. Rufus' original version does not survive; but Agnellus was likely working with that original. Agnellus' version includes the detail, not found in Galen, that the Atlas patient was an astronomer; Agnellus goes on to say that the patient died of a seizure. He tells the story in the past imperfect and perfect tenses (the patient kept on saying, the patient died); this is a departure from his grammar in the other examples from the Rufus passage, where the patients believe, sing, shout, and say in the present tense. It sounds like Rufus' story of the Atlas patient was a case history, perhaps something Rufus saw himself; in any case Rufus told the story as something that really happened to an individual, not just as a general example.

Galen twice tells a story about an Atlas patient as something he witnessed himself, and, as is typical for him, is precise in describing his relationship to the events — Galen is not the one who questioned the patient, and may not have been treating the patient at the time; he seems to know the patient socially, and

---

9 Ermancora, Forthcoming.
10 Aëtius 6.9=Rufus fr. 11, Pormann 2008, and below, nn. 22–23; Galen, *In Hipp. 2 Epid. comm.* 207 Wenkebach and Pfaff; Galen, *In Hipp. 6 Epid. comm.* 485–486 Wenkebach and Pfaff.
11 οἶδα γὰρ αὐτός ποτε θεασάμενος.

the problem and diagnosis came up in conversation. Galen's story lacks Rufus' detail that the patient was an astronomer; it adds the detail that the patient was from Cappadocia. Perhaps this is because Galen's patient, unlike that of Rufus, was from Cappadocia and was not an astronomer. In the version of the story that Alexander tells, the patient actually believes he is Atlas; Alexander may have been influenced by a similar patient he saw himself, who believed she had the world balanced on her middle finger.

I think the most likely interpretation of the Atlas tradition is that Rufus and Galen both saw a patient who was worried about Atlas, and Alexander saw a patient who thought she had the world balanced on her finger, which struck him as similar to the delusions recorded by Rufus and Galen. The Atlas patient might be a psychiatric folktale and it might also be something that physicians saw from time to time. Based on these few examples, we can say that when physicians recounted stories that conformed to what they knew from oral or written tradition, they tended to insert language describing their relationship to the story (I saw it, I encountered it, a man was in my presence) and to add or omit details to conform to the specific case they knew (Aetius' hysterical patient was not a widow, Galen's melancholic patient was from Cappadocia). Folklore has been one way of making sense of psychosis since classical times and perhaps much earlier.

2 *Melancholia*

Why is the Atlas patient important? First, this story illustrates Galen's understanding of the disease of melancholia. The last line of the version that survives in Greek reads: "And when he said this, we deduced that this was the beginning of melancholy (*melancholia*)." Galen saw something that enabled him to make a definitive diagnosis: the delusion, that became obvious when the patient's friends questioned him about his insomnia and anxiety. In this story, the delusion is the index symptom for melancholia. In the first place, Galen had read Rufus and knew that Rufus had a melancholic patient who was worried about Atlas — he made an easy diagnosis from a classic sign. But there is more to be learned from the story.

One of the most important passages for Galen's understanding of melancholia is Hippocratic aphorism 6.23, "if fear or depressed mood (*dusthumia*) persist for a long time, it is something melancholic." Commenting on this aphorism, he distinguishes fear caused by an apparent or obvious reason from fear that is not caused by something obvious. Galen believes that irrational fear has a darker prognosis, but even fears that seem reasonable can signify *melancholia*, if they are last a long time.¹² In the Arabic version of the story, it appears that the Atlas patient meets the criterion for irrational fear exactly — Galen here describes the patient's anxiety as ridiculous. (Similarly, a psychiatrist diagnosing schizophrenia by the criteria of the fourth edition of the *Diagnostic and Statistical Manual of Mental Disorders* had to make a judgment about whether a patient's delusions were "bizarre;" the fifth edition still contains a discussion of the term *bizarre* but has removed it from the diagnostic criteria for schizophrenia.)¹³ Had the Atlas patient been beset by fears Galen considered more reasonable, he might instead have diagnosed something milder, perhaps the disease associated with *lupê* that he describes in several places. Galen constructs *lupê* as a sort of chronic fear, roughly equivalent to the modern term anxiety as it is used by psychiatrists.¹⁴ In Galen, anxiety can lead to melancholia, presumably by raising a person's internal temperature, cooking the yellow bile and turning it black.¹⁵ The disorder caused by anxiety, which is bad enough on its own and can be deadly, can become the more serious condition of melancholia, and that may be what he believes has happened to the Atlas patient.

Delusions and hallucinations play an important role in many ancient descriptions of melancholia, beginning much earlier than Galen and Rufus. In the Hippocratic Corpus, to say someone is melancholic is roughly to say that person is crazy. The words *ekstasis* and variations of *mania* and *mainomai* are frequently linked to black bile; a person in one case history is "raving with black bile,"

---

12 *In Hipp. Aph. comment.* 23 (18A.35–36K); on the aphorism and on fear without a reason, also *Sympt. caus.* 2.7, 7.264K. The Hippocratic Corpus also contains references to unreasonable fears and also unreasonable distress (*lupê*). In *Reg.* 1.35.7 (154.7–11 Joly=4.286 Jones), people whose souls have too much water "lament because of nothing, are afraid of things that are not frightening, are distressed (*lupeontai*) at what does not affect them" (see Jouanna 2013, 102). A well-known female patient from *Epid. III* 3.3.17(11) suffers from "*lupê* with a cause", implying a contrast to *lupê* without cause; Galen's commentary on the case does not discuss this formulation, but refers to the patient as phrenetic and melancholic (*In Hipp. 3 Epid. comm.* 17A.777K). Two patients in *Epid. V* suffer from irrational fears (one of flute girls, one of heights; 5.81–82, 7.86–87 and King 2013). Caelius Aurelianus' chapter on *mania* (*Chron.* 5) also mentions irrational fears, for example of caves, or falling into a ditch (150, 538 Drabkin).
13 American Psychiatric Association 2000: 299, 312; American Psychiatric Association 2013: 87.
14 Mattern 2016.
15 On the connections among worry or anxiety, yellow bile, fever, and melancholia, see *De locis affect.* 3.9–10 (8.177–178K, 184–185K, 193K). On *lupê* and *phrontis* as causes of fever more generally in Galen, see e.g. *De cris.* 2.13 (9.697–700K), *De praesag. ex puls.* 3.8 (9.388K), *In Hipp. Progn. comm.* 3.23 (18B.273K), and Mattern 2016: 208–209, 212–214.

for example.[16] We find similar references in Aristophanes and Plato, suggesting that the concept of melancholic psychosis was not only a medical one but part of popular culture.[17] Cicero believed that the equivalent term to *melancholia* in Latin was *furor*.[18]

In the famous passage from Aristotle's *Problems* that discusses both melancholic types and melancholic pathologies (this passage was likely written by another author, perhaps Aristotle's student Theophrastus, and interpolated later), examples of melancholics include Ajax, Heracles, and Bellerophon; Orestes is also sometimes cited as melancholic by other writers.[19] The relevant stories reached their most lurid form in the plays of Euripides and these are probably the versions that the author of *Problems* had in mind: Ajax, deluded by Athena, murders livestock believing they are his enemies Agamemnon and Menelaus; Heracles, deluded by Hera, kills his own wife and children. Orestes saw Furies pursuing him, when others could not see them (the example of Bellerophon is a bit different and will be discussed later.) The idea that the delusions of Orestes were melancholic delusions is attested in Cicero, and seems to have been prominent in the Stoic tradition, which saw melancholia as a specific, medicalized version of the kind of insanity that by nature afflicts us all.[20] A passage about melancholia from the obscure physician of the second century BCE, Marcellus of Side, on werewolves, was reproduced in all of the late-antique medical encyclopedists; the idea of melancholic lycanthropy — delusions of being a wolf — persisted through the Arabic medical tradition and into the modern period.[21]

In any case, the Galen/Rufus tradition drew on an old and very popular association of melancholia with bizarre or terrifying delusions and hallucinations; moreover, the influence of the Galen/Rufus picture of melancholia remained robust through late antiquity (and indeed through the modern period). Aëtius of Amida's chapter on melancholia (6.9) credits "Galen and Rufus and Poseidonius," the latter an obscure fourth-century physician. Flight from other people, baseless fears, religious delusions, demonic possession, and the conviction that one has taken poison are all melancholic symptoms in this passage. Aëtius also

---

16 *Epid.* 5.2 (5.204 Littré); see Thumiger 2013 and 2017: 39–40.
17 Flashar 1966: 37–39; Kazantzidis 2013: 245.
18 *Tusc.* 3.11; Graver 2003: 48–49; Kazantzidis 2013.
19 *Pr.* 30.1; other melancholics in this passage are Socrates, Plato, and Empedocles. Orestes: Cicero *Tusc.* 4.38 (mentioning Athamas, Alcmaeon, Ajax, and Orestes); cf. Sextus Empiricus *Adv. Math.* 7.245–247.
20 On psychosis in the Stoic tradition and the example of Orestes, see Graver 2003 and 2007, chap. 5.
21 Aët. 6.11; Oribasius *Syn.* 8.9; Paul of Aegina 3.16; Metzger 2011: 150–170 and 2013.

mentions the story of the man who thought he had no head.[22] In the sixth century, Alexander of Tralles' discussion of melancholia reflects and builds on this long tradition. I have already discussed his version of the Atlas story; Alexander also offers the fullest version of the story of the headless man, telling us that the patient believed he had been beheaded by a tyrant, and that he was cured when the physician Philotimos gave him a lead crown to wear. (Later, Ishaq ibn Imran, in his treatise on melancholy, says he has seen a case of this delusion himself.) Alexander adds other bizarre delusions to the canon of melancholic delusions, including a woman who thought she had been turned into a nightingale like the mythical Procne.[23]

Besides hallucinations and delusions, another important theme in the tradition about melancholia was social avoidance and irrational suspicion. Bellerophon was the mythical prototype of this behavior. Ps-Aristotle quotes a passage from Homer that is also quoted much later by the pseudo-Galenic *Introductio*, in its discussion of melancholy: "He wandered across the Aleian plane, eating his heart out, shunning the beaten paths of men."[24] In the myth, Bellerophon's behavior is the result of overwhelming grief; Cicero compares his case to that of Niobe as an example of *aegritudo* and *dolor animi* (*Tusc.* 3.63), and thus Bellerophon illustrates melancholia's connection with *dusthumia*. It is therefore interesting that for the author of the *Introductio*, Bellerophon exemplifies fear and avoidance rather than grief; people with melancholia are "suspicious of everything, and they hate people, and take pleasure in deserted places, just as is said of Bellerophon."[25]

This association of melancholia with social avoidance and irrational suspicion is also attested for example in Aretaeus of Cappadocia, where symptoms of *melancholia* include extreme fear, terrifying visions, irrational hostility, and isolation: "sometimes suspicious of poison, sometimes seeking out solitude because they hate people, sometimes tormented by a superstitious fear of the gods, sometimes hating life itself."[26] We see similar symptoms in Galen's discussion of melancholia in *De locis affectis*, and in Caelius Aurelianus' translation of the Methodist Soranus, where signs of melancholia are "anxiety and distress of the mind, sadness together with silence and animosity toward friends … suspi-

---

22 Aët. 6.81; Flashar 1966: 120–122.
23 Alexander of Tralles' chapter on "melancholia arising from melancholic blood" (he recognized different types of melancholia attributable to the other humors) is *Therapeutica* 1.17 (1.605–607 Puschmann). Ishaq ibn Imran: Pormann 2008 F 12.
24 *Pr.* 30.1, 953a; Ps-Galen, *Introd.* 13.24; cf. Cicero, *Tusc.* 1.80 and 3.61–63.
25 Ps.-Galen, *Introd.* 13.24.
26 Aretaeus, *De causis et signis diuturnum morborum* 1.5.

cions that conspiracies are being set up against him, meaningless weeping, senseless muttering" (1.6.180).[27]

Other psychological symptoms of melancholia not as relevant to the Atlas patient include epileptic seizures, catatonia, seeing visions, foretelling the future, listlessness or avolition, inappropriate affect, of which the random laughter of the philosopher Democritus was the most famous example, and a number of speech problems including talkativity, aphasia, stuttering, or (as in the above quotation from Caelius Aurelianus) incoherent muttering.[28] Some authors (Aristotle, Aretaeus) divided melancholic syndromes into two different types, excited and depressed (Aretaeus considers *mania* a more intense form of the same disease as melancholia, but he describes this variability for both conditions). Today's psychiatry recognizes similar dichotomies in the different phases of bipolar disorder,[29] or — though this is unremarked in modern scholarship — in the "positive" and "negative" symptoms of schizophrenia. Celsus seems to represent a different tradition that classed melancholia as a disease of sadness; here Ajax and Orestes are afflicted not by melancholia but by a different kind of psychic disorder to which he does not give a name.[30] But for most ancient authors, Orestes and Ajax were melancholics.

For Galen, psychotic symptoms were the main indicator of a melancholic disturbance of the brain, and furthermore, and if he saw a person who was having disturbing hallucinations or bizarre delusions, who was suspicious or hostile and avoided social contact, or who imagined plots against his life, melancholia would be his diagnosis. In the case of the Atlas patient, once Galen becomes aware that the patient has what he believes is a bizarre delusion, he changes his diagnosis to melancholia from what he might otherwise describe as a different kind of psychic disorder. That the delusion was about Atlas, and that Rufus had also treated a melancholic patient worried about Atlas, made the diagnosis easier.

---

27 Caelius Aurelianus 1.6.181.
28 Lethargy, listlessness: Arist. *Pr.* 30.1 954a–b; Rufus *Krankenjournale* 13 (Ullmann 96–98); Aretaeus *De causis et signis diuturnum morborum* 1.5. Inspiration, divination: Arist. *Pr.* 30.1 954a; Arist. *Div. somn.* 463b; Cic. *Div.* 1.81 and *Tusc.* 1.80; Flashar 1966: 47; Pigeaud 2008: 187–191; Kazantzidis 2013: 252–255. Epilepsy: Arist. *Pr.* 954b, and epilepsy is closely related to melancholy in many sources, e.g. Galen, *De locis affect.* 3.9 (8.180, 185K); see Flashar 1966: 23, 47. Apoplexy, catatonia, paralysis: Arist. *Pr.* 31.1 954b; Hipp. *Aph.* 7.40; see Kazantzidis 2013: 261. Speech problems: Flashar 1966, 47, 61. Laughter/Democritus: Flashar 1966: 68–70; the main source is the *Letters of Hippocrates* 10–17.
29 Marneros 2001; Pies 2007.
30 Celsus 3.18.17.

This argument contributes to a growing consensus that the type of "severe, persistent break with reality" usually called schizophrenia today, as problematic as that diagnosis is,[31] is recognized as a pathology in every society in which people have looked for it, including societies that are not very modernized.[32] Symptoms may be interpreted differently, however. In societies where discourse about psychotic illness is based not on the self-report of patients but on their interactions with others, or where hearing voices, interacting with spirits, and similar experiences are more accepted, these symptoms may not receive the same emphasis; it is failures in social functioning and behavior that signal psychosis.[33] That Galen and other writers do not emphasize auditory hallucinations in their descriptions of melancholia may reflect one or both of these factors. Also, although consensus holds today that schizophrenia is not the product of modernity it was once thought to be,[34] finding traces of it in past populations – as opposed to today's traditional populations – is difficult because of the nature of the evidence; all the problems with retrospective diagnosis are even worse for mental disorders.[35] But if we want to add a historical dimension to our understanding of these disorders, we have to try.

Ancient views on melancholia, which were also very influential in the early modern period in Europe, may seem like quaint and unsophisticated relics of the age before Emil Kraepelin revolutionized psychiatry by dividing psychotic diseases without a clear "organic" cause into manic-depression and *dementia praecox* in the early twentieth century. Kraepelin distinguished the latter by its early onset and degenerative course, but also established the principle, still foundational to psychiatry today, that schizophrenia (the taxonomic descendant of *dementia praecox*) is primarily defined by its positive symptoms of delusions and hallucinations. Emotions are not central to its definition; or rather, a pathological absence of emotion, the blunting or absence of affect that are among its negative symptoms, is thought typical of schizophrenia. Bipolar disorder, on the other hand, is a disorder of moods, with emotions central to its definition.[36] This has never been an easy dichotomy to maintain. Delusions are

---

31 Jablensky 2010.
32 Luhrmann 2016; quotation from p. 2.
33 Luhrmann 2016; Marrow 2016.
34 The classic argument associating schizophrenia with modernity is Torrey 1980.
35 A few studies, inadequate in my mind, have attempted this for pre-modern societies: Jeste et al. 1985; Ellard 1987; Howells 1991; Evans, McGrath, and Milns 2003. A more substantial effort is Kroll and Bachrach 1982.
36 Shorter (1997: 99–109) is a concise history of Kraepelin's contribution; see also Jablensky 2010.

common in bipolar disorder's manic episodes, and several blended categories — "schizoaffective disorder," "depression with psychotic features" — are canonized in the *Diagnostic and Statistical Manual of Mental Disorders*. In recent years, the neo-Kraepelian classification of psychotic disorders has been undermined and seems likely to be abandoned soon, for example as psychiatrists have discovered genetic overlap between schizophrenia, bipolar disorder, and other diagnoses.[37] More than one line of inquiry suggests multiple underlying causes of similar, overlapping psychotic symptoms, unrelated to current diagnostic categories.[38] Psychiatrists also are rethinking the concept of psychosis, recognizing that many delusions are benign or culturally normal, and that many people have "subclinical" psychotic experiences.[39] Psychotic patients *suffer* from their delusions, either because they are more severe, or more distressing; emotions and moods are potentially important to defining psychotic disorders, and in particular, psychotic delusions are usually terrifying.[40] Thus the relationship between schizophrenia, fear, and anxiety/depression is much more complex than it used to be.

From the perspective of transcultural psychiatry, the most interesting feature of Galen's melancholia is its close connection with the negative emotion of fear. Melancholic delusions are fearful delusions — they include what a modern psychiatrist would call persecutory delusions, among the most common schizophrenic delusions cross-culturally today.[41] In this context, Galen's and Rufus' system seems less unsophisticated and more like one of many valid ways of approaching psychosis — is schizophrenia a disorder of the emotion of fear? Part of what the Atlas patient teaches us is that Galen and Rufus did not draw the same boundary between psychotic disorders and mood disorders that modern psychiatry does. The Atlas patient probably would not meet modern criteria for schizophrenia (though Alexander of Tralles' female patient with the world balanced on her finger would be a better candidate). Modern psychiatrists would more likely see an anxiety disorder. But while they define the boundaries

---

37 Jablensky 2010; see Witt et al. 2017 for a recent study that adds Borderline Personality Disorder to the group of clinical disorders with similar genetic links (schizophrenia, bipolar disorder, and major depressive disorder).
38 Arnedo et al. 2015; Clementz et al. 2016.
39 van Os et al. 2009; Pierre 2010.
40 Cf. Jenkins 2004, 41–47; Corin, Thara, and Padmavati 2004.
41 Stompe et al. 2003. "Persecutory syndrome" and "poisoning syndrome" are among seven distinct hallucinatory-delusional syndromes identified by Stompe 2007; "apocalyptic guilt syndrome" (Alexander's Atlas patient) and "coenasthetic hypochondria syndrome" (headless patient, women who swallowed snake) are also especially relevant for this discussion.

between disorders differently, they are not necessarily correct to do so, and we can learn much from studying where different societies drew those distinctions.

Bibliography

American Psychiatric Association 2000. *Diagnostic and Statistical Manual of Mental Disorders.* Fourth Edition, Text Revision. Arlington, VA: American Psychiatric Association.
American Psychiatric Association 2013. *Diagnostic and Statistical Manual of Mental Disorders.* Fifth Edition. Arlington, VA: American Psychiatric Association.
Arnedo, Javier/Dragan M. Svrakic/Coral del Val/Rocío Romero-Zaliz/Helena Hernández-Cuervo/Ayman H. Fanous/Michele T. Pato/Carlos N. Pato/Gabriel A. de Erausquin/Robert Cloninger/Igor Zwir 2015. "Uncovering the Hidden Risk Architecture of the Schizophrenias: Confirmation in Three Independent Genome-Wide Association Studies", *American Journal of Psychiatry* 172: 139–153.
Bell, Matthew. 2014. *Melancholia: The Western Malady.* Cambridge: Cambridge University Press.
Clementz, Brett A./John A. Sweeney/Jordan P. Hamm/Elena I. Ivleva/Lauren E. Ethridge/Godfrey D. Pearlson/Matcheri S. Keshavan/Carol A. Tamminga 2016. "Identification of Distinct Psychosis Types Using Brain-Based Biomarkers", *American Journal of Psychiatry* 173: 373–384.
Corin, Ellen/Rangaswami Thara/Ramachandran Padmavati. 2004. "Living Through a Staggering World: The Play of Signifiers in Early Psychosis in South India", in: Janis Hunter Jenkins and Robert John Barrett (eds.), *Schizophrenia, Culture, and Subjectivity*, 110–145. Cambridge: Cambridge University Press.
Debru, Armelle 1992. "La suffocation hystérique chez Galien et Aetius: réécriture et l'emprunt de 'je'", in: Antonio Garzya (ed.), *Tradizione e ecdotica dei testi medici tardoantichi e bizantini*: 79–89. Naples: M. d'Auria.
Ellard, J. 1987. "Did Schizophrenia Exist before the Eighteenth Century?", *Australian and New Zealand Journal of Psychiatry* 21: 306–318.
Ermancora, Davide (Forthcoming). "The Bosom Serpent in a Toga: Rufus of Ephesus, Galen, Trallianus, and the Snake Trick Between Folklore and Psychopathology", *La Ricerca Folklorica.*
Evans, K./J. McGrath/R. Milns 2003. "Searching for Schizophrenia in Ancient Greek and Roman Literature: A Systematic Review", *Acta Psychiatrica Scandinavica* 107: 323–30.
Fischer, Klaus-Dietrich 2010. "De fragmentis Herae Cappadocis atque Rufi Ephesii hactenus ignotis", *Galenos* 4: 173–183.
Flashar, Helmut 1966. *Melancholie und Melancholiker in den medizinischen Theorie der Antike.* Berlin: de Gruyter.
Garbers, K. (ed.) 1977. *Isḥāq ibn 'Imrān: Maqāla fi-l-mālīḫūliyā (Abhandlung über die Melancholie) und Constantini Africani: Libri duo de melancholia.* Hamburg: H. Buske.
Graver, Margaret 2003. "Mania and Melancholy: Some Stoic Texts on Insanity", in: Geoffrey W. Bakewell and James B. Sickinger (eds.), *Gestures: Essays in Ancient Literature, History, and Philosophy Presented to Alan L. Boegehold*: 40–54. Oxford: Oxbow.
Graver, Margaret 2007. *Stoicism and Emotion.* Chicago: University of Chicago Press.

Harris, William V. 2001. *Restraining Rage: The Ideology of Anger Control in Classical Antiquity*. Cambridge, MA: Harvard University Press.

Howells, John G. (ed.) 1991. *The Concept of Schizophrenia: Historical Perspectives*. Washington, D.C.: American Psychiatric Press.

Jablensky, Assen 2010. "The Diagnostic Concept of Schizophrenia: Its History, Evolution, and Future Prospects", *Dialogues in Clinical Neuroscience* 12: 271–287.

Jackson, Stanley W. 1986. *Melancholia and Depression: From Hippocratic Times to Modern Times*. New Haven, CT: Yale University Press.

Jenkins, Janis Hunter 2004. "Schizophrenia as a Paradigm Case for Understanding Fundamental Human Processes", in: Janis Hunter Jenkins and Robert John Barrett (eds.), *Schizophrenia, Culture, and Subjectivity*: 29–61. Cambridge: Cambridge University Press.

Jeste, Dilip V./Rebecca del Carmen/James B. Lohr/Richard J. Wyatt 1985. "Did Schizophrenia Exist before the Eighteenth Century?", *Comprehensive Psychiatry* 26: 493–503.

Jouanna, Jacques 2013. "The Typology and Aetiology of Madness in Ancient Greek Medical and Philosophical Writing", in: W.V. Harris (ed.), *Mental Disorders in the Classical World*, 97–118. Columbia Studies in the Classical Tradition 38. Leiden: Brill.

Kazantzidis, George 2013. "'Quem nos furorem, μελαγχολίαν illi vocant': Cicero on Melancholy", in: W.V. Harris (ed.), *Mental Disorders in the Classical World*, 245–264. Columbia Studies in the Classical Tradition 38. Leiden: Brill.

King, Helen 2011. "Galen and the Widow: Toward a History of Therapeutic Masturbation in Ancient Gynecology", *Eugesta* 1: 25–235.

King, Helen 2013. "Fear of Flute Girls, Fear of Falling", in: W.V. Harris (ed.), *Mental Disorders in the Classical World*: 265–284. Columbia Studies in the Classical Tradition 38. Leiden: Brill.

Kroll, Jerome/Bernard Bachrach 1982. "Medieval Visions and Contemporary Hallucinations", *Psychological Medicine* 12: 709–721.

Luhrmann, T.M. 2016. "Introduction", in: T.M. Luhrmann and Jocelyn Marrow (eds.), *Our Most Troubling Madness: Case Studies in Schizophrenia Across Cultures*: 1–25. Berkeley: University of California Press.

Luhrmann, T.M./R. Padmavati 2016. "Voices That Are More Benign: The Experience of Auditory Hallucinations in Chennai", in: T.M. Luhrmann and Jocelyn Marrow (eds.), *Our Most Troubling Madness: Case Studies in Schizophrenia Across Cultures*: 99–112. Berkeley: University of California Press.

Marneros, Andreas 2001. "Origin and Development of Concepts of Bipolar Mixed States", *Journal of Affective Disorders* 67: 229–240.

Marrow, Jocelyn 2016. "Vulnerable Transitions in a World of Kin: In the Shadow of Good Wifeliness in India", in: T.M. Luhrmann and Jocelyn Marrow (eds.), *Our Most Troubling Madness: Case Studies in Schizophrenia Across Cultures*: 56–70. Berkeley: University of California Press.

Mattern, Susan P. 2008. *Galen and the Rhetoric of Healing*. Baltimore, MD: Johns Hopkins University Press.

Mattern, Susan P. 2016. "Galen's Anxious Patients: *Lype* as Anxiety Disorder", in: Georgia Petridou and Chiara Thumiger (eds.), *Homo Patiens: Approaches to the Patient in the Ancient World*: 203–223. Leiden: Brill.

Metzger, Nadine 2011. *Wolfmenschen und nächtliche Heimsuchungen. Zur kulturhistorischen Verortung vormoderner Konzepte von Lykanthropie und Ephialtes*. Remscheid: Gardez.

Metzger, Nadine 2013. "Battling Demons with Medical Authority: Werewolves, Physicians, and Rationalization", *History of Psychiatry* 24: 341–355.
van Os, J./R. J. Linscott/I. Myin-Germeys/P. Delespaul/L. Krabbendam 2009. "A Systematic Review and Meta-Analysis of the Psychosis Continuum: Evidence for a Psychosis Proneness-Persistence-Impairment Model of Psychotic Disorder", *Psychological Medicine* 39: 179–195.
Pierre, Joseph M. 2010. "Hallucinations in Nonpsychotic Disorders: Toward a Differential Diagnosis of 'Hearing Voices'", *Harvard Review of Psychiatry* 18: 22–35.
Pies, Ronald 2007. "The Historical Roots of the 'Bipolar Spectrum': Did Aristotle Anticipate Kraepelin's Broad Concept of Manic-Depression?", *Journal of Affective Disorders* 100: 7–11.
Pigeaud, Jackie 2008. *Melancholia: Le malaise de l'individu*. Paris: Payot & Rivages.
Pigeaud, Jackie 2010. *Folie et cures de la folie chez les médecins de l'antiquité gréco-romaine: La manie*. 2nd ed. Paris: Les Belles Lettres.
Pormann, Peter E. (ed.) 2008. *Rufus of Ephesus On Melancholy*. Tübingen: Mohr Siebeck.
Pritchet, C.D. 1982. *Johannis Alexandrini Commentaria in librum de sectis Galeni*. Leiden: Brill.
Shorter, Edward 1997. *A History of Psychiatry from the Era of the Asylum to the Age of Prozac*. New York: Wiley.
Stompe, T./G. Ortwein-Swoboda/K. Ritter/H. Schanda 2003. "Old Wine in New Bottles? Stability and Plasticity of the Contents of Schizophrenic Delusions", *Psychopathology* 36: 6–12.
Stompe, Thomas/S. Bauer/Hanna Karakula/Palmira Rudaleviciene/Nino Okribelashvili/Haroon Rashid Chaudhry/E.E. Idemudia/S. Gschaider 2007. "Paranoid-Hallucinatory Syndromes in Schizophrenia: Results of the International Study on Psychotic Symptoms", *World Cultural Psychiatry Research Review* Apr/Jul 2007: 63–68.
Thumiger, Chiara 2013. "The Early Greek Medical Vocabulary of Insanity", in: W.V. Harris (ed.), *Mental Disorders in the Classical World*: 61–96. Columbia Studies in the Classical Tradition 38. Leiden: Brill.
Thumiger, Chiara 2017. *A History of the Mind and Mental Health in Classical Greek Medical Thought*. Cambridge: Cambridge University Press.
Toohey, Peter 2004. *Melancholy, Love, and Time: Boundaries of the Self in Ancient Literature*. Ann Arbor: University of Michigan Press.
Torrey, E. Fuller 1980. *Schizophrenia and Civilization*. New York: Aronson.
Ullmann, Manfred 1978. *Krankenjournale* (Rufus of Ephesus). Weisbaden: Harassowitz.
Westerink, L.G. 1981. *Agnellus of Ravenna: Lectures on Galen's De Sectis*. Buffalo, NY: Arethusa Monographs 8.
Witt, S.H./F. Streit/M. Rietschel 2017. "Genome-Wide Association Study of Borderline Personality Disorder Reveals Genetic Overlap with Bipolar Disorder, Major Depression, and Schizophrenia", *Translational Psychiatry* 7: e1155; doi:10.1038/tp.2017.115.

List of Contributors

Elizabeth Craik is Honorary Professor, School of Classics, University of St Andrews, Scotland. She has published widely on tragedy, social history, and history of medicine in ancient Greece, focusing in particular on the Hippocratic Corpus. She has produced critical editions and translations of four Hippocratic treatises, *Places in Man* (1998), *On Sight and On Anatomy* (2006), and *On Glands* (2009). She is also the author of *The 'Hippocratic' Corpus* (2015).

Julien Devinant is Associate professor in the Department of Medical Humanities at the University of Lille. He holds a PhD in Ancient Philosophy and Greek Philology (Paris-Sorbonne and Berlin Humboldt) and has published on Graeco-Roman medicine and epistemology, primarily on Galen's ideas on the mind, human physiology and pathology.

David Kaufmann is Associate Professor of Philosophy and Classics, at Transylvania University, US. He is specializing on ancient philosophy, Greek and Roman literature and ancient medicine. His publications include "Seneca on the Analysis and Therapy of Occurrent Emotions" (in *Seneca Philosophus*, eds. Colish / Wildberger) and "Galen on the Therapy of Distress and the Limits of Emotional Therapy" (*OSAP* 47).

George Kazantzidis is Assistant Professor of Latin Literature at the University of Patras. His monograph *Lucretius on Disease: The Poetics of Morbidity in De Rerum Natura* was published by De Gruyter (Trends in Classics) in 2021. In collaboration with Dimos Spatharas, he edits the book series *Trends in Classics- Ancient Emotions*. He is currently working on a book project provisionally entitled: *Ancient Paradoxography: Science, Horror, the Sublime*.

Jennifer Kosak is Associate Professor of Classics at Bowdoin College, US. She is author of *Heroic Measures: Hippocratic Medicine in the Making of Euripidean Tragedy* (Brill, 2004), and of numerous articles on ancient Greek tragedy and Hippocratic medicine. She is currently working on a book provisionally entitled: *Unmanned: Masculinity and Disease in Ancient Greek Society*, in which she examines the impact of disease on the performance of masculinity in ancient Greece.

Susan Mattern is Distinguished Research Professor of History at the University of Georgia in the United States. She has published books on Roman imperialism, on the physician Galen, and on the history of menopause.

Spyridon Rangos is Professor of Ancient Greek Literature and Philosophy in the University of Patras, Greece. His research focuses on the interrelationships between philosophy and religion in Greek antiquity. A recently completed monograph on the conceptual triptych "Wonder – Perplexity – Philosophy" is forthcoming in Greek.

P.N. Singer (Birkbeck, University of London) works on ancient medical and philosophical conceptions of the mind, mental illness, the emotions and time. Publications include three volumes of Galen translations (with OUP and CUP); Mental Illness in Ancient Medicine (co-edited with C. Thumiger, Brill); and Time for the Ancients (de Gruyter, forthcoming).

Dimos Spatharas is an Associate Professor at the University of Crete, Greece. He is the author of *Emotions, Persuasion, and Public Discourse in Classical Athens* (De Gruyter, 2019) and of several articles on the Sophists, Greek oratory and Athenian law, and ancient emotions. He is the co-editor of a volume entitled *The Ancient Emotion of Disgust* (OUP, 2016). In collaboration with George Kazantzidis, he edits the book series *Trends in Classics- Ancient Emotions*.

Chiara Thumiger is a classicist and historian of science, currently working as a Research Fellow within the Cluster of Excellence ROOTS at Kiel University. On the medical side of her research, her interests lie in the areas of history of psychiatry and of the representations of mental health. As a classicist, she has worked on Greek tragedy, ancient views about the self, and ancient animals. Recent publications are *A History of the Mind and Mental Health in Classical Greek Medical Thought* (Cambridge, 2017); *Mental Illness in Ancient Medicine* (co.-ed. w. P. Singer, Leiden, 2018); *Ancient Holism*, edited for Brill (2020). Her monograph about the ancient disease *phrenitis* and its afterlife in the Western medical tradition is now forthcoming with CUP, while she is working on a series of publications under the heading "Ancient Guts".

Teun Tieleman (PhD 1992) is Professor of Ancient Philosophy and Medicine at Utrecht University. He has published mainly on Galen of Pergamum, Stoicism, and, from a thematic perspective, ancient theories of emotion and moral psychology, epistemology, and methodology (dialectic). He is the director of the Utrecht Galen Project (2015-2021) and co-directs the Anchoring Innovation Research Program (2018-2028). As from 2022 he is chair of OIKOS, the national research school in classical studies in the Netherlands.

Index Rerum et Nominum

Selected Greek Terms

Terms which appear transliterated in the General index are normally not included here.

ἀθυμία   119 n.8, 125, 135
αἰσχρομυθεῖν   176 n.11, 182 n.26
αἰσχρός   25, 126 with n.8, 137, 138, 162
ἀκρατής   130, 163
ἁμάρτημα
– in Galen   232 n.9, 259 n.50
ἀμφιβάλλειν   133 n.27
ἀμφιεννύναι   133 n.27
ἀπορεόμενα   99, 105
ἀφροδίσια   164 n.52
διάνοια   80, 84–85, 259, 260 with n.57, 264 n.79
διδαχή   53
δυσάνιος   177–178, 181, 193
δυσθυμίη (–α)   125, 174–175 with 175 n.3, 176 n.8, 180–181, 182, 185, 186, 262, 279
δύσκριτος   91 n.60
δυσοργησίη   124
δυσχαλίνωτος   193
ἔκφορος   239
ἐπιβάλλειν   133
ἐπιτίθημι   133
εὐδαιμονία   75
εὐεμπτωσία   219–220 with n.58
εὔλογχος   52–53 with n.21
θερμός (and θερμασία)   38–39, 97, 174, 176 n.6

(ἐγ/συγ)καλύπτειν ('covering')   132, 133 with n.26, 134, 159, 161
– κάλυμμα/καλυπτήρ   133 nn.26–27
καταπλάττειν   133 n.27
μαχλοσύνη   164 n.52
μεθίστημι   49, 53–54
παθητικὴ ὁλκή   221
παράκαιρος   133
παραφέρομαι   133, 163
περιβάλλειν   133 n.27
περιέργεια   195 with n.68
περιστέλλειν   133 with n.27, 134 n.30, 158–160
(ἐκ/ἐμ)πίπτω   119 n.8, 214 n.45
πρόφασις   93 with n.65, 177
ῥυσμός   53 n.23
σκέπη   158 with n.42
συγκυρίη   124
συνδιατρίβω   110–111
τόπος ἐκ τῶν ἐναντίων   (argumentum ex contrariis)   81
ὑπόθεσις   98–100 with 98 n.78 and 99 n.81, 100, 102–103
φανερός (ἀφανής)   45
φαντασία   216
– in Galen   259, 263 with n.76, 264 with n.78
(περι)ψυχρός   97, 134 n.30, 158, 176 n.6, 180, 185, 186

General Index

abortion   185 with n.38
Aëtius of Amida   274
Agathinus of Sparta   208 with nn.27–28
Agnellus of Ravenna   273–275
air   94, 203 with n.8, 223 n.65, 256 n.40
Alexander of Aphrodisias   206 n.22

amathia   46, 55
ananke (necessity)   50 with n.17
– and 'need' (χρείη)   105
Anaxagoras   22, 47 n.12
Anaximander   107

anger/rage 4, 5, 17, 20, 27, 34–38, 118, 119, 124–125, 127, 128, 131, 133, 134, 146 n.5, 150, 157 n.37, 174, 178, 199, 215, 229, 235, 236, 238–239, 241, 248, 250, 254 n.29
– and the heart 256, 258
– as *energeia* in Galen
– as θυμός 6, 38
– as mild madness 251
– as ὀξυθυμία 155
– freedom of (ἀοργησία) in Galen 234
– frothing 38
Antiochus of Ascalon 244 with n.42
anus 165
anxiety (and anxiety disorders) 119, 150 n.18, 173, 175, 186, 250, 254 n.28, 276, 279, 282
– and death 261
– as ἀγωνία 38
– as chronic fear in Galen 277
– as *phrontis* 37, 212 n.41, 243 with n.39, 256 n.41, 277 with n.15
apatheia 13, 35 n.30
aphasia 280
Apollodorus of Tarsus (=Apollodorus Calvus) 209 n.35
apoplexy 280 n.28
apostasis 3 with n.2
appraisal mechanisms 125 n.4
Archigenes of Apamea 257 with n.45
Atomists 50–53
Bacon, Francis 65
baskania 51–52
bile
– black 14, 118, 176 n.6, 178, 181, 186, 187, 215–216, 271–272, 277
– and *ekstasis* 277
– yellow 256, 277 with n.15
bipolar disorder (or manic depression) 199, 280–282
– and *DSM* 282 with n.37
blood 49, 121, 184, 204
– and *pneuma* 222 n.61
– composition of in animals 216
– hematopoietic disturbances 259
– menstrual 175 n.5
Boethus (Peripatetic) 215 n.50

Borderline Personality Disorder 282 n.37
bowel movements 130
brain 37, 45 n.6, 94, 120, 230, 247, 248, 249, 253, 257–263, 271, 272, 280
– and the stomach 272
– *enkephalos* 118
bregma 181
Cælius Aurelianus 254 n.27
– and *mania* 265 with n.83, 277 n.12
Cambridge Changes 68 with n.16, 79, 107
cardiocentrism 257
catatonia 280 with n.28
Chrysippus 7, 12, 26, 29, 31 n.25, 32 n.26, 202, 205 with nn.16–17, 206, 207 n.23, 209, 215 with n.49, 217 n.52, 219–223, 225, 232, 252, 253
Cicero 209 with n.35, 215 n.50, 241, 278
Cleanthes 215
Cleopatra 211 n.38
clitoris (νύμφα) 164–165
Coenasthetic Hypochondria Syndrome 282 n.41
coma 161, 175, 180, 185
Combat Trauma 5
cosmology 99 with n.80, 101, 103, 105
crocydism 160
delirium 88, 134, 140, 159, 176 n.11, 180, 182 n.26, 186, 236 n.19, 248 n.2, 257, 263 n.74, 272
– delirious disorder (παραφροσύνη) 263, 264 n.78
delusions 14, 272, 273, 276, 277, 278, 279, 281, 282
dementia praecox 281
Democritus 47 n.12, 106 n.91
deontology 149 n.15, 162 n.48
depression 1, 118, 119, 126, 135 with n.33, 173, 174, 175 n.3, 180, 182, 185, 282
– with psychotic features in *DSM* 282
Descartes, René 65
diabetic 162
Diagnostic and Statistical Manual of Mental Disorders (*DSM*)
– and depression with psychotic features 282

- and schizoaffective disorder 282
- and schizophrenia 277
diaphragm 121
diarrhoea 220 n.58
diet 98, 102, 104, 105, 106, 107, 158
Diocles of Carystus 262, 272
Diodorus the Grammarian
- and epilepsy 262
Diodotus of Sidon 215 n.50
Dioscurides Phakas 211 n.38
disgust 125 with nn.3 and 6, 128, 152 n.22, 162, 163, 179 n.22
- ἀηδέα 136
dissoi logoi (double arguments) 81
doctors
- and emotional detachment 53 n.22, 179 with n.22
- and female patients 138 n.38
- and male gazes 193
- and shame 127, 149 n.15
- and the sophists 101, 103, 104
- as disembodied entities 2, 4, 187, 190
- as story-tellers 188
- from Pamphylia in Rome 208 n.29
Dodds, Eric 146
dreams 119, 120, 213 with n.45, 214 n.45
drugs/*pharmakon* 37, 43, 45 n.6, 204, 265 n.84
- analogy with persuasion in Gorgias 45–48, 52, 55–56
- *taxis* of in Gorgias 47
dunamis 7, 44, 45 n.6, 47–49, 54, 93 with n.65
- of the soul in Galen 251
eidôla
- in Democritus and Gorgias 50–53
eikos 46
Ekman, Paul 62, 125 n.4, 128 n.12
ekplêxis 54, 84 n.41
embarrassment
- of epileptics 166
embodied cognitivism 146 n.5
emetics (and vomit) 118, 120, 121, 163, 231 n.5, 275
emotion scripts 127 with n.10, 129
Empedocles 49 n.16, 50, 101, 103 with n.87, 278 n.19

- Love and Strife 60 n.2
Empiricist school 211
energeia
- *kata phusin* and *para phusin* in Galen 33
- of the soul in Galen 24, 32, 33, 34, 239, 251
envy 4, 28, 49 n.16, 51, 130–131, 150, 217, 255
Epictetus 26, 210 n.36, 253 n.24
epilepsis (ἐπίληψις/ἐπίληψίη) 90 with n.59, 129, 131, 155, 156, 162, 250, 254 n.26, 259, 260, 262, 280 with n.28
epistemic injustice 182
epithumia ('desire' and *epithumêtikon*) 20, 23, 26, 27, 34, 124, 125
Erasistrarus 275
erection 163–164 with n.52, 165
erôs/erotic love 49 n.16, 53 n.23, 54, 55, 60 with n.2, 61, 67 n.15, 88, 91, 108, 125 n.7, 146 n.5, 192
- as a disease 4–5, 46
- lust 164 n.52
- sex and sexuality 26, 34, 61, 125 n.7, 151, 158, 162–165 with n.57, 184, 230–231, 265 n.84
- symptomatology of 184 n.34
êthikos
- in Galen 259 with n.50
eyes 4, 49, 50, 63, 99 n.80, 130, 159
facial expressions 63, 128 n.12
fasting 262
fear (φόβος/δεῖμα) 1, 3, 4, 6, 10, 20, 22, 36, 38, 44, 46, 48, 123, 124, 125 with n.3, 128, 130, 131 with n.18, 121–122, 133, 134, 150, 155, 174, 178, 179, 180, 183, 185, 187, 213, 214 n.45, 215, 216, 236, 248, 250, 254 n.29, 258, 261, 262 with nn.66 and 68–69, 263
- and/of death 119, 138, 261, 272, 278, 279, 282
- and depression 182
- and δυσθυμία 176, 186, 276
- and the heart 258
- and melancholia 276–277 with n.12
- and miscarriage 185
- and vision 48
- as a cold emotion 222

– Nicanor's of flute girls 140
– opposed to shame 156
fetus 185
fever 6, 11, 38, 91, 133, 134 with n.27, 159 with n.43, 161 n.45, 175, 176, 178 n.16, 180, 186, 191, 200 n.58, 214, 222 n.62, 252, 254 n.29
– and covering 160
– and delirium 248 n.2, 272
– and exhaustion 262 n.66
– and melancholia 277 n.15
– and shivering 133, 160, 178 n.16
– and sunstroke 262 n.66
Gaius Piso 213
genitals
– female (αἰδοῖα) 140, 165, 274
  – external 164
– male 164
gnômê 118, 119, 120, 163
grief 3, 38 with n.33, 118, 119, 124, 133, 156, 157 with n.37, 161, 187, 242, 279
– and veiling 131
guilt 128, 146, 150
– apocalyptic guilt syndrome 282 n.41
Hadrian 29
hallucinations 120, 254 with n.29, 264, 271, 277–279
– auditory 281
– 'bestial' in Galen 272
– hallucinatory–delusional syndromes 282 n.41
happiness/joy 5, 38, 76, 124, 125, 154, 178, 217 n.52, 261
headache 181, 257
hêdone 20, 124
– hedonic valence 52
Heidegger, Martin 65, 109
hemorrhage 3
hexis 21, 33, 221 n.58
hierê nosos 131, 132, 135, 139, 140
Hobbes, Thomas 65
humours 3, 47–49 with 48 n.13, 56, 123, 164 n.52, 178, 204, 265 n.8, 279
– imbalance of 49, 182, 273
Hunayn ibn Isḥāq 203 n.5, 240 n.28
hydrophobia 254 n.27
'hysterical' blindness 5

impulse 28, 31, 164 n.52, 192 n.61, 221 with n.60, 222, 231, 253, 255
infants (and children) 71, 155–156 with n.32, 221 n.60
insanity/mental disorders 4, 5, 88, 120, 248 n.1, 249
– and lethargy 214, 250, 254 n.29, 280 n.28
– and listlessness 280 with n.28
– and paralysis 250, 259, 280 n.28
– and môrôsis 250, 257
– as possession 242, 243, 254 n.26, 278
– mania 6, 13, 36, 37, 120, 153, 248, 250, 254 nn.26–27, 255 n.30, 265, 277 with n.12, 280
– melancholia/melancholy 13, 14, 36, 37, 160, 178, 186, 216, 248, 250, 254 n.29, 255 n.30, 260, 262 with nn. 66 and 68–69, 263–265 with 264 n.79 and 265 n.84, 266, 278
– paraphrosunê 36, 118
– phrenitis 13, 36, 160, 248 with n.2, 250, 255 n.30, 257, 266
– seizures 261
Iris 64 with n.11
Ishaq ibn Imran 279 with n.23
Jason (son of Menecrates) 209 n.35
jaundice 259
kardia (heart) 33, 38, 118, 119, 121, 124, 184, 222 n.61, 230, 238, 248, 253, 256, 257, 258–259 with 258 n.48, 261, 262, 263
katharsis 10, 117, 121
– purifier (καθαρτής) 92 with n.62
kinesis (motion) 31–34, 216, 221 n.60, 233 with n.12, 238, 261
kôma 257
kosmos/kosmios 46, 140 n.40
Kraepelin, Emil 281 with n.36
krisis 25
Lack (Πενία) 91
laughter 120, 153, 154, 160, 195
– and shame 127
– involuntary 236 n.19
– of Democritus 280 with n.28
Lazare, Aaron 126–127, 147 nn.8–9, 149 nn.13 and 15, 156 n.34

liver 230, 256, 258–259 with 258 n.48, 259, 260
logismos 45, 54, 190
logistikon
– in Galen 37, 258, 264 n.79
longing (πόθος) 52–54
Lucius Annaeus Cornutus 208 n.27
lupê/lupêma 20, 30 n.23, 124, 133, 174, 177, 178 n.16, 181, 194, 252, 255, 277 with nn.12 and 15
– and doctors 189 n.49
– and women 175 n.4, 177, 184
– as anxiety 150 n.18, 186, 277
– as distress 38, 254 n.29
– as grief/sadness 124, 125, 128, 133, 258
– as sorrow 248, 250
– γνώμης 124 n.1
magic 91–92, 94
– incantations/spells 45, 49, 53, 91
Marc Antony 211 n.38
Marcel, Gabriel 65
Marcus Aurelius 26, 253 n.24
Mass Psychology 51 n.18
McTaggart, John 68 n.16
Medical Psychology 6 n.10
memory
– in Galen 259
menstruation 175 n.5, 181
metaphor 1, 4–5, 8, 55–56, 124–125
Middle Platonists 30
morbus 18 n.1, 252 n.21
mors immatura 191 n.58
mortality 185 n.36
nausea 181
Niccolò da Reggio 203 n.5
pain
– doctors' responses to 2, 179
– endurance of 138, 241
– fear of 44
– in metaphors 55, 71–72
palpitations (of the heart) 124, 259
panic 3, 4, 7, 51–52
passio 18
patients
– doctors' empathy for 53 n.22
– community of in the *Epidemics* 186

– fear for medical practices 45
– female 175–176, 183
– metaphor for agents of emotions 6
– 'objectification' of 6–7, 178–179 with n.19, 190
– 'silencing' of 189
– subjectivity of 193
– unreliability of 187 with n.44
Peripatetics 13, 241, 244
persecutory syndrome 282 n.41
Philodemus 241
phlegm 48 n.13, 94, 163
phrikê 53, 123
phronêma 51, 120
phusis 48 n.13, 50, 55, 85, 93 n.65, 95, 106 with n.93, 121, 163, 175 n.4, 184
physiology 46, 118, 125 n.4, 151, 162, 256
– and psychology 8
– of fevers 160
– of the soul 264
pity (ἔλεος) 7, 20
– in Aristotle 10, 117, 118, 122
– in Gorgias 53
Plato 232, 236, 244
plêsmonê 120
Pliny the Elder 208
Plutarch 26, 253 n.24, 254
pneuma 218, 222, 223 n.65, 224
– in Athenaeus 210
– in Galen 39, 203, 261
– in Pneumatist pathology 204 n.12
poisoning syndrome 282 n.41
Pompey 209 with n.35
praemeditatio malorum 28
preventive medicine 255 n.33
pride 27, 137, 139, 145
– *vulnus* 149 n.15
psuchê
– as ally (σύμμαχος) to reason in Galen 240
– as spirit 118
– contraction/expansion of 222
– *nosêma* of 252
– right blend (εὐκρασία) of 222 n.62
– strength (ἰσχύς) of in Galen 234, 252
– symmetry (συμμετρία) of 222 n.62

- tripartition of 115 n.49, 221 n.60, 258–259
psychotropic medication 43
psychopathology 264–265 with n.84
Ptolemy (Auletes?) 211 with n.38
PTSD (Post Traumatic Stress Disorder) 5
pulse 33, 38, 186, 203 n.7, 252
Pythagoras 233 n.11
respiration 222 n.65
rhetoric (ῥητορική) 44
pus 191
reputable opinions (*endoxa*) 82
Resourcefulness (Πόρος) 91
Rufus of Ephesus 210 n.38, 265 n.84, 273
Russell, Bertrand 68 n.16
satyriasis 164 n.52
schêmata 47 n.12
schizophrenia 277, 280–281
– and anxiety 282
– and depression 282
– and fear 282
– schizoaffective disorder 282
self-restraint
– in Galen 235, 236
shaking 124
shame (αἰδώς) 10, 11, 38, 119, 124, 125 with n.8, 128, 130, 131, 139, 140 with n.43, 250
shivering 133
Simplicius 206 n.22
skin 132 n.25
sleep/sleeplessness (and insomnia) 88, 119, 175, 185, 186, 212–214, 254, 276
Sontag, Suzan 1 n.1, 55 n.30
stasis 21
– and illness in Galen 252
stilus 29
Stoics 6, 8, 12, 13, 18, 29, 31, 36 with n.30, 216, 244, 249
– and *apatheia* 241
– and causal theory 205
– and preferred 'indifferents' 217
suicide 121, 126, 140 n.41

surprise 125, 128
symptoms 53 n.23, 174, 178, 180–181, 183, 186, 192–193
– in tragedy 140 n.41
– shameful 126
syncope 258, 261
sweat 124, 254
tarachê/tarassô 47 n.12, 49, 52, 240
technê 97–98, 99 n.81
tekmêria (symptoms)
– in Galen 271
tension (τόνος) 203 n.7
tetanus 162
Thales of Miletus 73 n.23
Thaumas 64 with n.11
theôria 74 n.26
therapeia 21
thumos (and *thumoeides*)
– as a seat of cognition 118
– as spirit 118
– in Galen 27, 34–35
– in Plato 34
– in Plato and Galen 27
– in the Hippocratic Corpus 125 n.7
Tiberius 208
tremor 215, 252 n.18, 254 with n.29, 261 with n.64
tuchê 50 with n.17, 52
tupos 50
urination 140, 162, 164, 165
uterus 121, 181
veiling 131–132 with 131 n.19, 133–134, 157–158
virginity 184, 192
– virginal hymen 184 n.35
Zeno of Citium 32 n.26, 215
Zopyrus 210 with n.37, 211
weeping (and crying) 119, 133, 154, 272, 280
–involuntary 236 n.19
Wittgenstein, Ludwig 65

Index Locorum

Aeschylus
Eumenides
407 — 63

Aetius of Amida
Libri Medicinales
16.70 — 274
16.118 — 164

Alexander of Tralles
Therapeutica
1.17 — 273

[Andronicus]
De passionibus
1 — 31–2

Antiphanes
3 G–P — 183

Apollonius of Citium
CMG XI.1.1, p.12 — 210

Aretaeus of Cappadocia
De causis et signis diuturnorum morborum
1.4 — 130–1
1.5 — 162
1.6 — 162
2.12 — 163
De curatione diuturnorum morborum
1.4 — 131

Aristotle
De anima
403a16–33 — 20
403a–b — 118
De caelo
294a12–16 — 84–5
297b7–12 — 81–2
De partibus animalium
645a4–24 — 85
De respiratione
480b26–30 — 106

De sensu
436a19–b1 — 106
De somniis
406b4–16 — 6
Ethica Nicomachea
1147a12–18 — 6
1177b1–4 — 75
[Mechanics]
847a11–13 — 62
Metaphysics
981b14–15 — 76
982b7 — 79
982b11–19 — 73
982b14–15 — 77
982b19–27 — 74
983a12–21 — 78
995a24–b4 — 80
1028b2–4 — 108 n.94
Poetics
1448b11–17 — 75
1452a3–11 — 77–8
[Problemata Physica]
877a — 119
953a15–16 — 90
Rhetoric
1371a31–34 — 85
Topics
101a35–36 — 82
145b1–2 — 82

Demosthenes
54.11–12 — 2–3

Galen
Ars medica
24 (1.371 K.) — 255
Comm.Hipp.Epid.I
17a.213–4 K. — 272
Comm.Hipp.Epid.III
17a.500 K. — 194
17a.778 K. — 177, 180
17a.789 K. — 160
Comm.Hipp.Epid.VI
487 Wenkebach/Pfaff — 272

De affectuum dignotione
3 (5.7 K.)	28, 232, 236
5 (5.24 K.)	237, 251
6 (5.28–9 K.)	27, 234
9 (5.50 K.)	242
10 (5.52 K.)	239

De indolentia
65–66 BJP	243

De locis affectis
3.6 (8.162 K.)	258
3.10 (8.190 K.)	272–3

De methodo medendi
12 (10.841 K.)	261

De moribus
1 (27–8 Kraus)	28

De placitis Hippocratis et Platonis
5.2 (5.434 K.)	35, 219
5.2.2–3 (5.434 K.)	233
5.21 (5.463 K.)	221
5.22–29 (5.463–4 K.)	223
6.1 (5.506–7 K.)	32–3
6.1 (5.507 K.)	33

De praenotione ad Epigenem
6 (14.630–33)	186

De sanitate tuenda
1.5 (6.28 K.)	37
2.9 (6.138 K.)	38

De sectis ingredientibus
Westerink 1981, 118	273

De symptomatum causis
2.5 (7.191 K.)	39
2.5 (7.191–4 K.)	38
2.7 (7.203 K.)	263

De symptomatum differentiis
2 (7.53–4 K.)	33

Glossarium
19.94 K.	193–4

On Cohesive Causes
2.1–3 (p.45.4–24 Lyons)	203–4

Gorgias
Encomium of Helen
9–10	53
13–14	55
14	47, 48
15	48, 50
16	52
18	48, 51
19	49, 88

Herodotus
2.35.1	62

Hippocrates
Aphorismi
2.6 (4.470 L.)	118
3.24 (4.496 L.)	119
6.23 (4.470 L.)	118
7.9 (4.580 L.)	118

De articulis
30 (3.524 L.)	137
37 (4.166 L.)	138
44 (4.188 L.)	137
64 (4.274 L.)	137
78 (4.312 L.)	137

De flatibus
1 (6.90 L.)	136
14 (6.112–4 L.)	49

De humoribus
9 (5.488–90 L.)	118–9, 123–4

De interioribus affectibus
48 (7.284 L.)	120

De morbis
2.72 (7.108–10)	120

De morbo sacro
1 (6.362 L.)	120
1.1–3 (6.352–4 L.)	89–90
1.4 (6.354 L.)	92
12 (6.382–4 L.)	129–30, 155
14 (6.386–8 L.)	120
18.1 (6.394 L.)	93
18.2–3 (6.394 L.)	94–5

De mulierum affectibus
1.62 (8.126 L.)	138–9
1.70 (8.148 L.)	185
2.72 (8.364–6)	181

De natura hominis
5 (6.42 L.)	48 n.13

De vetere medicina
1.1–3 (1.570–2 L.)	97, 98
3.1 (1.574 L.)	105–6
9.3 (1.590 L.)	97
13.1–3 (1.598–600 L.)	98
15.1–2 (1.604–6 L.)	98

20.1–2 (1.620–2 L.)	100	*Meno*	
De victu		79e–80b	70–1
1.21 (6.494 L.)	120	*Phaedo*	
1.35 (6.512 L.)	120	83c–d	23
1.35 (6.518 L.)	120	96a	22
4.93 (6.660 L.)	120–1	96e–97b	67
De victu acutorum morborum		97a–b	67–8
1 (2.224 L.)	189–90	*Phaedrus*	
De virginum morbis		229e–230a	86
1 (8.466–70 L.)	121, 184	250d	87
Epidemiae		270d	22
2.2.22 (5.94 L.)	133, 159	*Philebus*	
3.1.3 (3.42 L.)	158–9	33d2–34a5	23
3.6. (3.50–2 L.)	119	35c6–d2	23
3.11 (3.60–2 L.)	119, 185	*Republic*	
3.17.11 (3.134 L.)	174–5	524d–525a	68–69
3.17.15 (3.142 L.)	133, 160	*Sophist*	
4.15 (5.152 L.)	140	242b	72
5.50 (5.326 L.)	191	244a	72
5.81–83 (5.250 L.)	119	*Symposium*	
6.8–9 (5.346 L.)	119	174d–175d	67
6.8.17 (5.350 L.)	190	174e	22
6.8.23 (5.352 L.)	158	175b	67
7.11 (5.384–6 L.)	119, 133, 160–1	189a	60
7.25 (5.394–8 L.)	133–4, 159	210e	87
7.80 (5.436 L.)	140	220c–d	67
7.83 (5.440 L.)	134	*Theaetetus*	
7.86 (5.444 L.)	140	149a–151d	69–70
7.87 (5.444 L.)	140	151c	71
7.89 (5.446 L.)	135	154c	66
Praecepta		155c–d	63–4
6 (9.258 L.)	137	210b–c	71
Prorrheticon		*Timaeus*	
2.12 (9.34–6 L.)	136	44a–b	22

Paul of Aegina
De re medica libri septem
6.70   165

Plato
Euthyphro
15e   70
Gorgias
456a7–c7   6, 43–4
525c   22
Laches
194a–b   70

Plotinus
Enneads
3.6.1.33–7   24
3.6.3.1–15   25
4.4.19.8–13   24–5

Plutarch
Aemilius Paulus
1.4   51 n.21
Marius
45.3–7   211–2

Moralia
419A	52 n.21
682F–683A	51

De libidine et aegritudine
6	214–5

Seneca
De ira
1.7.1	241

Epistles
87.31	217–8

Sextus Empiricus
Adversus Mathematicos
9.19	52 n.21

Sophocles
Ajax
317–25	154
356–480	153–4
471–2	154

Stobaeus
2.88–90	31

Strabo
2.3.8	206

Thucydides
2.39.5	62
2.41.4	62

www.ingramcontent.com/pod-product-compliance
Lightning Source LLC
Chambersburg PA
CBHW020222170426
43201CB00007B/285